OXFORD COMPARATIVE CONSTITUTIONALISM

Foreign Relations Federalism

OXFORD COMPARATIVE CONSTITUTIONALISM

Comparative constitutional law has a long and distinguished history in intellectual thought and in the construction of public law. As political actors and the people who create or modify their constitutional orders, they often wish to learn from the experience and learning of others. This cross-fertilization and mutual interaction has only accelerated with the onset of globalization, which has transformed the world into an interconnected web that facilitates dialogue and linkages across international and regional structures. Oxford Comparative Constitutionalism seeks to publish scholarship of the highest quality in constitutional law that deepens our knowledge of local, national, regional, and global phenomena through the lens of comparative public law.

ALSO PUBLISHED IN THIS SERIES

Responsive Judicial Review
Democracy and Dysfunction in the Modern Age
Rosalind Dixon

Outsourcing Rulemaking Powers
Constitutional limits and national safeguards
Cedric Jenart

Abusive Constitutional Borrowing
Legal globalization and the subversion of liberal democracy
Rosalind Dixon and David Landau

A Theory of African Constitutionalism
Berihun Adugna Gebeye

Eternity Clauses In Democratic Constitutionalism
Silvia Suteu

Deliberative Peace Referendums
Ron Levy, Ian O'Flynn, Hoi L. Kong

Scales of Memory Constitutional Justice and Historical Evil
Justin Collings

The Global South and Comparative Constitutional Law
Edited by Philipp Dann, Michael Riegner, and Maxim Bönnemann

Foreign Relations Federalism

The EU in Comparative Perspective

THOMAS VERELLEN

Assistant Professor, Utrecht University

OXFORD
UNIVERSITY PRESS

OXFORD
UNIVERSITY PRESS

Great Clarendon Street, Oxford, OX2 6DP,
United Kingdom

Oxford University Press is a department of the University of Oxford. It furthers the University's objective of excellence in research, scholarship, and education by publishing worldwide. Oxford is a registered trade mark of Oxford University Press in the UK and in certain other countries

First Edition published in 2023

Published in the United States of America by Oxford University Press
198 Madison Avenue, New York, NY 10016, United States of America

British Library Cataloguing in Publication Data

Data available

Library of Congress Control Number: 2023932453

ISBN 978–0–19–284456–9

DOI: 10.1093/oso/9780192844569.001.0001

Printed and bound in the UK by
TJ Books Limited

Preface

This book is a revised and updated version of a PhD thesis I defended at KU Leuven in September 2019. I owe a tremendous amount of gratitude to my PhD supervisor, Professor Geert De Baere; my co-supervisor, Professor Stefan Sottiaux; the members of my PhD supervisory committee Professors Koen Lenaerts and Daniel Halberstam; and the members of my PhD defence committee Dr Kathleen Gutman and Professors Robert Schütze and Gleider Hernández.

The initial PhD research was generously funded by Research Foundation—Flanders (FWO). Thank you to Professor Geert De Baere and Dr Tina Van den Sanden for their efforts in obtaining the initial FWO grant. Writing the PhD and the ensuing book would not have been possible without the financial support of the Belgian American Educational Foundation and the hospitality extended to me by the entire academic community at KU Leuven's Law Faculty, by Professor Daniel Halberstam at the University of Michigan Law School, by Professor Stéphane Beaulac at the *Université de Montréal*, and by Professor Koen Lenaerts at the Court of Justice of the EU.

I am grateful also to Professors Robert Schütze and Richard Albert for accepting my book as part of Oxford University Press' Comparative Constitutionalism Series, and to Professor Cedric Ryngaert for supporting my request to spend a full academic year in the United States so shortly after the start of my employment at Utrecht University. To Oxford University Press, I am grateful for their support and assistance throughout the publication process.

To my parents: thank you for your love and support throughout my studies. To my parents-in-law: thank you for your hospitality and support; and to my father-in-law: thank you for your editing help in those intense months in the run-up to the PhD submission deadline. And, finally, to Laura: this would not have been possible without you. I love you, always.

Contents

Case-law

EUROPEAN UNION

Cases

Opinions

UNITED STATES

CANADA

BELGIUM

OTHER

Legal instruments and other documents

EUROPEAN UNION

Basic Treaties

Directives

Protocols

Declarations

Rules of Procedure

Regulations

Council Decisions

UNITED STATES

Legislation

Bills

Congressional resolutions

Compacts

Rules and regulations

Other documents

CANADA

Legislation

Bills

Intergovernmental agreements

Other documents

BELGIUM

Legislation

Intergovernmental agreements

Rules of Procedure

Other Documents

OTHER

INTERNATIONAL TREATIES AND CONVENTIONS

International Treaties and Conventions

UN Documents

UNESCO Documents

1
Introduction

How are foreign relations constitutionally structured in federal unions? How does the foreign affairs constitution of the EU—itself a federal union in all but name[1]—compare to that of other federal unions? This book addresses these questions. It offers a comparative analysis of the constitutional framework in which foreign relations are conducted in four federal unions: the US, Canada, Belgium, and the EU. The EU takes up a special position in the book. By looking at the constitutional experience of other federal unions—two longstanding (the US and Canada), one of more recent pedigree (Belgium)—this book informs and contributes to debates on how the EU's 'foreign affairs constitution' should be structured. Over a decade since the Treaty of Lisbon entered into force, the EU's foreign affairs constitution continues to evolve. New institutional practices emerge and cases continue to be brought before the Court of Justice of the European Union that require the Court to interpret Treaty provisions on how the EU and the Member States are to conduct foreign relations. In this sense, the EU's foreign affairs constitution—as is the case for the EU's constitution as a whole—remains very much a fast-moving target. The pace of constitutional change is high, and there is a sustained need for critical and constructive legal analysis of that change. This book represents my effort to fulfil this need.

1. A Comparative Perspective on EU Foreign Relations Federalism

Comparative law has an important contribution to make to the study of the EU's foreign affairs constitution. The EU is a unique project, but so is every other federal union. By acknowledging that the EU, despite its many differences, shares

[1] In this sense, see eg Olivier Beaud, *Théorie de la fédération* (Presses Universitaires de France—PUF 2007).

Foreign Relations Federalism. Thomas Verellen, Oxford University Press. © Thomas Verellen 2023.
DOI: 10.1093/oso/9780192844569.003.0001

key features with federations such as the US, Canada, or Belgium, it becomes possible to engage in a meaningful analysis of those differences and similarities.[2] This analysis creates a critical distance. It allows me—and hopefully the reader—to question assumptions and imagine alternative ways to structure the EU's foreign affairs constitution.[3] It allows me to zoom out, rather than to focus on the narrower, technical questions that EU lawyers address as they engage with the Court's external relations case law. To be clear, these technical questions matter. They are the bread and butter of EU external relations law, as it is through incremental change rather than wholesale constitutional reform that the EU's foreign affairs constitution develops. Be that as it may, it is the job of the academic lawyer to look at the bigger picture and to try to make sense of the EU's foreign affairs constitution as a whole.

This book, then, is an effort at zooming out and at thinking the EU's foreign affairs constitution as a whole. By examining the EU and three other federations within an integrated theoretical framework, the book offers an understanding of the EU's foreign affairs constitution that moves beyond the issues of the day as they arise with the ebb and flow of the case law. Instead, I want to examine how the EU's foreign affairs constitution addresses classic questions of constitutional law as they play out in federal unions. The questions are simple (it is in answering them that the challenge lies). What powers do the EU institutions hold to engage in foreign relations? What limits do the Treaties impose on the exercise of those powers? How does the EU's foreign affairs constitution balance unity and diversity in a federal polity in which both levels of governance can engage in foreign relations? How are conflicts prevented or resolved between levels of governance? What voice do member units have in the federal foreign policy-making process? What space is there for government-to-government collaboration and interaction? And if such space exists, how does the constitution govern that collaboration and interaction?

[2] There is a rich tradition of comparative legal research that includes the EU. For an early contribution, see Mauro Cappelletti, Monica Seccombe, and Joseph Weiler, *Integration Through Law: Europe and the American Federal Experience* (Walter de Gruyter 1985). More recently, in the narrower field of foreign relations law, see eg Robert Schütze, *Foreign Affairs and the EU Constitution: Selected Essays* (Cambridge University Press 2014); Geert De Baere and Kathleen Gutman, 'Federalism and International Relations in the European Union and the United States: A Comparative Outlook' in Elke Cloots, Geert De Baere, and Stefan Sottiaux (eds), *Federalism in the European Union* (Hart 2012).

[3] On comparative law as an effort to create critical distance and imagine alternative realities, see Mark Tushnet, 'The Possibilities of Comparative Constitutional Law' (1999) 108 Yale Law Journal 1225, 1308.

2. Federalism as a Combination of Self-Rule and Shared Rule

The theoretical framework within which I examine how foreign relations are conducted in the US, Canada, Belgium, and the EU is inspired by the definition of federalism offered by Daniel Elazar. Elazar, a political scientist, defined federalism as a combination of self-rule and shared rule. 'Federalism,' he argued, 'involves the linking of individuals, groups, and polities in lasting but limited union in such a way as to provide for the energetic pursuit of common ends while maintaining the respective integrities of all parties.'[4] 'As a political principle', he continued,

> federalism has to do with the constitutional diffusion of power so that the constituting elements in a federal arrangement share in the processes of common policy making and administration by right, while the activities of the common government are conducted in such a way as to maintain their respective integrities. Federal systems do this by constitutionally distributing power among general and constituent governing bodies in a manner designed to protect the existence and authority of all. In a federal system, basic policies are made and implemented through negotiation in some form so that all can share in the system's decision-making and executing processes.[5]

Elazar's definition brings together two traditions in the study of federalism: the 'dual' or 'categorical' tradition, and the 'cooperative' or 'Althusian' tradition. What do these traditions entail? And what do they tell us about the meaning of 'federalism' as a concept in constitutional theory? I briefly look at these questions before I conclude this introduction by sketching the structure of the book and the book's main argument.

Federalism is an essentially contested concept.[6] Commentators have advanced different definitions, each drawing on their knowledge of and experience with a specific set of manifestations of the 'federal' phenomenon.[7]

[4] Daniel Elazar, *Exploring Federalism* (University of Alabama Press 1987) 5.

[5] ibid 5–6.

[6] On essentially contested concepts, see Jeremy Waldron, 'Is the Rule of Law an Essentially Contested Concept (in Florida)?' (2002) 21 Law and Philosophy 137, 148, referring to WB Gallie who defined 'essentially contested concepts' as concepts 'the proper use of which inevitably involves endless disputes about their proper uses on the part of their users'.

[7] For an analysis of the meaning of federalism, see eg Solomon Rufus Davis, *The Federal Principle: A Journey Through Time in Quest of a Meaning* (University of California Press 1978). More recently, see also Beaud (n 1); Michael Burgess, *In Search of the Federal Spirit: New Theoretical and Empirical Perspectives in Comparative Federalism* (Oxford University Press 2012).

Commentators have characterized 'federalism' as a means to strike a balance between unity and diversity within compound polities. For example, writing within the tradition of EU legal scholarship, Koen Lenaerts and Amaryllis Verhoeven defined federalism as 'a means to structure the relationship between interlocked authorities in such a way that a balance can be achieved between the need for common action in order to pursue efficiently a set of common values, and the need to see the identity of the different actors taking part in the common action being preserved'.[8] Similarly, Pierre Pescatore submitted in a contribution to a 1982 book that 'federalism is a political and legal philosophy which adapts itself to all political contexts on both the municipal and the international level, wherever and whenever two basic prerequisites are fulfilled: the search for unity, combined with genuine respect for the autonomy and the legitimate interests of the participant entities'.[9] These definitions are quite similar to those articulated within other traditions. In its *Quebec Secession Reference*, for example, the Supreme Court of Canada defined federalism succinctly as 'the political mechanism by which diversity could be reconciled with unity'.[10]

To define federalism as a 'means' to strike a 'balance' between unity and diversity says little about how this balance is to be attained, let alone maintained, however. Roughly two answers have been formulated to this question. Both answers can be understood as models or ideal types for the ways in which the 'federal principle' is to be implemented. One model—the dual or categorical model—involves dividing powers between two orders of governance with the view of empowering these governments to act in full independence within their own sphere of authority; the other—the cooperative or Althusian model—entails a search for means to ensure that common issues are decided by common accord.

The first model is perhaps best known today. Kenneth Wheare captured its essence very well when he defined the federal principle as 'the method of dividing power so that the general and regional governments are each, within a sphere, co-ordinate and independent'.[11] It is an approach of establishing a 'federal balance' that looks primarily at the division of powers between orders of governance. The approach is sometimes referred to as one of 'classical' federalism (perhaps alluding to the approach's popularity in the US and Canada in

[8] Koen Lenaerts and Amaryllis Verhoeven, 'Institutional Balance as a Guarantee for Democracy in EU Governance' in *Good Governance in Europe's Integrated Market Pages* (Oxford University Press 2002) 43.

[9] Pierre Pescatore, 'Preface' in Terrance Sandalow and Eric Stein (eds), *Courts and Free Markets*, vol II (Clarendon Press 1982) ix–x.

[10] *Reference re Secession of Quebec*, [1998] 2 SCR 217, 1998 CanLII 793 (SCC) [43].

[11] Kenneth C Wheare, *Federal Government* (Oxford University Press 1963) 10.

the late nineteenth century),[12] 'dual'[13] federalism, or 'categorical' federalism.[14] The classical model can be understood as an effort at reconciling the existence of multiple orders of government with theories of popular sovereignty that emerged in the second half of the eighteenth century. By establishing separate spheres of authority, each government—and thus each 'people'—could remain 'sovereign', and 'govern itself' through processes of democratic will-formation. The approach is visible, for example, in late nineteenth and early twentieth-century case law on the scope of the federal power to regulate interstate and interprovincial commerce in the US and Canada.[15]

The model of dividing powers between orders of governance can be distinguished from a different, much older, model of federalism, which harks back to the writings of Johannes Althusius, a seventeenth-century German jurist and Calvinist political philosopher.[16] Althusius asserted that in compound polities '[w]hat touches all ought to be approved by all'.[17] Althusius argued for a constitutional model in which the different member units of a federation decide on common matters by consensus. Perhaps not coincidentally, Althusius

[12] Bruce Ryder, 'The Demise and Rise of the Classical Paradigm in Canadian Federalism: Promoting Autonomy for the Provinces and First Nations' (1990) 36 McGill Law Journal 308. In the US specifically, see in more general terms Duncan Kennedy, *The Rise and Fall of Classical Legal Thought* (Beard Books 2006), referring to an era of 'classical legal thought' characterized by categorical thinking as opposed to the balancing of competing values and interests which came to characterize more recent US legal thought influenced by the legal realist tradition.

[13] Ernest Young, 'The Puzzling Persistence of Dual Federalism' [2012] Faculty Scholarship <http://scholarship.law.duke.edu/faculty_scholarship/2689> accessed 21 June 2017. See also Robert Schütze, *From Dual to Cooperative Federalism: The Changing Structure of European Law* (Oxford University Press 2013); Jean-François Gaudreault-DesBiens, 'From Dualism to Cooperative Federalism and Back?: Evolving and Competing Conceptions of Canadian Federalism' in Peter Oliver, Patrick Macklem, and Nathalie Des Rosiers (eds), *The Oxford Handbook of the Canadian Constitution*, vol 1 (Oxford University Press 2017).

[14] Judith Resnik, 'Categorical Federalism: Jurisdiction, Gender, and the Globe' (2001) 111 Yale Law Journal 619.

[15] In Canada, see seminally *Citizens Insurance Co of Canada v Parsons*, 1881 WL 18745 (1881):

> Sects. 91 and 92 of the British North America Act, 1867, must, in regard to the classes of subjects generally described in sect. 91, be read together, and the language of one interpreted and, where necessary, modified by that of the other, so as to reconcile the respective powers they contain and give effect to all of them. Each question should be decided as best it can, without entering more largely than is necessary upon an interpretation of the statute.

In the U.S., see for example *A.L.A. Schechter Poultry Corporation v. U.S.*, 295 U.S. 495 (1935) ('Power of Congress to control intrastate transactions on the ground that they affect interstate commerce is confined to transactions directly affecting such commerce, and, where the effect on interstate commerce is merely indirect, such transactions remain within domain of state's power').

[16] On the life and work of Johannes Althusius, see eg Thomas Hueglin, 'Johannes Althusius: Medieval Constitutionalist or Modern Federalist?' (1979) 9 Publius: The Journal of Federalism 9. As pointed out to me by Andrew Cecchinato, Althusius in turn drew on a tradition that harks back to the private law of Justinian. See generally Orazio Condorelli, '«Quod Omnestangit, Debet Ab Omnibus Approbari». Note Sull'origine e Sull'utilizzazione Del Principio Tra Medioevo e Prima Età Moderna' (2013) 53 Ius Canonicum 101.

[17] Althusius, as cited in Thomas O Hueglin and Alan Fenna, *Comparative Federalism: A Systematic Inquiry, Second Edition* (University of Toronto Press 2015) 82.

wrote several decades before theories of popular sovereignty became widespread in Europe. He wrote against the backdrop of a fragmented constitutional and political landscape characterized by multiple levels of governance. In this landscape, the town, the county or principality, and the empire exercised overlapping powers.

For many years, the Althusian conception of federalism did not receive much attention, overshadowed as it was by the influence of the US as the politically, economically, and culturally most powerful modern federal-type polity. In recent decades, however, commentators have rediscovered the Althusian model.[18] As Althusius had done before, contemporary theorists of 'cooperative' of 'collaborative' federalism emphasize the attractiveness of decision-making through negotiation and consensus-formation.[19] Likewise, within the EU scholarly tradition, theorists of 'subsidiarity' draw on the work of Althusius, leading one Althusius scholar to state that '[t]he rediscovery, discussion, and entrenchment of federalism and subsidiarity as organizational principles in the post-Maastricht European Union may have finally propelled Althusius from obscurity to the forefront of (some!) academic curiosity'.[20]

This brings us back to Daniel Elazar. Elazar can be credited for bringing together both traditions of federal thought in an elegant definition of federalism as a combination of self-rule and shared rule.[21] As mentioned, Elazar's definition is relevant to this book as it accommodates both the 'dual' or 'categorical' conception of federalism and its Althusian counterpart. The reference to self-rule evokes the constitutional division of authority with the view of establishing a space for the different governments to 'rule themselves'. The reference to shared rule, in turn, evokes the Althusian maxim that '[w]hat touches all ought to be approved by all', which typically takes the form of mechanisms of intergovernmental relations or of member unit representation within the

[18] In this sense, see Thomas Hueglin, 'Federalism at the Crossroads: Old Meanings, New Significance' (2003) 36 Canadian Journal of Political Science/Revue canadienne de science politique 275.

[19] In the EU context, see eg Christophe Hillion, 'Mixity and Coherence in EU External Relations: The Significance of the "Duty of Cooperation"' in Christophe Hillion and Panos Koutrakos (eds), *Mixed Agreements Revisited: The EU and its Member States in the World* (Hart 2010) 110, arguing that a shift towards a system of overlapping powers subjected to a duty of sincere cooperation is 'more in line with, and certainly more apposite to, the inherent features of the Union's system of external relations. The latter's functioning and ultimate efficiency depend less on its successful obliteration of plurality through exclusivity, than on its aptitude to live with and exploit the fortune of diversity.' Note, furthermore, that the very term 'cooperative federalism' has a normative undertone: how could anyone be against cooperation?

[20] Thomas O Hueglin, *Early Modern Concepts for a Late Modern World: Althusius on Community and Federalism* (Wilfrid Laurier Univ Press 2006) vii.

[21] See seminally Daniel Elazar, *Exploring Federalism* (University of Alabama Press 1987).

federal political institutions. The constitutional architecture of most contemporary federations displays elements of both traditions.

Elazar's definition of federalism is agnostic on the issue of the locus of *Kompetenz-Kompetenz*—a question which has preoccupied European commentators and constitutional courts alike.[22] Starting from the premise that what makes a federation 'federal' is the fact that the question of *Kompetenz-Kompetenz* is left in abeyance and that the federal constitution is ultimately a contract or—to speak with Elazar: a 'covenant',[23] in this book I do not aim to make a contribution to the theoretical literature on *Kompetenz-Kompetenz* or the constitutional theory of the EU more generally. Where recourse to hierarchy is necessary—as it is, in particular, when conflicts between federal and member unit norms need to be resolved—such hierarchy can be justified in functional as opposed to ontological terms.[24] It is this functional approach that I take in this book.

3. Defining the 'Foreign' in Foreign Relations

What do I mean by 'foreign relations'? Stephan Keukeleire and Tom Delreux, two political scientists, defined the closely related concept of 'foreign policy' as 'that area of politics which is directed at the external environment with the objective of influencing that environment and the behaviour of other actors within it, in order to pursue interests, values and goals'.[25] How to further operationalize this definition? In her 2002 book on the intergovernmental pillars of the EU, Eileen Denza, an international law professor, identified the following as instruments that a sovereign state can deploy to engage in foreign policy:

> The State by its nature has international legal personality; it may conclude treaties, become a member of international organizations, send and receive diplomatic and consular missions, defend its external interests by domestic legislation and its physical and political integrity by arms and weapons. By

[22] For a useful starting point for discussions on the issue of the locus of sovereignty, see Neil Walker (ed), *Sovereignty in Transition* (Hart 2006).

[23] Michael Burgess, 'Daniel J. Elazar and Federalism as Covenant' in *In Search of the Federal Spirit: New Theoretical and Empirical Perspectives in Comparative Federalism* (Oxford University Press 2012).

[24] See on this eg Mathias Kumm, 'How Does European Union Law Fit into the World of Public Law? Costa, Kadi and Three Conceptions of Public Law' in Jürgen Neyer and Antje Wiener (eds), *Political Theory of the European Union* (Oxford University Press 2011).

[25] Stephan Keukeleire and Tom Delreux, *The Foreign Policy of the European Union* (Palgrave Macmillan 2014) 1.

exploiting its natural and human resources it has money at its disposal which may be used for internal as well as external purposes.[26]

In this book I focus on two of the instruments Denza identified: (i) the power to negotiate and conclude agreements with third countries, and (ii) the power to engage in external representation. Some of the other instruments listed by Denza I do not address head-on, but they appear in the analysis when discussing which add value. In Chapter 2, for example, I discuss the EU's competence to set up a common defence. I address this topic as defence policy in the EU—in contrast to the other three federations—has an important federal dimension. Similarly, in Chapters 6 and 7 I look at the power to tax and spend as part of a broader assessment of how member units can acquire a direct or indirect voice in the federal foreign policy-making process. Likewise, I do not focus directly on the power to adopt legislation, but this power will come into the picture when I explore the pre-emption doctrines in the US and the EU. Finally, I fully take into account the informalization of international law by including in the analysis not only treaties in the meaning of the Vienna Convention on the Law of Treaties, but also non-binding informal agreements such as memoranda of understanding.[27] Doing so is crucial as informal instruments play a central role in the foreign relations of many of the governments—federal and member unit alike—I look at in this book.

4. The Book's Structure: Two Parts, Four Building Blocks

The book is constructed around the two pillars of federalism as defined by Daniel Elazar, namely the combination of self-rule and shared rule. I regard both elements of Elazar's definition as complementary perspectives on federalism. These dimensions do not necessarily play an equally significant role in all four of the federations examined. Yet for analytical reasons it is useful to examine the constitutional framework on foreign relations in all four federations from this two-fold angle.

[26] Eileen Denza, *The Intergovernmental Pillars of the European Union* (Oxford University Press 2002) 86.

[27] On this development, which raises accountability challenges, see eg in the specific context of the EU's immigration policy: Caterina Molinari, 'The EU and Its Perilous Journey Through the Migration Crisis: Informalisation of the EU Return Policy and Rule of Law Concerns' (2019) 44 European Law Review 824, 826–27. And more generally, see Andrea Ott, 'Informalization of EU Bilateral Instruments: Categorization, Contestation, and Challenges' (2021) 39 Yearbook of European Law 569.

Here again, further operationalization was required. Self-rule as understood in this book has two dimensions. First, if a member of the federation—be it a member unit or the federal government—is to exercise self-rule, it must first be empowered to exercise public authority. The constitutions of the four federal unions in this book allocate these powers to the different governments involved. A first dimension of self-rule, then, is that of *power allocation*. Secondly, if powers overlap, a risk of conflict arises. Depending on the nature of the powers allocated, the means to resolve such conflicts differ. In a system of exclusive powers, conflicts are resolved by delineating the boundaries between areas of exclusive powers.[28] In a system in which powers formally overlap, conflict resolution mechanisms must exist that provide answers to the question of what to do when two norms or policies clash. The second dimension of self-rule, then, is that of *conflict resolution*. In the first part of the book, I focus on the self-rule dimension of foreign relations federalism. It consists of four chapters: two chapters on the allocation of powers (Chapters 2 and 3), and two chapters on conflict resolution (Chapters 4 and 5).

In addition to self-rule, I also look at the shared rule dimension of federalism. Shared rule refers to the need for governments to work together to address issues that affect all members of the federation—both federal and member unit. It points to the cooperative dimension of federalism, capturing the phenomenon that governments within compound polities must work together to attain common objectives.[29] Cooperation between federal and member unit governments can take place in two ways. First, it can occur within the federal political process. By granting the member units a voice within that process—be it formal or informal—member units can influence what happens at the federal level and ensure that their interests and values are respected by the federal authorities. Drawing on US literature on the topic, I refer to this first dimension of shared rule as the *political safeguards of federalism*. Secondly, cooperation can also take place on a government-to-government basis, through processes

[28] Note that by allocating exclusive powers, the framers of federal constitutions intended to prevent conflicts from occurring in the first place. In this sense, see eg Schütze (n 13) 94: 'In a dual federalist universe, legislative conflicts should never arise as each "sovereign" enjoys exclusive powers within "its" sphere of jurisdiction. Rival legislative claims will be arbitrated at the competence level.'

[29] Hueglin and Fenna (n 17) 238: '[I]ntergovernmental relations came to drive modern federal systems as much as, or even more than, the formal constitutional set-up of divided powers and the bicameral legislative process.' In the US, Heather Gerken has argued for greater emphasis on what I call the shared rule dimension of federalism. In a 2014 contribution, for example, she urged the Supreme Court to abandon its emphasis on autonomy and sovereignty and instead acknowledge the important role states play in implementing federal policy. This role, Gerken argues, grants the states leverage also at the policy-making phase. See Heather Gerken, 'Slipping the Bonds of Federalism' (2016) 128 Harvard Law Review 85.

Table 1.1 Theoretical framework of the book

Foreign relations federalism			
Self-rule		*Shared rule*	
Power allocation	Conflict resolution	Political safeguards of federalism	Intergovernmental relations

of *intergovernmental relations*. The former dimension of shared rule will be discussed in Chapters 6 and 7; the latter in Chapters 8 and 9.

This book thus has four building blocks: (i) power allocation; (ii) conflict resolution; (iii) political safeguards of federalism; and (iv) intergovernmental relations. The former two building blocks pertain to what Elazar referred to as the self-rule dimension of federalism; the latter two to its shared rule dimension. Each building block consists of two chapters—one offering a comparative analysis of the three federal states; a second focused on the EU which draws on the comparative analysis of the three federal states conducted earlier. This approach allows for a book that consists of eight chapters (in addition to an introductory and concluding chapter), structured along the lines set out in the table below (see Table 1.1).

5. The Book's Findings: Different Approaches to Foreign Relations Federalism

This book thus offers a comparative analysis of the foreign affairs constitution of four federal unions: the EU plus three other federal unions. I look at key features of those constitutions through the prism of the four abovementioned building blocks. This framework allows me to evaluate the four federal unions under review along four axes. The book does not aim to introduce a taxonomy of different types or models of 'foreign relations federalism' that has a validity that extends beyond the four cases explored in this book. (The sample is too small to undertake such a task.) That said, as the table below demonstrates (see Table 1.2), each federation's approach to each of the four parameters does make for a unique combination of features, which allows me to rank all four federations on a unity–diversity axis.

From a comparative perspective, the EU's approach to foreign relations federalism is thus best understood as one of 'diversity ++'. Compared to the other three federations explored in the book, the balance between unity and diversity

Table 1.2 Overview of the findings of the book

	Power allocation	**Conflict resolution mechanisms**	**Political safeguards of federalism**	**Intergovernmental relations**	**Type of foreign relations federalism**
United States	Broad federal powers, limited member unit powers	Well-developed political and judicial mechanisms	Weak formal and weak informal safeguards	No constitutional protection of intergovernmental relations	Unity +
Canada	Broad federal powers, limited member unit powers	Underdeveloped political and judicial mechanisms	Weak formal and strong informal safeguards	No constitutional protection of intergovernmental relations	External unity, internal diversity
Belgium	Broad federal *and* member unit powers	Well-developed political mechanisms; underdeveloped judicial mechanisms	Strong formal and strong informal safeguards	Constitutional protection of intergovernmental relations	Diversity +
European Union	Broad federal *and* member unit powers	Well-developed judicial mechanisms; underdeveloped political mechanisms	Strong formal and strong informal safeguards	Constitutional obligation to cooperate, but limited by the autonomy of EU law	Diversity ++

in the EU's foreign affairs constitution tilts heavily towards the latter. As I will discuss, the EU Treaties did put in place constitutional principles that safeguard the autonomy of the EU—and thus its ability for self-rule. Yet these principles have to be understood in conjunction with an institutional framework that provides few checks on the institutions that represent Member State interests, that is, the Council and the European Council. The interplay of a constitutional framework that aims to protect the autonomy of the EU with an institutional framework that protects the autonomy of the member units of the EU makes for an overall approach to foreign relations federalism that tilts heavily towards the pole of diversity on the unity–diversity spectrum.

The EU's 'diversity ++' approach can be contrasted with that of the US foreign affairs constitution. The US Constitution pursues a 'unity +' approach to foreign relations federalism. As is the case for the EU, the US foreign affairs constitution protects the ability of the federal government to act autonomously.

Federal powers are broad, and the federal government has instruments at its disposal to resolve conflicts with state law in favour of the former. In contrast to the EU Treaties, however, the US Constitution neither provides for meaningful political safeguards of federalism, nor does it constitutionally protect intergovernmental relations that take place between the federal and member unit governments. As a result, US foreign relations federalism is a federalism that primarily protects the ability of self-rule of the federal government and does little to protect the interests of the fifty state governments in the foreign policy-making process.

In between the positions of the EU and the US on the extremities of the unity–diversity spectrum, we find Canada and Belgium. Canada's approach to foreign relations federalism can best be understood as one of 'external unity, internal diversity': external powers are held exclusively by the federal government whereas the internal power to adopt legislation remains divided. As in the US, Canada's constitution offers few political safeguards of federalism. This makes intergovernmental relations a core feature of Canadian foreign relations federalism and Canadian federalism more generally. That said, the many contacts that exist between federal and member unit governments are not constitutionally protected in Canada. While shared rule is encouraged, each government's authority to rule itself prevails in Canada. This means, in practice, that legislatures in Canada can always unilaterally override intergovernmental agreements concluded with other Canadian governments.

When it comes to the constitutional protection of intergovernmental relations, Canada differs from Belgium. The Belgian foreign affairs constitution requires federal and member unit governments to conclude intergovernmental agreements with one another to facilitate cooperation and joint external action. Intergovernmental cooperation is much needed in Belgium since Belgian governments—as is the case for the EU—often conclude mixed agreements. In Belgium, as in the EU, both levels of governance hold treaty-making powers. This raises questions of shared rule, which in Belgium are addressed through a constitutional obligation to cooperate which trumps the autonomy Belgian governments enjoy through the allocation of exclusive internal and external competences. The greater weight carried by shared rule over self-rule in Belgium provides for an interesting comparison with the EU: the EU Treaties, too, require the different levels of governance to cooperate, in accordance with the duty of sincere cooperation. However, whereas in Belgium that duty is reciprocal, in the EU it limits the autonomy of the member units, but it does not trump the autonomy of the EU, which remains capable—as is the case in Canada—of exercising its competences in accordance with the decision-making rules in the Treaties.

The concluding chapter of the book finishes on a normative note: I critically assess the EU's 'diversity ++' approach to foreign relations federalism from the vantage point of democratic legitimacy. In all four of the federal unions under review in this book, federalism is combined with democracy, turning them into what Sergio Fabbrini has referred to as 'compound democracies'.[30] Canada and Belgium combine federalism with parliamentary democracy. In the US, both Congress and the President infuse the federal political process with direct democratic legitimacy; and the EU Treaties proclaim that the 'functioning of the Union shall be founded on representative democracy'[31]—a constitutional principle realized through the role of the directly elected European Parliament and the indirectly elected Council and European Council in the EU political process. Yet, as I discuss in the concluding chapter, the EU's constitutional and institutional set-up makes it difficult for voters to hold decision-makers accountable as the latter engage in foreign relations. In particular, the scarcity of checks on the Member States risks insulating Member States from democratic control—both at EU and at Member State level. Constitutional principles—in particular, the principle of exclusivity and the duty of sincere cooperation—preclude individual Member States from acting unilaterally on the international stage. Instead, they must either act collectively within the EU framework or alongside the EU. In either scenario, there are few checks on the Member States that ensure that decision-makers in EU foreign relations are held democratically accountable. Instead, to speak with Peter Mair, there is a risk that Member State executives operate collectively in a sphere in which policy-making can evade the constraints imposed by representative democracy.[32]

To remedy the democratic deficit at the heart of the EU's foreign affairs constitution, I put forward three avenues for reform. First, by interpreting narrowly the options Member States have to transform EU external action into mixed action, the full effectiveness of EU decision-making rules, and thus of the institutional balance that protects the prerogatives of the European Parliament, can be ensured. Secondly, by normalizing the Common Foreign and Security Policy, the European Parliament and the Court of Justice could be allowed to play a more meaningful role in this corner of EU foreign relations.

[30] Sergio Fabbrini, *Compound Democracies: Why the United States and Europe Are Becoming Similar* (Oxford University Press 2010).

[31] TEU, art 10.

[32] Peter Mair, 'Popular Democracy and the European Union Polity' (EUROGOV 2005) C-05-03 5.

Thirdly, by merging the offices of European Council president and European Commission president, and by democratizing the resulting merged office, an element of direct democratic legitimation can be introduced in the cockpit of the EU political process. As a result, the political course set by the European Council would be the product of a compromise between the interests of the twenty-seven Member States, represented by their heads of state or government, and the EU citizenry, represented by a merged European Council/ Commission president. If implemented, these reforms would do much to remedy the democratic deficit to which the current foreign affairs constitution of the EU has given rise.

PART I
SELF-RULE

2
Power Allocation in the US, Canada, and Belgium

> Foreign relations are national relations . . . And yet, despite careless, flat statements to the contrary, the foreign relations of the United States are not in fact wholly insulated from the states, are not conducted exactly as though the United States were a unitary state.
>
> Louis Henkin[1]

1. Introduction

James Madison, one of the Founding Fathers of the American republic, argued that, '[i]n framing a government which is to be administered by men over men, the great difficulty lies in this: you must first enable the government to control the governed; and in the next place oblige it to control itself'.[2] Being a central component of the self-rule dimension of federalism, this chapter and the next focus on the allocation of powers onto governments, that is, the first leg of Madison's equation.[3] In the foreign relations context, a widespread assumption has been that *foreign* relations are inherently *national* relations. As the same James Madison put it in Federalist Paper No 42: 'If we are to be one nation

[1] Louis Henkin, *Foreign Affairs and the United States Constitution* (2nd edn, New York; Oxford University Press 1996) 150.

[2] See Alexander Hamilton, James Madison, and John Jay, *The Federalist (The Gideon Edition), Edited with an Introduction, Reader's Guide, Constitutional Cross-Reference, Index, and Glossary by George W. Carey and James McClellan* (George W Carey and James McClellan eds, Liberty Fund 2001) 273. Allocating public authority to institutional actors is one of the main functions of constitutional law, alongside subjecting the subsequent exercise of that authority to external limits. On the former function, see generally Martin Loughlin, *Foundations of Public Law* (Oxford University Press 2010) 11–12, pointing to the role of institutional structures as means to generate 'political power'. On the latter function, see eg S Sottiaux, *Grondwettelijk Recht* (Intersentia 2016), using as the cover of his book the image of Odysseus tied on the deck of his ship when sailing past the Sirens. Constitutional law, Sottiaux argues, is an act of self-binding.

[3] It plays a central role in the philosophy of federalism espoused by commentators such as Kenneth Wheare, who, as mentioned, defined the 'federal principle' as 'the method of dividing power so that the general and regional governments are each, within a sphere, co-ordinate and independent'. See Kenneth C Wheare, *Federal Government* (Oxford University Press 1963) 10.

Foreign Relations Federalism. Thomas Verellen, Oxford University Press. © Thomas Verellen 2023.
DOI: 10.1093/oso/9780192844569.003.0002

in any respect, it clearly ought to be in respect to other nations.' In Madison's view, then, only the federal government of the newly established American republic should have the necessary authority, derived from its status as a sovereign state, to engage in foreign relations. More recent federations have followed a different approach from that of Madison, however, and have extended the internal division of powers to the external sphere. This is the case, in particular, in Belgium and—as will be discussed in the following chapter—the EU. But, as Louis Henkin pointed out in his seminal book *Foreign Affairs and the United States Constitution*, even in the US, states have a role to play in the foreign relations sphere.

This chapter and the next add further nuance to what at first glance appear opposite understandings of the degree to which internal diversity should be extended onto the international stage.[4] In the US and Canada, member units have become increasingly active on the international stage, defying the characterization of foreign affairs as an exclusively federal affair. Yet, in Belgium and the EU the promise of endowing both orders of government with a capacity to act autonomously on the international stage has not been fully delivered upon as external action in these federations often takes the form of joint or 'mixed' action. Also in the context of foreign relations, then, in all of the federations under review *both* orders of governance have a role to play as areas of jurisdiction increasingly overlap and both orders of governance are endowed with external powers. In such a context, the quintessentially federal question arises as to how these orders of governance interact with one another in a manner that strikes a balance between the protection of diversity, on the one hand, and the safeguard of a sufficient degree of unity, on the other. This question will be addressed in later chapters (in particular Chapters 4 and 5 on the resolution of conflicts).

In keeping with the conception of 'foreign relations power' presented in the introduction to the book, I understand these powers to include the following: (i) the power to negotiate and conclude international agreements; (ii) the power to implement those agreements, if necessary by means of internal legislation; and (iii) the power of external representation, which includes the power to speak on the international stage on behalf of the federation, be it with

[4] The labels 'open' and 'closed' federations are sometimes used to characterize these two approaches. See Bardo Fassbender, *Der offene Bundesstaat: Studien zur auswärtigen Gewalt und zur Völkerrechtssubjektivität bundesstaatlicher Teilstaaten in Europa* (Mohr Siebeck 2007) and also Robert Schütze, 'Federalism and Foreign Affairs: Mixity as a (Inter)National Phenomenon' in Christophe Hillion and Panos Koutrakos (eds), *Mixed Agreements Revisited: The EU and its Member States in the World* (Hart 2010) 59–72.

third country governments (bilateral) or on international fora (multilateral). Taken together, these powers cover much of the spectrum of instruments used to engage in foreign relations.[5]

This chapter provides a comparative overview of the allocation of foreign relations powers in the US, Canada, and Belgium. Chapter 3 focuses on the EU.

2. The United States: 'federal, but not wholly insulated from the states'

The US Constitution allocates foreign relations powers to the federal government. Some of these powers are exclusive in nature; others are concurrent. The following observations are significant: (i) that only the federal government in the US has the ability to *incur* international legal obligations; the individual states are unable to do so; (ii) that the federal government possesses broad powers to *implement* treaty obligations, which ensures the federal government is able to meet its promises towards third countries; and (iii) that only the federal government is empowered to engage in diplomatic relations with third countries. These features of the division of powers in the US do much to protect the ability of the federal government to speak with one voice on the international stage. That said, it is important also to be mindful of the opportunities US states have to engage in foreign relations of their own. They can adopt legislation on the basis of their residuary powers and they can engage in different forms of non-binding paradiplomatic activities. As will become apparent in Chapter 6, it would be mistaken to dismiss these state powers too easily as they allow US states to play a meaningful role on the international stage alongside and sometimes in competition with the federal government.

2.1 Only the President Concludes International Agreements, but States Can Make Compacts

The US Constitution allocates the power to conclude international agreements to the President. Article II §2 Cl 2 of the US Constitution provides that '[the President] shall have Power, by and with the Advice and Consent of the Senate, to make Treaties, provided two thirds of the Senators present concur'.

[5] In this sense, see also Eileen Denza, *The Intergovernmental Pillars of the European Union* (Oxford University Press 2002) 85–86.

International agreements adopted on this basis are referred to as *Article II treaties*. In addition, Congress may empower the President to conclude international agreements on any matter that falls within Congress' powers, or it may retroactively authorize agreements made by the President.[6] Such agreements are called *Congressional executive agreements*. And finally, the President may also conclude international agreements on matters that fall within the President's sole constitutional powers, such as his power to command the military.[7] Such agreements are called *sole executive agreements*.

The constitutional authority of the President to conclude Congressional or sole executive agreements is concomitant with the scope of Congress' and the President's powers. By contrast, the US President can make Article II treaties on subjects that fall outside of the scope of Congress' internal legislative powers and outside of the scope of his own independent constitutional powers. In the 1920 Supreme Court case of *Missouri v Holland*, Justice Holmes held for the majority that the limits of the federal government's authority to conclude international agreements (to 'make treaties') must be determined in a different way compared to the limits of Congress' domestic legislative powers.[8] Holmes held: 'Acts of Congress are the supreme law of the land only when made in pursuance of the Constitution, while treaties are declared to be so when made under the authority of the United States.'[9]

What did Holmes mean? What distinction did he draw between the 'Constitution' and 'the United States'? Holmes here invoked a theory that was popular at the time, according to which every sovereign state ought to be endowed with the powers that come with that status.[10] These include, amongst others, the power to conclude international agreements on a very broad, if

[6] In this sense, see 'Restatement (Third) of Foreign Relations Law of the United States' (American Law Institute 1987) para 303. The State Department's *Foreign Affairs Manual*, which lays down the policies adhered to by that department, distinguishes between Article II treaties and 'international agreements other than treaties'. Congressional executive agreements and sole executive agreements both fall within that category. See Bureau of Public Affairs Department of State, The Office of Website Management, *Foreign Affairs Manual* (US Department of State 2007) para 11 FAM 723.2–1 <https://fam.state.gov/> accessed 3 May 2022. The manual adds that Article II treaties previously concluded by the President can also empower the President to conclude executive agreements. See ibid, 11 FAM 723.2-2(A). Confirming the President's authority to conclude international agreements outside of the framework of the Article II process, see *US v Belmont*, 301 US 324 (1937) and *US v Pink*, 315 US 203 (1942).

[7] 'Restatement (Third) of Foreign Relations Law of the United States' (n 6) para 303. See eg

[8] 252 US 416 (1920).

[9] ibid 433.

[10] For an example, see *Chae Chan Ping v US ('Chinese Exclusion Case')*, 130 US 581 (1889), 604:

> [T]he United States, in their relation to foreign countries and their subjects or citizens, are one nation, invested with powers which belong to independent nations, the exercise of which can be invoked for the maintenance of its absolute independence and security throughout its entire territory. The powers to declare war, make treaties, suppress insurrection, repel invasion, regulate foreign commerce, secure republican governments to the states, and admit subjects of other nations to citizenship, are all sovereign powers, restricted in their exercise

not unlimited, number of issues.[11] To limit the scope of the President's power to make treaties to those issues that fall within Congress' legislative powers, Holmes seemed to suggest, would undermine the status of the US as a sovereign state. Sixteen years later, the Supreme Court made the point in even starker terms. In the case of *Curtiss-Wright*, Justice Sutherland stated for the majority that:

> It results that the investment of the federal government with the powers of external sovereignty did not depend upon the affirmative grants of the Constitution. The powers to declare and wage war, to conclude peace, to make treaties, to maintain diplomatic relations with other sovereignties, if they had never been mentioned in the Constitution, would have vested in the federal government as necessary concomitants of nationality.[12]

As a consequence of the 'external sovereignty' theory, the treaty-making power was deemed not to be limited by the same constitutional constraints that limit Congress' authority to legislate domestically.

Today, the 'external sovereignty' theory has been abandoned.[13] The Supreme Court has held in related contexts that the powers to engage in foreign relations are also conferred upon the federal government by the Constitution.[14] However, *Missouri v Holland* continues to be understood as standing for the proposition that the Tenth Amendment does not apply to the treaty-making power, and that, as a consequence, the scope of the federal government's treaty-making power is not subject to the same limitations as Congress' authority to adopt legislation.[15] In its most recent restatement on the foreign relations law

only by the constitution itself and considerations of public policy and justice which control, more or less, the conduct of all civilized nations.

[11] Note that Holmes did not rule out the existence of some restrictions on the Treaty Power. Possible limits on the treaty-making power should be ascertained in a 'different way', Holmes nonetheless held, somewhat cryptically. See *State of Missouri v Holland*, 252 US 416 (1920), 433.

[12] *US v Curtiss-Wright Export Corporation*, 299 US 304 (1936), 57 S Ct 216, 81 L Ed 255, 318. For a full exposition of Sutherland's theory, see George Sutherland, *Constitutional Power and World Affairs* (1st edn 1919, HardPress Publishing 2013), eg at 20: 'In all matters of external sovereignty the powers of the nation are not only supreme but exclusive, and the question whether a given power in this field shall be exercised by the general government of by the states, can never arise.' For an inquiry into the genesis and subsequent development of the theory, see Sarah H Cleveland, 'Powers Inherent in Sovereignty: Indians, Aliens, Territories, and the Nineteenth Century Origins of Plenary Power over Foreign Affairs' (2002) 81 Texas Law Review 1, 268–69.

[13] Although some continue to invoke the theory. See in particular Adrian Vermeule, *Common Good Constitutionalism* (1st edin, Polity 2022) 137–43.

[14] See eg *Zschernig v Miller*, 389 US 429 (1968), 436, referring to foreign affairs and international relations as 'matters which *the Constitution* entrusts solely to the Federal Government' (emphasis added).

[15] In this sense, see eg Henkin (n 1) 191. In a similar sense, see Thomas Healy, 'Is "Missouri v. Holland" Still Good Law? Federalism and the Treaty Power' (1998) 98 Columbia Law Review 1726, 9.

of the US, the American Law Institute (ALI) agrees: 'The treaty power is conferred in Article II of the Constitution, separate from Congress's legislative authority,' the Restatement holds, 'and it may be used to address matters falling outside the scope of that authority.'[16] (Restatements by the ALI carry much weight in the US. They are formulated over several years with extensive input from law professors, practising attorneys, and judges. They are meant to reflect the consensus of the American legal community as to what the law is.[17])

The Constitution thus allocates a treaty-making power to the President. But what is the nature of that power? Does the US Constitution not only empower the President to conclude international agreements, but also preclude US states from doing so? In its Article I §10 Cl 1, the US Constitution characterizes the President's treaty-making power as an exclusive power, in the sense that it precludes US states from concluding a 'Treaty, Alliance, or Confederation'.[18] That said, Article I §10 Cl 3 of the Constitution does empower US states to enter into 'agreements' or 'compacts' with 'foreign Powers', provided that Congress approves. How do these two constitutional provisions interact? We know that only the President can make 'treaties', and that states can make 'agreements' or 'compacts'. But what are 'agreements' or 'compacts'? By answering this question, we get an understanding of the constitutional space US states have to engage in relations with third countries.

In *Holmes v Jennison*, a very old case involving a decision by Vermont authorities to extradite an individual to Canada, the Supreme Court interpreted the notion of 'agreement' broadly as encompassing 'every agreement, written or verbal, formal or informal, positive or implied, by the mutual understanding of the parties'.[19] This broad definition suggests states have a broad power to make deals with third countries. However, the broad *Holmes v Jennison* definition does not allow us to distinguish 'agreements' or 'compacts', which US states may conclude, from 'treaties', which they may not. Half a century later, in the 1893 case of *Virginia v Tennessee*, a challenge brought against an agreement between two US states, the US Supreme Court held that 'the prohibition [against the conclusion of inter-state compacts] is directed to the formation

[16] 'Restatement (Fourth) of Foreign Relations Law' (American Law Institute 2018) para 312. Some commentators as well as a minority of Supreme Court justices have argued in favour of federalism restrictions on the federal treaty power. See in particular *Bond v United States*, 572 US 844, 134 S Ct 2077, 189 L Ed 2d 1 (2014), 879 (Scalia J, concurring), and Curtis A Bradley, 'The Treaty Power and American Federalism' (1998) 97 Michigan Law Review 390, 394.

[17] Paul B Stephan and Sarah H Cleveland (eds), *The Restatement and beyond: The Past, Present, and Future of U.S. Foreign Relations Law* (Oxford University Press 2020) 1.

[18] US Constitution, art I §10 cl 1. The abovementioned Restatement confirms the point. See 'Restatement (Fourth) of Foreign Relations Law' (n 16) para 312(c).

[19] *Holmes v Jennison*, 39 US 540 (1840), 14 Pet 540, 10 L Ed 579, 572.

of any combination tending to the increase of political power in the states, which may encroach upon or interfere with the just supremacy of the United States.'[20] This second definition is helpful as it delineates the category of 'agreements' and 'compacts' that are subject to the requirement of Congressional approval. Agreements or compacts that do not meet the threshold do not require Congressional approval.

In *Virginia* and subsequent case law, US courts have articulated a test to determine whether or not an 'agreement' or 'compact' increases the political power of the states and encroaches on the just supremacy of the US. The test was introduced in the interstate context, but in 2020 a federal district court applied it also to an agreement between California, a US state, and Quebec, a Canadian province. This judgment concurs with the State Department's position on the issue.[21] According to the *Virginia* test, for a state agreement to encroach on the just supremacy of the US, the agreement must meet three requirements. First, it must authorize states to exercise powers they could not exercise in its absence. Secondly, it must delegate sovereign power to an outside organization. And thirdly, it must preclude each state from withdrawing at any time.[22] This is a high threshold, which suggests there are quite a number of agreements that US states can conclude freely without there being a need for prior Congressional approval.

Relevant for our purposes is that agreements which all parties regard as non-binding are not likely to meet the threshold for Congressional approval.[23] This opens the door for US states to conclude memorandums of understanding with, for example, their Canadian neighbours on issues related to the shared border, with Quebec to link cap-and-trade emissions trading schemes, or with the UK to promote business investment.[24] Conversely, it would seem—but the

[20] 148 US 503 (1893), 519. The Compact Clause is discussed further in Chapter 8 on intergovernmental relations.

[21] See Letter of William H Taft, IV, Legal Adviser of the Department of State to Senator Byron L Dorgan of North Dakota regarding a Memorandum of Understanding signed by the State of Missouri and the Province of Manitoba, 20 November 2001, <https://2009-2017.state.gov/s/l/22720.htm> accessed 29 April 2022 ('When [foreign compacts] are called to the Department's attention, such arrangements have generally been analyzed under the Virginia standard, with particular attention to whether such texts would interfere with the President's foreign relations responsibilities').

[22] *US Steel Corp v Multistate Tax Commission*, 434 US 452 (1978), 473.

[23] An alternative reading would be that non-binding agreements constitute a distinct category of agreements, apart from 'treaties' and 'agreements/compacts', not covered by either of the two constitutional provisions, and that, as a consequence, states are free to conclude non-binding agreements. In this sense, see Ryan M Scoville, 'The International Commitments of the Fifty States' [2022] UCLA Law Review 51, 9–10. As the matter is of little practical significance (Congress does not often approve interstate compacts), little effort has been made by US commentators to clarify the distinction. See however the references to older literature in Henkin (n 1) 152.

[24] 'Brexit: UK Signs First US State-Level Trade Agreement with Indiana' *BBC News* (27 May 2022) <www.bbc.com/news/uk-politics-61604784> accessed 2 June 2022.

point has never been confirmed by a US court—that only the federal government is constitutionally empowered to conclude agreements which both parties regard as being subject to *international* law. If a US state were to take such a step, the agreement would likely be deemed unconstitutional, either because it constitutes a 'treaty' in the meaning of Article I §10 Cl 1 of the US Constitution, or because by doing so the state would unlawfully interfere with the federal government's foreign affairs powers—or perhaps both. (I return to the latter issue in Chapter 4, where I discuss how conflicts between federal and state powers are resolved in the US.)

2.2 Congress Has the Necessary Powers to Implement Treaty Obligations

Treaty compliance was a central concern of the framers of the US Constitution. During the Confederation era, individual states refused to comply with treaty obligations incurred by the federal government.[25] An important aim of the 1787 Constitution was to avoid such risks from materializing again. To this end, the Supremacy Clause covers not only federal legislation, but also federally concluded treaties—a category which has been understood to include both Article II treaties and (Congressional) executive agreements.[26] Treaty provisions that are self-executing are part of the law of the land in the US. They are binding as a matter of domestic law, and they prevail over state law in the event of a conflict.[27] If an Article II treaty provision is self-executing when the text and context of the provision are consistent with an understanding by the US treaty-makers that the provision would be directly enforceable in courts in the US, then the abovementioned Restatement holds.[28]

By contrast, when treaty provisions are not self-executing—as they often are since the Supreme Court's 2008 ruling in the case of *Medellín v Texas*[29]—they

[25] On the shortcomings of the Articles of Confederation in this area, see the Articles by John Jay in the Federalist Papers: George W Carey, *The Federalist (The Gideon Edition), Edited with an Introduction, Reader's Guide, Constitutional Cross-Reference, Index, and Glossary by George W. Carey and James McClellan* (Liberty Fund 2001) N) 2–5.

[26] In this sense see *American Insurance Association v Garamendi*, 539 US 396 (2003), 416 ('Generally, then, valid executive agreements are fit to pre-empt state law, just as treaties are . . . ').

[27] *Medellín v Texas*, 552 US 491 (2008) ('While a treaty may constitute an international commitment, it is not binding domestic law unless Congress has enacted statutes implementing it or the treaty itself conveys an intention that it be "selfexecuting" and is ratified on that basis').

[28] 'Restatement (Fourth) of Foreign Relations Law' (n 16) para 310.

[29] Samuel Estreicher, 'Taking Treaty-Implementing Statutes Seriously' in Paul B Stephan and Sarah H Cleveland (eds), *The Restatement and Beyond* (Oxford University Press 2020) 107. On the growing hostility towards international law in the U.S., see generally Jens David Ohlin, *The Assault on International Law* (Oxford University Press USA 2015).

are not binding as a matter of *domestic law*, even though they of course remain binding as a matter of *international* law. If existing US law is at variance with the content of the treaty, domestic law will have to be amended to ensure compliance with the treaty. This may entail the adoption of legislation by Congress. In *Missouri v Holland*, mentioned earlier, the Supreme Court made clear that all powers required to implement US treaty obligations are 'necessary and proper', and that Congress thus has an implied power to implement all US treaty obligations regardless of whether or not the issues covered by the treaty fall within the scope of Congress' internal law-making powers. As Justice Holmes stated: 'If the treaty is valid there can be no dispute about the validity of the statute under Article 1, Section 8, as a necessary and proper means to execute the powers of the Government.'[30]

In the not so distant past, the Supreme Court has made efforts to limit the reach of its holding in *Missouri* that Congress always has the necessary legislative powers to implement US treaty obligations. In the 2014 decision in *Bond v United States*, a majority of Supreme Court justices held that if Congress wishes to adopt treaty-implementing legislation that benefits from the protection of the Supremacy Clause and which thus pre-empts state law, Congress must expressly indicate its intent to do so by means of a clear statement (a 'clear indication', the opinion states).[31] If Congress does not clearly express a wish to pre-empt state legislation, US courts are under an interpretative obligation to uphold state legislation as much as possible, and the federal treaty-implementing statute will be interpreted as not giving expression to a Congressional intention to pre-empt state law. I return to the issue of pre-emption in Chapter 4.

Bond runs counter to the spirit of *Missouri*. While *Missouri* purported to grant Congress exceptionally broad authority to implement treaty obligations, *Bond* restricts that authority without however overturning *Missouri* itself.[32] Despite the justices' reluctance to overturn *Missouri*, *Bond* may have a

[30] *State of Missouri v Holland*, 252 U.S. 416 (1920), 432. Contra, see generally Nicholas Quinn Rosenkranz, 'Executing the Treaty Power' (2005) 118 Harvard Law Review 1867.

[31] 572 US 844 (2014), p 14 ('[I]n this curious case, we can insist on a clear indication that Congress meant to reach purely local crimes, before interpreting the statute's expansive language in a way that intrudes on the police power of the States.').

[32] In this sense, see Michael J Glennon and Robert D Sloane, 'The Sad, Quiet Death of *Missouri v Holland*: How *Bond* Hobbled the Treaty Power' (2016) 41 Yale Journal of International Law 51 and subsequently Michael J Glennon and Robert D Sloane, *Foreign Affairs Federalism: The Myth of National Exclusivity* (Oxford University Press 2016) 204–17. As Heather Gerken put it: '[O]ne cannot help but suspect that the conservative majority fully intended to limit *Missouri v Holland* but discovered that it could not write such an opinion without flouting the dictates of craft. Some dogs don't hunt; some opinions don't write.' See H Gerken, 'Slipping the Bonds of Federalism' (2016) 128 Harvard Law Review 85, 93.

chilling effect on *Missouri*. One can imagine that federal treaty-implementing statutes will less easily be relied upon before courts post-*Bond* than before. That being said, it should be borne in mind that Congress' Article I powers are in themselves very broad.[33] In this sense, the significance of a possible future overturning of *Missouri* on Congress' ability to adopt legislation required to implement treaty obligations incurred by the President should not be overstated.

2.3 The President as the 'Sole Voice' of the Nation

External representation is the third type of foreign relations power that I examine. 'Sub-state diplomacy' or 'paradiplomacy' has become a topic of interest for international relations scholars in recent decades.[34] They emphasize the role played by sub-state actors such as US states in tackling societal challenges such as climate change. However, while economically and politically significant, from a legal perspective such activities must be distinguished from traditional diplomacy governed by the Vienna Convention on Diplomatic Relations (VCDR) and by customary international law. I look at both forms of external representation in turn.

As far as diplomatic relations are concerned, the US President maintains an exclusive power to engage in diplomatic relations on behalf of the US.[35] The theory underpinning this claim is known as the 'one voice' or 'sole organ' theory.[36] It finds support in the 1937 case of *Curtiss-Wright*, mentioned earlier, in which Justice Sutherland held that '[i]n this vast external realm, with its important, complicated, delicate and manifold problems, the President alone has the power to speak or listen as a representative of the nation'.[37] Sutherland in turn relied on a speech by John Marshall in the House of Representatives,

[33] Pointing to Congress' broad Article I powers as a means to avoid controversies surrounding the scope of Congress' treaty implementing power, see M Hakimi, 'The Bond Court's Institutional Truce' (2014) 108 American Journal of International Law 90.

[34] See eg R Tavares, *Paradiplomacy: Cities and States as Global Players* (Oxford University Press 2016) as well as Julia Spiegel, 'Embracing Foreign Affairs Federalism in a Post-Trump Era' (*Lawfare*, 3 March 2021) <www.lawfareblog.com/embracing-foreign-affairs-federalism-post-trump-era> accessed 27 October 2021, calling on the Biden administration to 'embrace the role that states and localities play as force multipliers and divisors of solutions to the foreign policy dilemmas the global community faces.'

[35] The federal government defended this position, eg in the case of *Zivotofsky v Kerry*, where Secretary of State John Kerry held in an amicus brief, with a reference to *Curtiss-Wright*, that '[t]he Constitution ... establishes the Executive as the sole organ of the federal government in the field of international relations, with exclusive authority to conduct diplomatic relations' (internal quotation marks omitted). See *Zivotofsky v Kerry*, 2014 WL 4726506 (U.S., 2014), 18.

[36] On the principle, see critically L Fisher, *The Law of the Executive Branch: Presidential Power* (Oxford University Press USA 2014) 465–68.

[37] *US v Curtiss-Wright Export Corporation*, 299 US 304 (1936), 318.

in which the then still future Supreme Court Chief Justice had asserted that '[t]he President is the sole organ of the nation in its external relations, and its sole representative with foreign nations'.[38]

Subsequent Supreme Court majorities have refused to endorse this sweeping understanding of the 'sole organ' theory, however. In its 2015 ruling in *Zivotofsky v Kerry*, on the (lack of) authority of Congress to legislate that US citizens born in Jerusalem can, upon request, have 'Israel' be listed as their place of birth on their passport, Justice Kennedy held for the majority that the President holds an exclusive power to recognize foreign governments—a conclusion Justice Kennedy grounded in the text and structure of the US Constitution, institutional practice, as well as in functional considerations that favour Presidential action.[39] He immediately added, however, that the Supreme Court was not taking a position on the broader question of whether the President possesses an exclusive power to engage in diplomatic relations more broadly considered. Rather to the contrary, Justice Kennedy mentioned that *Curtiss-Wright*, mentioned earlier, does not support a 'broader definition of the Executive's power over foreign relations that would permit the President alone to determine the whole content of the Nation's foreign policy'.[40] It does not do so, he submitted, since *Curtiss-Wright* addressed the legality of a delegation of powers by Congress to the President, not the constitutionality of independent Presidential action. As such, *Zivotofsky* cannot be relied on to support the sweeping contention that the President has an independent, exclusive power to engage in diplomatic relations broadly considered.[41]

Zivotofsky v Kerry confirms that the President has an exclusive power to recognize foreign governments. For other aspects of diplomacy, the constitutional landscape is less clear. The President can appoint and dismiss ambassadors.[42] The logic of *Zivotofsky* would seem to suggest that such a power is exclusive to the President as well.[43] Regardless, relevant for our present purposes is that it certainly is a power that cannot be exercised by individual US states. Having been allocated to the President, the Tenth Amendment implies that the power no longer lies with the individual states. Similarly, the US Constitution grants

[38] John Marshall, as quoted in *US v Curtiss-Wright Export Corporation*, 299 US 304 (1936), 318.
[39] *Zivotofsky ex rel. Zivotofsky v Kerry*, 576 US 1 (2015).
[40] ibid 3.
[41] See ibid 21.
[42] US Constitution, art II § 2 cl 2.
[43] Criticizing the ruling on this basis, see J Goldsmith, 'Zivotofsky II as Precedent in the Executive Branch' (2015) 129 Harvard Law Review 112, arguing that the judgment provides the executive branch with further arguments in support of a broad reading of the President's exclusive powers over foreign affairs. The ambiguities surrounding the limits of the recognition power only bolster the executive in making that type of argument.

the President the authority to represent the US on the international stage, for example within international organizations such as the United Nations, without however necessarily granting him an exclusive power to determine what is to be said.[44] (Exclusivity should be understood here in horizontal terms as exclusive vis-à-vis Congress.) Here as well, however, there are no restrictions on the content of the President's representations on the international stage that derive from the federal structure of the US.

That said, US states have ample opportunity to engage in relations with third country governments, as long as in doing so they do not claim to be engaging in *diplomatic* relations. US states can engage in bilateral relations with third country governments or in multilateral fora which do not purport to adopt decisions or norms regarded as binding under international law, such as the Conference of Great Lakes and St Lawrence Governors and Premiers. Their actions and communications will not benefit from the protections provided for in the VCDR, however, and the outcome of their deliberations will not be binding as a matter of international law.

* * *

In conclusion, in the US the federal government, and in particular the President, has an exclusive power to conclude international agreements governed by international law, and Congress has the necessary powers to implement any international commitments incurred by the President. For the individual US states, the following arrangement applies: agreements that touch upon the just supremacy of the federal government require prior Congressional approval; agreements that do not, do not require such approval. Non-binding agreements are very unlikely to touch upon the just supremacy of the federal government. States can thus conclude non-binding agreements independently, without prior Congressional approval. By contrast, states cannot conclude international agreements governed by international law. Finally, the President has the necessary constitutional authority to engage in diplomatic relations on behalf of the US. There is some uncertainty on whether Congress, too, can play a role in this area. It is clear, however, that US states cannot engage in diplomatic relations. That said, here too, they have ample opportunity to engage in less formal, paradiplomatic relations with third countries. The table below summarizes how foreign relations powers are allocated in the US (see Table 2.1).

[44] L Fisher, *The Law of the Executive Branch: Presidential Power* (Oxford University Press USA 2014) 268.

Table 2.1 Allocation of foreign relations powers in the US

	Conclude international agreements	**Implement international agreements**	**Represent on the international stage**
Federal	Yes	Yes	Yes
Member unit	No	No	No

3. Canada: External Unity, Internal Diversity

Canada's Constitution Act, 1867 allocates broad foreign relations powers to the federal government. The federal government of Canada alone can conclude international agreements and represent Canada within the diplomatic system. On these two issues, the Constitution of Canada thus aligns closely with that of the US. By contrast, on the matter of treaty implementation, Canada diverges from the US. Pursuant to a decision of the Judicial Committee of the Privy Council (JCPC), the London-based judicial body which until 1949 operated as Canada's court of final appeal on many matters,[45] the federal government of Canada does not hold a general treaty-implementing power akin to the power recognized by the US Supreme Court in *Missouri v Holland*. Instead, the power to implement treaty obligations depends on the subject matter of the treaty and rests with either a federal or provincial head of legislative power, depending on which level of government has jurisdiction over that area. This absence of a federal treaty-implementing power in Canada is all the more significant given Canada's 'dualist' constitutional tradition, which in many instances requires treaties to be implemented through legislation.

3.1 Treaty-Making as a Federal Royal Prerogative

Canada inherited much of its constitutional tradition from the UK.[46] Following this tradition, the power to negotiate and conclude international agreements is

[45] *An Act to amend the Supreme Court Act*, S.C. 1949 (2nd sess.), *c.* 37, s. 3. Appeals in criminal matters were abolished in 1933. See *An Act to amend the Criminal Code*, S.C. 1932–33, *c.* 53, s. 17.

[46] See the preamble to the Constitution Act, 1867: 'Whereas the Provinces of Canada, Nova Scotia, and New Brunswick have expressed their Desire to be federally united into One Dominion under the Crown of the United Kingdom of Great Britain and Ireland, *with a Constitution similar in Principle to that of the United Kingdom*...' (emphasis added).

part of the royal prerogative.[47] AV Dicey, a nineteenth-century British constitutional scholar, defined the royal prerogative as 'the residue of discretionary or arbitrary authority, which at any given time is legally left in the hands of the Crown.'[48] Many commentators regard the prerogative as a product of the common law,[49] although an argument can also be made that it predates the common law.[50] The royal prerogative covers most of the foreign relations powers discussed in this book. It empowers the Crown to negotiate and conclude international agreements and to represent the country on the international stage by exercising the *ius legationis*.[51] It covers, in other words, the exercise of public authority on the international stage, and can thus be contrasted with the exercise of domestic authority. Externally, the Crown can act independently from Parliament by relying directly on the prerogative. By contrast, internally the Crown's powers are more circumscribed: Parliament can change the law of the land, and it has legislated to displace much of the Crown's domestic prerogative powers.[52]

What impact, if any, does Canada's federal architecture have on the prerogative power to conclude international agreements? Conflicting theories have been offered. As the 'first principle of Canadian government',[53] the Crown is divisible.[54] It has many incarnations: it can act on behalf of 'Canada' (the 'Crown in right of Canada'), or on behalf of a particular province (eg the 'Crown in right of New Brunswick'). The matter of whether not only the federal Crown, but also the provincial Crowns can exercise the foreign affairs prerogative has never been settled authoritatively by a court of law. The federal government as well as a majority of commentators maintain that the right to advise

[47] A Gottlieb, *Canadian Treaty-Making* (Butterworths 1968) 4.

[48] AV Dicey, *Introduction to the Study of the Law of the Constitution* (Reprint Originally published: 8th edn London: Macmillan, 1915, Liberty Classics 1982), 424.

[49] In this sense, see eg A Gottlieb, *Canadian Treaty-Making* (Butterworths 1968), 4.

[50] In this sense, in the UK context, see generally HWR Wade, 'The Basis of Legal Sovereignty' [1955] The Cambridge Law Journal 172.

[51] Blackstone included the following powers: the power to appoint and receive ambassadors, to make treaties with foreign states, the sole power to make war and peace, the power to exact reprisals for injury of the King's subjects by foreign states, and the power to grant safe conduct for foreigners entering the nation. See Blackstone as summarized in C McLachlan, *Foreign Relations Law* (Cambridge University Press 2014), 116. Notably, for most of these matters, the royal prerogative has not been displaced by federal legislation in Canada. In this sense, see eg Craig Forcese, 'The Executive, the Royal Prerogative, and the Constitution' in P Oliver, P Macklem, and N des Rosiers (eds), *The Oxford Handbook of the Canadian Constitution*, vol 1 (Oxford University Press 2017) 164. ('In Canada, too, the conduct of foreign affairs is still a prerogative power').

[52] On the power of Parliament to displace the prerogative, see ibid 155–58.

[53] DE Smith, *The Invisible Crown: The First Principle of Canadian Government* (University of Toronto Press 2013).

[54] A Twomey, 'Responsible Government and the Divisibility of the Crown' [2008] Public Law 742, 742 ('It has long been recognised by courts that the Crown is divisible').

the Crown on matters pertaining to foreign relations, including the power to conclude international agreements, has been transferred from the Imperial Crown (ie the British Crown) to the Crown in right of Canada.[55] As a consequence, only the federal executive can advise the Crown on the desirability of concluding international agreements. The 1947 Letters Patent, which empower the Governor General, the representative of the Queen in Canada's capital, 'to exercise all powers and authorities lawfully belonging to Us [the King] in respect of Canada', are often invoked in support of this proposition.[56]

A minority of commentators maintain that the provincial executives, too, can advise the Crown in its exercise of the royal prerogative over foreign relations. If this is indeed the case, Canadian provincial governments, too, could conclude binding international agreements.[57] The argument is made in different ways. Quebec-based commentators have contended that a gradual process of emancipation of Quebec from Canada has endowed Quebec with treaty-making rights—rather like the process that has led Canada to acquire external sovereignty a few decades before.[58] Another argument advanced in support of a provincial treaty-making power is teleological: to give full effect to the provincial power to implement international agreements by means of legislation, it is necessary also for the provincial executives to have the power to conclude such agreements. As former Quebec education minister Paul Gérin-Lajoie put it in a speech to the Montreal-based consular corps: 'Why would the state who implements an agreement be unable to negotiate and sign the agreement itself? Is an agreement not first and foremost concluded to be applied, and is it not for those who implement the agreement to define its terms?'[59] (The

[55] For the federal government, see P Martin, *Federalism and International Relations* (The Queen's Printer 1968). Amongst commentators, see eg PW Hogg, *Constitutional Law of Canada* (5th edn supplemented, Thomson/Carswell 2007) 11–12; S Beaulac, 'Myth of Js Tractatus in La Belle Province: Quebec's Gerin-Lajoie Statement, The' (2012) 35 Dalhousie Law Journal 237. See also the review of Hugo Cyr's book (referred to below) by a former director of the administrative and constitutional law unit of the Justice Department of the federal government: M Freeman, 'Canadian Federalism and Treaty Powers: Organic Constitutionalism at Work' (2011) 37 Commonwealth Law Bulletin 210. In the same sense, assuming without explaining: Alexander Bolt and Philippe Lagassé, 'Beyond Dicey: Executive Authorities in Canada' (2021) 3 Journal of Commonwealth Law 1, 27.

[56] See eg PW Hogg, *Constitutional Law of Canada* (5th ed supplemented, Thomson/Carswell 2007) 11–12.

[57] See eg J-Y Morin, 'La personnalité internationale du Québec' (1984) 1 Revue Québécoise de droit international 163, and somewhat more recently also G Van Ert, 'The Legal Character of Provincial Arrangements with Foreign Governments' (2001) 42 Les Cahiers de Droit 1093, and H Cyr, *Canadian Federalism and Treaty Powers: Organic Constitutionalism at Work* (Peter Lang 2009). For a presentation of the provincial position, see also G Van Ert, *Using International Law in Canadian Courts* (Irwin Law, Incorporated 2008) 107–11.

[58] See in particular J-Y Morin, 'La personnalité internationale du Québec' (1984) 1 Revue Québécoise de droit international 163, 199ff. On the process through which Canada acquired independence, see AM Jacomy-Millette, *Treaty Law in Canada* (University of Ottawa Press 1975) ch 1.

[59] See Gérin-Lajoie P, 'Allocution du ministre de l'Éducation, M. Paul Gérin-Lajoie, aux membres du Corps consulaire de Montréal, lundi, le 12 avril à 12h30 de l'après-midi, à l'hôtel Windsor' <www.

theory that provincial crowns can conclude international agreements would become known in Quebec as the *Gérin-Lajoie doctrine*.)

It is important to point out that, while the theoretical disagreement persists, no Canadian court has ever endorsed the minority position.[60] Rather, albeit in *dicta*, some courts have indicated support for the majority view. In its 2010 judgment in *Khadr*, for example, the Supreme Court of Canada mentioned in *dicta* that '[t]he prerogative power over foreign affairs has not been displaced ... and continues to be exercised by the federal government'.[61] Further back in time, in its 1967 *Offshore Mineral Rights Reference*, the Supreme Court rejected an argument advanced by the province of British Columbia that the provincial government has jurisdiction over offshore mineral rights.[62] The Court did not agree; it held that 'the rights in the territorial sea arise by international law and depend upon recognition by other sovereign states. Canada is a sovereign state recognized by international law and thus able to enter into arrangements with other states respecting the rights in the territorial sea.'[63] From this perspective, it is relevant to note also that no third country has ever gone as far as to conclude an agreement with a Canadian province which it expressly characterized as governed by international law.[64] These different *dicta* point in the same direction, that is, against a provincial treaty-making power, and in favour of an exclusive federal treaty-making power.

mrif.gouv.qc.ca/content/documents/fr/discours_gerin_lajoie.pdf > accessed 28 October 2021. Translation TV. Original in the French: 'Pourquoi l'État qui met un accord à exécution serait-il incapable de le négocier et de le signer lui-même? Une entente n'est-elle pas conclue dans le but essentiel d'être appliquée, et n'est-ce pas à ceux qui la doivent mettre en œuvre qu'il revient d'abord d'en préciser les termes?'.

[60] Writing in 2008: G Van Ert, *Using International Law in Canadian Courts* (Irwin Law, Incorporated 2008) 111 ('No Canadian court has yet answered the question of the capacity of provincial governments to bind their provinces by treaty at international law.')

[61] *Canada (Prime Minister) v Khadr*, [2010] 1 SCR 44, 2010 SCC 3 (CanLII). Similarly, see the decision of the Quebec Superior Court in *UL c Canada*: 'En droit canadien, seul le gouvernement fédéral a le pouvoir de conclure des traités internationaux et ce, en vertu de la prérogative royale dont est revêtu le cabinet fédéral comme détenteur du pouvoir exécutif.' (*UL Canada inc. c. Québec (Procureur général)*, 1999 CanLII 11667 (QC CS) [83]).

[62] *Reference Re: Offshore Mineral Rights*, [1967] SCR 792, 1967 CanLII 71 (SCC).

[63] Ibid. Note that the theory is similar to the one encountered in the US in the cases of *Curtiss-Wright*. In both contexts, international law is turned to in support of the view that only the federal government can undertake certain actions.

[64] Gaullist France at one point came close to doing so. On this episode of Canadian-French relations, see E Baraton, *De Gaulle ou l'hypothèque française sur le Canada* (L'Harmattan 2013) and the comments in footnote in G Van Ert, *Using International Law in Canadian Courts* (Irwin Law, Incorporated 2008) 117. Another, more recent, example was provided by Germany, which in the early 2000s agreed to insert an arbitration clause governed by international law in an agreement with Quebec. As reported by Armand de Mestral and Hugo Cyr, following objections by the Canadian federal government, Germany quickly withdrew the clause. See Hugo Cyr and Armand de Mestral, 'International Treaty-Making and Treaty Implementation' in *The Oxford Handbook of the Canadian Constitution* (Oxford University Press 2017) 598.

As in the US and, as will be discussed, in Belgium, but contrary to the arrangements in the EU, the member units of the Canadian federation do have the constitutional authority to conclude non-binding agreements. The latter point was confirmed, albeit implicitly, by the Canadian Supreme Court in the 1956 case of *Ontario v Scott*.[65] At issue in that case was the constitutionality of a memorandum of understanding between the Ontario and UK governments. The applicant argued the memorandum constituted an international agreement and was therefore unconstitutional. The Court dismissed the argument, submitting that the agreement was merely a non-binding agreement and that the 'essentials of a treaty [were] absent'. The Canadian Supreme Court thus interpreted narrowly the scope of the foreign affairs prerogative in order to avoid the constitutional issue of the possible division of the treaty-making power in Canada. In doing so, the court implicitly gave its blessing to the proposition that provincial governments can conclude non-binding agreements with third country governments.[66]

All Canadian provinces have been involved in the business of concluding non-binding agreements,[67] but Quebec in particular has been keen to make arrangements with third countries.[68] While the Quebec government labels such agreements '*ententes*' rather than 'treaties' or 'international agreements' (a practice which appears to suggest Quebec itself accepts that the agreements it concludes do *not* constitute international agreements), the government of Quebec nonetheless maintains it has the constitutional authority to conclude binding international agreements.[69] Quebec's position is not without its ambiguities: to persuade the federal government and its third country partners,

[65] *Ontario v Scott* ([1956] SCR 137, 1955 CanLII 16 (SCC)).

[66] In the same sense, see also *Bazylo c Collins*, 1984 CanLII 2861 (QC CA), where the Quebec Court of Appeals read down an 'entente' concluded by the Quebec government with a third country, considering it constituted not a treaty, but mere administrative arrangements. The decision has been criticised by commentators of a 'sovereignist' persuasion such as former Bloc québecois MP Daniel Turp. See Turp D, 'L'arrêt Bazylo c. Collins et la nature juridique des ententes internationales du Québec' [1985] Revue québécoise de droit international <www.sqdi.org/fr/larret-bazylo-c-collins-et-la-nature-juridique-des-ententes-internationales-du-quebec/> accessed 2 November 2017.

[67] JT McHugh, 'Paradiplomacy, Protodiplomacy and the Foreign Policy Aspirations of Quebec and Other Canadian Provinces' (2015) 0 Canadian Foreign Policy Journal 1.

[68] Quebec's quest for recognition as a distinct nation is not alien to the efforts by subsequent Quebec governments to develop relations with third country governments. On this aspect, see L Bélanger, 'The Domestic Politics of Quebec's Quest for External Distinctiveness' [2002] The American Review of Canadian Studies 195.

[69] See eg C St-Pierre, 'La Doctrine Gérin-Lajoie, un socle solide' Le Devoir (14 April 2015) <www.ledevoir.com/politique/quebec/437068/la-doctrine-gerin-lajoie-un-socle-solide> accessed 31 March 2016 ('La doctrine Gérin-Lajoie, en somme, demeure aussi pertinente et actuelle qu'elle l'était il y a 50 ans').

the Quebec government must accept that *ententes* it concludes with foreign governments are not governed by international law, whereas to domestic audiences it continues to feel compelled to insist on the agreements' binding character.[70]

Despite the continued popularity of the *Gérin-Lajoie* doctrine in Quebec[71]—the issue of a possible division of the treaty-making power in Canada has remained largely theoretical. As a former Director of Constitutional and Administrative Law of the federal Department of Justice concluded his review of a book defending the provincial case for a divided treaty-making power:

> Treaty-making in Canadian constitutional law is an intriguing topic. The actual state of the law remains somewhat uncertain and the courts have managed to avoid the issue for many years. Nevertheless, this has not had a great impact on the way the world of international relations and treaty-making has operated for Canadians. In practice, the Government of Canada does exercise a monopoly in this field.[72]

Despite the ongoing controversy, only the federal government of Canada, and in particular the federal executive, can advise the Crown to negotiate and conclude international agreements. However, as is the case in the US, this exclusive federal power does not preclude provincial executives from concluding non-binding agreements with foreign governments. These agreements are non-binding both under international law and under domestic Canadian law, and can thus not be enforced by Canadian courts.

[70] As argued by Stéphane Beaulac, Quebec's insistence on possessing an independent power to conclude international agreements has something of a 'heroic myth', i.e. a widely held but false belief or idea which nonetheless has powerful rhetorical force amongst its intended audience (in this case the population of the province of Quebec). The *Gérin-Lajoie* doctrine, after the aforementioned Quebec education minister, has operated as a political tool to garner popular support precisely for that which is claimed to already exist: a provincial power to conclude international agreements. See S Beaulac, 'Myth of Js Tractatus in La Belle Province: Quebec's Gerin-Lajoie Statement, The' (2012) 35 Dalhousie Law Journal 237.

[71] See eg a 2015 op-ed by Quebec minister of international relations Christine St-Pierre in defence of the doctrine: Christine St-Pierre, 'La Doctrine Gérin-Lajoie, un socle solide' *Le Devoir* (14 April 2015) <www.ledevoir.com/politique/quebec/437068/la-doctrine-gerin-lajoie-un-socle-solide> accessed 28 October 2021. The doctrine is treated also as a legitimate topic of scholarly inquiry amongst international relations scholars in Quebec. See eg S Paquin, *Les relations internationales du Québec depuis la doctrine Gérin-Lajoie (1965–2005): le prolongement externe des compétences internes* (Presses Université Laval 2006).

[72] M Freeman, 'Canadian Federalism and Treaty Powers: Organic Constitutionalism at Work' (2011) 37 Commonwealth Law Bulletin 210, 213.

3.2 Implementing Treaties: 'There is no such thing as treaty legislation as such'

Canada is, as far as international agreements are concerned, a so-called 'dualist' jurisdiction.[73] As is the case with non-self-executing international agreements in the US or international agreements without direct effect in Belgium or the EU, in many instances domestic legislation must be adopted for treaty obligations to be given effect within Canada's domestic legal order.[74] Here again, a federalism question arises: which legislature(s)—federal or provincial—is/are empowered to enact treaty obligations incurred by Canada's federal government? On this issue, Canadian constitutional law has charted a different course from its neighbour to the south. In the 1937 *Labour Conventions* reference, the JCPC held that the Constitution Act, 1867 does not provide for a distinct treaty-implementing power. As Lord Atkin submitted:

> For the purposes of ss. 91 and 92, i.e., the distribution of legislative powers between the Dominion and the Provinces, there is no such thing as treaty legislation as such. The distribution is based on classes of subjects; and as a treaty deals with a particular class of subjects so will the legislative power of performing it be ascertained. No one can doubt that this distribution is one of the most essential conditions, probably the most essential condition, in the inter-provincial compact to which the [Constitution Act 1867] gives effect.[75]

At the time, *Labour Conventions* was regarded as a significant setback for the Canadian federal government. Without a *Missouri*-type implied federal legislative power to implement treaty obligations, commentators feared Canada

[73] See Stéphane S Beaulac and JH Currie, 'Canada' in Dinah Shelton (ed), *International Law and Domestic Legal Systems: Incorporation, Transformation, and Persuasion* (Oxford University Press 2011) 126 as well as Gib van Ert, 'The Domestic Application of International Law in Canada' in Curtis A Bradley (ed), *The Oxford Handbook of Comparative Foreign Relations Law* (Oxford University Press 2019) 502. In contrast to international agreements, which must be implemented to be effective within Canada's domestic legal order, customary international law does not require implementation. It is in this sense that, as van Ert mentions, that Canada is 'not wholly' a dualist system. For an example, see *Nevsun Resources Ltd. v Araya*, 2020 SCC 5, [90] ('Canada has long followed the conventional path of automatically incorporating customary international law into domestic law via the doctrine of adoption, making it part of the law of Canada').

[74] In this sense, see eg *UL Canada inc. c. Québec (Procureur général)*, 1999 CanLII 11667 (QC CS) [82] ('Au plan conceptuel, il importe de ne pas confondre l'approbation d'un traité, qui est du ressort exclusif du cabinet fédéral, avec la mise en œuvre du traité en droit interne. Un traité n'ayant pas, en principe, une valeur juridique contraignante dans l'ordre juridique interne canadien, sa mise en œuvre nécessite l'adoption d'un instrument juridique reconnu par le droit interne, ce qui suppose, dans la plupart des cas, l'intervention du Parlement, de l'Assemblée nationale ou des législatures provinciales.').

[75] *Attorney General for Canada v Attorney General for Ontario... ('Labour Conventions')*, [1937] AC 326 (1937), 351.

would prove itself untrustworthy vis-à-vis its treaty partners. Francis Scott, for example, argued in a 1937 contribution that 'the conduct of Canada's foreign relations will henceforth be impossibly handicapped; the Dominion Cabinet and Parliament will always be in doubt as to their jurisdiction save in those increasingly rare cases when the Imperial Crown enters into treaties binding the whole Empire'.[76]

With the benefit of hindsight, Scott's fears have proven themselves to be overstated. While it is impossible to pinpoint how many treaty obligations Canada did not incur due to its constitutional set-up, it is nonetheless important to emphasize the wide scope of the federal Parliament's legislative powers, irrespective of the existence of a specific treaty-implementing power. Key in bolstering the federal Parliament's ability to adopt treaty legislation has been the development by the Supreme Court of Canada of a series of 'federalism doctrines'. These doctrines govern the way Canadian courts analyse federalism cases above and beyond the interpretation of the various heads of power.[77] The Supreme Court has referred to these doctrines as the 'dominant tide' of 'modern' or 'flexible' Canadian federalism. As Chief Justice Dickson held in the 1987 *OPSEU* case:

> The history of Canadian constitutional law has been to allow for a fair amount of interplay and indeed overlap between federal and provincial powers. It is true that doctrines like interjurisdictional and Crown immunity and concepts like 'watertight compartments' qualify the extent of that interplay. But it must be recognized that these doctrines and concepts have not been the dominant tide of constitutional doctrines; rather they have been an undertow against the strong pull of pith and substance, the aspect doctrine and, in recent years, a very restrained approach to concurrency and paramountcy issues.[78]

These doctrines purport to uphold the validity of legislation enacted by both federal and provincial legislatures. As Justices Binnie and LeBel held in the 2007 *Canadian Western Bank* ruling:

[76] FR Scott, 'The Consequences of the Privy Council Decisions' (1937) XV Canadian Bar Review 485, 487.

[77] PC Oliver, 'The Busy Harbours of Canadian Federalism: The Division of Powers and Its Doctrines in the McLachlin Court' in David A Wright and Adam M Dodek (eds), *Public Law at the McLachlin Court: The First Decade* (Irwin Law 2011) 169.

[78] *Ontario (Attorney General) v OPSEU*, [1987] 2 SCR 2, 1987 CanLII 71 (SCC) [27]. On this development, see generally Wade K Wright, 'Facilitating Intergovernmental Dialogue: Judicial Review of the Division of Powers in the Supreme Court of Canada' (2010) 51 Supreme Court Law Review 625, as well as B Ryder, 'Demise and Rise of the Classical Paradigm in Canadian Federalism: Promoting Autonomy for the Provinces and First Nations, The' (1990) 36 McGill Law Journal 308.

> The 'dominant tide' finds its principled underpinning in the concern that a court should favour, where possible, the ordinary operation of statutes enacted by both levels of government. In the absence of conflicting enactments of the other level of government, the Court should avoid blocking the application of measures which are taken to be enacted in furtherance of the public interest.[79]

In the context of treaty implementation, the dominant tide works one-way only, however. Because only the federal government can conclude international agreements, only the federal Parliament can make use of the flexibility offered by the 'dominant tide' of Canadian federalism to enact legislation that may in part overlap with provincial powers. As a consequence, as will be discussed in a later chapter, the leverage provincial governments might have obtained at one point from the *Labour Conventions* principle—while still meaningful[80]—is less significant today than it might have been at the time of Francis Scott's contribution.

3.3 External Representation: Federal in Principle, Shared in Practice

The power to represent Canada on the international stage is also covered by the royal prerogative and can thus only be exercised by the federal executive. However, as in the US, the exclusive power of the federal government is best understood as limited to the power to engage in *diplomatic* external representation. An interpretation of the prerogative against the backdrop of the constitutional principle of federalism—recognized as such by the Supreme Court in its 1998 *Quebec Secession Reference*[81]—points in this direction. In that reference, the Canadian Supreme Court held that constitutional principles 'assist in the interpretation of the text and the delineation of spheres of jurisdiction,

[79] *Canadian Western Bank v Alberta*, [2007] 2 SCR 3, 2007 SCC 22 (CanLII) [37]. For a more recent affirmation, see *References re Greenhouse Gas Pollution Pricing Act*, 2021 SCC 11 [50]: 'Although early Canadian constitutional decisions by the Judicial Committee of the Privy Council applied a rigid division of federal-provincial powers as watertight compartments, this Court has favoured a flexible view of federalism—what is best described as a modern form of cooperative federalism—that accommodates and encourages intergovernmental cooperation.'

[80] Pointing to the continued influence of provincial governments on the implementation of treaty obligations in Canada, see AJ VanDuzer, 'Could an Intergovernmental Agreement Increase the Credibility of Canadian Treaty Commitments in Areas of Provincial Jurisdiction?' (2012) 68 International Journal 536.

[81] *Reference re Secession of Quebec*, [1998] 2 SCR 217, 1998 CanLII 793 (SCC).

the scope of rights and obligations, and the role of [Canada's] political institutions'.[82] Federalism is such a principle.[83] Assuming that the royal prerogative, which grants the federal executive an independent power to exercise public authority, can be considered a form of 'jurisdiction', the *Quebec Secession Reference* suggests that the scope of the federal royal prerogative should be read in a way that is respectful of the provinces' own spheres of jurisdiction. By restricting the scope of the federal royal prerogative to diplomatic relations, provincial governments retain the option of engaging in non-diplomatic exchanges with third country governments on topics that, as a matter of legislative competence, fall within the provincial legislatures' jurisdiction. Thus, for example, Canadian provincial governments are empowered to discuss issues of education with third country governments, which the Constitution Act, 1867 allocates for the most part to the provincial legislatures,[84] provided these discussions are understood not to constitute diplomatic negotiations.

Moreover, exclusive federal authority to exercise the *ius legationis* within international organizations does not necessarily preclude provincial governments from playing a role within such organizations. In some instances, the government of Canada has authorized provincial governments to participate. This has been the case for example with UNESCO. In 2006, the federal government concluded an agreement with the Quebec government which provided for the inclusion of a representative of the Quebec government within the delegation of Canada to UNESCO. This agreement allows Quebec to participate—albeit indirectly—in the workings of a UN body.[85] As will be discussed in Chapter 7 on intergovernmental relations, it should immediately be emphasized, however, that this arrangement is contingent on a federal willingness to involve provincial governments such as Quebec within its delegation. Provincial governments are not constitutionally entitled to involvement of this type, and the agreements concluded between them and the federal government are again non-binding. Neither can an argument be made that agreements of this type establish 'legitimate expectations' the betrayal of which entitles provincial governments to a judicial remedy, as in Canada only the legitimate expectations of individuals or corporations can give rise to a justiciable

[82] ibid [52].
[83] ibid [32].
[84] Section 93 of the Constitution Act, 1867.
[85] Agreement between the Government of Canada and the Government of Quebec Concerning the United Nations Educational, Scientific and Cultural Organization (UNESCO), 5 May 2006, <www.mrif.gouv.qc.ca/content/documents/en/accord-unesco.pdf> accessed 29 April 2022.

Table 2.2 Allocation of foreign relations powers in Canada

	Conclude international agreements	**Implement international agreements**	**Represent on the international stage**
Federal	Yes	Yes	Yes
Member unit	No	No	No

controversy.[86] The table below summarizes how foreign relations powers are allocated in Canada (see Table 2.2).

4. Belgium: *in foro interno, in foro externo*

Belgium differs from both Canada and the US in the degree of diversity the framers of the Belgian Constitution were willing to project onto the international stage. In contrast to both North American federations, the Belgian member units hold treaty-making powers of their own.[87] In this sense, Belgium takes up an exceptional position in the comparative federalism landscape: no other federal *state* has been willing to go as far as to pierce the metaphorical veil of external sovereignty and to fully project externally the internal diversity that characterizes the polity.[88] (In the next chapter we will see, however, that the EU does project its internal diversity onto the external sphere as well.)

However, this external projection of internal diversity has important limitations. The product of a political compromise between defenders of increased member unit autonomy and defenders of a strong Belgian state, the 1993 round of constitutional reform placed emphasis both on projecting internal diversity onto the international stage and on maintaining the coherence of Belgian foreign relations.[89] The latter is visible in particular in the express

[86] The Canadian Supreme Court repeated this point in its 2015 *Firearms Registry II* decision, where it considered that 'a province's legitimate expectation of action that the federal government would or would not undertake . . . cannot bind Parliament's legislative action . . . ' See *Quebec (Attorney General) v Canada (Attorney General) ('Firearms Registry II')*, [2015] 1 SCR 693, 2015 SCC 14 (CanLII) [25].

[87] Belgian federalism is characterized by the co-existence of two types of member units: regions and communities (on the distinction, see eg S Sottiaux, *Grondwettelijk Recht* (Intersentia 2016) 225–26. Throughout this book, I will refer to both types of units as 'member units.'

[88] In this sense, see eg L Van den Brande, 'The International Legal Position of Flanders: Some Considerations' in Karel Wellens (ed), *International Law: Theory and Practice. Essays in Honour of Eric Suy* (Kluwer Law International 1998) 146.

[89] In this sense, see Frank Ingelaere, 'De Nieuwe Wetgeving Inzake de Internationale Betrekkingen van de Gemeenschappen En de Gewesten' [1993] Tijdschrift voor Bestuurswetenschappen & Publiekrecht

recognition by the framers of mixed agreements, that is, international agreements to which both federal and member unit governments are a party, and on the continued centralization of authority over diplomatic external relations at the federal level.

4.1 Treaty-Making in Belgium: *in foro interno, in foro externo*

The 1831 Constitution as amended in 1993 divides the power to conclude international agreements between the different orders of government. Article 167 §1 of the Belgian Constitution holds: 'The King directs international relations, notwithstanding the competence of Communities and Regions to regulate international cooperation, including the concluding of treaties, for those matters that fall within their competences in pursuance of or by virtue of the Constitution.'[90] The third paragraph of the same provision adds: 'The Community and Regional Governments ... conclude, each one in so far as it is concerned, treaties regarding matters that fall within the competence of their Parliament.' Article 167 of the Belgian Constitution thus introduces a parallelism between the internal division of legislative powers and the external division of treaty-making powers. Whenever a government has the power to legislate with regard to a given subject matter, it can also conclude international agreements on that same subject matter. This parallelism principle is commonly referred to in Belgium by the Latin adage of *in foro interno, in foro externo*.[91]

The recognition of member unit powers to conclude international agreements requires Belgian governments to determine the division of powers between the federal, regional, and community governments whenever a Belgian government wishes to conclude an international agreement. To facilitate this determination, the Special Law on Institutional Reform (SLIR)—a quasi-constitutional statute adopted by supermajority in the federal Parliament[92]—called for the conclusion of an intergovernmental agreement (IGA) between

807, 811; Jan Velaers, '"In foro interno et in foro externo": de internationale bevoegdheden van gemeenschappen en gewesten' in Godfried Geudens and Frank Judo (eds), *Internationale betrekkingen en federalisme: Staatsrechtconferentie 2005—Vlaamse Juristenvereniging* (Uitgeverij Larcier 2006) 4–5.

[90] An English-language version of the Belgian Constitution is available at <www.dekamer.be/kvvcr/pdf_sections/publications/constitution/GrondwetUK.pdf> accessed 1 November 2021.

[91] See generally Velaers (n 89). Or, more recently, Karel Reybrouck and Stefan Sottiaux, *De federale bevoegdheden* (Intersentia 2019) s 1219.

[92] On quasi-constitutional statutes (*bijzondere meerderheidswetten* or *lois à majorité spéciale*), see Article 4 of the Belgian Constitution.

the different Belgian governments.[93] This IGA needed to contain more precise rules on the conclusion of international agreements touching on competences of the federal and member unit governments. In an IGA dated 8 March 1994, the different governments decided on the establishment of a working group on mixed agreements within the Inter-ministerial Conference on Foreign Relations (ICFR).[94] This working group consists of representatives of the federal, regional, and community executives.[95] An IGA—which within Belgium is regarded as a binding agreement upon the parties involved[96]—requires the working group to make a recommendation to the ICFR on the nature of a proposed international agreement (mixed or not).[97] The ICFR in turn makes a determination on the issue.[98]

When the agreement is sent to the legislature(s) for ratification, the legislative division of the Council of State, Belgium's highest administrative court which also operates as an advisory body to Belgian law-makers, will ordinarily issue an opinion.[99] This opinion will cover the issue of the division of powers.[100] The issue is a vital one, as the determination has an important impact on the nature of the autonomy enjoyed by the different Belgian governments as they conclude the agreement. If the determination leads to a characterization of the agreement as a federal-only or member unit-only agreement, the government involved has the capacity to act independently.[101] If, by contrast, the determination leads to a characterization as a mixed agreement, the governments involved possess a less complete form of autonomy: instead of being able to independently determine the content of the agreement—together with the third country treaty partners, that is—each Belgian government involved will hold only a veto power over the agreement, which will be concluded jointly by all governments whose powers are involved.

[93] Art. 92bis §4ter of the Special Law on Institutional Reform ('SLIR') (Bijzondere Wet van 8 augustus 1980 tot hervorming der instellingen, *Moniteur belge* 15 augustus 1980).

[94] Art 3 of the Cooperation Agreement 'Mixed treaties' (*Accord de coopération entre l'Etat fédéral, les Communautés et les Régions, relatif aux modalités de conclusion des traités mixtes (Moniteur belge 19 July 1996)*).

[95] Ibid.

[96] See Chapter 8 on intergovernmental relations.

[97] Art 4 of the Cooperation Agreement 'Mixed treaties'.

[98] Ibid.

[99] Art 3 of the Coordinated Statutes on the Council of State (*Lois sur le Conseil d'État, coordonnées le 12 janvier 1973*), *Moniteur belge* 21 March 1973.

[100] This is the case even if the government 'fast tracks' the request for an opinion. See ibid art 3 §2.

[101] The member unit governments must however keep the federal government informed about the initiation of negotiations and every subsequent step in the treaty making process. This is necessary to enable the federal government to make use of the suspension mechanism, which I discuss in Chapter 4 on conflict resolution mechanisms. See art 81 §1 SLIR.

In its division of treaty-making powers analysis, the Belgian Council of State applies what one member of the Council of State has referred to as a 'pastis' approach.[102] Pastis is an alcoholic beverage often associated with France's Mediterranean coast. It consists of a combination of water and anis liquor. Add but a single drop of anis liquor to a glass of water and the beverage turns an untransparent, milky white. Similarly, for the Belgian Council of State, a single provision of, for example, regional competence in an otherwise entirely federal international agreement transforms the agreement from a federal-only agreement into a mixed federal-regional agreement.[103] Given the fragmented division of competences in Belgium, it comes as no surprise that a large number of agreements are mixed rather than federal-only or member unit-only.

The Council of State's Legislative Division's opinions are non-binding but highly persuasive.[104] If disregarded, a contracting government may expose itself to criticism within the political process as well as to a risk of litigation. For, once enacted, it remains possible under the Special Law on the Constitutional Court (SLCC) to challenge the constitutionality of the ratification statute before Belgium's Constitutional Court.[105] A successful challenge in turn exposes Belgium to a risk of international responsibility, as annulment of the ratification statute annuls Belgium's ratification of the international agreement. The international legal personality of the member units of the Belgian federation is only partial: while they can *conclude* international agreements, they cannot be *held liable* in the event of non-fulfilment of the international legal obligations in those agreements. The federal government will incur international responsibility instead.[106] By concluding most international agreements as mixed

[102] The metaphor of the pastis, referred to by a member of the legislative division of the Council during an interview in 2015, was introduced by Advocate General Kokott. In her opinion in the *Vietnam* case, she mentioned that '[j]ust as a little drop of pastis can turn a glass of water milky, individual provisions, however secondary, in an international agreement ... can make it necessary to conclude a shared agreement.' See Opinion of AG Kokott in Case C–13/07 *Commission v Council ('Vietnam')*, EU:C:2009:190, para 121.

[103] In this sense, see eg J Van Nieuwenhove, 'Bevoegdheidsverdeling en verdragen' in Godfried Geudens and Frank Judo (eds), *Internationale betrekkingen en federalisme: Staatsrechtconferentie 2005*—Vlaamse Juristenvereniging (2006) 94.

[104] S Sottiaux, *Grondwettelijk Recht* (Intersentia 2016) 467 as well as Jan Velaers, *De Grondwet en de Raad van State, afdeling Wetgeving: vijftig jaar adviezen an wetgevende vergaderingen in het licht van de rechtspraak van het Arbitragehof* (Maklu 1999) 34.

[105] Article 3 §2 of the SLCC (*Moniteur belge* 7 January 1989) allows for direct constitutional challenges against ratification statutes to be brought during a six month period after the statute's adoption. Yet even after the six-month period, Belgian courts can make requests for preliminary rulings on the validity of ratification statutes (except for those statutes ratifying amendments to the EU Treaties or the European Convention on Human Rights). See Article 26 §1 and §1bis SLCC. These two exceptions notwithstanding, a ratification statute is thus never entirely protected against constitutional challenges after its adoption.

[106] In this sense, see J Wouters and L De Smet, 'The Legal Position of Federal States and Their Federated Entities in International Relations—The Case of Belgium' (Institute for International Law (KU Leuven) 2001) Working Paper 7, 27–28.

agreements, the risk of a mismatch between the government that concludes agreements and the government that incurs responsibility in case of non-compliance is foreclosed.[107] In the 1993–2013 period, the Flemish government concluded twenty-seven non-mixed agreements. Twelve of these agreements were concluded with the Netherlands. By contrast, in the 1993–2004 period alone, the Flemish government became a party to 246 mixed agreements.[108] Statistics for the number of mixed and non-mixed agreements to which the federal government is a party are not readily available. Presumably, the ratio between mixed and non-mixed agreements is not very different.

In addition to international agreements governed by international law, Belgian governments—including the member unit governments—also have the authority to conclude non-binding agreements. This authority is derived from Article 167 §1 of the Belgian Constitution, which empowers the member units to 'regulate international cooperation'.[109] Much depends on the intention of the authors of the agreement. If the agreement is not intended to be governed by international law, it will not constitute an international agreement even if it is concluded between two international legal subjects, such as the Belgian member units and, for example, a foreign state.[110] By opting for this type of instrument, the procedural strictures of the mixed agreement can be avoided: no parliamentary ratification is required, no information must be shared between governments, and coordination within the ICFR is not required.[111] In the 1994–2004 period, the Flemish government concluded forty-seven such non-binding agreements.[112]

4.2 Treaty Implementation: Parallelism All the Way Down

Once properly ratified by the affected legislatures, international agreements are binding within the Belgian legal order.[113] They rank above legislation and in the

[107] In this sense with regard to multilateral agreements, see also J Wouters, *Internationaal recht in kort bestek* (2nd edn, Intersentia 2017) 26, noting that it is exceptional for multilateral agreements to touch only upon member unit powers.
[108] Velaers (n 89) 37.
[109] In this sense, see ibid 29.
[110] Velaers suggests that in light of the definition of an international agreement in Article 2(1)(a) of the VCLT, the category of non-binding (or transnational) agreements will not be very large (ibid, 28). I would question this proposition. As the intention of the parties is what ultimately determines the nature of the agreement, whether an agreement is binding under international law really is up to the parties themselves.
[111] In this sense: Velaers (n 89) 26–27.
[112] ibid 37.
[113] Belgian Constitution, art 167.

view of the Supreme Court even above the Belgian Constitution.[114] However, it must immediately be added that Belgian courts will enforce only those treaties (or provisions thereof) that have 'direct effect'. If a treaty provision does not have direct effect, legislatures, not courts, are responsible for its implementation. In contrast in particular to the US, where US courts have become increasingly reticent to recognize the self-executing character of treaty provisions,[115] Belgian courts appear to continue to maintain an open attitude vis-à-vis international legal obligations lawfully ratified by the federal and/or member unit governments.[116] Writing over thirty years ago, Marc Maresceau argued:

> In the great majority of cases where treaties are applied by Belgian courts, the direct effect issue is not mentioned. In other words, treaties, if approved under the procedures as analysed, are very often simply applied. By their application and to the extent they are applied treaties implicitly receive the characteristics of direct effect.[117]

While I am not aware of an empirical study on the issue of self-execution in Belgium, I have discerned no signals in legal doctrine that Belgian courts have become more hesitant to recognize the direct effect of treaty obligations since Maresceau's contribution.[118] Moreover, it is important to keep in mind that a large share of international treaty law that affects Belgium makes its way into the Belgian legal order through EU legislation that implements mixed agreements to which the EU and the Member States (including Belgium) are a party. In this way, Belgium's membership of the EU makes the question of the direct

[114] The matter of the position of international agreements within the Belgian hierarchy of norms has been the object of a *guerre des juges* between, on the one hand, the Supreme Court and, on the other, the Constitutional Court. Whereas the former considers international agreements to rank above the Constitution (see seminally Cass, 27 mei 1971 (*NV Fromagerie Franco-Suisse Le Ski*), Arr Cass, 1971, 959), the latter ranks international agreements above secondary legislation but below the Constitution. However, it should immediately be added that by mid-2016 the Constitutional Court has not yet invalidated a provision of a treaty for being contrary to the Belgian Constitution. See W Verrijdt, 'EU Integration and the Belgian Constitution' in Stefan Griller, Monica Claes, and L Papadopoulou (eds), *Member States' Constitutions and EU Integration* (Hart 2016) §28. For an example of constitutional review in which the Constitutional Court concluded that the agreement at issue was compatible with the Constitution, see the ruling on the European Stability Mechanism Treaty: GH nr 62/2016 of 28 April 2016, <www.const-court.be/public/n/2016/2016-062n.pdf> accessed 1 November 2021.

[115] On the broader development, see generally Ohlin (n 29).

[116] In the US, see in particular *Medellín v Texas*, 552 US 491 (2008).

[117] Marc Maresceau, 'Belgium' in Francis Geoffrey Jacobs, Shelley Roberts, and United Kingdom National Committee of Comparative Law (eds), *The Effect of Treaties in Domestic Law* (Sweet & Maxwell 1987) 16.

[118] In 2002, Dries Van Eeckhoutte and Arne Vandaele mentioned in a working paper that Belgian courts typically spend very little time examining the direct effect of treaty provisions. See Dries Van Eeckhoutte and Arne Vandaele, *Doorwerking van internationale normen in de Belgische rechtsorde* (Instituut voor Internationaal Recht, KU Leuven 2002) Working Paper 33 para 13.

effect of international agreements within the Belgian legal order to an important extent moot. This would explain why in Belgium, in contrast to, for example, the US, questions on the status of international agreements in the domestic legal order do not arise often.

If treaty-implementing legislation would nonetheless turn out to be necessary—for example if the language of a treaty unambiguously calls for the adoption of such legislation—the power to adopt such legislation remains divided, in keeping with the division of legislative powers set out in the Constitution and the SLIR and the principle of a parallelism between internal and external powers discussed earlier.[119] In other words, as in Canada, there is no such thing as 'treaty legislation' in Belgium. In comparison with Canada, however, the different legislatures can be expected to be more willing to enact the necessary implementing legislation as these same legislatures have already attached their consent to the agreement in the ratification process. This is not the case in Canada, where the federal executive can conclude international agreements without parliamentary approval and neither provincial executives nor legislatures are involved in the federal treaty-making process.[120] Consequently, in Belgium, implementing legislation does protect the autonomy of the member unit governments in the same way as it does in Canada, and the likelihood of political conflicts erupting at this juncture is limited.

4.3 External Representation: Federal in Principle, Shared in Practice

Article 167 §1 of the 1831 Belgian Constitution empowers the King (ie the federal executive) to 'direct international relations'. This power aims to ensure that, despite the abovementioned parallelism, 'coherence' is maintained in the foreign relations of Belgium.[121] The power is best understood as an exclusive federal competence to exercise the *ius legationis*: it encompasses a power to recognize foreign states and governments; to appoint diplomatic and consular representatives of Belgium abroad and to receive such representatives in Belgium; to represent Belgium before international tribunals, including in

[119] In this sense, see Reybrouck and Sottiaux (n 91) s 1222.

[120] The federal government of Canada adheres to a policy of tabling treaties in Parliament. See <https://treaty-accord.gc.ca/procedures.aspx?lang=eng> accessed 29 April 2022. However, this is a mere executive policy, which the government can rescind. The policy also contains exceptions on grounds of urgency or negative repercussions for Canada's national interest.

[121] Velaers (n 89) 4–5.

matters touching on the powers of the member units; and to become a member of international organizations, including those that deal with matters falling within the scope of the member units' powers.[122]

The fact that membership of Belgium in international organizations is thus restricted to membership of the *federal* executive raises the prospect of the federal executive participating in discussions within multilateral or bilateral fora on subject matters which, as an internal matter, are covered by member unit powers. To protect the autonomy of the Belgian member units also in this regard, the Belgian federal government voluntarily concluded IGAs with the member unit governments. The agreements provide for a member unit representation within the Belgian delegations to certain international organizations[123] (most importantly the EU)[124] and within the Belgian embassies in third countries.[125] These member unit representatives receive orders directly from their own governments. As will be discussed in Chapter 7, while concluded voluntarily, such agreements are nonetheless binding on all parties: once enacted, the federal government cannot unilaterally modify or cancel the agreement. The agreements thus allow the member unit governments to independently engage in contacts with third country governments, while benefiting from diplomatic protection as members of the Belgian representation or embassy.

The representatives of the member unit governments are often housed in the same building as the Belgian representation or embassy.[126] This is not necessarily always the case, however. The representation of Flanders in the US, for example, is housed in a different city (New York) from the Belgian embassy (Washington DC). Organically, the head of the Flemish office is nonetheless a member of the Belgian consulate in New York, which allows them to

[122] ibid 10–11. In the same sense, see A Feyt, 'Les Communautés et Les Régions Peuvent-Elles Se Doter d'une Diplomatie Propre?' [2002] Chroniques de Droit Public—Publiekrechtelijke Kronieken (CDPK) 25, 26.

[123] See Cooperation Agreement 'International Organizations' (*Accord-cadre de coopération entre l'Etat fédéral, les Communautés et les Régions portant sur la représentation du Royaume de Belgique auprès des organisations internationales poursuivant des activités relevant de compétences mixtes, Moniteur belge* 19 November 1994).

[124] See Cooperation Agreement 'European Union' (*Accord de coopération entre l'Etat fédéral, les Communautés et les Régions modifiant l'accord de coopération du 8 mars 1994 entre l'Etat fédéral, les Communautés et les Régions relatif à la représentation du Royaume de Belgique au sein du Conseil des Ministres de l'Union européenne, Moniteur belge* 4 March 2010).

[125] See Cooperation Agreement 'Diplomatic Representation' (*Accord de coopération entre l'Etat fédéral, les Communautés et les Régions relatif au statut des représentants des Communautés et des Régions dans les postes diplomatiques et consulaires, Moniteur belge* 16 November 2014).

[126] On these activities, see eg D Criekemans, 'Foreign Policy and Diplomacy of the Belgian Regions: Flanders and Wallonia' (Netherlands Institute of International Relations Clingendael' 2010) or, for Wallonia specifically: Grégoire Gayard, 'Projection internationale des entités fédérées: les politiques internationales du climat du Québec et de la Région wallonne' [2020] Études canadiennes/Canadian Studies 301.

Table 2.3 Allocation of foreign relations powers in Belgium

	Conclude international agreements	**Implement international agreements**	**Represent on the international stage**
Federal	Yes	Yes	Yes
Member unit	Yes	Yes	No

benefit from the protections provided by the Vienna Convention on Consular Relations (VCCR).[127] Similarly, the head of the representation of the French-speaking Community on Paris' Left Bank is recognized as a member of the Belgian embassy near the Place Charles de Gaulle, which allows them to benefit from the protections provided by the VCDR.

The arrangements between the federal and member unit governments set out in legally binding IGAs provide the member units of the Belgian federation with more robust legal means to engage in paradiplomacy than those at the disposal of US states or Canadian provinces, the staff of which typically operate as private individuals.[128] If member units fail to come to an agreement with the Belgian federal government on the inclusion of member unit representatives within the Belgian representations or embassies abroad, it remains possible for the Belgian member units to engage in non-diplomatic relations with third country governments. As is the case for US states and Canadian provinces: this type of representation is not covered by the VCDR or the VCCR. The table below summarizes how foreign relations powers are allocated in Belgium (see Table 2.3).

5. Conclusion: Open versus Closed Federations

This first chapter provided an overview of the division of foreign relations powers in the US, Canada, and Belgium, which operates as the first dimension of self-rule in the conception of federalism set out in the introduction to the

[127] 'Kris Dierckx Mag Blijven in Flanders House' *deredactie.be* (20 July 2010) <http://deredactie.be/cm/vrtnieuws/binnenland/1.829218> accessed 1 November 2021.

[128] But see the status of the representatives of Quebec in Paris, which on the basis of a unilateral decision by the French government benefit from the same privileges and immunities as those enjoyed by Canadian diplomats in France. See in this sense Cour de cassation (FR), civile, Chambre sociale, 4 novembre 2009, 08-60.593, publié au bulletin, on the applicability of French labour law on employees of the *Délégation générale* of Quebec in Paris.

book. Before turning to the EU, it is worth highlighting the extent to which within all three federations the division of foreign relations powers represents a compromise between the competing requirements of (i) ensuring that the federal government is capable of acting effectively on the international stage to defend the values and interests of the federation as a whole, and (ii) the autonomy—that is, the capacity of self-rule—of the member units of the federation on the other.

In the US and Canada, this compromise has taken the form of—to use a concept introduced by Bruno Fassbender—a 'closed' federation whereby the federal government has exclusive control over the bulk of the federation's foreign relations powers.[129] The member units do have the authority to adopt measures that affect foreign relations. US states can, for example, adopt legislation that affects aliens or they can engage in paradiplomacy with third country governments. Similarly, Canadian provinces can legislate to implement treaty obligations touching on subject matters under provincial jurisdiction. But—as will be developed further in later chapters—the exercise of such authorities is, to some extent, subject to federal control. In the US, the federal government can pre-empt state law, while in Canada the power to implement treaty obligations is dependent on the prior conclusion of an international agreement by the federal government.

By contrast, in Belgium, the internal diversity of the federation is projected onto the international stage by virtue of the parallelism between domestic legislative powers and external treaty-making powers. This turns the Belgian federation into a particularly 'open' federal arrangement. However, for the sake of protecting the unity and coherence of Belgian foreign relations, most agreements are mixed agreements. In addition, the federal government retains much of the responsibility to conduct formal diplomatic relations. Openness, in other words, is not without limits in the Belgian foreign affairs constitution.

Having provided a comparative overview of the division of foreign relations powers in federations other than the EU, the next chapter focuses on the EU and the differences and similarities between the allocation of these powers in the EU, the US, Canada, and Belgium.

[129] Bardo Fassbender, *Der offene Bundesstaat: Studien zur auswärtigen Gewalt und zur Völkerrechtssubjektivität bundesstaatlicher Teilstaaten in Europa* (Mohr Siebeck 2007). The distinction has also been used by Robert Schütze, eg in Schütze (n 4) 58.

3

Power Allocation in the EU

> [T]he Community is to be considered as a new subject in international relations vested with powers and responsibilities of considerable scope with a view to performing the tasks set by the Treaties. These tasks must be performed by the Community itself, acting on its own and through its own institutions, and not to be assumed by any combination whatsoever of the Member States.
>
> Pierre Pescatore, 1979[1]

1. Introduction

How do the EU Treaties allocate foreign relations competences?[2] How does the EU compare to the three federations examined in the previous chapter? This chapter makes two interrelated points. First, the EU holds broad external competences. Often, these competences overlap with those of the Member States. In this sense, the EU fits within broader developments in federal systems from arrangements characterized by categorical distinctions between spheres of powers—dual federalism—towards paradigms in which different governments operate within overlapping areas of jurisdiction—cooperative federalism.[3] Secondly, while the EU holds broad external competences, these competences are not always exercised. This leaves space for Member States to act externally. As a consequence of the Council's ability to not exercise bits of EU competence, EU external action often takes the form of mixed action.[4]

[1] Pierre Pescatore, 'External Relations in the Case-Law of the Court of Justice of the European Communities' (1979) 16 Common Market Law Review 615, 642.

[2] The EU Treaties speak of 'competences' rather than 'powers', which is the more commonly used term in the English language. I will use the EU terminology.

[3] On the distinction, see generally Robert Schütze, *From Dual to Cooperative Federalism: The Changing Structure of European Law* (Oxford University Press 2013).

[4] Mixity has been much debated (and criticized) in the EU. See Claus-Dieter Ehlermann, 'Mixed Agreements—A Set of Problems' in David O'Keeffe and Henry G Schermers (eds), *Mixed Agreements* (Kluwer Law and Taxation Publishers 1983); N Neuwahl, 'Joint Participation in International Treaties and the Exercise of Power by the EEC and Its Member States: Mixed Agreements' (1991) 28 Common Market Law Review 717. For a positive appraisal, see Joseph HH Weiler, 'The External Legal Relations of Non-Unitary Actors: Mixity and the Federal Principle' in *The Constitution of Europe: Essays on the*

Foreign Relations Federalism. Thomas Verellen, Oxford University Press. © Thomas Verellen 2023.
DOI: 10.1093/oso/9780192844569.003.0003

Mixed action is external action undertaken jointly by the EU and some or all of the EU Member States. While exceptional in comparative terms, mixity is not unique to the EU.[5] As discussed in the previous chapter, mixity is a prominent phenomenon also in Belgium. However, in Belgium mixity flows from the fragmented division of exclusive competences between the federal and member unit governments. By contrast, as will be discussed below, in the EU mixity is often the product of a political choice by the Council on whether or not to exercise shared EU competence.

This chapter is structured along the same lines as the previous chapter. It focuses, in order of appearance, on (i) the competence to negotiate and conclude international agreements, (ii) the competence to implement those agreements, and (iii) the competence to ensure the external representation of the federation. As will become apparent, compared to the federal *states* explored in this book, it is more challenging to offer an integrated account of the division of foreign relations competences in the EU. As Deirdre Curtin argued shortly after the coming into force of the Maastricht Treaty in 1993, but to some extent the point remains valid today: the EU is a polity 'of bits and pieces'.[6] It consists of distinct policy areas that are each subject to different constitutional arrangements. In the context of foreign relations, the distinction between the Common Foreign Security Policy (CFSP) and other areas of EU external action gives the EU division of foreign relations competences a distinctly 'bipolar' flavour.[7] Throughout the analysis, it will be important to bear the distinction between CFSP and non-CFSP competence in mind, even though the Lisbon Treaty

Ends and Means of European Integration (Cambridge University Press 1999). More recently, see also Christophe Hillion and Panos Koutrakos (eds), *Mixed Agreements Revisited: The EU and Its Member States in the World* (Hart 2010). The CETA controversy has sparked renewed attention. See eg Guillaume Van der Loo and Ramses A Wessel, 'The Non-Ratification of Mixed Agreements: Legal Consequences and Solutions' (2017) 54 Common Market Law Review 735; Gesa Kübek, 'The Non-Ratification Scenario: Legal and Practical Responses to Mixed Treaty Rejection by Member States' (2018) 23 European Foreign Affairs Review 21; Thomas Verellen, 'On Hybrid Decisions Mixed Agreements and the Limits of the New Legal Order: Commission v Council ("US Air Transport Agreement")' (2016) 53 Common Market Law Review 741.

[5] Characterizing mixity as the EU's 'near-unique contribution to true federalism', see Weiler (n 4) 130.

[6] Deirdre M Curtin, 'The Constitutional Structure of the Union: A Europe of Bits and Pieces' (1993) 30 Common Market Law Review 17.

[7] In this sense, see also Alan Dashwood, 'The Continuing Bipolarity of EU External Action' in Inge Govaere and others (eds), *The European Union in the World: Essays in Honour of Marc Maresceau* (Martinus Nijhoff Publishers 2014). The bipolarity of EU foreign relations was much discussed prior to the Lisbon Treaty. See eg Ramses A Wessel, *The European Union's Foreign and Security Policy: A Legal Institutional Perspective* (Martinus Nijhoff Publishers 1999), and shortly before the Lisbon Treaty also Geert De Baere, *Constitutional Principles of EU External Relations* (Oxford University Press 2008) ch 6. For a more recent critique of the continued bipolarity of EU external action, see generally Graham Butler, *Constitutional Law of the EU's Common Foreign and Security Policy: Competence and Institutions in External Relations* (Hart 2019).

framers formally dispensed with the pillar architecture which had been put in place at Maastricht and formally integrated the CFSP into a unified 'European Union'.

Contrary to the previous chapter, in this chapter I also include a section—a coda—on the division of competences in the military sphere. In Belgium, the US, and Canada, the use of military force is a federal responsibility. Not so in the EU, where the EU Treaties make provision for the establishment of a 'common defence' for the Union, but where few steps have been undertaken to make this constitutional vision a reality. To provide a comprehensive overview of the division of external competences in the EU, it is important to also look at how the EU Treaties allocate competences to engage in military activities.

2. Broad Treaty-Making Powers

When can the EU conclude international agreements? And, when the EU Treaties do empower the EU to conclude international agreements, what does the allocation of such competence mean for the ability of Member States to continue to conclude their own agreements? I look at both questions in turn. The first question goes to the *existence* of EU competence; the second to its *nature*.

2.1 The Existence of EU External Competence: Not So Limited

As is the case in the US, the EU's competences are conferred competences.[8] As required by the principle of conferral, the EU can only act on those issues over which the EU Treaties have allocated a competence to the EU.[9] In contrast to the US, however, the power to conclude international agreements is not allocated wholesale to the 'federal' level of governance, leaving US states unable to make binding international agreements altogether. Instead, the EU Treaties allocate to the EU a competence to conclude international agreements in a number of circumstances. Outside of those circumstances, Member States retain their ability to make treaties—an ability that flows from their status as sovereign states.

[8] TEU, art 4(1).
[9] TEU, art 5(2).

Article 216(1) of the Treaty on the Functioning of the European Union (TFEU) exhaustively lists the circumstances in which the EU is allocated a competence to conclude international agreements. The provision holds:

> The Union may conclude an agreement with one or more third countries or international organisations where the Treaties so provide or where the conclusion of an agreement is necessary in order to achieve, within the framework of the Union's policies, one of the objectives referred to in the Treaties, or is provided for in a legally binding Union act or is likely to affect common rules or alter their scope.

The provision thus provides for four avenues through which the EU acquires a competence to negotiate and conclude international agreements: (i) the Treaties allocate such a power expressly; (ii) the conclusion of an agreement is 'necessary in order to achieve, within the framework of the Union's policies, one of the objectives referred to in the Treaties'; (iii) the conclusion of an agreement is provided for expressly in a 'legally binding Union act'; or (iv) the conclusion of an agreement is 'likely to affect common rules or alter their scope'. I take a brief look at each of these scenarios in turn.

The *first scenario* does not require much explanation. It is the traditional scenario in a polity subject to the principle of conferral.[10] Article 191(4) first paragraph TFEU on environmental policy offers a good example. This provision provides that '[t]he arrangements for Union cooperation may be the subject of agreements between the Union and the third parties concerned'. Similarly, within the CFSP, Article 37 TEU expressly empowers the EU to conclude international agreements on issues falling within the sphere of the CFSP.

The *second scenario* is familiar to students of comparative federalism. It recognizes the existence in EU law of a doctrine of implied competences.[11] We have encountered implied powers also in the US, where, following the Supreme Court ruling in *Missouri v Holland*, the powers of Congress to implement treaty obligations incurred by the President are considered 'necessary and proper' for carrying into execution the President's Treaty Power. In a similar spirit, the EU has an external competence to conclude international agreements when

[10] It reaffirms the importance of what Alan Dashwood described as 'the drafting technique that entails the specific and detailed attribution of competences to the Union, through provisions that constitute the legal basis authorising action in a determined policy area or in pursuance of a determined objective, and no other'. See Alan Dashwood, 'The Relationship between the Member States and the European Union/European Community' (2004) 41 Common Market Law Review 355, 357–58.

[11] The doctrine finds its origins in Opinion 1/76 ('Laying-up Fund'), EU:C:1977:63.

conclusion of an agreement is 'necessary in order to achieve, within the framework of the Union's policies, one of the objectives referred to in the Treaties'. Implied competence is relevant, in particular, where the EU Treaties empower the EU to adopt internal legislative acts but do not expressly empower it to conclude international agreements. In such cases, the EU can rely on Article 216(1) TFEU to conclude an international agreement on the issue on which it can legislate internally, provided that concluding such an agreement is 'necessary'. 'Necessary' is to be construed flexibly in this context. It is enough for the conclusion of an international agreement to *contribute to* or to *facilitate* the attainment a Treaty objective.[12] This is a relatively low threshold. Read in conjunction with the EU's broad internal legislative competences, this second scenario empowers the EU to conclude international agreements on a wide range of issues.[13] We will see later on that this 'necessity' requirement is to be interpreted more restrictively when the *nature* rather than the *existence* of competence is at issue.

The *third* and *fourth scenarios* are best understood as referring to one and the same principle—the ERTA principle—according to which the EU acquires a(n) (exclusive) competence to conclude international agreements on issues that are closely connected to topics on which it has legislated internally.[14] I discuss this principle further below when I look at the nature of the EU's competence to conclude international agreements. I return to it also in Chapter 5 on conflict resolution mechanisms in EU foreign relations. As we will see, ERTA competence is always exclusive to the EU. On this point, ERTA competence

[12] In this sense, see Case C-600/14 *Germany v Council ('OTIF')*, EU:C:2017:935, para 58, in which the Court held that the EU possessed a power to adopt a position on the amendment of a previously concluded international agreement on the basis of the second avenue of Article 216(1) TFEU because doing so 'contribute[s] to the achievement of the common transport policy, within the framework of the competence conferred on the Union by Article 91(1) TFEU'. In the literature, see already Alan Dashwood, 'The Attribution of External Relations Competence' in Alan Dashwood and Christophe Hillion (eds), *The General Law of E.C. External Relations* (Sweet & Maxwell 2000) 133–34, as well as De Baere (n 7) 26.

[13] In this sense, see Allan Rosas, 'Exclusive, Shared and National Competence in the Context of EU External Relations: Do Such Distinctions Matter?' in Inge Govaere and others (eds), *The European Union in the World: Essays in Honour of Marc Maresceau* (Brill 2014) 33–34.

[14] In this sense, see also Marcus Klamert, *The Principle of Loyalty in EU Law* (Oxford University Press 2014) 153. The third scenario finds its origins not in the *ERTA* judgment, but in Opinion 1/94 on the accession of the EU to the WTO. In that opinion, the Court of Justice held that '[w]henever the Community has included in its legislative acts provisions relating to the treatment of non-member countries or expressly conferred on its institutions powers to negotiate with non-member countries, it acquires exclusive external competence in the sphere covered by those acts' (Opinion 1/94 ('WTO'), EU:C:1994:384, para 95). As Klamert points out, however, this language could also be read more broadly as empowering the EU legislature to expressly empower the EU to conclude international agreements regardless of whether the requirements of ERTA exclusivity are met. Such a reading would be at odds with the conferral principle. In this sense, see also Robert Schütze, *European Union Law* (Cambridge University Press 2015) 273 ('Theoretically, it is difficult to accept that the Union can expand its competences without Treaty amendment through the simple adoption of internal Union acts').

differs from the first and second scenarios, which can give rise to either shared or exclusive competence.

* * *

Taken together, these four scenarios offer the EU many opportunities to conclude international agreements. This is a remarkable conclusion in light of the fact that the Treaty framers have historically been reluctant to allocate express treaty-making competences to the EU, and that until today the number of express legal bases empowering the EU to conclude international agreements remains limited—especially when compared to the number of legal bases empowering the EU to enact internal legislation.[15]

2.2 The Nature of EU External Competence: Shared, Most of the Time

The EU thus holds broad treaty-making competences. But what impact does the allocation of these broad competences to the EU have on the autonomy of the Member States? Did the allocation of a treaty-making power to the 'federal' level of governance (here, the EU) entail a concomitant loss of treaty-making powers at the member unit level, as in the US? Or did EU Member States retain competences to conclude international agreements despite the allocation of such competences to the EU?

As a general rule, the EU's competences are shared, and EU competence is only exclusive when the Treaties provide for exclusivity.[16] Article 3 TFEU lists the scenarios in which the EU is allocated an exclusive competence to conclude international agreements. Article 3(1) TFEU lists a number of areas in which the EU's competence is exclusive. Geert De Baere referred to these areas as areas of a priori exclusivity.[17] They include: (i) the customs union; (ii) the establishing of the competition rules necessary for the functioning of the internal market; (iii) monetary policy for the Member States whose currency is the euro; (iv) the conservation of marine biological resources under the common fisheries policy; (v) common commercial policy (CCP). In the external sphere, the CCP represents the most significant exclusive competence

[15] The Rome Treaty empowered the EU only to conclude commercial agreements and association agreements. See EEC, ex arts 113 and 238.

[16] TFEU, art 4(1).

[17] De Baere (n 7) 39.

of the EU.[18] As the external mirror image of the internal market, the EU has historically been particularly active in international trade. The EU's efforts to conclude free trade agreements with foreign markets such as Canada, Japan, Mexico, Mercosur, and so forth are examples of the EU's activities in this area.

In addition to a priori exclusive competences, the TFEU envisages other types of EU exclusivity as well. In particular, Article 3(2) TFEU provides that:

> [t]he Union shall also have exclusive competence for the conclusion of an international agreement when its conclusion is provided for in a legislative act of the Union or is necessary to enable the Union to exercise its internal competence, or in so far as its conclusion may affect common rules or alter their scope.

The language of Article 3(2) TFEU is reminiscent of that in Article 216(1) TFEU, discussed above. It codifies Court of Justice case law on the subject of external EU competences. As was the case for Article 216(1) TFEU on the existence of an EU competence to conclude international agreements, Article 3(2) TFEU on the nature of such competence also introduces several scenarios in which the EU acquires an exclusive competence. First, exclusivity can be provided for in a legislative act. Secondly, it can be necessary to enable the Union to exercise its internal competence. And thirdly, exclusivity arises in so far as the conclusion of the international agreement may affect common rules or alter their scope.

The *first* and *third scenarios* are best understood as referring to the ERTA principle.[19] As mentioned, I will discuss this principle in depth in Chapter 5 on conflict resolution mechanisms, as the ERTA principle is best understood as a pre-emption mechanism that allocates an exclusive competence to conclude international agreements on issues that may affect pre-existing internal EU rules or alter their scope. In this sense, the doctrine shares features with the US pre-emption doctrine, which I will discuss in Chapter 4.

The *second scenario* is reminiscent of the second scenario offered by Article 216(1) TFEU on the existence of an implied EU competence to conclude international agreements. Both scenarios suggest that the EU has such a competence when it is 'necessary'. As discussed, 'necessary' in Article 216(1) TFEU

[18] On the CCP, see generally Michael Hahn and Guillaume Van der Loo (eds), *Law and Practice of the Common Commercial Policy: The First 10 Years after the Treaty of Lisbon* (Brill Nijhoff 2020).

[19] In this sense, see Marise Cremona, 'EU External Competence—Rationales for Exclusivity' in Sacha Garben and Inge Govaere (eds), *The Division of Competences between the EU and the Member States: Reflections on the Past, the Present and the Future* (Hart 2017) 145.

means necessary 'to attain a Treaty objective'. By contrast, in Article 3(2) TFEU 'necessary' means necessary for the EU 'to exercise its internal competence'. The third scenario finds its origins in Opinion 1/76, an opinion issued by the Court of Justice in 1977.[20] In that opinion, the Court held that participation of Switzerland in a legislative scheme to regulate traffic on the Rhine river was necessary to enable the EU to exercise its competence since non-participation of Switzerland would make the scheme entirely ineffective. 'Necessary' in this context should be construed more narrowly than in the Article 216(1) TFEU context. Whereas it is sufficient for a treaty-making competence to *contribute to* the attainment of a Treaty objective for such a competence to come into being, the competence must be *indispensable* for the exercise of internal EU legislative competence for it to become exclusive in nature.[21]

* * *

When the EU acquires an exclusive competence, Member States are no longer permitted, as a matter of EU law, to exercise their own powers in the area covered by that exclusive competence.[22] Litigation is regularly brought before the Court in which the scope of the exclusive competence of the EU is at issue. Such litigation tends to revolve around the scope of Article 207 TFEU on the CCP, or around the scope of a possible ERTA pre-emptive effect.[23] Over time, the Court of Justice's position on the scope of the exclusive competence of the EU has shifted, ranging from a broad interpretation in the early years of the (then) EEC,[24] to a narrower reading during the 1990s,[25] only to return to a

[20] Opinion 1/76 ('Laying-up Fund'), EU:C:1977:63.

[21] In this sense, see eg De Baere (n 17) 26; Dashwood (n 12) 134.

[22] De Baere (n 17) 33. ('[T]he exclusivity principle does prevent the Member States from entering into certain international obligations damaging to the Community's interests').

[23] Discussing the latter, see Mirka Kuisma and Joris Larik, 'The Continuing Contestation of ERTA' in Nicolas Levrat and others (eds), *The EU and its Member States' Joint Participation in International Agreements* (Hart 2022) 47–53; Merijn Chamon, 'Implied Exclusive Powers in the ECJ'S Post-Lisbon Jurisprudence: The Continued Development of the ERTA Doctrine' (2018) 55 Common Market Law Review 1101; Thomas Verellen, 'The ERTA Doctrine in the Post-Lisbon Era: Note under Judgment in Commission v Council (C-114/12) and Opinion 1/13' (2015) 21 Columbia Journal of European Law 383. Discussing the former, see Allan Rosas, 'Mixity and the Common Commercial Policy after Opinion 2/15: An Overview' in Michael Hahn and Guillaume Van der Loo (eds), *Law and Practice of the Common Commercial Policy: The First 10 Years after the Treaty of Lisbon* (Brill Nijhoff 2020).

[24] See most clearly Opinion 1/75 ('OECD Understanding on a Local Cost Standard'), EU:C:1975:145, at 1362, where the Court of Justice held that the concept of the CCP has 'the same content whether it is applied in the context of the international action of a State or to that of the Community'.

[25] See most clearly Opinion 1/94 ('WTO'), EU:C:1994:384. Highlighting how the Court in Opinion 1/94 was more receptive to Member State concerns regarding their sovereignty, see generally Nicholas Emiliou, 'The Death of Exclusive Competence?' (1996) 21 European Law Review 294. Criticizing the same opinion for its narrow construction of the EU's competence, see generally Pierre Pescatore, 'Opinion 1/94 on "Conclusion" of the WTO Agreement: Is There an Escape from a Programmed Disaster?' (1999) 36 Common Market Law Review 387.

broader reading in more recent years.[26] In May 2016, in Opinion 2/15 on the nature of the competence of the EU to conclude the EU-Singapore Free Trade Agreement, for example, the Court of Justice ruled that the vast majority of the provisions of this 'second generation' trade agreement were covered either by Article 207 TFEU or by an ERTA pre-emptive effect—both of which lead to a recognition of an exclusive external competence for the EU.[27] Only the provisions on dispute resolution and non-direct foreign investment fell outside of the scope of EU exclusive competence, the Court held.[28]

Despite the broad scope of Article 207 TFEU and of ERTA pre-emption in Opinion 2/15, it is important to be mindful of the limits of EU exclusivity. As Piet Eeckhout mentioned in a 2013 contribution: 'More often than not the exclusive competence is limited to a particular part of a treaty or agreement, or even to some specific provisions.'[29] Other provisions of the agreement may be covered by EU shared or parallel competence, or by no EU competence at all.

When the EU has a *shared competence* in a field, both the EU and the Member States may conclude international agreements in that field. But when the EU acts, Member States can no longer act.[30] This applies both internally and externally. Hence, if an issue falls within the scope of the EU's shared competence, either the EU or the Member States can conclude an international agreement on that issue. That said, the Council has interpreted 'issue' narrowly: it makes an assessment of whether the EU should act on a provision-by-provision basis.[31] For those provisions for which the Council decides not to exercise EU shared competence, the EU Member States can exercise their own

[26] Referring to the Court's construction of the CCP in Opinion 2/15 as 'expansive', see Marise Cremona, 'Shaping EU Trade Policy Post-Lisbon: Opinion 2/15 of 16 May 2017: ECJ, 16 May 2017, Opinion 2/15 *Free Trade Agreement with Singapore*' (2018) 14 European Constitutional Law Review 231, 257.

[27] Opinion 2/15 ('EU-Singapore FTA'), EU:C:2017:376, in particular paras 33–167 for the analysis of the scope of the CCP, and paras 168–258 for the analysis of the scope of ERTA-type pre-emption. For an analysis of the opinion, see Guillaume Van der Loo, 'The Court's Opinion on the EU-Singapore FTA: Throwing off the Shackles of Mixity?' (CEPS 2017) 2017/17. For a reaffirmation of this broad reading of the scope of the CCP, see also Case C-389/15 *Commission v Council ('Lisbon Agreement')*, EU:C:2017:798.

[28] Opinion 2/15 ('EU-Singapore FTA'), EU:C:2017:376, paras 225–56 for the section on non-direct investment and paras 285–304 for the section on dispute resolution.

[29] Piet Eeckhout, 'Exclusive External Competences: Constructing the EU as an International Actor' in Court of Justice of the European Union (ed), *The Court of Justice and the Construction of Europe: Analyses and Perspectives on Sixty Years of Case-law* (TMC Asser Press 2013) 634.

[30] TFEU, art 2(2).

[31] To get a sense of the complexities that flow from this approach, see the view of AG Hogan in Opinion 1/19 ('Istanbul Convention'), EU:C:2021:198, in which AG Hogan accepted that the Council may exercise EU shared competence only for parts of a proposed international agreement, which leads the EU to accede for some parts of the agreement, and the Member States for other parts. This is difficult to reconcile with international law, which does not allow for a 'partial' accession to a treaty. Instead, when a party accedes to a treaty, it is bound by the entire treaty, and a party may not invoke the provisions of its internal law as justification for its failure to perform a treaty. See VCLT, art 27.

competences. When Member States do so, the EU together with its Member States can jointly conclude the proposed international agreement. The agreement will be a mixed agreement. If none of the Member States exercises its own competences, the agreement cannot be concluded in its current form. If some Member States exercise their own powers, the agreement could perhaps be concluded as a so-called 'incomplete' mixed agreement, that is, an agreement to which, in addition to one or several third country parties, the EU and *some* of its Member States are parties.[32] This would be an option, in particular, if the text of the agreement allows for that agreement to enter into force prior to its ratification by all parties. If, by contrast, ratification by all parties is required for the agreement to enter into force, a refusal by one Member State to ratify means the agreement will not enter into force. Incomplete mixity does not work in such a scenario.

When the EU has a *parallel competence* in a field, both the EU and the Member States can act in that field. Contrary to the arrangement for shared competence, on issues of parallel competence the EU and the Member States can act simultaneously.[33] They can both conclude international agreements on the same subject matter and Member States will not be precluded from doing so because the EU has already exercised its competence on the issue concerned. Development cooperation and humanitarian aid fall under EU parallel competence, as do research, technological development, and space policy.[34] The EU's competence to conclude international agreements on CFSP issues can also be considered a case of parallel competence.[35]

The EU and its Member States thus both hold competences to conclude international agreements, and the allocation of a competence to the EU as a general rule does not lead to a concomitant loss of competence by the Member States. As in Belgium, the fact that both levels of governance hold treaty-making competences has led governments to conclude mixed agreements. As discussed in the previous chapter, mixed agreements are international agreements to which, in addition to one or several third country parties, both levels of governance

[32] See generally Van der Loo and Wessel (n 4).

[33] For an explanation of the rationale behind parallel competences in the field of development aid, see also Opinion of AG Kokott in Case C-13/07 *Commission v Council ('Vietnam')*, EU:C:2009:190, para 70: 'Independent action by the Member States in that field, whether collectively, individually or jointly with the Community, can share out the financial and technical burdens of development cooperation in Europe over several shoulders. Overall, this may result in more intensive development cooperation than would be the case if the Community alone had the right to conclude treaties in this area with non-member countries.'

[34] See TFEU, art 4(3) and (4). On the EU's competence in the field of development policy, see generally Tina Van den Sanden, 'Between Constitutional Strictures and Policy Objectives: An Examination of the Legal Framework of EU Development Cooperation' (PhD thesis, Leuven University 2018) ch 2.

[35] In this sense, see eg Butler (n 7) 41.

are a party. In Belgium, this means the federal and member unit governments. In the EU, it means the EU and its Member States. As discussed in the previous chapter, mixed agreements are a constitutional necessity in Belgium. The fragmented division of exclusive competences, coupled with the extension of the internal division of competences to the external sphere in accordance with the *in foro interno, in foro externo* principle, means that many international agreements cut across areas of jurisdiction in Belgium. To enable Belgium to conclude such agreements, the federal and member unit governments must act jointly. The ensuing agreement will be a mixed agreement.

A similar situation may arise in the EU. It is conceivable that the EU lacks the necessary competence—exclusive or shared—to conclude a proposed international agreement. In such cases, Member States must 'supplement' EU competence to enable the EU to become a party to the proposed agreement. This scenario is referred to in the literature as one of *mandatory mixity*.[36] In addition, and on this point EU law differs from the Belgian constitutional arrangement, it is possible also that the EU has been allocated sufficient shared competence, but that the Council refuses to exercise that competence. In such a scenario, Member States also have to 'supplement' EU competence to enable the EU to conclude the agreement. This scenario is referred to in the literature as one of *facultative mixity*.[37] In contrast to mandatory mixity, facultative mixity is the result of a political choice made by the Member States in the Council rather than the result of a lack of EU competence to conclude the agreement.[38] This element of political discretion explains why the EU's 2017 association agreement with Ukraine was concluded as a mixed agreement, whereas the 2021 trade agreement between the UK and the EU following Brexit was concluded

[36] On these scenarios, see Allan Rosas, 'The European Union and Mixed Agreements' in Alan Dashwood and Christophe Hillion (eds), *The General Law of E.C. External Relations* (Sweet & Maxwell 2000).

[37] On the subject of facultative mixity, see the contributions in Merijn Chamon and Inge Govaere (eds), *EU External Relations Post-Lisbon: The Law and Practice of Facultative Mixity* (Brill Nijhoff 2020).

[38] In this sense, see Case C–600/14 *Germany v Council ('OTIF')*, EU:C:2017:935, para 68. Note that, in exceptional circumstances, mixity may also be constitutionally required because the EU cannot alone exercise its competence for reasons of international law. In the 2018 case of *Antarctica MPAs*, the Court held that, in order to ensure compliance with public international law, the Council was right to act 'with the participation of the Member States' rather than to act without it. The case involved the representation of the EU and its Member States in an international body, not the conclusion of an international agreement. The same principle arguably applies to both contexts, however. See Joined Cases C–626/15 and 659/16 *Commission v Council ('Antarctica MPAs')*, EU:C:2018:925. On the 'AMP Antarctique Effect', see generally Merijn Chamon and Marise Cremona, 'The Representation of the EU and Its Member States in Multilateral Fora' in Nicolas Levrat and others (eds), *The EU and its Member States' Joint Participation in International Agreements* (Hart 2022).

as an EU-only agreement, despite both agreements being adopted on the same legal basis.[39]

Mixed agreements raise questions of shared rule: as the EU and its Member States jointly conclude international agreements, questions arise on how both the EU and the Member States can effectively protect their own interests and how in the process the interests of the federation as a whole can be safeguarded. I tackle these questions in Chapter 9 on intergovernmental relations in the EU, where I zoom in on the management of mixity as an important challenge faced by the EU in this area.

2.3 Non-Binding Agreements

In the US and Canada, governments not endowed with treaty-making powers may nonetheless conclude agreements that are not binding under international law. In Belgium, all governments are empowered to conclude non-binding agreements on subject matters within the scope of their legislative and treaty-making competences. By contrast, they cannot conclude such agreements on issues outside of the scope of their legislative and treaty-making competences. However, as neither the arrangements set out in intergovernmental agreements nor the procedure which allows the Belgian Council of State to advise on the division of powers applies to non-binding agreements, the instrument of the non-binding agreement arguably gives Belgian governments a greater space than the space they have at their disposal in the ordinary treaty-making context. In this sense, the non-binding agreement is a central instrument for Belgian member unit governments to engage in paradiplomacy, as is the case also in the US and Canada.

Can the EU conclude non-binding agreements? Article 216(1) TFEU, discussed earlier, only empowers the EU to conclude *international agreements*, a notion best understood as referring to treaties in the meaning of the 1986

[39] See respectively Council Decision (EU) 2017/1247 of 11 July 2017 on the conclusion, on behalf of the European Union, of the Association Agreement between the European Union and the European Atomic Energy Community and their Member States, of the one part, and Ukraine, of the other part, with the exception of the provisions relating to the treatment of third-country nationals legally employed as workers in the territory of the other party, [2017] OJ L181/1, and Council Decision (EU) 2021/689 of 29 April 2021 on the conclusion, on behalf of the Union, of the Trade and Cooperation Agreement between the European Union and the European Atomic Energy Community, of the one part, and the United Kingdom of Great Britain and Northern Ireland, of the other part, and of the Agreement between the European Union and the United Kingdom of Great Britain and Northern Ireland concerning security procedures for exchanging and protecting classified information, [2021] OJ L149/2.

Vienna Convention on the Law of Treaties between States and International Organisations or between International Organisations (the 1986 VCLT). This emphasis on the adoption of formal, binding legal acts should not be read as suggesting that the EU institutions can adopt non-binding agreements on issues that would have fallen outside of the EU's competence had the agreement been a treaty in the meaning of the 1986 VCLT. There is no reason to believe that the principle of conferral would apply only to acts with formal legal effects under international law and not to informal acts that are not binding under international law.[40]

There is some evidence that the Court of Justice agrees. In a dispute between Commission and Council on the power of the Commission to independently conclude non-binding agreements with third countries, the Court annulled a Commission decision because it violated the principle of conferral as it applies *between* the EU institutions (in this case, Commission and Council).[41] The Court considered that the Commission had infringed on the Council's powers to make policy for the EU—a power laid down in Article 16(1) of the Treaty on European Union (TEU). Thus, the principle of conferral applies to the relations between the EU institutions also when concluding non-binding agreements with third countries. A fortiori, and as a preliminary matter, it would seem that the principle also applies to the relations between the EU and the Member States. In her opinion in the same case, Advocate General Sharpston drew attention to the distinction where she mentioned that '[l]ogically, indeed, the question whether the Union has substantive competence must precede the question of the distribution of powers between the Union institutions as regards matters for which the Union is competent'.[42] Similarly, in an earlier case, the Court itself had rejected an argument made by the Commission that the fact that a measure is not binding is sufficient to confer on that institution the competence to adopt it. Instead, the Court held that '[d]etermining the conditions under which such a measure may be adopted requires that the division of powers *and* the institutional balance established by the Treaty in the field of the common commercial policy be duly taken into account' (emphasis added).[43]

[40] In this sense, see Andrea Ott, 'Informalization of EU Bilateral Instruments: Categorization, Contestation, and Challenges' (2021) 39 Yearbook of European Law 569, 587.

[41] Case C–660/13 *Commission v Council ('Swiss MoU')*, EU:C:2016:616.

[42] Opinion of AG Sharpston in Case C–660/13 *Council v Commission ('Swiss MoU')*, EU:C:2015:787, para 75.

[43] Case C–233/02 *France v Commission ('EU-US Guidelines on Regulatory Cooperation and Transparency')*, EU:C:2004:173, para 40. In a similar sense, see also Linda AJ Senden, 'Soft Law and Its Implications for Institutional Balance in the EC' (2005) 1 Utrecht Law Review 79, 86. And more recently, see Valerie Demedts and Merijn Chamon, 'The Commission Back on the Leash: No Autonomy to Sign Non-Binding Agreements on Behalf of the EU: Council v. Commission' (2017) 54 Common Market Law Review 245, 258.

Hence, also when concluding non-binding international agreements, EU institutions must identify a legal basis in the EU Treaties. As the EU Treaties do not expressly make provision for the conclusion of non-binding international agreements, an approach by analogy should be followed.[44] The legal bases empowering the EU to 'adopt measures' are the most obvious candidates to fulfil this function. Thus, when the EU wants to conclude a non-binding agreement with a third country that contains policy commitments, it must identify a substantive legal basis—for example Article 192(1) TFEU on environmental policy—as well as a procedural legal basis, most likely Article 16(1) TEU, which empowers the Council to 'carry out policy-making… functions'.

Before proceeding to the issue of the external representation of the EU, one qualification needs to be made to the above conclusion. While the principle of conferral thus applies both to binding and non-binding agreements made by the EU, Member States do in practice have opportunities to conclude informal, non-binding agreements even in areas of EU competence, including EU exclusive competence. Such action is incompatible with the division of competences set out above. However, it is difficult to challenge such non-binding agreements before the Court of Justice, especially if all Member States are a party to them. In such a scenario, there may not be an act that can be challenged before the Court of Justice through an annulment action.[45] Bringing an infringement action may be an option, but the Commission cannot bring a single infringement action against multiple, let alone all, Member States.[46] In any case, an infringement action will only offer the Commission declaratory relief; it cannot invalidate an agreement concluded by the Member States.

The abovementioned procedural difficulties explain why the challenge brought against the European Council concerning the legality of the agreement between the EU or its Member States on the one hand, and Turkey on the other, on the managing of refugee flows across the Aegean Sea (the so-called 'EU-Turkey Statement') failed. The 2016 EU-Turkey Statement was negotiated by the EU Member States meeting in the European Council and Turkey. There was a degree of ambiguity—a *flou artistique*—surrounding the identity of the parties: did the EU or the Member States make the agreement?[47] Was the

[44] Case C–233/02 *France v Commission ('EU-US Guidelines on Regulatory Cooperation and Transparency')*, EU:C:2004:173, para 45 in which the Court concluded that because the agreement at issue did not constitute an international agreement, it did not fall within the scope of (then) art 300 EC, (current) art 218 TFEU on the procedure to negotiate and conclude international agreements.

[45] TFEU, art 263 limits the target of annulment actions to EU acts that are 'intended to produce legal effects vis-à-vis third parties'.

[46] In this sense, see Koen Lenaerts and others, *EU Procedural Law* (Oxford University Press 2014) 184.

[47] On this question, see generally Carmelo Danisi, 'Taking the "Union" out of "EU": The EU-Turkey Statement on the Syrian Refugee Crisis as an Agreement Between States under International Law'

agreement even binding under international law?[48] The General Court considered the application brought by affected refugees to be inadmissible because the contested decision was not a decision of the European Council and thus not a reviewable act.[49] This case demonstrates how EU procedural law offers Member States opportunities to evade legal accountability.[50] This is regrettable as the EU-Turkey agreement arguably ran afoul of multiple EU norms: it may have violated EU exclusive competence and it may have infringed on the Charter rights of asylum seekers.

3. Implementing Treaties: No European *Missouri v Holland*

In early case law, the Court of Justice determined that validly concluded international agreements become an 'integral part' of EU law.[51] For international agreements to become binding within the EU legal order, no additional implementing legislation seemed necessary. The Court of Justice here took an approach akin to that pursued by the Belgian Supreme Court. Both high courts adopted a 'monist' approach to the reception of international agreements within the domestic legal order.[52] This approach could be contrasted with the 'dualist' approach prevalent, for example, in Canada.[53]

That said, despite the characterization of EU agreements as an integral part of EU law, in many instances the EU does adopt internal legislation to implement treaty obligations.[54] This is unsurprising as many international agreements are drafted in such a way that further legislative action is unavoidable.[55]

(*EJIL:Talk!*, 20 April 2017) <www.ejiltalk.org/taking-the-union-out-of-eu-the-eu-turkey-statement-on-the-syrian-refugee-crisis-as-an-agreement-between-states-under-international-law/> accessed 28 April 2022.

[48] Maarten den Heijer and Thomas Spijkerboer, 'Is the EU-Turkey Refugee and Migration Deal a Treaty?' (*EU Law Analysis*, 7 April 2016) <http://eulawanalysis.blogspot.be/2016/04/is-eu-turkey-refugee-and-migration-deal.html> accessed 29 July 2016.

[49] Order of the General Court in Case T–257/16 *NM v European Council*, EU:T:2017:130, para 70.

[50] Criticizing how the flight into informality allows EU institutions to avoid both democratic and judicial accountability, see Caterina Molinari, 'The EU and Its Perilous Journey Through the Migration Crisis: Informalisation of the EU Return Policy and Rule of Law Concerns' (2019) 44 European Law Review 824, 837–39.

[51] Case C–181/73 *Haegeman*, EU:C:1974:41, para 5.

[52] Cass, 27 mei 1971, *N.V. Fromagerie Franco-Suisse Le Ski*, Arr Cass, 1971, 959.

[53] See *Attorney General for Canada v Attorney General for Ontario . . . ('Labour Conventions')* [1937] AC 326, 347.

[54] Mario Mendez, *The Legal Effects of EU Agreements* (Oxford University Press 2013) xviii ('There is . . . a large body of EU legislation seeking to implement EU . . . Agreements (or parts thereof)').

[55] See on this André Nollkaemper, 'The Duality of Direct Effect of International Law' (2014) 25 European Journal of International Law 105, 119 ('Of course, it is rare that states conclude a treaty that

In addition, the Court of Justice has in recent years been reticent to recognize the direct effect of provisions of international agreements to which the EU is a party.[56] Furthermore, by incorporating treaty obligations into domestic EU legislation, the EU legislature is able to mobilize the enforcement mechanisms of EU law and thus bypass controversies related to the direct enforcement of treaty obligations within the EU.[57] In many instances, these factors and developments make it necessary for the EU legislature to enact legislation to implement obligations the EU incurred by concluding international agreements.

Who can adopt treaty-implementing legislation within the EU? Do the EU Treaties provide for a *Missouri v Holland*-type of 'treaty-implementing power' that ensures that the EU legislature can implement whichever international obligation the EU treaty-maker has incurred? Or does the legislative competence to implement treaty obligations in the EU remain divided, as is the case in Canada? When addressing these questions, it is important to be mindful of the structure of the division of legislative competences in the EU Treaties and how this division compares to its American and Canadian counterparts. As is the case in the US, if treaty-implementing legislation is required, the EU legislature will often have the necessary authority to adopt such legislation.[58] This will be the case not only because the EU holds broad internal legislative competence akin to the US Congress' authority to enact legislation affecting interstate commerce,[59] but also because the scope of the EU's external competence is closely aligned with that of its internal competence. (Remember how many of the EU's treaty-making competences are implied by the EU's internal legislative competences, as per Article 216(1) TFEU.) This means that, if the EU lacks sufficient domestic legislative competence to implement an international agreement, it is likely to have lacked also the external competence to conclude it in the

requires the contracting parties to ensure that all or some of its provisions have the status of directly applicable law and must be enforced by their domestic courts').

[56] In this sense, see Mario Mendez, 'The Application of International Law by the Court of Justice of the European Union' in Curtis A Bradley (ed), *The Oxford Handbook of Comparative Foreign Relations Law* (Oxford University Press 2019) 613–17.

[57] See Thomas Verellen, *Federalism and Treaty Enforcement in the European Union. Letters from America* (City University 2017) 1/2017 <www.city.ac.uk/__data/assets/pdf_file/0005/357854/Thomas-Verellen.pdf> accessed 15 November 2021.

[58] But see Gracia Marín Durán, 'Sustainable Development Chapters in EU Free Trade Agreements: Emerging Compliance Issues' (2020) 57 Common Market Law Review 1051, arguing that the EU has an external competence to conclude free trade agreements on labour law issues, but that it lacks internal competence to implement International Labour Organization agreements. This mismatch creates a risk of international responsibility for the EU.

[59] For a comparison, see generally José A Gutierrez-Fonz, 'Transatlantic Adjudication Techniques. The Commerce Clause and the EU's Internal Market Harmonization Clause in Perspective' in Elaine Fahey and Deirdre Curtin (eds), *A Transatlantic Community of Law: Legal Perspectives on the Relationship Between the EU and US Legal Orders* (Cambridge University Press 2014).

first place. Moreover, in the case of mixed agreements, for those provisions for which the EU lacks external competence, or for which the Council chose not to exercise EU shared competence, Member States that ratify the mixed agreement are under an international legal obligation to adopt the necessary implementing legislation in accordance with the *pacta sunt servanda* principle. In this sense, taken together, the EU and the Member States will always be in a position to implement the mixed agreements to which they are joint parties.

When it comes to treaty implementation, the EU thus shares features with the US, the Canadian, as well as the Belgian constitutional frameworks. As is the case in Canada, and in contrast to the US, the EU Treaties do not provide for a distinct 'treaty-implementing power'. As in the US, and to a lesser degree in Canada, the EU Treaties typically do provide for sufficiently broad legislative competences to enable the EU legislature to implement treaty obligations. Conversely, no situation is likely to arise in which the EU might lack the necessary internal legislative competence to implement its treaty obligations. Finally, as in Belgium, the practice of mixity ensures that there is always at least one order of governance that has the necessary competence to implement international agreements concluded jointly by the EU and the Member States.

4. External Representation in a Westphalian International Order

Who can represent the EU on the international stage? The EU Treaties empower the EU to engage in both bilateral and multilateral diplomacy. Article 15(6) TEU provides that '[t]he President of the European Council shall, at his level and in that capacity, ensure the external representation of the Union on issues concerning its common foreign and security policy, without prejudice to the powers of the High Representative of the Union for Foreign Affairs and Security Policy'. Furthermore, Article 17(1) TEU holds that, '[w]ith the exception of the common foreign and security policy, and other cases provided for in the Treaties, [the Commission] shall ensure the Union's external representation'. Article 221(1) TFEU empowers the delegations of the EU to represent the EU abroad: 'Union delegations in third countries and at international organisations shall represent the Union.' Similarly, Article 220(1) TFEU holds that:

> [t]he Union shall establish all appropriate forms of cooperation with the organs of the United Nations and its specialised agencies, the Council of Europe, the Organisation for Security and Cooperation in Europe and the

> Organisation for Economic Cooperation and Development. The Union shall also maintain such relations as are appropriate with other international organisations.

Similarly, in the sphere of the CFSP, Article 27(2) TEU provides that '[t]he High Representative shall represent the Union for matters relating to the common foreign and security policy. He shall conduct political dialogue with third parties on the Union's behalf and shall express the Union's position in international organisations and at international conferences.'

In addition to these *procedural* legal bases, activities of external representation also need to have a *substantive* legal basis in the Treaties. This is relevant in all instances, but perhaps in particular outside of the CFSP context, where the TFEU provides for more narrowly tailored legal bases. The same principles apply as in the treaty-making context. In areas covered by EU exclusive competence, only the EU can act. In areas covered by parallel competence, both the EU and its Member States can act. In areas covered by shared competence, the Member States can act for as long as the EU has not acted. Here, too, institutional practice has been characterized by a lack of willingness amongst some Member States to exercise EU shared competence. The UK government was perhaps the best-known—albeit anno 2022 somewhat less relevant—example. In the UK government's 2013 review of the balance of competences between the EU and its Member States, it was reported: 'The Government has taken the firm position that any statement containing issues where competence is shared between the EU (that is, the institutions) and the Member States, must make clear that it is delivered on the Member States' behalf as well as on the EU's.'[60] I return to the issue of how EU law manages the interactions between EU institutions and Member States within international bodies in Chapter 9 on intergovernmental relations.

Characteristic of the external representation of the EU as compared to that of the other federal unions examined in this book are the external difficulties the EU experiences when trying to exercise its competences within a state-centric international order.[61] In the *bilateral context*, the process has been relatively

[60] Foreign & Commonwealth Office (UK), 'Review of the Balance of Competences between the United Kingdom and the European Union' (2013), 40 <www.gov.uk/government/consultations/foreign-policy-report-review-of-the-balance-of-competences> accessed 15 November 2021.

[61] See on this Gerd Droesse, *Membership in International Organizations: Paradigms of Membership Structures, Legal Implications of Membership and the Concept of International Organization* (Asser Press, Springer 2020) 11–12; Jed Odermatt, *International Law and the European Union* (Cambridge University Press 2021) 25.

smooth.[62] Since the EU is not a sovereign state, the Vienna Convention on Diplomatic Relations (VCDR) is not applicable to it. As a consequence, the EU does not automatically benefit from the rights and privileges provided for in that convention.[63] However, as Sanderijn Duquet and Jan Wouters described in a 2012 contribution, through a series of bilateral agreements between the EU and host states the EU has been able to contract itself into many of the protections provided for in the VCDR. This led the authors to conclude that, '[a]lthough the EU is not a party to the Vienna Convention ... the Vienna Convention is being applied to the widest extent possible in the EU's bilateral diplomatic relations via multiple agreements'.[64]

In the *multilateral context*, external representation has been more challenging for the EU.[65] In many international organizations, including organizations within the UN system such as the International Labour Organization (ILO) or the International Maritime Organization (IMO), full membership is restricted to sovereign states.[66] In other organizations, such as the United Nations itself, the EU has only limited possibilities to participate. (The EU is not a member of the UN, while all the Member States are full members. Since the 2010s, however, the EU is able to partake in meetings of the General Assembly.[67]) In other organizations, such as the Food and Agriculture Organization (FAO) or the World Trade Organization (WTO) the EU and its Member States are both full members. In all of these settings, it is challenging for the EU to exercise its external competences effectively as Member States often try to leverage their full

[62] See however the 'downgrading' of the EU ambassador to the US in 2019 (Steven Erlanger, 'U.S. Downgraded E.U.'s Diplomatic Status (but Didn't Say Anything)' *The New York Times* (8 January 2019) <www.nytimes.com/2019/01/08/world/europe/eu-us-diplomatic-status.html> accessed 16 November 2021, and of the EU ambassador to the UK in 2020 (Daniel Boffey, 'EU-UK Inaugural Meeting "postponed" after Bloc Ambassador's Status Downgrade' *The Guardian* (28 January 2021) <www.theguardian.com/world/2021/jan/28/eu-uk-inaugural-meeting-postponed-after-bloc-ambassadors-status-downgrade>accessed 16 November 2021.

[63] The VCDR is drafted to apply only to states. See eg art 2 ('The establishment of diplomatic relations between States, and of permanent diplomatic missions, takes place by mutual consent') as well as art 48 ('The present Convention shall be open for signature by all States Members of the United Nations or of any of the specialized agencies Parties to the Statute of the International Court of Justice, and by any other State invited by the General Assembly of the United Nations to become a Party to the Convention ...') and art 50 ('The present Convention shall remain open for accession by any State belonging to any of the four categories mentioned in article 48. The instruments of accession shall be deposited with the Secretary-General of the United Nations').

[64] Sandrijn Duquet and Jan Wouters, 'The EU and International Diplomatic Law: New Horizons?' (2012) 7 The Hague Journal of Diplomacy 31, 32.

[65] On this subject, see generally Odermatt (n 61) ch 4; Geert De Baere, 'EU Status in Other International Organizations' in Robert Schütze and Takis Tridimas (eds), *Oxford Principles of European Union Law—Volume I: The European Union Legal Order* (Oxford University Press 2018).

[66] Note that since 20 October 2017 the EU does have a form of observer status within the ILO.

[67] On the role of the EU within the UN, see UN General Assembly Resolution 65/276, *Participation of the European Union in the work of the United Nations*, 10 May 2011, A/RES/65/276 <https://digitallibrary.un.org/record/705589> accessed 4 January 2023.

membership of organizations to prevent the EU from exercising its own external competence.[68]

The challenges the EU faces in this area of foreign relations are the mirror image of those faced by the member units of the other federal unions explored in this book. To return to an example offered in the previous chapter: it proved difficult for the Canadian province of Quebec to participate in UNESCO without federal assistance. This is unsurprising, considering that membership of UNESCO is restricted to states, and Quebec does not constitute a state.[69] The EU runs into the opposite difficulty: it may want to become a full member of an international organization. However, membership of the organization may be restricted to states, whereas the field in which they are active falls within EU competence. At the same time, several or all EU Member States may already be full members. To allow the EU to participate, Member State efforts to facilitate EU accession to the organization are needed. However, the Member States concerned may not be willing to give up their privileged role within the organization. And even if the EU gets to accede, it may only be able to accede along with those Member States, without however replacing them.

Parallel membership of the EU and the Member States of an international organization in turn raises challenges of shared rule.[70] As will be discussed in Chapters 5 and 9, the principle of sincere cooperation does some work to prevent individual Member States and the EU from acting in conflict with one another as they engage in parallel external representation. Yet an insistence on remaining visible does occasionally lead to controversies on who gets to take the floor or who gets to vote within the international body at issue (the Commission, the Council Presidency, or even individual Member States).[71] Such controversies can be addressed in different ways, including through a clarification of the division of competences between the EU and its Member States or through pragmatic collaboration. I discuss the latter strategy in Chapter 9 on intergovernmental relations in the EU. On the former, suffice

[68] Such disputes sometimes make their way to the Court of Justice. See eg Case C–161/20 *Commission v Council ('IMO')*, EU:C:2022:260 on the decision of the Council to authorize the Council Presidency rather than the Commission to act on behalf of the EU in the IMO. Central to the controversy was the ambiguous position of the Commission in the IMO: the Commission is an observer in the IMO, whereas the EU does not have a formal status.

[69] Art II(1) of the UNESCO Constitution restricts membership to UN members. UN membership is open only to states. See art 3 of the UN Charter.

[70] On such challenges, see Odermatt (n 61) 148–59.

[71] Such disputes sometimes make their way to the Court of Justice. See eg Case C–161/20 *Commission v Council ('IMO')*, EU:C:2022:260 on the decision of the Council to authorize the Council Presidency rather than the Commission to act on behalf of the EU in the IMO. Central to the controversy was the ambiguous position of the Commission in the IMO: the Commission is an observer in the IMO, whereas the EU does not have a formal status.

it to say that declarations of competence do not have a good track record when it comes to clarifying the division of competence between the EU and its Member States towards third countries. As Andrès Delgado Casteleiro has made clear in his work on the subject, declarations of competence suffer from important weaknesses. They are often vague and they do not take into account the dynamic nature of the division of competences as they are rarely updated.[72] (In particular, the EU acquires exclusive competences through the enactment of internal common rules, as provided for by Article 3(2) TFEU.) These features of declarations of competence make them less than ideal instruments to manage the cooperation between the EU and its Member States as they engage in multilateral external representation.

5. Coda: Towards a Common EU Defence?

In the previous chapter, I did not cover how the constitutions of Belgium, Canada, and the US allocate the power to deploy the military. The reason for not doing so is simple: in all three federations, the military is primarily a federal responsibility, with little to no member unit involvement.[73] The constitutional arrangement in the EU is different—the reason for which I do cover the issue in this chapter as a coda.[74] Dreams of a 'European Army' are as old as the European integration process itself, but have repeatedly failed to materialize.[75] The present EU Treaties also make provision for the establishment of a 'common defence'.[76] Article 42(2) TEU, in particular, provides:

[72] Andrés Delgado Casteleiro, *The International Responsibility of the European Union From Competence to Normative Control* (Cambridge University Press 2016) 127–28. In a similar sense, see Peter Olson, 'Mixity from the Outside: The Perspective of a Treaty Partner' in Christophe Hillion and Panos Koutrakos (eds), *Mixed Agreements Revisited: The EU and its Member States in the World* (Hart 2010) 335–37.

[73] In the US, the National Guard can be called upon by state governors as well as the President. However, and crucially, the federal government has the ability to 'federalize' parts of the National Guard and integrate them into the US Army Reserve. Criticizing this possibility, see Robert Leider, 'Federalism and the Military Power of the United States' (Social Science Research Network 2013) SSRN Scholarly Paper ID 2330648 <https://papers.ssrn.com/abstract=2330648> accessed 3 October 2017.

[74] In (classical) music, a coda is the concluding passage of a piece or movement, typically forming an addition to the basic structure.

[75] See eg Gerhard Bebr, 'The European Defence Community and the Western European Union: An Agonizing Dilemma' (1955) 7 Stanford Law Review 169, 172–73. And more recently, Kiran Klaus Patel, *Project Europe: A History* (Cambridge University Press 2020) 61–63.

[76] For an analysis, see generally Luigi Lonardo, 'Integration in European Defence: Some Legal Considerations' (2017) 2 European Papers—A Journal on Law and Integration 887903.

> The common security and defence policy shall include the progressive framing of a common Union defence policy. This will lead to a common defence, when the European Council, acting unanimously, so decides. It shall in that case recommend to the Member States the adoption of such a decision in accordance with their respective constitutional requirements.

The TEU thus allows for a future possibility to establish a 'common defence', provided the European Council agrees to doing so by unanimity and all Member States in turn endorse a proposal in this sense in line with their domestic constitutional requirements. Thus far, Member States have not taken any steps in this direction.[77]

In the meantime, the EU Treaties are best understood as putting in place a legal framework that aims to facilitate coordination and cooperation between Member States in the area of security and defence policy.[78] The Treaty provisions on the topic radiate a constructivist belief that through cooperation, coordination, and information sharing, the interests of the different EU Member States would gradually come to converge, thereby paving the way for a genuine common defence policy to emerge at a later phase of the integration process.[79] As part of this endeavour, the Treaties provide for much prospective language. Article 42 TEU, in particular, provides that '[t]he common security and defence policy shall include the progressive framing of a common Union defence policy', and it 'shall provide the Union with an operational capacity drawing on civilian and military assets'. Furthermore, the 'Member States shall make civilian and military capabilities available to the Union for the implementation of the common security and defence policy, to contribute to the objectives defined by the Council', and '[t]hose Member States which together establish multinational forces may also make them available to the common security and defence policy.'[80] And finally: 'Member States shall undertake progressively to improve their military capabilities.'[81]

[77] But see the European Parliament resolution of 22 November 2016 on the European Defence Union (2016/2052(INI)), [2018] OJ C224/18.

[78] On the subject of defence cooperation within the EU, see generally Panos Koutrakos, *The EU Common Security and Defence Policy* (Oxford University Press 2013).

[79] Constructivist theories of international relations assert that features of the contemporary international system are historically and socially constructed, as opposed to being the necessary consequence of human nature or other factors of the international environment. On the theory, see generally Emanuel Adler, 'Constructivism in International Relations: Sources, Contributions, Debates' in Walter Carlsnaes, Thomas Risse, and Beth A Simmons (eds), *Handbook of International Relations* (SAGE 2012) ch 5.

[80] TEU, art 42(3) first para.

[81] TEU, art 42(3) second para.

In addition to the prospective language, the Treaty framers were adamant also on insisting that, whichever action is undertaken in the security and defence context, these actions would not diminish their own autonomy in this area of policy-making, which is regarded as lying at the heart of national sovereignty. Article 42(2) second paragraph TEU for example holds:

> The policy of the Union in accordance with this Section shall not prejudice the specific character of the security and defence policy of certain Member States and shall respect the obligations of certain Member States, which see their common defence realised in the North Atlantic Treaty Organisation (NATO), under the North Atlantic Treaty and be compatible with the common security and defence policy established within that framework.

Similarly, the Declarations Nos 13 and 14, attached to the EU Treaties, emphasize that the Member States retain a capacity to conduct their own foreign policies. The impression left by these declarations is that EU actions in the sphere of security and defence are voluntary: Member States do not surrender autonomy to the EU, as is the case in other areas of EU foreign relations, in particular those areas under exclusive EU competence such as the CCP. Rather, the actions undertaken at EU level are cooperative in nature: effectiveness can be attained only if all Member States agree on a given course of action.

At the same time, and despite the fact that the EU Treaties contain much language to protect the autonomy of Member States, the EU Treaty framers did consider it necessary to define the limits of the type of defence-related activities in which the EU can engage. Article 43(1) TEU provides in that regard:

> The tasks referred to in Article 42(1), in the course of which the Union may use civilian and military means, shall include joint disarmament operations, humanitarian and rescue tasks, military advice and assistance tasks, conflict prevention and peace-keeping tasks, tasks of combat forces in crisis management, including peace-making and post-conflict stabilisation. All these tasks may contribute to the fight against terrorism, including by supporting third countries in combating terrorism in their territories.

While the text does allow for an interpretation of this list as being merely illustrative of the types of activities in which the EU can engage, the provision can also be read as providing a broad yet exhaustive list of such activities. This would mean that, even if participation in EU security and defence policy is voluntary, the TEU does impose restrictions on what can be achieved within the

EU framework. It would follow, for example, that it would be impermissible for the EU to engage in an offensive military operation. (It is unsurprising, in that regard, that the EU Treaties do not provide for a power to declare war, as exists for example in the US.)[82]

Relevant for present purposes is the possibility provided for in Articles 42(6) and 46 TEU for Member States to engage in a form of enhanced cooperation catered to the context of external security known as 'permanent structured co-operation'. This type of enhanced cooperation designed specifically for the EU's common security and defence policy (CSDP) introduces an element of asymmetrical federalism into the realm of security and defence policy in the EU. It allows those Member States with sufficient capabilities to do more and it takes away the ability of the other Member States to veto initiatives. In December 2017, a formal decision to trigger permanent structured cooperation was adopted.[83] In the same fashion, in the course of 2017 the Commission introduced a number of measures—a European Defence Fund—aimed at strengthening the industrial base of the EU, which in turn serves to facilitate the joint procurement of military equipment.[84] In doing so, the EU aims to strengthen the military capabilities of its Member States, as is required by Article 42(3) second paragraph TEU.

Initiatives of this type are a far cry, however, from a genuine military capability—a 'European Defence Union' as the European Parliament called for in a 2016 resolution[85]—which would include an EU capacity to deploy common military forces. Within the context of the CSDP, military missions have been undertaken, albeit that most of them have been limited in scope and typically situate themselves at the 'softer' end of the military spectrum.[86] Crucially, Member States are responsible for providing sufficient capabilities (military and financial) to allow for a CSDP action to be undertaken. Thus far, they have done so on an ad hoc basis. Initiatives to construct an EU operational capacity thus far have not been very successful. EU battlegroups represent the closest the EU has come to establishing a permanent military force. While the

[82] US Constitution, art I §8 cl 11.

[83] Council Decision (CFSP) 2017/2315 of 11 December 2017 establishing permanent structured co-operation (PESCO) and determining the list of participating Member States, [2017] OJ L331/57.

[84] Regulation (EU) 2018/1092 of the European Parliament and of the Council of 18 July 2018 establishing the European Defence Industrial Development Programme aiming at supporting the competitiveness and innovation capacity of the Union's defence industry, [2018] OJ L200/30, now replaced by Regulation (EU) 2021/697 of the European Parliament and of the Council of 29 April 2021 establishing the European Defence Fund and repealing Regulation (EU) 2018/1092 (Text with EEA relevance), [2021] OJ L170/149.

[85] See n 63.

[86] For an overview, see Michael E Smith, *Europe's Common Security and Defence Policy* (Cambridge University Press 2017) 36–37.

EU has maintained such battlegroups of 1,500 troops since 2017, they have never been deployed.[87] In the meantime, several larger EU Member States—including France and Germany—have launched separate initiatives outside of the EU framework to integrate military units. Germany has launched the 'Framework Nations Concept', a framework in which Dutch, Czech, and Romanian brigades have been integrated within the *Bundeswehr*.[88] France has taken steps in a similar direction with its 'European Defence Initiative'[89]—an initiative that eight other Member States, including Germany, endorsed in June 2018.[90]

It is important to note that these Member State initiatives take place outside of the EU framework altogether. (In his October 2017 speech at the Sorbonne University, French President Macron revealingly spoke of a *European*, not an *EU* Defence Initiative.) The aforementioned CSDP initiatives will not change this. PESCO focuses on building capabilities (eg the establishment of a military training centre) and harmonizing standards (eg in the areas of procurement or military radio communications). At this point, and to the regret of some, no operational capabilities are being created within PESCO.[91] The same holds true for the European Peace Facility, which enabled the EU to finance the acquisition of weaponry which could then be made available to Ukraine following the Russian invasion of that country in 2022.[92] Taking these elements into account, it would be mistaken to draw an equivalence between CSDP military missions, which require cooperation between the militaries of the different EU Member States, and the deployment of the US military, which is a single military force financed by federal fiscal resources and controlled by the federal President and Congress. For the foreseeable future, CSDP military actions remain dependent

[87] See Robin Emmott, 'EU to Aim for Rapid Deployment Force without U.S. Assets by 2025, Document Says' *Reuters* (16 November 2021) <www.reuters.com/business/aerospace-defense/eu-aim-rapid-deployment-force-without-us-assets-by-2025-document-says-2021-11-16/> accessed 16 November 2021.

[88] H Lunde Saxi, 'British and German Initiatives for Defence Cooperation: The Joint Expeditionary Force and the Framework Nations Concept' (2017) 17 Defence Studies 171.

[89] Claudia Major and Christian Mölling, 'France Moves From EU Defense to European Defense' *Carnegie Europe* (7 December 2017) <http://carnegieeurope.eu/strategiceurope/74944?lang=en> accessed 15 November 2021.

[90] Daniel Boffey, 'Nine EU States Sign off on Joint Military Intervention Force' *The Guardian* (25 June 2018) <www.theguardian.com/world/2018/jun/25/nine-eu-states-to-sign-off-on-joint-military-intervention-force> accessed 15 November 2021.

[91] See Andrew Sparrow, 'Jean-Claude Juncker Calls for EU Army' *The Guardian* (8 March 2015) <www.theguardian.com/world/2015/mar/08/jean-claude-juncker-calls-for-eu-army-european-commission-miltary> accessed 15 November 2021.

[92] Council Decision (CFSP) 2022/339 of 28 February 2022 on an assistance measure under the European Peace Facility to support the Ukrainian Armed Forces, [2022] OJ L61/1.

on ad hoc Member State commitments to make military capabilities available to the EU.

6. Conclusion: A Very Open Federation

In this chapter I set out to explore two questions. How do the EU Treaties allocate foreign relations competences? And how does the EU compare to the three federations examined in the previous chapter? I explained that the EU holds broad external competences. These competences are, as a general rule, shared rather than exclusive. This means that EU law, in contrast with the US and Canadian constitutions, to an important extent preserves the ability of Member States to continue to engage in foreign relations. Member States continue to be able to conclude international agreements and they remain participants in the workings of many international bodies. It is only when the EU holds an exclusive competence that EU law completely precludes Member States from acting unilaterally on the international stage.

The division of competences sketched in this chapter portrays an image of the EU and its Member States as constituting a particularly 'open' system of multilevel governance. In contrast to both the US and Canada, but as is the case also in Belgium, *both* levels of governance can conclude treaties in the meaning of the VCLT. The openness of the EU's foreign affairs constitution has important implications. As the EU and its Member States operate in the same fields, EU law must put in place mechanisms to either avoid or resolve conflicts between the different governments and institutions involved in this complex foreign relations space. I look at these mechanisms in the following chapters. In keeping with the structure of the book as consisting of two parts, one dedicated to *self-rule* and another to *shared rule*, in the following two chapters (Chapters 4 and 5) I comparatively explore how conflicts between exercises of EU/federal and member unit competences are resolved. In the second part of the book on shared rule, I look at how conflicts can be avoided. This can be achieved in two ways: by granting member units a (formal or informal) voice in the federal foreign policy-making process (Chapters 6 and 7), or by encouraging and in turn regulating the relations that exists between the different governments as they engage in foreign relations (Chapters 8 and 9).

4

Conflict Resolution in the US, Canada, and Belgium

> I do not think the United States would come to an end if we lost our power to declare an Act of Congress void. I do think the Union would be imperiled if we could not make that declaration as to the laws of the several states.
>
> Oliver Wendell Holmes Jr, 1921[1]

1. Introduction

When federal and member unit governments can act within the same policy area, a potential for conflict arises. To protect the integrity of the polity, it is important that a conflict rule or a conflict resolution mechanism is in place should such situations arise.[2] This chapter focuses on this second dimension of self-rule as it plays out in the foreign relations context. A conflict resolution mechanism is a mechanism that resolves a conflict between federal and member unit action in a categorical fashion rather than through pragmatic accommodation as occurs in the federal political process (discussed in Chapters 6 and 7) or in the framework of intergovernmental relations (discussed in Chapters 8 and 9). In other words, the application of a conflict rule or a conflict resolution mechanism leads to winners and losers as the preferences of one government will prevail over those of another.

In this chapter, I offer a comparative overview of the instruments and mechanisms to resolve conflicts between federal and member unit foreign relations actions in the US, Canada, and Belgium. I explain how, in particular in the US—in part as a result of the pre-1789 experience under the Articles of

[1] Oliver Wendell Holmes, *Collected Legal Papers* (Harcourt, Brace and Company 1920) 295–96.

[2] In this sense, see also Ernest A Young, '"The Ordinary Diet of the Law": The Presumption Against Pre-emption in the Roberts Court' (2012) 2011 The Supreme Court Review 253, 254 ('In this world of concurrent jurisdiction, the key task of federalism is to manage the overlap of state and federal law.' Internal quotation marks omitted).

Foreign Relations Federalism. Thomas Verellen, Oxford University Press. © Thomas Verellen 2023.
DOI: 10.1093/oso/9780192844569.003.0004

Confederation—the Constitution emphasizes the ability of the federal government to enforce its decisions, including its foreign policy determinations, on the state governments. The doctrine of pre-emption plays a vital role in this regard. By contrast, the Canadian and Belgian constitutions are less forthcoming on the matter of conflict resolution. The Canadian constitution is silent on the issue. The Belgian constitutional arrangements do contain two mechanisms that respectively allow the federal government to substitute itself to the member unit governments and to suspend the negotiation and implementation of member unit international agreements. However, neither of these two mechanisms can be used by the Belgian federal government on a discretionary basis. Instead, their application depends on the fulfilment of objective criteria—criteria which, institutional practice demonstrates, are difficult to fulfil.

In the following chapter (Chapter 5), I will explore the mechanisms in the EU Treaties to resolve conflicts between the EU and its Member States in the conduct of foreign relations. I will argue that, in comparison especially with Belgium and Canada, the EU Treaties provide for relatively elaborate conflict resolution mechanisms. These mechanisms are not at the disposal of the political institutions at EU level: nowhere do the Treaties—or secondary EU legislation, for that matter—provide for a 'federal' veto against Member State initiatives. By contrast, through a series of rulings dating back to the 1970s, the Court of Justice has developed two closely related constitutional doctrines that aim to resolve conflicts between the EU and Member States, namely the ERTA pre-emption doctrine and the duty of sincere cooperation. Consequently, the EU courts, and ultimately the Court of Justice, are charged with the responsibility of resolving conflicts between Member States and the EU, including in the conduct of EU foreign relations.

For the sake of exposition, in this chapter I first look at conflict resolution mechanisms developed in Canada and Belgium, where, as mentioned, conflict resolution mechanisms do not figure prominently in the constitution, and then turn to the US, where federal–state conflict resolution was a central concern of the framers. Discussing the US after Belgium and Canada facilitates the comparative analysis with the EU, which follows in the next chapter. In an effort to theorize the differences and similarities between the three federal states I look at in this chapter, I compare the different conflict resolution mechanisms in terms of the degree of *formality* of each mechanism, and in terms of the *institution* that holds responsibility for resolving the conflict (the courts or the political institutions). We will see that in Canada, conflict resolution mechanisms are informal and political; in Belgium, they are formal and political; and in the

US, they are formal and judicial. Overall, it will become apparent that conflict resolution plays a central role, in particular in the US where, in keeping with the principles of dual sovereignty, the supremacy of federal law and policy over conflicting state law carries much weight. By contrast, the scarcity of conflict resolution mechanisms in both Canada and Belgium, and their informal nature in Canada, help to explain why intergovernmental relations have become so important in both Belgium and Canada. Because the Belgian and Canadian federal governments cannot easily impose their preferences on the member units, collaboration and cooperation become all the more important.

2. Canada: Political and Informal Mechanisms

The Canadian foreign affairs constitution does not provide for formal mechanisms to resolve conflicts between federal foreign policy and individual provincial initiatives that—in the view of the federal government—negatively affect Canadian foreign policy. The only obvious means to challenge provincial initiatives at the disposal of the federal government consists in challenging the *vires* of provincial legislation under the division of legislative powers set out in sections 91 and 92 of the Constitution Act, 1867, or in invoking an infringement of the Canadian Charter of Rights and Freedoms, which is part of the Constitution Act, 1982.[3] Unlike its American counterpart, the Canadian constitution does not provide for a pre-emption doctrine capable of leading to an invalidation of provincial legislation due to a conflict with federal foreign policy. The paramountcy doctrine empowers Canadian courts to disapply (not invalidate) provincial law in the event of a conflict with federal law. This doctrine has however never been interpreted in such a way as to include federal policy determinations as a reference norm.[4] As for conflicts between federal

[3] Canada's written constitution consists of two documents: (i) the British North America Act, 1867, now known as the Constitution Act, 1867, and (ii) the Constitution Act, 1982, which includes the Canadian Charter of Rights and Freedoms.

[4] See *Alberta (Attorney General) v Moloney*, [2015] 3 SCR 327, 2015 SCC 51 (CanLII) [16]:

> [The doctrine of federal paramountcy] recognizes that where laws of the federal and provincial levels come into conflict, there must be a rule to resolve the impasse . . . When there is a genuine inconsistency between federal and provincial *legislation*, that is, when the operational effects of provincial *legislation* are incompatible with federal *legislation*, the federal law prevails. (Internal quotation marks omitted, italics added)

On the effects of applying the doctrine, see ibid [29]:

> Such a conflict results in the provincial law being inoperative, but only to the extent of the conflict with the federal law . . . In practice, this means that the provincial law remains valid, but will be read down so as to not conflict with the federal law, though only for as long as the conflict exists.

legislation, or even federally concluded international agreements on the one hand, and provincial *ententes* (ie non-binding agreements between a Canadian province and a third country government) on the other: the non-binding nature of the latter precludes conflicts from arising between such norms. From the perspective of Canadian courts, the latter do not exist.[5] Likewise, in legal terms a conflict between a federally concluded international agreement and a provincial statute cannot arise either, as international agreements—while binding under international law—are not a source of domestic law in Canada.[6]

Canada's federal government could ask the Supreme Court of Canada to clarify the scope of the federal foreign affairs prerogative so as to get more clarity on who can do what in the event of a conflict between federal and provincial foreign policy action.[7] As discussed in Chapter 2, the outer limits of the prerogative are ill-defined. The ensuing ambiguity has allowed the federal and provincial governments to engage in processes of pragmatic mutual accommodation. If, however, matters were to come to a head, the federal government could consider it useful to clear up this ambiguity and obtain greater legal certainty about the precise scope of its prerogative powers. A case could be made that the exclusive nature of the federal foreign affairs prerogative precludes provincial governments from undertaking foreign relations-related activities if the federal government considers such activities harmful to federal foreign policy. As an early commentator put it: 'If there is a clear conflict with national foreign policy ... the federal government should have the executive power under the constitution to prohibit, nullify, or veto the provincial activity by order-in-council.'[8] The Canadian federal government has never taken such a step, however. As will be discussed further in Chapter 8, federal–provincial relations remain characterized by pragmatism and mutual trust.

Only in the late 1960s did federal–provincial antagonism breach the threshold of open conflict. In this period, Quebec experienced its 'Quiet Revolution'. The Quiet Revolution was a period of economic modernization, rising Quebec nationalism, and generally an increased emphasis on the distinctiveness of Quebec society within Canada.[9] During this period, successive

[5] In this sense, see eg *Ontario v Scott* ([1956] SCR 137, 1955 CanLII 16 (SCC), discussed in Chapter 1.

[6] In this sense, see eg Stéphane Beaulac, 'Arrêtons de dire que les tribunaux au Canada sont liés par le droit international' (2004) 38 Revue juridique Thémis 359.

[7] Section 53(d) of Canada's Supreme Court Act empowers the Governor in Council (ie the federal executive) to refer to the Supreme Court 'important questions of law or fact' concerning the powers of the governments.

[8] Ronald G Atkey, 'The Role of the Provinces in International Affairs' (1970) 26 International Journal 261, 270.

[9] On the Quiet Revolution, see generally Réjean Pelletier, 'La Révolution Tranquille' in Gérard Daigle and Guy Rocher (eds), *Le Québec en jeu. Comprendre les grands défis* (Les Presses de l'Université

Quebec governments became increasingly assertive, including on foreign relations-related issues.[10] Part of this assertiveness consisted in strengthening ties with Gaullist France, which was keen to engage with Quebec City and ready to bypass Ottawa if such an action was considered beneficial for France.[11] For his part, Pierre Elliot Trudeau, Canada's Prime Minister at the time, believed in a bilingual, federal Canada in which Quebec was treated equally to the other provinces. Trudeau's style and approach, moreover, was of a more confrontational type.[12]

In the late 1960s, the Quebec and federal governments clashed on a number of issues. For example, when the Quebec government organized Saint-Jean-Baptiste Day celebrations in Montreal on 24 June 1968, federal Prime Minister Trudeau was not invited, even though invitations to numerous foreign diplomats had been issued.[13] When the Prime Minister put pressure on foreign ambassadors not to attend the celebrations, many of them complied. This eventually led the Montreal authorities to retract the invitations. In this case, the federal strategy was effective, perhaps in part due to the power of the federal government (in turn derived from the foreign affairs prerogative, coupled with the recognition of the federal government as the holder of external sovereignty) to declare ambassadors *persona non grata* in Canada.[14] In similar fashion, in 1968 the Trudeau government threatened to end diplomatic relations with the African country of Gabon when the latter had invited the Quebec government to attend a conference in Libreville, Gabon's capital, on education without also having issued an invitation to the federal government of Canada.[15] Here again, the federal government exercised diplomatic pressure on the third country (in this case Gabon) to prevent the province of Quebec from acting in a manner

de Montréal 1992) as well as Geneviève Zubrzycki, *Beheading the Saint: Nationalism, Religion, and Secularism in Quebec* (University of Chicago Press 2016). For the impact of the Quiet Revolution on Canadian foreign relations law, see Edward McWhinney, 'Canadian Federalism, and the Foreign Affairs and Treaty Power. The Impact of Quebec's "Quiet Revolution"' [1969] The Canadian Yearbook of International Law 3. On the significance of sub-state diplomacy to Quebec's identity, see generally Stéphane Paquin, 'Identity Paradiplomacy in Québec' (2018) 66 Quebec Studies 3.

[10] On the role of the domestic considerations in Quebec's international activities, see eg Louis Bélanger, 'The Domestic Politics of Quebec's Quest for External Distinctiveness' [2002] The American Review of Canadian Studies 195 (referred to in fn 177).

[11] On this episode, see generally Edouard Baraton, *De Gaulle ou l'hypothèque française sur le Canada* (L'Harmattan 2013).

[12] On the life of one of Canada's most celebrated and despised prime ministers, see generally John English, *Just Watch Me: The Life of Pierre Elliott Trudeau* (1st edn, Alfred A Knopf 2006).

[13] On this episode, see McWhinney (n 9) 24–26.

[14] Vienna Convention on Diplomatic Relations, art 9.

[15] On this episode, see McWhinney (n 9) 12–16.

that the federal government considered to run contrary to Canadian foreign policy.[16]

As mentioned, the actions of the federal government of Canada in the late 1960s were unusual. Since that time, the Canadian federal government has never again pursued a strategy of open confrontation. Instead, pragmatic co-operation has taken place, including with successive Quebec governments. As will be discussed in Chapter 8 on intergovernmental relations, provincial governments have occasionally called for the establishment of formal frameworks of federal–provincial consultation and collaboration.[17] However, Canada's federal government has never responded favourably to such proposals. Arguably, the ambiguities surrounding the scope of the federal foreign affairs prerogative—in particular, does the prerogative preclude Canadian provinces from engaging in non-binding para-diplomatic activities?—coupled with the fact that only the federal government is recognized by the international community as the holder of Canadian sovereignty, benefit the federal government over the provinces. This combination of factors allows the federal government to externalize conflicts if they arise and rally the international community behind the federal cause.

The absence of formal conflict resolution mechanisms aimed at safeguarding the effectiveness of Canadian federal foreign policy is not surprising, considering that Canada's constitution was drafted at a time when Canada was still firmly part of the British Empire. When the Trudeau government amended Canada's constitution in the early 1980s, questions regarding foreign relations were left out of the process, and commentators have been sceptical as to the chances of success were the federal government ever to try and write its understanding of Canada's foreign affairs constitution into Canada's Constitution Act.[18] By contrast, when the Belgian Constitution was amended in the early

[16] On this episode, see eg Robin S Gendron and David Edward Tabachnik, 'The Libreville Conference and Federalism in Canadian Foreign Relations' in Michael K Hawes, Andrew C Holman, and Christopher Kirkey (eds), *1968 in Canada: A Year and Its Legacies* (University of Ottawa Press 2021).

[17] See eg Carl Meyer, 'Provinces Want Trade Role Outlined in Writing' *Embassy* (August 2011) <http://canada-europe.org/en/pdf/Provinces%20Want%20Trade%20Role%20Outlined%20in%20Writing%20-%20August%202011.pdf> accessed 24 November 2021. See further also Yulia Minaeva, 'Canadian Federalism Uncovered: The Assumed, the Forgotten and the Unexamined in Collaborative Federalism' (PhD Thesis, University of Ottawa 2012) 168.

[18] In this sense, writing in 1988, see eg John Zeigel, 'Treaty-Making and Implementation Powers in Canada: The Continuing Dilemma' in Georg Schwarzenberger, Edward D Brown, and Bin Cheng (eds), *Contemporary Problems of International Law: Essays in Honour of Georg Schwarzenberger on his Eightieth Birthday* (Taylor & Francis 1988) 347 ('Even if the parties were minded to make an attempt and to re-allocate the treaty-making and implementing powers, the prospects of meeting the amendment formula's requirements . . . are slight.' There is no reason to believe Zeigel's statement would hold less true today. On the difficulties involved in amending Canada's constitution, see eg Richard Albert, 'The Difficulty of Constitutional Amendment in Canada' (2015) 53 Alberta Law Review 85.

1990s, foreign relations were a central component of the reform package. Together with the objective of extending the autonomy of the Belgian member units onto the international stage, the framers wished to maintain the 'coherence' of Belgian foreign relations.[19]

3. Belgium: Political and Formal Mechanisms

Intergovernmental relations and consensus-based joint decision-making are the primary means to protect the coherence of Belgian foreign relations. This is a sensible approach in light of the structure of Belgian federalism, which is characterized by a fundamental equality between the federal and member unit levels of governance.[20] Absent a Belgian 'Supremacy Clause', it is not surprising that intergovernmental relations are an important method of conflict resolution.[21] However, despite this equality, the 1993 framers did insert two elements of hierarchy into Belgium's foreign affairs constitution to resolve conflicts: first, a *suspension mechanism* that allows the Belgian federal government in certain objectively defined circumstances to suspend the negotiation and implementation of member unit international agreements; and secondly, a *substitution mechanism* that allows the Belgian federal government to take measures to ensure compliance with Belgium's international obligations even in areas of member unit exclusive competence. I look at each mechanism in turn.

3.1 The Suspension Mechanism

The suspension mechanism is a first conflict resolution mechanism that the 1993 framers of the Belgian Constitution introduced. It empowers the Belgian federal government to suspend the negotiation or implementation of a member unit international agreement if such an agreement threatens to undermine the coherence of federal foreign relations. In particular, the Special Law on

[19] Jan Velaers, '"In foro interno et in foro externo": de internationale bevoegdheden van gemeenschappen en gewesten' in Godfried Geudens and Frank Judo (eds), *Internationale betrekkingen en federalisme: Staatsrechtconferentie 2005—Vlaamse Juristenvereniging* (Uitgeverij Larcier 2006) 4–5.

[20] Jürgen Vanpraet and Yannick Peeters, 'Autonomie en samenwerking in het federale België' in E Vandenbossche and Xavier Delgrange (eds), *Evoluties in het Belgisch cooperatief federalisme = : Évolutions dans le fédéralisme coopératif belge* (Die Keure 2015) 107, referring to the 'principled equality between the federal, regional and community governments'.

[21] But see ibid, where the authors point to an early Council of State opinion which endorsed a principle of federal supremacy. The Constitutional Court as well as the majority of commentators rejected this proposition (see ibid 108 and the references to case law and literature there).

Institutional Reform (SLIR) authorizes the Belgian federal government to suspend the negotiation and, if necessary, the application, of member unit international agreements.[22] A suspension takes place in two phases. In a first phase, the federal government informs the Interministerial Conference on Foreign Policy (ICFP) that it objects to the intention of one or several member unit governments to conclude an international agreement.[23] The expression of such an objection suspends the negotiating process for a thirty-day period. During this 'cool-off' period, the different governments discuss the matter and look for a consensus. If no consensus is reached, the federal government can suspend the negotiation of the proposed member unit agreement for an indefinite amount of time, provided at least one of the following conditions is met:

- (i) Belgium has not recognized the third country-treaty partner;[24]
- (ii) Belgium does not maintain diplomatic relations with the third country-treaty partner;
- (iii) it can be discerned from a decision or act of the federal government that relations between Belgium and the third country-treaty partner are interrupted, suspended, or imperilled; or
- (iv) the proposed agreement violates the international or supranational obligations of Belgium.[25]

The substitution mechanism thus endows the federal government with a power to suspend the exercise of member unit treaty-making powers. The use of the mechanism is however restricted to four objectively identifiable sets of circumstances. Consequently, it is not possible for the federal government to wield this power on the basis of a claim that a member unit agreement violates the 'national interest' or similar open-textured notions. As will be discussed further later in this chapter and in the next, this mechanism is thus not as far-reaching as the pre-emption doctrine in the US, which precludes states from interfering with federal executive foreign policy, or the EU's ERTA pre-emption doctrine, which forever precludes Member States from acting on certain issues on which the EU has adopted internal legislation. The Belgian suspension mechanism has other limitations as well. In particular, its scope of

[22] SLIR, art 81 §§ 3–4.
[23] ibid §3. On the ICFP, see Chapter 7.
[24] Belgium typically only recognizes states, not governments. In this sense, see Marc J Bossuyt and Jan Wouters, *Grondlijnen van internationaal recht* (Intersentia 2005) 207 (Translation TV: 'A number of countries, including Belgium and the Netherlands, as a general rule do not recognize governments: to them only the question of whether a government exercises effective control over the territory counts').
[25] SLIR, art 81 §4.

application is limited to legally binding international agreements. The federal government thus cannot rely on the mechanism to suspend the negotiation or application of non-binding agreements, or to prevent member unit governments from visiting third country governments or multilateral organizations. The mechanism has never been used since its introduction in 1993.

3.2 The Substitution Mechanism

The substitution mechanism is a second conflict resolution mechanism which the framers of the Belgian Constitution put in place during the 1993 round of constitutional reform. This mechanism operates at the level of the implementation of the international obligations incurred by Belgium's member units. It empowers the Belgian federal government to take measures to ensure compliance with Belgium's international obligations, even if such measures encroach on the member units' exclusive internal competence. Such a mechanism was considered necessary to address the risk that Belgian member units fail or refuse to take measures Belgium committed itself to take in the EU legislative process or in international negotiations outside of the EU context, as well as the risk that member units fail to implement international obligations they themselves incurred but for which Belgium, that is, the federal government, remains liable under international law. In either context, as mentioned in the first chapter of this book, only the state of Belgium is exposed to a risk of international liability. The substitution mechanism aims to foreclose this risk.

The mechanism finds its legal basis in the Belgian Constitution and is further developed in the SLIR.[26] The SLIR makes use of the substitution mechanism by the Belgian federal government subject to a number of conditions:[27]

(i) Belgium's liability must have been established by an international or supranational court;
(ii) the federal government has to warn the member unit government three months in advance by means of a royal decree;
(iii) the member unit must have been involved throughout the legal proceedings before the abovementioned international or supranational court;

[26] Belgian Constitution, art 169.
[27] SLIR, art 16 §3.

(iv) the federal government must be in compliance with its obligations under the applicable intergovernmental agreement that imposes obligations of information sharing and cooperation on Belgium's governments (a topic discussed further in Chapter 7 on intergovernmental relations).

As with the suspension mechanism, the substitution mechanism has not yet been put to use; leading commentators consider it to be of more symbolic than practical value.[28]

Perhaps mindful of how difficult it is for the above requirements to be met, in 2014, in the framework of the sixth round of constitutional reform since 1970, the SLIR was amended to make it easier for the federal government to substitute itself for the member units to ensure compliance with Belgium's international obligations related to climate change.[29] In this context, a decision by the monitoring body established by the United Nations Framework Convention on Climate Change (UNFCC) or a reasoned opinion by the European Commission is sufficient to trigger the substitution mechanism.[30] No final judgment by an international tribunal is needed. The SLIR imposes a number of other procedural requirements, including a waiting requirement and an obligation to discuss the issue in the Concertation Committee, which is the intergovernmental body that brings together the heads of the various Belgian governments. As is the case for the general substitution mechanism, the federal government has not yet made use of this climate change-specific substitution mechanism, and commentators have questioned the mechanism's overall effectiveness.[31]

Could the Belgian federal government follow the lead of Canadian Prime Minister Trudeau and pursue a strategy of 'internationalizing' a federal–member unit conflict? Arguably not. First, for such a conflict to escalate, it is necessary for incongruent coalitions to be in office within the different governments in Belgium. Since typically at least one political party will be in office at both levels of government, the scenario is less likely to materialize in Belgium than it is in Canada where coalition government has yet to occur and the party system is split along federal–provincial lines. Secondly, in Belgium most

[28] Karel Reybrouck and Stefan Sottiaux, *De federale bevoegdheden* (Intersentia 2019) para 1257.

[29] SLIR, art 16 §4. On the sixth round of constitutional reform, see generally Jurgen Goossens and Pieter Cannoot, 'Belgian Federalism after the Sixth State Reform' (2015) 7 Perspectives on Federalism 29.

[30] The Commission issues reasoned opinions in the run up towards bringing an infringement action before the Court of Justice.

[31] See in particular 'Syntheserapport Belgisch "Klimaat-Governance"' (Université Saint Louis Bruxelles 2018) 9–10 <https://klimaat.be/doc/KlimGov_Synth_NL.pdf> accessed 3 June 2022.

international agreements must be ratified not only by the federal Parliament, but also by the member unit legislatures. These constitutional entitlements, which stand on legally firmer ground than those enjoyed by the Canadian provincial governments, preclude the Belgian federal government from pursuing a strategy of confrontation with the member units as confrontation will lead to gridlock.

The controversy surrounding the signing and provisional application of CETA, the EU-Canada trade agreement, which captured headlines across Europe and Canada in the autumn of 2016, is illustrative of how conflicts between the federal and member unit governments play out in Belgium. When the governments of Wallonia and the French-speaking Community refused to authorize the federal executive to sign CETA and allow for its provisional application within the Council of the EU, the Belgian federal government did not seek confrontation with the member unit governments. Instead, it sought a negotiated solution.[32] While some political party leaders publicly argued for overriding the Walloon and French-speaking Communities' objections, most stakeholders rejected such a radical—and arguably unconstitutional—approach, and negotiations were considered the only viable course of action.[33] Interestingly, however—and in this sense the Belgian approach is reminiscent of the approach pursued by Canadian Prime Minister Trudeau in the late 1960s—the negotiations with the Belgian member unit governments involved not only the federal government, but also the European Commission, the European Parliament, and even Canadian government ministers.[34] Clearly, external pressure did play a role in persuading the member units to change course in this case.

Overall, it would appear that, while political pressure often does play a role, resolving conflicts through coercion or hierarchy is not a viable course of action in the present configuration of Belgian foreign relations federalism. The few opportunities to do so (ie the suspension and substitution mechanisms) have at the time of writing never been used. Instead, negotiations between the

[32] For the outcome of those negotiations, see S Ta, 'CETA: les détails de l'accord intrabelge' *La Libre Belgique* (26 October 2016) <www.lalibre.be/actu/politique-belge/ceta-les-details-de-l-accord-intrabelge-5812577ccd70958a9d5906be> accessed 25 November 2021.

[33] Sylvie Van Ginneken and Wim Winckelmans, 'Het geduld van Rutten is op' *De Standaard* (20 October 2016) <www.standaard.be/cnt/dmf20161019_02528737> accessed 25 November 2021. Criticizing the suggestion to sign CETA regardless of intra-Belgian constitutional restrictions, see Raf Geenens and others, 'Walen blokkeren continent? Naast de kwestie' *De Standaard* (21 October 2016) <www.standaard.be/cnt/dmf20161020_02531035> accessed 25 November 2021.

[34] Jennifer Rankin, 'EU-Canada Trade Deal in Crisis as Canadian Minister Walks Out' *The Guardian* (22 October 2016) <www.theguardian.com/world/2016/oct/21/eu-canada-ceta-trade-deal-meltdown-canadian-minister-walks-out> accessed 25 November 2021.

different governments have always been the preferred course of action—even if failing to reach a consensus means no action can be undertaken at all.[35]

4. United States: Judicial and Formal Mechanisms

In contrast to Canada and Belgium, conflict resolution mechanisms take centre stage in the foreign affairs constitution of the US. As mentioned earlier, this is not surprising. For some of the framers of the US Constitution, the experience under the Articles of Confederation had been one of frustration and disappointment with state governments which refused to live up to their commitments vis-à-vis the central government.[36] Decisions of states such as Virginia to not honour pre-revolution debt obligations to British creditors were deemed particularly problematic. (In retaliation, Britain had retained possession of a series of forts along the US-Canadian border.[37]) To remedy the above shortcomings of the Articles of Confederation, the 1787 United States Constitution provides for two mechanisms to resolve conflicts between federal and state law: first, under the Compact Clause,[38] the federal Congress has the authority to veto State 'compacts', and second, under the Supremacy Clause,[39] in case of a conflict between federal and state law, the former prevails, and the latter is invalid to the extent of the conflict. The former mechanism is discussed further in Chapter 8 on intergovernmental relations in the US; the latter is discussed here.

4.1 Introducing: Pre-emption

Pre-emption is the mechanism whereby state law is invalid to the extent of a conflict with federal law.[40] As mentioned, the pre-emption principle finds its

[35] See eg Wim Winckelmans, 'Belgisch klimaatakkoord is voor een andere keer' *De Standaard* (10 November 2021) <www.standaard.be/cnt/dmf20211109_97712641> accessed 25 November 2021, reporting that the Belgian governments were not able to reach an agreement on how to divide emission reduction targets among the different Belgian governments before the 2021 COP26 summit in Glasgow.

[36] On this episode, see eg Ron Chernow, *Alexander Hamilton* (Penguin 2005) 394–95. See also Office of the Historian, 'Articles of Confederation, 1777–1781' <https://history.state.gov/milestones/1776-1783/articles> accessed 25 November 2021 ('[T]he Articles did not allow Congress sufficient authority to enforce provisions of the 1783 Treaty of Paris that allowed British creditors to sue debtors for pre-Revolutionary debts, an unpopular clause that many state governments chose to ignore').

[37] ibid.

[38] US Constitution, art II s 10 cl 3.

[39] US Constitution, art VI cl 2.

[40] On pre-emption, see generally William W Buzbee, *Pre-emption Choice: The Theory, Law, and Reality of Federalism's Core Question* (Cambridge University Press 2008).

foundation in the Supremacy Clause of the US Constitution. The Supremacy Clause provides that:

> [t]his Constitution, and the Laws of the United States which shall be made in Pursuance thereof; and all Treaties made, or which shall be made, under the Authority of the United States, shall be the supreme Law of the Land; and the Judges in every State shall be bound thereby, any Thing in the Constitution or Laws of any State to the Contrary notwithstanding.[41]

In comparison with its Canadian or EU counterparts—the principles of paramountcy and primacy, respectively—the US pre-emption principle is further-reaching in its effects. Whereas Canadian and EU courts merely *disapply* conflicting provincial or Member State law, US courts *invalidate* conflicting state law (or, more precisely, they confirm the existence and clarify the scope of a pre-emptive effect).[42] Furthermore, in contrast in particular to the EU, in institutional terms enforcement of the pre-emption principle is relatively effective due to the existence of a federal court system charged with the responsibility of interpreting and enforcing federal law, including by means of preliminary injunctions by which US federal courts can preclude state authorities from enforcing a state law pending a constitutional challenge.[43] The combination of these features led Mark Tushnet to conclude in a 2017 book chapter that '[t]he question of the enforcement of national law against subnational units in the [United States] is of some theoretical interest, but rather little practical importance.'[44]

While pre-emption is an important doctrine of US constitutional law in domestic cases—former US Supreme Court Justice Breyer has referred to it as the

[41] United States Constitution, art VI cl 2. Confirming that pre-emption is rooted in the Supremacy Clause, see *Murphy v National Collegiate Athletic Ass'n*, 138 S Ct 1461 (2018), 1479 ('Preemption is based on the Supremacy Clause ...'). The point was not always as well established as it appears today. Contrast the view that pre-emption is rooted in the Supremacy Clause, see eg Stephen A Gardbaum, 'Nature of Pre-emption' (1993) 79 Cornell Law Review 767.

[42] See eg *Am Ins Ass'n v Garamendi*, 539 US 396, 123 S Ct 2374, 156 L Ed 2d 376 (2003), consistently speaking of the 'invalidation' of the conflicting state law. See similarly *Crosby v Nat'l Foreign Trade Council*, 530 US 363, 120 S Ct 2288, 147 L Ed 2d 352 (2000), 366 ('The issue is whether the Burma law of the Commonwealth of Massachusetts ... is invalid under the Supremacy Clause of the National Constitution').

[43] On the conditions for ordering a preliminary injunction, see *Winter v Nat Res Def Council, Inc*, 555 US 7, 129 S Ct 365, 172 L Ed 2d 249 (2008), 374 ('[P]laintiffs seeking preliminary relief are required to demonstrate that irreparable injury is likely in absence of injunction').

[44] Mark Tushnet, 'Enforcement of National Law against Subnational Units in the US' in András Jakab and Dimitry Kochenov (eds), *The Enforcement of EU Law and Values: Ensuring Member States' Compliance* (Oxford University Press 2017) 316.

'ordinary diet of the law'[45]—pre-emption also plays a role in foreign relations. In this area, US courts have not shied away from taking up cases pitting the federal government against individual states. Preliminarily, it should be acknowledged that, because of the exclusive nature of the treaty-making power allocated to the federal government, conflicts between federal *legislation* and state *treaties* are not an issue in the US. The US differs in this respect from the EU, where both orders of governance (the EU institutions and the Member States) hold treaty-making powers, thereby creating a risk of conflict between Member State treaty obligations and EU law. That being noted, even outside of the sphere of state treaty-making, conflicts between federal law or policy on the one hand, and state law on the other, can arise.[46] It is possible, for example, for a state law to affect and even conflict with a treaty concluded by the federal government. The pre-emption principle resolves such conflicts in favour of the federal government.

How does pre-emption work? Pre-emption is a fact-dependent doctrine. Whether or not a conflict exists between federal law or policy on the one hand and state law on the other cannot be answered in the abstract.[47] That said, a number of principles can nonetheless be discerned that are relevant for our purposes. First, a pre-emptive effect can be triggered not only by federal legislation, but also by provisions of federally concluded treaties (provided they are self-executing), and even by federal executive foreign policy. Secondly, US courts have historically been more willing to recognize pre-emptive effects in cases with a foreign relations component as compared to strictly domestic cases. Commentators have referred to this tendency as one of the features of 'foreign affairs exceptionalism', defined by Curtis Bradley as the view that the federal government's foreign affairs powers are subject to a different, and generally more relaxed, set of constitutional constraints compared to those that govern its domestic constitutional powers.[48] Thirdly and finally, while US courts have recognized pre-emption in the foreign relations context, it must also be acknowledged that pre-emption of state law in the face of federal

45 See Young (n 2) 253, quoting Justice Breyer in *Egelhoff v Egelhoff ex rel Breiner*, 532 US 141, 121 S Ct 1322, 149 L Ed 2d 264 (2001), at 1335.

46 Emphasizing the relevance of EU–US comparisons on the subject of foreign affairs pre-emption, see Geert De Baere and Kathleen Gutman, 'Federalism and International Relations in the European Union and the United States: A Comparative Outlook' in Elke Cloots, Geert De Baere, and Stefan Sottiaux (eds), *Federalism in the European Union* (Hart 2012) 137.

47 Emphasizing this point, see Young (n 2) 253.

48 Curtis Bradley, 'A New American Foreign Relations Law?' (1999) 70 Colorado Law Review 1090, 1096. More recently, see also Ganesh Sitaraman and Ingrid Wuerth, 'The Normalization of Foreign Relations Law' (2015) 128 Harvard Law Review 1897, arguing that a shift away from foreign affairs exceptionalism can be discerned in more recent Supreme Court decisions. But in contrast to the 'normalization' thesis, see Stephen I Vladeck, 'The Exceptionalism of Foreign Relations Normalization' (2014) 128 Harvard Law Review Forum 322.

foreign policy executive action does not necessarily lead to states being pushed altogether out of policy areas in which the federal government has acted. It is possible, for example, for a court to recognize a pre-emptive effect only with respect to a number of provisions of a state statute, while other provisions remain intact. What happens within the federal political process is very relevant in this regard: if Congress enacts relatively little legislation, or if the President instructs departments and agencies to pre-empt state law as little as possible, states acquire a broader space for independent action. At the same time, this observation points to another: as a pre-emptive effect often hinges on the intent of Congress or the President, the space for independent state action is always fragile, and state action that is lawful today may be pre-empted tomorrow. I unpack these propositions below. Taken together, they provide a comprehensive picture of how the US foreign affairs constitution addresses conflicts between federal foreign policy and state law by means of a clear conflict rule, which is enforceable by US federal courts.

4.2 Federal Legislation, Federal Treaties, and Even Federal Executive Foreign Policy Can Pre-empt State Law

Pre-emption triggered by *federal legislation* is the *locus classicus* of pre-emption in the US. The scope of a pre-emptive effect depends on the intention of Congress. As the Supreme Court regularly holds: '[T]he purpose of Congress is the ultimate touchstone in every pre-emption case.'[49] The Supremacy Clause gives effect to this Congressional purpose.[50] Sometimes such intent is easy to discern. In particular, when Congress includes a pre-emption clause (or conversely, an express savings clause) in a statute, a conclusion in favour (or against) pre-emption is easy to draw.[51]

Federal treaties can also pre-empt state law, albeit that in the treaty context an additional threshold requirement must be met. For a treaty provision to be

[49] *Wyeth v Levine*, 555 US 555 (2009), 565.

[50] See on this Robert Schütze, 'Supremacy Without Pre-Emption? The Very Slowly Emergent Doctrine of Community Pre-Emption' (2006) 43 Common Market Law Review 1023, 1044. ('[T]he pre-emption doctrine determines what constitutes a conflict, whereas the supremacy clause decides how that conflict is to be resolved').

[51] For an example of a pre-emption clause, see (now defunct) 15 USC § 1392(d) (1988 ed): 'Whenever a Federal motor vehicle safety standard established under this subchapter is in effect, no State or political subdivision of a State shall have any authority either to establish, or to continue in effect, with respect to any motor vehicle or item of motor vehicle equipment[,] any safety standard applicable to the same aspect of performance of such vehicle or item of equipment which is not identical to the Federal standard.' For an example of a case in which the Supreme Court concluded against pre-emption of

covered by the Supremacy Clause and thus potentially have a pre-emptive effect, it must be 'self-executing'.[52] As mentioned earlier, since the 2008 judgment in the case of *Medellín v Texas* in which the Supreme Court considered a judgment by the International Court of Justice to not be binding within the US, it has become increasingly exceptional for provisions of treaties to be characterized as 'self-executing'.[53] This renders treaty pre-emption less significant in practical terms. In many instances, legislation will be required to implement treaty obligations. Whether or not such legislation has a pre-emptive effect again depends on the intent of Congress.[54] By contrast, if the treaty provision is self-executing, it is not the intention of Congress that determines the scope of a pre-emptive effect. Instead, a self-executing treaty provision will pre-empt state law if the latter clearly conflicts with the former.[55]

Especially relevant in the context of foreign relations is the holding—first expressed by the Supreme Court in the 1969 case of *Zschernig*[56] and reaffirmed in the 2004 decision in *Garamendi*[57]—that a (mere) federal executive foreign *policy* can pre-empt state *law*, provided it has more than an incidental effect that conflicts with federal foreign policy. It is worth explaining how pre-emption of state law by federal executive policy works by looking at the *Garamendi* case. At issue in that case was the constitutionality of a California statute imposing disclosure requirements on insurance companies who serviced clients in Nazi-era Germany and Austria.[58] The contested statute was part of a broader Californian effort to force insurance companies to pay damages to Holocaust survivors. At

a state statute due to the presence of an express savings clause in the federal statute, see *Chamber of Commerce of the United States v Whiting*, 563 US 582 (2011).

[52] 'Restatement (Fourth) of Foreign Relations Law' (American Law Institute 2018) § 308.

[53] *Medellin v Texas*, 552 US 491, 128 S Ct 1346, 170 L Ed 2d 190 (2008). See also *ESAB Grp, Inc v Zurich Ins plc*, 685 F 3d 376, 387 (4th Cir 2012) ('[T]here is an emerging presumption against finding treaties to be self-executing'). Criticizing *Medellín* on this basis, see generally Carlos Manuel Vázquez, 'Treaties as Law of the Land: The Supremacy Clause and the Judicial Enforcement of Treaties' (2008) 122 Harvard Law Review 599.

[54] See in this regard the Supreme Court judgment in *Bond v United States*, 572 US 844, 134 S Ct 2077, 189 L Ed 2d 1 (2014), requiring a clear Congressional statement of intent to pre-empt state law.

[55] In this sense, see 'Restatement (Fourth) of Foreign Relations Law' (n 52) § 308, 2.

[56] *Zschernig v Miller*, 389 US 429, 88 S Ct 664, 19 L Ed 2d 683 (1968).

[57] *Am Ins Ass'n v Garamendi*, 539 US 396, 123 S Ct 2374, 156 L Ed 2d 376 (2003).

[58] It is worth mentioning at this juncture that the constitutional foundations of what commentators often refer to as 'foreign affairs pre-emption' remain contested. From a textual perspective, it is not persuasive to argue that the Supremacy Clause itself renders federal executive *policy* part of the supreme *law* of the land. More is required. Some commentators have suggested that foreign affairs pre-emption can be understood as a form of pre-emption triggered by the constitutional grants of authority to the federal government—not unlike the practice of pre-empting state law that impedes on interstate commerce (see seminally *Cooley v Bd of Wardens of Port of Philadelphia, to Use of Soc for Relief of Distressed Pilots, Their Widows & Child*, 53 US 299, 13 L Ed 996 (1851)). The authority of courts to pre-empt state law even in the absence of federal law in order to protect the authority of Congress to enact legislation

the same time as the adoption of the California statute, the President was involved in negotiations with the German authorities with the view to setting up a foundation, funded by German capital, which was to process damage claims by Holocaust survivors. The foundation was to work with the International Commission on Holocaust Era Insurance Claims, a non-profit organization with a mission to negotiate with European insurers to provide information about and settlement of unpaid insurance policies, and which had set up procedures to that end.

At issue in *Garamendi* was an alleged conflict between, on the one hand, a federal executive foreign policy of arriving at a negotiated settlement with Germany to ensure payment of damages to Holocaust survivors and, on the other, a California statute which aimed to unilaterally impose such payments on German insurance companies. At first sight, the issue appeared straightforward: it was well established that claims settlement agreements such as the one concluded between Germany and the US could be equated with treaties for pre-emption purposes.[59] Consequently, such executive agreements can pre-empt state law in the same way as treaties. Crucially, however, the German-US agreement did not contain a 'pre-emption clause', that is, a clause expressing an intention to pre-empt state law. Rather than deriving an intention in favour of pre-emption from other aspects of the agreement itself, the Supreme Court relied on the precedent set in *Zschernig* to derive a pre-emptive effect directly from the federal executive foreign policy of which the agreement was yet to become a product. In particular, the Court concluded in favour of pre-emption since the state law at issue 'impair[ed] the effective exercise of the Nation's foreign policy'. And the Court added that 'the likelihood that state legislation will produce something more than incidental effect in conflict with express foreign

in the future and to preclude states from interfering with interstate commerce is referred to as the 'negative' or 'dormant' Commerce Power (on this subject, see Donald H Regan, 'The Supreme Court and State Protectionism: Making Sense of the Dormant Commerce Clause' (1986) 84 Michigan Law Review 1091). In a similar sense, one can argue that foreign affairs pre-emption represents the 'negative' or 'dormant' dimension of the federal government's powers over foreign affairs (see eg Leanne M Wilson, 'The Fate of the Dormant Foreign Commerce Clause after Garamendi and Crosby' (2007) 107 Columbia Law Review 746). In contrast to the negative Commerce Power, however, the negative Foreign Affairs Power does not have a clear textual basis: there is no 'Foreign Affairs Clause' in the US Constitution. This lack of constitutional text arguably explains the ongoing controversy surrounding the doctrine's foundations. For my own purposes, it is not necessary to take a stance on the issue: it is sufficient to point out how, regardless of the principle's exact constitutional foundation, the federal government is capable of pre-empting state law by articulating a policy on a given issue.

59 In this sense, see *United States v Belmont*, 301 US 324, 57 S Ct 758, 81 L Ed 1134 (1937) and *United States v Pink*, 315 US 203, 62 S Ct 552, 86 L Ed 796 (1942).

policy of the National Government would require pre-emption of the state law'.[60]

In *Garamendi*, the Supreme Court reaffirmed the holding first introduced in *Zschernig* thirty-five years earlier that state law with more than an 'incidental effect in conflict with express foreign policy of the National Government' triggers a pre-emptive effect. A federal executive policy can thus pre-empt a state statute adopted by a democratically elected legislature.[61] The justification for such pre-emptive effect is functional: with several references to Alexander Hamilton and James Madison in the Federalist Papers, the *Garamendi* Court emphasized the importance of protecting the ability of the federal government to speak with one voice on the international stage.[62] State laws that would undermine the federal government's ability to do so would have to be pre-empted.[63] This justification can be contrasted with the justification for pre-emption triggered by federal legislation and federally concluded treaties: for both categories of instruments, the intention of its author determines the existence and extent of a pre-emptive effect. Not so for federal foreign policy, where the degree to which state law interferes with such foreign policy guides the pre-emption analysis.[64]

Garamendi was decided by the Supreme Court in 2003. Since *Garamendi*, no case of 'foreign affairs pre-emption'—as the *Zschernig* and *Garamendi* holdings have become known—has been decided by the Supreme Court. It follows that, in keeping with the doctrine of *stare decisis*, lower federal courts remain bound to apply *Garamendi*'s holding on the issue of foreign affairs pre-emption. And as Steve Vladeck, a law professor, pointed out in a 2014 contribution, US

[60] *AmIns Ass'n v Garamendi*, 539 US 396, 123 S Ct 2374, 156 L Ed 2d 376 (2003), 419–20.

[61] I refrain from discussing the different interpretations of the *Zschernig* holding, whereby some have read *Zschernig* as requiring a conflict between federal foreign policy and state law, whereas others have read the decision as precluding state action in the field of foreign relations even in the absence of a conflict. (It was notable in *Zschernig* that the federal government had intervened to inform the court that it did not have any objections against the Oregon intestate statute at issue in *Zschernig*.) For a discussion, see the opinion by the Court of Appeals for the 9th Circuit in *Movsesian v Victoria Versicherung AG*, 670 F 3d 1067 (2012), 1072.

[62] A 'functional' justification focuses on the consequences of a course of action. In this case, the need for vigorous and unified foreign relations action was considered a necessary feature of the American Republic. To ensure this outcome, it was necessary to articulate a broad notion of conflict.

[63] Commentators have been critical about the 'one voice' doctrine in US foreign relations law. See eg Sarah H Cleveland, 'Crosby and the One-Voice Myth in US Foreign Relations' (2001) 46 Villanova Law Review 975 and David H Moore, 'Beyond One Voice' (2013) 98 Minnesota Law Review 953.

[64] Pointing to the difference, see eg Jack Goldsmith, 'Statutory Foreign Affairs Preemption' (2000) 2000 The Supreme Court Review 175, 177, pointing out that pre-emption doctrines can be compared along two dimensions: (i) the degree to which the political branches have spoken to the pre-emption issue, and (ii) the extent to which pre-emption doctrines require courts to engage in an independent assessment of the state laws' effect on US foreign relations.

courts—especially lower courts—remain very willing to apply expansive, functionally driven, pre-emption principles.[65]

4.3 A Foreign Relations Component Makes Pre-emption More Likely

Often, it is not easy to discern whether or not Congress intended to pre-empt state law. When courts cannot identify any Congressional intent, they have recourse to presumptions.[66] In cases without a clear foreign relations component in which Congressional intent was not clear, US courts have at times endorsed a presumption against pre-emption.[67] The presumption applies in particular when Congress legislates on issues that touch on 'traditional areas of state responsibility' such as family law or criminal law. The Supreme Court made this point in the 1947 case of *Rice v Santa Fe Elevator Corporation*, where it held: '[W]e start with the assumption that the historic police powers of the States were not to be superseded by the Federal Act unless that was the clear and manifest purpose of Congress.'[68] US courts have repeated the point on multiple occasions even though they have not always been consistent in applying the presumption.[69] Relatedly, in the past federal courts have not been

[65] Vladeck (n 48) 322. For a lower court decision applying *Garamendi*, see *Movsesian v Victoria Versicherung AG*, 670 F 3d 1067 (9th Cir 2012), 1071 ('Under the foreign affairs doctrine, state laws that intrude on this exclusively federal power are pre-empted'). That said, US courts have also distinguished cases from *Garamendi*, thereby limiting its scope. See eg the DC District Court in *Beaty v Republic of Iraq*, 480 F Supp 2d 60 (2007), distinguishing the case from *Garamendi* on two grounds: (i) at the federal level a statute had been enacted, and (ii) the state law at issue (a common law created tort) did not affect US foreign relations and did not lead the state of Oklahoma to 'weigh in on knotty issues of international consequence'. See also, more recently, *United States v California*, not reported in Fed Supp (2020) 2020 WL 4043034, in which a federal district court rejected the Trump administration's claim that California's participation in Quebec's cap-and-trade scheme violated pre-emption principles as it did not impermissibly intrude on the federal government's foreign affairs power because it did not substantially circumscribe or compromise the federal government's ability to conduct foreign policy. The Fourth Restatement further nibbles away at *Zschernig* and *Garamendi* by suggesting that *Garamendi* implies that states may act within the areas of their traditional competence even if the action has foreign-policy implications, as long as no conflict with federal law exists. See 'Restatement (Fourth) of Foreign Relations Law' (n 52) § 403 reporters' note 5.

[66] On the importance of presumptions, see generally Randy E Barnett, 'Foreword: The Power of Presumptions' (1994) 17 Harvard Journal of Law & Public Policy 613.

[67] When Congress includes a clause explicitly expressing its intention to pre-empt (an 'express pre-emption clause'), there is no presumption against pre-emption. In this sense, see *Puerto Rico v Franklin California Tax-Free Trust*, 136 S Ct 1938 (2016), 1946.

[68] *Rice v Santa Fe Elevator Corp*, 331 US 218 (1947), 230. For a more recent affirmation, see *Hillman v Maretta*, 133 S Ct 1943 (2013), 1950 ('The regulation of domestic relations is traditionally the domain of state law . . . There is therefore a "presumption against pre-emption" of state laws governing domestic relations').

[69] Jay B Sykes and Nicole Vanatko, 'Federal Preemption: A Legal Primer' (Congressional Research Service 2019) CRS Report R45825 2–3.

alone in presuming a federal intent to *not* pre-empt state law. When President Obama took office in 2009, he issued a memorandum in which he instructed federal departments and agencies to adhere to a presumption against (the desirability of) pre-emption in their activities, and not be too sweeping when deciding whether or not to pre-empt state law.[70]

By contrast, in cases touching on US foreign relations, the presumption against pre-emption does not apply.[71] To the contrary, US Supreme Court case law suggests that courts should be more, rather than less, willing to recognize pre-emption in cases with a foreign relations component compared to cases with a strictly domestic focus. For example, in its 1941 decision in *Hines v Davidowitz*, the Supreme Court ruled in favour of pre-emption of a Pennsylvania statute imposing registration requirements on aliens. The Court held that 'it is of importance that this legislation is in a field which affects international relations, the one aspect of our government that from the first has been most generally conceded imperatively to demand broad national authority'.[72] Here, as in *Garamendi*, functional considerations related to the need for the federal government to be able to speak with one voice justified pre-emption of the Pennsylvania statute.

The 1968 case of *Zschernig*, mentioned earlier, points in the same direction. In that case, without using the language of pre-emption, the Supreme Court invalidated an Oregon statute stating the conditions under which alien persons, that is, persons who are not US citizens, not residing in the US can take property in Oregon by succession or testamentary disposition. In *Zschernig*, the Supreme Court neither identified a conflict between the Oregon statute and a federal law or executive policy, nor did it rely on a Congressional intention to pre-empt state law. Instead, the fact that the Oregon statute 'intru[ded] in the field of foreign affairs, which the Constitution entrusts to President and Congress' was sufficient for the Supreme Court to rule in favour of pre-emption. *Zschernig* shares features with *Hines* as well as *Garamendi*. In all three cases the Supreme Court expressed a concern with safeguarding the ability of Congress and President to conduct an effective foreign policy. In the words of Justice Douglas, writing for the majority in *Zschernig*: '[The Oregon statute] has a direct impact upon foreign relations and may well adversely affect the

[70] The White House, Office of the Press Secretary, Memorandum for the Heads of Executive Departments and Agencies, 'Pre-emption' (20 May 2009) <https://obamawhitehouse.archives.gov/the-press-office/presidential-memorandum-regarding-preemption> accessed 26 November 2021. The Trump and Biden administrations have not (yet) articulated a pre-emption policy.

[71] See 'Restatement (Fourth) of Foreign Relations Law' (n 52), § 308 reporters' note 2 ('The Court has indicated that [the] presumption might not apply to statutes that concern foreign affairs').

[72] *Hines v Davidowitz*, 312 US 52 (1941), 68.

power of the central government to deal with those problems.' For this reason, the Supreme Court declared the Oregon statute to be unconstitutional.

More recently, again in the context of immigration policy, the Supreme Court reaffirmed *Hines* when in the 2012 case of *Arizona v United States* it held that the federal government must enjoy broad discretion in the conduct of its immigration policy, and that, to safeguard this discretion, parts of an Arizona statute that dealt with the enforcement at state level of federal immigration law were unconstitutional.[73] One justification for this broad discretion, the Supreme Court held, was federal immigration policy's link with international relations:

> Some discretionary decisions involve policy choices that bear on this Nation's international relations. Returning an alien to his own country may be deemed inappropriate even where he has committed a removable offense or fails to meet the criteria for admission. The foreign state may be mired in civil war, complicit in political persecution, or enduring conditions that create a real risk that the alien or his family will be harmed upon return. The dynamic nature of relations with other countries requires the Executive Branch to ensure that enforcement policies are consistent with this Nation's foreign policy with respect to these and other realities.[74]

The justification for pre-emption provided in this opinion written by Justice Kennedy is again similar to the one put forward in *Zschernig* and *Garamendi*, namely: to protect the ability of the federal government to conduct an effective foreign policy. Hence, and while the Supreme Court has never endorsed a presumption in *favour of* pre-emption in foreign relations cases,[75] the presence of a foreign relations component does seem to make a decision recognizing a pre-emptive effect more likely. At the very least, the presence of a foreign relations component in a pre-emption case adds additional weight to the federal argument in favour of pre-emption.[76]

[73] *Arizona v United States*, 567 US 387, 132 S Ct 2492, 183 L Ed 2d 351 (2012).

[74] ibid 396–97.

[75] Arguing that the early twenty-first-century Supreme Court endorsed a presumption *in favour of* pre-emption, see generally Mary J Davis, 'Unmasking the Presumption in Favor of Preemption' (2001) 53 South Carolina Law Review 967.

[76] Kerry Abrams used the metaphor of a scale to examine the pre-emption case law of the Supreme Court in cases touching on foreign relations. See Kerry Abrams, 'Plenary Power Pre-emption' (2013) 99 Virginia Law Review 601, 603.

4.4 But Pre-emption Is Not Always Complete and Often Fragile

Even though pre-emption is thus more likely to be recognized in foreign relations cases than it is in domestic contexts, it would be mistaken to assume that whenever the President or Congress enter a policy field by engaging in interactions with third country governments, individual US states are automatically precluded from acting. Two factors account for this observation. First, despite the Supreme Court's reliance on functional considerations, the presence of a foreign relations aspect does not necessarily lead US courts to conclude in favour of pre-emption of the entirety of a state statute. US courts adhere to a retail as opposed to a wholesale approach: they determine on a provision-by-provision basis whether or not a state legislative provision is pre-empted. Secondly, even if in foreign relations-related cases the intent of the federal decision-maker is not determinative, Congress and the President continue to play a central role in determining the extent to which federal law and policy pre-empts state law. In particular, if Congress has not exhaustively covered a field through legislation,[77] US courts are less likely to rule in favour of pre-emption. Similarly, if the President pursues a policy of deference towards and collaboration with state governments, he or the federal agencies that depend on him will be hesitant to pre-empt state law through rule-making.

The following two cases are examples of both phenomena. First, in *Arizona v United States*, mentioned earlier, the Supreme Court pre-empted only part of an Arizona immigration statute labelled the 'Support Our Law Enforcement and Safe Neighborhoods Act', leaving another part intact.[78] Secondly, the Clean Air Act of 1970 and the Clean Power Plan adopted by the Obama administration expressly provide for federal–state cooperation.[79] This emphasis on state involvement restricted the scope of a pre-emptive effect of federal law.

The state statute at issue in *Arizona v United States* aimed to 'discourage and deter the unlawful entry and presence of aliens and economic activity by persons unlawfully present in the United States'.[80] Four of the provisions of the Arizona statute were contested: (i) Section 3, which made failure to comply with federal alien registration requirements a state misdemeanour; (ii) Section

[77] See generally James H Read, 'Constitutionalizing the Dispute: Federalism in Hyper-Partisan Times' (2016) 46 Publius: The Journal of Federalism 337.

[78] *Arizona v United States*, 567 US 387, 132 S Ct 2492, 183 L Ed 2d 351 (2012).

[79] 42 USC ch 85, subch I § 7401ff.

[80] Note following Ariz Rev Stat Ann §11–1051 (West 2012), as quoted in *Arizona v United States*, 567 US 387, 132 S Ct 2492, 183 L Ed 2d 351 (2012).

5, which made it a state misdemeanour for an unauthorized alien to seek or engage in work in the State; (iii) Section 6, which authorized officers to arrest without a warrant a person whom 'the officer has probable cause to believe ... has committed any public offence that makes the person removable from the United States'; and (iv) Section 2(B), which provided that officers who conduct a stop, detention, or arrest must in some circumstances make efforts to verify the person's immigration status with the federal government.

The Supreme Court pre-empted the first three of these provisions, but left the final provision standing. The methodology is interesting. Despite the functional justification for pre-emption in the area of immigration policy mentioned earlier, the Court did examine the four provisions of the statute separately, and ultimately came down in favour of pre-emption of three of the provisions, but not all four. Justice Kennedy, who wrote the majority opinion, was careful to emphasize the central role of the federal government in conducting the federal government's immigration policy. Yet at the same time he was careful also to acknowledge the importance of immigration policy to the states in general. 'The problems posed to the State by illegal immigration must not be underestimated', he submitted, adding that '[t]hese concerns are the background for the formal legal [pre-emption] analysis that follow[ed]'.[81] By deciding not to pre-empt one of the provisions, the Supreme Court confirmed that federal and state legislatures both continue to have a role to play in in the field of immigration law, even though the Court puts strong emphasis on the federal role and the requirement for unity in this area.[82]

The Clean Air Act and the Clean Power Plan are illustrative of how the federal political institutions can prevent state action from being pre-empted and can instead encourage and occasionally oblige states to act. In particular, the Clean Air Act calls for states to adopt implementation plans with a view to attaining federally set emission reduction targets.[83] The Clean Power Plan adopted by the Obama administration in 2015 by means of executive order pursued this strategy further. The Plan required states to adopt implementation plans that

[81] ibid 6–7.

[82] David Freeman Engstrom and Jeremy M Weinstein summarized the Supreme Court's approach as establishing an 'equilibrium granting states and localities latitude to regulate immigrants and immigrant services so long as they leave regulation of *immigration* to the feds'. See David Freeman Engstrom and Jeremy M Weinstein, 'What if California Had a Foreign Policy? The New Frontier of States' Rights' (2018) The Washington Quarterly 27, 40.

[83] See in particular 42 US Code § 7410, providing *inter alia* that '[e]ach State shall, after reasonable notice and public hearings, adopt and submit to the Administrator ... a plan which provides for implementation, maintenance, and enforcement of such primary standard in each air quality control region (or portion thereof) within such State'. On the practice of cooperative federalism in environmental policy, see generally John P Dwyer, 'The Practice of Federalism Under the Clean Air Act' (1995) 54 Maryland Law Review 1183.

demonstrate to the federal government how they would reduce emissions caused by power plants. If they failed to do so, a federal plan would apply to the state involved. The Clean Power Plan was an example of a regulatory scheme that expressly provided for state action.

Often, state initiatives in areas of concurrent jurisdiction are possible not because the federal government has not acted in an area (it typically has), but rather because the federal government expressly authorizes states to act. For example, the Clean Air Act allows the Environmental Protection Agency (EPA) to issue waivers to states. Waivers authorize states to undertake actions to lift environmental standards above those established at the federal level. For example, the Obama EPA had issued a waiver authorizing California to lift standards for tailpipe emissions.[84] In other instances, states can act precisely because the federal government has not acted. For example, California has been able to participate in the carbon emissions marketplace established by the Canadian province of Quebec because no federal rules on cap-and-trade had been adopted.[85] However, it must be kept in mind that, just as the federal government can choose to create a space for state governments to act by refusing to pre-empt state action, it can just as well pursue a different course and opt to pre-empt in a more far-reaching manner. In September 2019, for example, the Trump EPA retracted the abovementioned tailpipe emissions waiver.[86] Doing so immediately rendered the Californian tailpipe emission standards as well as similar standards adopted by other states mirroring the Californian example unlawful. In April 2021, the Biden EPA reversed course again and reinstalled the tailpipe emissions waiver. The episode demonstrates the fragility of state legislation adopted in a space in which the federal government has historically been relatively active.

Crucially, when an alleged conflict between federal and state law arises, provided justiciability, standing, and related threshold requirements are met,

[84] 42 US Code § 7543 (b), which, after having pre-empted state law on the matter of vehicle emissions, provides that:

> [t]he [EPA] shall, after notice and opportunity for public hearing, waive application of this section to any State which has adopted standards (other than crankcase emission standards) for the control of emissions from new motor vehicles or new motor vehicle engines prior to March 30, 1966, if the State determines that the State standards will be, in the aggregate, at least as protective of public health and welfare as applicable Federal standards.

[85] In 2009, the federal Congress considered adopting a federal cap-and-trade scheme. This scheme would have pre-empted the California-Quebec scheme. The House passed the bill, but the Senate did not. See Bryan Walsh, 'Why the Climate Bill Died' [2010] *Time* <http://science.time.com/2010/07/26/why-the-climate-bill-died/> accessed 25 November 2021.

[86] Chris Mills Rodrigo, 'Trump Administration Officially Revoked California Tailpipe Emissions Waiver' *The Hill* (19 September 2019) <https://thehill.com/policy/energy-environment/462142-trump-administration-officially-revokes-california-tailpipe> accessed 12 October 2021.

US courts have the authority to resolve the conflict, if necessary by ruling that the state norm has been pre-empted. In the final analysis, then, Congress and President have the ability to determine the amount of space states enjoy to engage in foreign relations. Environmental policy is a case in point—and a relevant one for the present purposes, as it has a significant external dimension—but the same holds true in other policy areas as well.

5. Conclusion

As discussed in the introduction, the balance between unity and diversity in federal systems can be maintained through mechanisms of self-rule and mechanisms of shared rule. In this first part of the book I look at the former set of mechanisms. Self-rule in turn has two dimensions: power allocation and conflict resolution. The constitutional charter first empowers governments to act (power allocation), which endows them with a degree of autonomy. When powers overlap—as they often do, be it *de jure* in systems of shared and overlapping powers or *de facto* in systems of exclusive powers in which the borders between areas of jurisdictions are not always clear—conflicts may arise. Such conflicts need to be resolved. This is where conflict resolution mechanisms, self-rule's second dimension, come in.

In this chapter, I examined the conflict resolution mechanisms in Canada, Belgium, and the US in terms of the degree of *formality* of the mechanism, and the *institution* that holds responsibility to resolve the conflict (the courts or the political institutions). Conflict resolution mechanisms in Canada were both informal and political: courts are not involved in resolving conflicts between the federal and provincial governments, and there has not been any formalization of the rules to resolve conflicts. Pragmatism and mutual accommodation are key, which explains why intergovernmental relations play a central role in Canadian foreign relations federalism. Belgium is similar to Canada in one respect, and different in another. It is similar to Canada, as in Belgium as well as in Canada courts are not involved in resolving conflicts between the federal and member unit governments that have a foreign relations component. Instead, the two mechanisms I discussed endow the federal executive with tools to resolve conflicts. In contrast to Canada, however, the Belgian conflict resolution mechanisms are highly formalized: they are included in the Belgian Constitution and in the SLIR, a quasi-constitutional statute. Finally, conflict resolution mechanisms in the US are both formal and judicial. The pre-emption doctrine is directly grounded in the US Constitution through the

Supremacy Clause, and courts are responsible for applying pre-emption principles and thus for resolving conflicts between the federal and state governments. In this sense, the US is the mirror image of Canada and differs from Belgium through its reliance on courts to resolve federal–state conflicts. As I will discuss in the next chapter, however, the US shares many features with the EU. The EU Treaties as well put much emphasis on resolving conflicts between EU and Member State law in an effort to preserve the full effectiveness of EU foreign policy.

5
Conflict Resolution in the EU

> Sweden did not let that decision-making process take its natural course and culminate in a Council decision ... Sweden should have engaged in the Community decision-making process until such a decision was reached, even if, politically, it felt that its efforts to achieve a common proposal ... were as doomed as lemmings heading towards the edge of a cliff.
>
> Advocate General Poiares Maduro in *PFOS*[1]

1. Introduction

What mechanisms do the EU Treaties provide to resolve conflicts between the EU institutions and the Member States in the conduct of their respective foreign relations? And how do those mechanisms compare to the ones in Canada, Belgium, and the US discussed in the previous chapter? The EU Treaties provide for two formal, judicial conflict resolution mechanisms: the ERTA preemption doctrine and the duty of sincere cooperation. In addition, secondary EU legislation endows the European Commission with a number of sector-specific political conflict resolution mechanisms. I look at both categories of mechanisms: first the latter, then the former. As we will see, compared to the other federal unions explored in this book, the conflict resolution mechanisms in the EU Treaties are primarily judicial and formal in nature. The Court of Justice plays a central role in resolving conflicts between the EU institutions and the Member States; and it does so on the basis of constitutional principles set out in the EU Treaties. The judicial and formal nature of conflict resolution mechanisms in the EU distinguishes the EU from both Belgium and Canada, which both rely on political mechanisms—in the former they are more formal; in the latter informal. And it highlights a commonality with the US. There, too,

[1] Opinion of AG Poiares Maduro in Case C-246/07 *Commission v Sweden ('PFOS')*, EU:C:2009:589, para 58.

Foreign Relations Federalism. Thomas Verellen, Oxford University Press. © Thomas Verellen 2023.
DOI: 10.1093/oso/9780192844569.003.0005

conflicts are resolved through the application of constitutional principles enforced by the (federal) courts.

2. Political Mechanisms

Before exploring the political mechanisms to resolve or prevent conflicts between the EU institutions and the Member States within the scope of EU law, it is useful to zoom out and have a look at EURATOM, the European Atomic Energy Community—an organization established in 1957, at the same time as the European Economic Community. EURATOM makes use of many of the EU's institutions, but is nonetheless legally distinct from it. Relevant for our purposes is that the EURATOM Treaty introduced an institutional mechanism of control by the EU institutions over Member State treaty-making reminiscent of the Belgian suspension mechanism, discussed in the previous chapter. Article 103 of the EURATOM Treaty provides that 'Member States shall communicate to the Commission draft agreements or contracts with a third State, an international organisation or a national of a third State to the extent that such agreements or contracts concern matters within the purview of this Treaty'.[2] And the provision continues in its following paragraphs:

> If a draft agreement or contract contains clauses which impede the application of this Treaty, the Commission shall, within one month of receipt of such communication, make its comments known to the State concerned. The State shall not conclude the proposed agreement or contract until it has satisfied the objections of the Commission or complied with a ruling by the Court of Justice, adjudicating urgently upon an application from the State, on the compatibility of the proposed clauses with the provisions of this Treaty. An application may be made to the Court of Justice at any time after the State has received the comments of the Commission.

Article 103 of the EURATOM Treaty grants the Commission and ultimately the Court of Justice a power to review draft agreements or contracts before they are adopted by the Member State concerned. The power is limited to a *legal* review: the Commission can express its concerns about 'clauses which impede the application of [the EURATOM] Treaty', and the Court of Justice can adjudicate 'on the compatibility of the proposed clauses with the provisions

[2] See similarly art 75 of the now defunct European Coal and Steel Community Treaty.

of [the EURATOM] Treaty'. As is the case with the Belgian suspension mechanism, discussed in the previous chapter, the EURATOM review power thus should not be understood as a veto power which would allow the Commission to review the desirability of a draft agreement on policy grounds. It is, rather, a mechanism to ensure that a EURATOM institution—the Commission and ultimately the Court of Justice—always has an opportunity to review the legality under the EURATOM Treaty of draft Member State agreements.

The EU Treaties do not provide for a similar mechanism to that of Article 103 of the EURATOM Treaty which allows an EU institution to comment on proposed Member State international agreements, and which requires the Member State concerned to 'satisfy' the institution's objections. Member States and EU institutions can request the Court of Justice to issue an opinion on the legality of a proposed international agreement that the EU wishes to conclude.[3] A similar option is not available for international agreements to which one or several Member State(s), but not the EU, wishe(s) to become a party.[4] That said, in specific fields the EU legislature did endow the Commission with *ex ante* screening powers over certain Member State actions with foreign policy repercussions. While these legislative acts do not endow the Commission with a veto power over Member State initiatives, their practical impact should not be underestimated either. I provide three examples of such mechanisms: one in the area of foreign direct investment (FDI), one in the area of energy policy, and another in the field of air transport policy.

2.1 The Framework for FDI Screening

In March 2019, the EU adopted a regulation establishing a framework for the screening of foreign direct investments into the Union (the FDI Screening Regulation).[5] The FDI Screening Regulation distinguishes between FDI that is 'likely to affect projects or programmes of Union interest' and FDI that is not.[6] On FDI projects in the former category, the Commission is empowered to issue an opinion. In that opinion, the Commission can take a stance on whether it believes the proposed investment is compatible with 'security' and

[3] TFEU, art 218(11).

[4] In this sense, see Koen Lenaerts and others, *EU Procedural Law* (Oxford University Press 2014) 554.

[5] Regulation (EU) 2019/452 of the European Parliament and the Council of 19 March 2019 establishing a framework for the screening of foreign direct investments into the Union [2019] OJ L79I/1.

[6] ibid arts 3–7.

'public order'. The Member State in which the investment will be or has been made must take 'utmost account' of that opinion.[7] On FDI projects in the latter category, the Commission—as well as certain Member States—may in some instances also have the opportunity to issue an opinion. Member States must 'give due consideration' to that opinion as they decide on whether to approve or reject the proposed investment.[8]

In neither case would the Commission hold a formal power to oppose proposed investments akin to the Commission's power under Article 103 of the EURATOM Treaty. That said, the requirement to take 'utmost account' of investments that affect projects or programmes of Union interest does come fairly close. 'Due consideration' certainly does not require a Member State to prohibit an investment if the Commission issues a negative opinion. However, the requirement to take 'utmost account' that applies to investments that are 'likely to affect projects or programmes of Union interest' puts the bar higher for Member States intent on deviating from a Commission opinion. As I argued elsewhere, to ensure that the distinction between 'due consideration' and 'utmost account' remains meaningful, the Court of Justice may be compelled to subject Member States' replies to Commission opinions to closer scrutiny if the investment concerned has a Union dimension as compared to investments without such a dimension.[9] At the very least, Member States would have to put forward substantive arguments explaining why they chose to disregard the Commission's opinion.[10] Over time, this requirement may very well come to operate as a de facto veto power in the hands of the Commission.

Thus, in this corner of the EU's investment policy the Commission does hold powers that enable it to put pressure on—and in some

[7] ibid art 8(2)(c).

[8] ibid arts 6(9) and 7(7).

[9] Thomas Verellen, 'When Integration by Stealth Meets Public Security: The EU Foreign Direct Investment Screening Regulation' (2021) 48 Legal Issues of Economic Integration 19, 28.

[10] See by analogy Case C-277/16 *Polkomtel sp z oo v Prezes Urzędu Komunikacji Elektronicznej*, EU:C:2017:989, involving Directive 2002/21/EC of the European Parliament and of the Council of 7 March 2002 on a common regulatory framework for electronic communications networks and services [2002] OJ L108/33 ('the Framework Directive'). The Framework Directive requires national regulatory authorities (NRAs) in the telecom sector to take 'utmost account' of recommendations issued by the European Commission on the appropriateness of imposing price control and cost accounting obligations on market participants. At para 37, the Court of Justice held that:

> it is for the NRA, when imposing obligations concerning price control and cost accounting ... to follow, as a rule, the guidance contained in Recommendation 2009/396. It is only where it appears to the NRA, in its assessment of a given situation, that the model advocated by that recommendation is not appropriate to the circumstances that it may depart from it, giving reasons for its position.

instances compel—Member States to refrain from taking a decision which the Commission believes would run counter to EU security or public order. This is an important observation in an era in which foreign policy is increasingly conducted through unilateral trade and investment instruments.[11]

2.2 The Information Exchange Mechanism in the Field of Energy

A second example of a mechanism that allows the European Commission to screen Member State actions can be found in the energy policy sphere. In 2017, the EU adopted a decision that subjects agreements between individual Member States and third country governments on oil and gas-related issues to Commission review.[12] The Commission can express its doubts regarding the proposed agreements' compatibility with EU law.[13] As under the FDI Screening Regulation as it applies to investments that affect programmes and projects of Union interest, the Member State must 'take utmost account' of the Commission's objections before concluding the agreement.[14] This means that, formally speaking, the Member States can still conclude the agreement despite the Commission's assessment.[15] Yet, as I argued is the case under the FDI Screening Regulation, the 'utmost account' requirement comes very close to a veto power for the Commission.[16] That said, the Commission's power under the 2017 decision is limited to a review of the legality of the proposed Member State agreement, rather than a more open-ended 'security and public order' assessment as we encountered under the FDI Screening Regulation.

[11] On this development, see generally Sophie Meunier and Kalypso Nicolaïdis, 'The Geopoliticization of European Trade and Investment Policy' (2019) 57 Journal of Common Market Studies 103; Thomas Verellen, 'Unilateral Trade Measures in Times of Geopolitical Rivalry' (*Verfassungsblog*, 25 May 2021) <https://verfassungsblog.de/unilateral-trade-measures-in-times-of-geopolitical-rivalry/> accessed 13 June 2021.

[12] Decision (EU) 2017/684 of the European Parliament and of the Council of 5 April 2017 on establishing an information exchange mechanism with regard to intergovernmental agreements and non-binding instruments between Member States and third countries in the field of energy, and repealing Decision No 994/2012/EU [2017] OJ L99/1.

[13] ibid art 5(1).

[14] ibid art 5(4) second para.

[15] ibid.

[16] In this sense, referring to the Commission's powers as a 'veto power', see Philipp Thaler and Vija Pakalkaite, 'Governance through Real-Time Compliance: The Supranationalisation of European External Energy Policy' (2021) 28 Journal of European Public Policy 208, 221.

2.3 The Air Service Agreements Screening Mechanism

A third example of a screening mechanism set up through secondary EU legislation can be found in the air transport field. In a set of judgments issued in the late 1990s, together referred to as the *Open Skies* judgments, the Court of Justice had clarified that parts of the bilateral agreements Member States had been concluding with the US to liberalize air traffic fell within the scope of EU exclusive competence.[17] For this reason, Member States were precluded from concluding such agreements independently. Instead, the EU needed to be a party alongside the Member State concerned. Following the *Open Skies* judgments, the EU legislature had adopted a regulation.[18] The regulation authorized Member States to conclude air service agreements with third countries, and it required Member States which intended to make use of this option to notify the Commission of their plans and to comply with certain substantive requirements. In particular, Member States could not introduce more restrictive arrangements,[19] and they should include a number of standard clauses in the agreement they intended to conclude.[20]

Relevant for our purposes is that the regulation requires Member States to notify the Commission of its intentions to conclude an air service agreement.[21] The Commission forwards the notification to the other Member States, which are invited to make comments. Within fifteen days of receipt of the notification, the Commission lets the Member State which intends to conclude an agreement know whether it believes the agreement is likely to 'undermine the objectives of Community negotiations underway with the third country concerned' or to 'lead to an agreement which is incompatible with Community law'.[22] Crucially, if the Commission considers that the intended agreement checks either of these two boxes, it cannot block the Member State from concluding the agreement—it merely informs the Member State there is a problem. In this sense, the air service agreements screening mechanism differs from the EURATOM mechanism, which does allow for an agreement to be blocked before it can be concluded. The air service agreements screening mechanism is less powerful, also, than the FDI screening mechanism or the information

[17] See eg Case C-467/98 *Commission v Denmark ('Open Skies')*, EU:C:2002:625.

[18] Regulation (EC) No 847/2004 of the European Parliament and the Council of 29 April 2004 on the negotiation and implementation of air service agreements between Member States and third countries [2004] OJ L157/7.

[19] ibid art 3.

[20] ibid art 1(1).

[21] ibid art 1(2) to (4).

[22] ibid art 1(4).

exchange mechanism in the field of energy. In contrast to both of these instruments, the air service agreements screening mechanism does not impose an obligation on the Member State to take account or to take 'utmost account' of the Commission's opinion.

***

Overall, the EU Treaties do not provide for such a strong political conflict resolution mechanism as the one encountered in the EURATOM Treaty or the suspension mechanism provided for in the Belgian foreign affairs constitution and discussed in the previous chapter. By contrast, at the level of EU secondary law, in the fields of investment policy, external energy policy, and air transport policy, the EU legislature has introduced political conflict resolution mechanisms that enable the Commission to screen Member State actions. In the investment policy field, the Commission conducts a review on fairly open-ended 'security and public order' grounds; in the energy field the review represents a compliance review whereby the Commission screens proposed Member State agreements in light of the pre-existing EU rules governing the internal energy market; and in the air transport field the mechanism combines a compliance aspect with a more forward-looking orientation whereby the Commission aims to prevent Member States from negotiating bilateral agreements while the Commission is negotiating a multilateral agreement with the same third country. In none of the three mechanisms does the Commission hold a power to suspend or block Member State agreements. That said, the requirement that Member States take 'utmost account' of the Commission's opinion included in the investment and energy policy instruments makes it difficult for Member States to ignore the Commission's views.

3. Judicial Mechanisms

3.1 ERTA Pre-emption to Protect Pre-existing Common EU Rules

The EU Treaties as well as secondary EU legislation thus provide for a number of sector-specific political conflict resolution mechanisms. In addition to these political mechanisms that give the Commission *ex ante* powers to review Member State actions before they are adopted, the EU Treaties provide for two cross-sectoral judicial conflict resolution mechanisms: the ERTA pre-emption doctrine and the duty of sincere cooperation. Internally, the principle of primacy operates as the primary conflict resolution mechanism between EU and Member State law.[23] Externally, in its early case law the Court of Justice has undertaken efforts to proactively avoid conflicts from arising.[24] This objective has been pursued primarily by characterizing EU competences as exclusive, either on an a priori basis or through ERTA-type pre-emption.[25] More recently, the Court has developed a 'duty of sincere cooperation' as a means to restrict the freedom of individual Member States to act once the EU has undertaken some form of action. I discuss these mechanisms in turn, and examine whether they are effective in achieving their stated aims. Where useful, I will draw parallels with US pre-emption principles discussed in the previous chapter. As we will see, both ERTA pre-emption and the duty of sincere cooperation show a certain family resemblance to pre-emption in the US foreign affairs constitution.

The ERTA pre-emption doctrine endows the EU with an exclusive treaty-making power to the extent that proposed Member State international agreements 'affect' pre-existing EU common rules. As the Court held in the 1971 *ERTA* case:

> [E]ach time the Community, with a view to implementing a common policy envisaged by the Treaty, adopts provisions laying down common rules, whatever form these may take, the Member States no longer have the right, acting individually or even collectively, to undertake obligations with third countries which affect those rules.[26]

Following *ERTA*, Member States were no longer in a position to negotiate and conclude the agreement at issue independently. Instead, they had to act within the EU framework, following instructions issued by the Council on the basis of EU exclusive competence. In this way, conflicts between the common EU interest and the interests of the Member States could be prevented. The ERTA pre-emption doctrine has been codified in the Treaty of Lisbon. Article 3(2) TFEU now holds that '[t]the Union shall ... have exclusive competence for the

[23] See Case C-6/64 *Costa v ENEL*, EU:C:1964:66.

[24] On this subject, see also Thomas Verellen, 'Convergence and Divergence in EU External Action: The Very Slowly Emerging Doctrine of Shared Competence' in Marjan Kos, Jaka Kukavica, and Maja Sahadžić (eds), *The Dialectics in Multilevel Systems—Mechanisms of Divergence and Convergence* (Hart 2023).

[25] The EU Treaties provide for other mechanisms tailored to specific circumstances, such as TFEU, art 351, on the relation between EU law and Member State agreements pre-dating the establishment of the EU or the accession of the Member State(s) involved. On this topic, see eg Robert Schütze, *Foreign Affairs and the EU Constitution: Selected Essays* (Cambridge University Press 2014) 123–34. Similarly, the primacy principle has been relied on directly in cases involving an alleged conflict between Member State agreements and provisions of EU law. See recently Case C-284/16 *Achmea*, EU:C:2018:158.

[26] Case C-22/70 *Commission v Council ('ERTA')*, EU:C:1971:32, paras 15–18.

conclusion of an international agreement in so far as its conclusion may affect common rules or alter their scope'.

The ERTA principle is a form of pre-emption.[27] As Robert Schütze has argued, the ERTA principle serves to identify the degree of conflict required to trigger a mechanism that resolves the conflict.[28] In the *internal* context, the primacy principle requires Member State courts to disapply national norms to the extent of a conflict with EU law.[29] In the *external* context, the Court of Justice devised a more rigorous approach: instead of a mere disapplication of the conflicting Member State norm, which leaves the conflicting national norm intact, the Court considered it necessary to proactively prevent conflicts from arising. This could be achieved by recognizing an exclusive EU competence covering the extent of the potential conflict.[30]

To explain how ERTA pre-emption works, it is useful to compare the doctrine with its US counterpart and to highlight a number of differences and similarities.[31] First, and as already discussed, one important difference stands

[27] In this sense, see also Piet Eeckhout, 'Exclusive External Competences: Constructing the EU as an International Actor' in Court of Justice of the European Union (ed), *The Court of Justice and the Construction of Europe: Analyses and Perspectives on Sixty Years of Case-law* (TMC Asser Press 2013); Koen Lenaerts, 'Les répercussions des compétences de la Communauté européenne sur les compétences externes des États Membres et la question de "pre-emption"' in Paul Demaret (ed), *Relations extérieures de la Communauté européenne et marché intérieur: aspects juridiques et fonctionnels: colloque 1986* (Story-Scientia 1988), and more recently also Marise Cremona, 'External Competences and the Principle of Conferral' in Robert Schütze and Takis Tridimas (eds), *Oxford Principles Of European Union Law: The European Union Legal Order: Volume I* (Oxford University Press 2018) 1129 ('AETR itself, is based on the existence of internal legislation, whether or not adopted within the framework of a common policy, and is founded on pre-emption'), and Amedeo Arena, 'Exercise of EU Competences and Pre-Emption of Member States' Powers in the Internal and the External Sphere: Towards "Grand Unification"?' [2016] Yearbook of European Law 1. In contrast to this characterization, see Marcus Klamert, *The Principle of Loyalty in EU Law* (Oxford University Press 2014) 115, arguing that pre-emption is a function of supremacy, which runs counter to the pluralist constitutional DNA of the EU which the author defends.

[28] Robert Schütze, 'Supremacy Without Pre-Emption? The Very Slowly Emergent Doctrine of Community Pre-Emption' (2006) 43 Common Market Law Review 1023–24.

[29] See eg Joined Cases C-10/97–22/97 *Ministero delle Finanze v IN.CO.GE.'90 Srl*, EU:C:1998:498, para 21.

[30] In this sense, see eg Geert De Baere, *Constitutional Principles of EU External Relations* (Oxford University Press 2008) 43 ('the Court took the specific character of external relations into account and opted for a more rigorous "conflict rule"'). Marise Cremona has pointed out that the Court of Justice pursued this course to avoid the challenge of clarifying the reach of the primacy principle in the external sphere. See Marise Cremona, 'The Doctrine of Exclusivity and the Position of Mixed Agreements in the External Relations of the European Community' (1982) 2 Oxford Journal of Legal Studies 393, 397–98. More recently, authors have argued that since the reach of the primacy principle to the external sphere is now settled, the very rationale underlying the ERTA principle has disappeared, and that as a consequence the doctrine has lost its purpose. See in this sense Piet Eeckhout, 'Bold Constitutionalism and Beyond' in Miguel Maduro and Loic Azoulai (eds), *The Past and Future of EU Law: The Classics of EU Law Revisited on the 50th Anniversary of the Rome Treaty* (Hart 2010).

[31] Comparative analyses have been undertaken in the past, including in the intra-EU context where pre-emption has been regarded as a useful concept to theorize the Court of Justice's case law on the freedom of movement. See eg Michel Waelbroeck, 'The Emergent Doctrine of Community Pre-Emption—Consent and Re-Delegation' in Terrance Sandalow and Eric Stein (eds), *Courts and Free Markets*, vol. II (Clarendon Press 1982); Daniel Eugene Cross, 'Pre-Emption of Member State Law in

out: pre-emption in the US affects the validity of (parts of) specific pieces of internal state legislation. By contrast, ERTA pre-emption in the EU grants the EU an exclusive external competence to conclude an international agreement. Or, from the perspective of the Member States, ERTA pre-emption precludes Member States from exercising their external powers to conclude the agreement. Secondly, as discussed in the previous chapter, in the US not only federal legislation and federally concluded treaties, but also federal executive policy can pre-empt state legislation. (This is the lesson of *Zschernig* and its progeny.) By contrast, only internal EU legislation can pre-empt Member States from acting. Conversely, a mere executive policy—for example a common EU strategy taken up in Council conclusions—cannot lead to pre-emption.[32] The same holds true for EU Treaty provisions: in Opinion 2/15—an opinion on the competence of the EU to conclude a trade agreement with Singapore—the Court of Justice ruled out the possibility that Article 65 TFEU, a provision of primary law on the free movement of capital, could in and by itself bring about an exclusive external EU competence by virtue of an ERTA pre-emptive effect.[33] This can again be contrasted with the US, where the Commerce Clause of the US Constitution has a 'dormant' pre-emptive effect that precludes states from legislating on issues that affect interstate commerce—even in the absence of Congressional legislation.[34] Thirdly, it is doubtful also whether an international agreement the EU has concluded in the past can have an ERTA pre-emptive effect.[35] This again differs from the US, where, as discussed, federally

the European Economic Community: A Framework for Analysis' (1992) 29 Common Market Law Review 447.

[32] As we will see, however, the duty of sincere cooperation does put limits on Member State autonomy once the EU has adopted a common strategy.

[33] Opinion 2/15 ('EU-Singapore FTA'), EU:C:2017:376, para 234:

> Regard would not be had to the reasoning inherent in the rule as to exclusive internal competence contained in the [*ERTA* judgment] . . . if the scope of that rule, currently laid down in the final limb of Article 3(2) TFEU, were extended to a situation which, as in the present instance, concerns not rules of secondary law laid down by the European Union in the exercise of an internal competence that has been conferred upon it by the Treaties, but a rule of primary EU law adopted by the framers of those Treaties.

[34] *Cooley v Bd of Wardens of Port of Philadelphia, to Use of Soc for Relief of Distressed Pilots, Their Widows & Child*, 53 US 299, 13 L Ed 996 (1851). On the subject, see generally Donald H Regan, 'The Supreme Court and State Protectionism: Making Sense of the Dormant Commerce Clause' (1986) 84 Michigan Law Review 1091.

[35] In this sense, see eg Mirka Kuisma and Joris Larik, 'The Continuing Contestation of ERTA' in Nicolas Levrat and others (eds), *The EU and its Member States' Joint Participation in International Agreements* (Hart 2022) 54 ('ERTA-based competence must be anchored to existing and foreseeable *internal* rule-setting) (emphasis added). In contrast, Marise Cremona mentioned in a 2014 contribution that ERTA pre-emption can also be triggered by the exercise of an external competence, although she immediately added that this is much less common (see Marise Cremona, 'EU External Relations: Unity and Conferral of Powers' in Loïc Azoulai (ed), *The Question of Competence in the European Union* (Oxford University Press 2014) 70).

concluded treaties can pre-empt state legislation if the federal government expressed an intention to this end. Taken together, these differences with pre-emption in the US make ERTA pre-emption a comparatively inward-looking doctrine geared more towards preserving the full effectiveness of previously enacted internal EU legislation, rather than towards protecting the EU's ability to pursue a specific foreign policy vis-à-vis a given third country as was the case, for example, in *Garamendi*, discussed earlier, where California legislation was pre-empted to safeguard the President's policy vis-à-vis Germany on the issue of Holocaust compensation payments.

In terms of similarities, it is worth comparing the criteria that trigger pre-emption in the EU and the US. In the previous chapter, I discussed how in the context of statutory pre-emption or treaty pre-emption (ie pre-emption caused, respectively, by Congressional legislation and federally concluded treaties), the intention of, respectively, Congress or the President determines whether or not state law is pre-empted. By contrast, pre-emption of state law caused by federal executive policy as in *Garamendi* is not caused by a Congressional or Presidential intention, but by the proximity of the state law at issue to that federal executive policy and the concomitant risk that the state law undermine the effectiveness of that federal policy. (As discussed, the California statute was pre-empted because it undermined the President's efforts of reaching a negotiated solution with California.)

A similar line of reasoning to the one at work in *Garamendi* in the US undergirds ERTA pre-emption in the EU. Article 3(2) TFEU, which codified the ERTA pre-emption doctrine as developed by the Court of Justice,[36] makes no reference to an intention of the EU legislature or treaty-maker to pre-empt. Instead, ERTA pre-emption occurs, and the EU thus acquires an exclusive external competence, when the commitments in a proposed international agreement 'affect common EU rules or alter their scope'. This is the case, the Court has clarified, when the commitments contained in the international agreement the EU intends to conclude 'fall within the scope of those [common] rules'.[37] And the Court has added that it is not necessary for those commitments to

[36] In this sense, see Opinion 1/13 ('Hague Convention'), EU:C:2014:2303, para 71 confirming that the question of whether commitments affect common rules contained in TFEU, art 3(2), must be assessed in light of the Court of Justice's case law dating back to the *ERTA* judgment.

[37] Opinion 1/13 ('Hague Convention'), EU:C:2014:2303, para 71. Contra, arguing that more than a mere overlap is needed, see Arena (n 27) 51 ('[E]very time the ECJ established subsequent external exclusivity it relied on at least one positive indicium in addition to scope overlap'). A more persuasive reading, I suggest, is one whereby the 'area largely covered' test operates as a rebuttable presumption that the proposed international agreement affects common rules or alters their scope. In this sense, see Thomas Verellen, 'Opinion 3/15 on the Marrakesh Treaty: The ECJ Reaffirms "Minimum Harmonisation" Exception to ERTA Principle' (2017) Revista General de Derecho Europeo 160.

match those common rules one-to-one; it is sufficient that they fall within the scope of an 'area that is largely covered' by common EU rules[38] and that the proposed commitments one way or another 'affect' those common rules.[39]

The US and EU pre-emption doctrines thus differ with respect to *which* federal or EU action the respective pre-emption doctrines aim to preserve—the President's foreign policy in the US versus the EU legislature's internal 'common rules'. However, they resemble one another in that both pre-emption doctrines aim to preserve the *effectiveness* of federal/EU action, rather than to give effect to the expressed *intention* of the federal/EU legislature or executive to pre-empt. The closer the member unit action is to the federal/EU action, the more likely a pre-emptive effect will be recognized. In the US, proximity to federal foreign policy action can directly pre-empt states from acting. By contrast, in the EU proximity to EU internal common rules triggers ERTA pre-emption. That said, indirectly ERTA pre-emption also protects the EU's policy space for external action. After all, ERTA pre-emption leads to a loss by the Member States of their ability to exercise their own external competence, to the benefit of the EU's ability to do so, and to conclude a proposed international agreement alone.[40]

A second similarity relates to the scope of pre-emption in both jurisdictions. As discussed in the previous chapter, in the US—including in cases with a foreign relations connection—the pre-emption analysis takes place at a retail as opposed to a wholesale level. As was the case in *Arizona v United States*, often individual provisions of state law rather than entire state statutes are pre-empted. A similar point can be made for the EU. Under EU law, too, a pre-emptive effect is often partial in the sense that it will not cover the entire international agreement the EU has concluded or intends to conclude.[41] Instead, ERTA pre-emption tends to leave other elements of the international agreement covered by a priori exclusive competence, non-exclusive competence, or no EU competence at all. The Court of Justice reached this conclusion, for example, in Opinion 2/15, mentioned

[38] Opinion 1/13 ('Hague Convention'), EU:C:2014:2303, para 73.

[39] See eg Opinion of AG Szpunar in Case C-161/20 *Commission v Council ('IMO')*, EU:C:2021:957, para 118, speaking of a 'tangible effect' of the commitment(s) on EU rules.

[40] On the ERTA principle as an instrument to construct the EU as a foreign policy actor, see Marise Cremona, 'Structural Principles and Their Role in EU External Relations Law' (2016) 69 Current Legal Problems 35, referring to the Court as being 'engaged in establishing and protecting an institutional space within which policy may be formed, in which the different actors understand and work within their respective roles'. The recognition in more recent ERTA case law that in the comparison of the proposed international agreement and the pre-existing common rules account should also be taken of the 'foreseeable future development' of the latter provides some support for Cremona's argument. See eg Opinion 1/13 ('Hague Convention'), EU:C:2014:2303, para. 74.

[41] In this sense, see Eeckhout (n 27) 634.

earlier.[42] In this opinion, the Court held that much of the proposed trade agreement between the EU and Singapore was covered by the EU's exclusive competence to conduct a common commercial policy. Several components of the agreement—including on transport policy—were covered by an ERTA pre-emptive effect. Yet others, including the sections on non-direct foreign investment, were covered by shared EU competence. As discussed, shared competence tends to translate into agreements being mixed—a consequence of a retail-level pre-emption analysis that, of course, is absent in the US as in that federation member unit governments do not hold treaty-making powers.

Is ERTA-type pre-emption an effective conflict resolution mechanism? Much depends on what one expects ERTA pre-emption to achieve. If ERTA pre-emption aims only to protect the full effectiveness of pre-existing internal EU legislation, it is quite effective as it prevents Member States from concluding agreements without EU involvement whenever such agreements affect the internal EU legislation concerned.[43] From this viewpoint, it is not problematic for ERTA pre-emption to be partial. What matters is that the EU, and in particular the Commission, sits at the negotiating table, allowing it to shape international agreements to ensure consistency with existing EU law.[44] If, by contrast, one understands ERTA pre-emption also as a means to protect the capacity of the EU to engage in autonomous external action and to pursue policies that cannot be reduced to the exportation of EU common rules to third countries, it is less successful. To make this second point, I distinguish between the different phases involved in treaty-making (and, by extension, external representation), and in particular between the phase of *negotiating* treaties and articulating common positions on the one hand, and the phase of *implementing*

[42] Opinion 2/15 ('EU-Singapore FTA'), EU:C:2017:376. Other examples were the GATS and TRIPS agreements, as decided in Opinion 1/94 ('WTO'), EU:C:1994:384, and the the EU-US Open Skies agreements, as decided in Case C–467/98 *Commission v Denmark ('Open Skies')*, EU:C:2002:625.

[43] But see Piet Eeckhout (n 30), arguing that while ERTA might be effective, it is not really necessary, as an ordinary application of the primacy principle would also ensure the full effectiveness of EU law vis-à-vis Member State agreements.

[44] ERTA pre-emption thus fits well with a conception of EU foreign relations as a 'mere' exportation of the internal *acquis* to third countries or an 'uploading' thereof to the international sphere. This process does not require political actorness or 'government'. Only 'governance' is required. For a conception of EU foreign relations in such terms, see Sandra Lavenex and Frank Schimmelfennig, 'EU Rules beyond EU Borders: Theorizing External Governance in European Politics' (2009) 16 Journal of European Public Policy 791 and again generally in Roman Petrov, *Exporting the Acquis Communautaire through European Union External Agreements* (Nomos Publishers 2011). For a conception of the EU as a foreign policy actor—a 'polity'—in its own right, see generally Robert Post, 'Constructing the European Polity: ERTA and the Open Skies Judgments' in Miguel Maduro and Loic Azoulai (eds), *The Past and Future of EU Law: The Classics of EU Law Revisited on the 50th Anniversary of the Rome Treaty* (Bloomsbury Publishing 2010).

treaties or decisions by multilateral organizations on the other. I start with the latter and then move to the former.

At the level of *implementation* of agreements and decisions, ERTA pre-emption is an effective mechanism to resolve conflicts between EU and Member State law. Since the areas covered by an ERTA pre-emptive effect fall within the exclusive competence of the EU, the Court of Justice has jurisdiction to interpret the provisions of a mixed agreement covered by such an effect.[45] Likewise, the Court has jurisdiction to enforce provisions covered by ERTA pre-emption vis-à-vis Member States, and if necessary to impose fines on these Member States.[46] In short: parts of an international agreement to which the EU is a party that are covered by an ERTA pre-emptive effect benefit from the enforcement mechanisms provided for in the EU Treaties. This observation is significant: had the Court not had jurisdiction to interpret and apply those agreements, it would have fallen to Member State courts to enforce the terms of the agreement against their own legislative and executive branches.[47] There would be less of a guarantee of an effective enforcement and uniform interpretation of mixed agreements throughout the EU.

By contrast, at the level of the *negotiation* of international agreements and the adoption of decisions within multilateral organizations, ERTA pre-emption has proven itself a less effective conflict resolution (or rather, conflict prevention) mechanism. As discussed in the previous chapter, as ERTA pre-emption typically does not cover the entirety of EU agreements, Member States at least potentially remain involved in the treaty negotiation process. Member States can mandate the Commission to represent them, but they are not obliged to do so.[48] They can mandate the Member State holding the rotating Presidency of the Council or they can themselves partake in the

[45] The Court of Justice has jurisdiction to interpret parts of mixed agreements within the scope of EU law. Areas covered by an ERTA pre-emptive effect certainly meet that condition. In this sense, see eg Case C-741/19 *Republic of Moldova v Komstroy LLC*, EU:C:2021:655, paras 24–27, confirming that the Court has jurisdiction to interpret the European Energy Charter since the EU has competence with regards to the concept of 'investment'.

[46] In this sense, see eg Case C-239/03 *Commission v France ('Étang de Berre')*, EU:C:2004:598, holding that the Court of Justice has jurisdiction to interpret and enforce the terms of a mixed agreement as the EU has an interest in ensuring compliance with those parts of the agreement over which the EU has competence. To determine whether the EU has competence, the Court looked at whether the field at issue has been covered 'in very large measure' by EU legislation.

[47] See eg Case C-240/09 *Lesoochranárske zoskupenie VLK v Ministerstvo životného prostredia Slovenskej republiky ('Slovak Brown Bear')*, EU:C:2011:125, para 32.

[48] In this sense, see Case C-161/20 *Commission v Council ('IMO')*, EU:C:2022:260, para 75, holding that there is no provision in the Treaties that requires Member States to give the Commission the task of ensuring their representation. See also Frank Hoffmeister, 'Of Presidents, High Representatives and European Commissioners—the External Representation of the European Union Seven Years after Lisbon' (2017) 1 Europe and the World: A Law Review 1, 46.

negotiations. Because Member States are involved in the negotiation process qua sovereign states in their own right, a risk of EU–Member State conflict remains with the EU and individual Member States pursuing different objectives or strategies. This risk arises both internally, when the EU determines its negotiation positions, and externally, when it defends those positions vis-à-vis its potential treaty partners. At the very least, as I discuss also in Chapter 9 on the management of mixity within the EU, mixed treaty negotiations typically mean that decisions will be taken by consensus amongst the Member States, even if the TFEU requires the Council to proceed by qualified majority vote (QMV). This is likely to be the case because each Member State will individually have to ratify the ensuing mixed agreement, thus turning each Member State into a veto player.[49] If ERTA pre-emption also ought to serve the purpose of protecting the full effectiveness of EU decision-making rules—in particular the qualified majority voting rule in the Council—and thus protecting the EU's ability to act as a foreign policy actor in its own right, it is not successful in attaining its aims.

In this sense, too, ERTA pre-emption remains an inward-looking doctrine aimed at protecting the internal *acquis communautaire* (ie the body of rules and principles that have been adopted throughout the history of the EU), rather than an outward-looking one that aims to protect the ability of the EU to effectively pursue the external policies it has autonomously decided upon.[50] (Marise Cremona has spoken of the role of EU foreign relations law in constructing the EU as a foreign policy actor.[51]) To address conflicts that might arise between the EU and its Member States in the exercise of their shared external competences, alternative conflict resolution mechanisms are thus required. The duty of sincere cooperation has been the main answer to these challenges.

[49] There is an important exception to this rule: multilateral agreements can often enter into force without all parties having ratified them. In this context, the EU can act independently, without unanimous consent among the Member States. In this sense, see Opinion 1/19 ('Istanbul Convention'), EU:C:2021:198, para 274.

[50] Pointing to the continued dependency of the ERTA principle on prior common EU rules: Cremona (n 35) 85:

> The link between internal and external competence is still strong. The Union is directed to pursue its general external objectives when developing and implementing the external dimension of its policies. External instruments are used to serve objectives that have an essentially internal focus. Pre-emption and exclusivity under art 3(2) TFEU are based on the adoption of legislation, requiring external unity to safeguard this internal *acquis*. As a matter of practice, rather than doctrine, the Union is more likely to choose to exercise its competence externally, and is perhaps more likely to be able to formulate a common external position, where a policy has already been formulated internally.

[51] Cremona (n 40) 35.

3.2 The Duty of Sincere Cooperation to Discipline Member States in Areas of Shared Competence

Ever since the Court of Justice approved the facultative mixity thesis discussed in Chapter 3 of this book, the Court has turned to the principle of sincere cooperation in the search for a means to address EU–Member State conflicts that arise in the context of mixed external action.[52] From the *principle* of sincere cooperation, set out in Article 4(3) TEU, the Court derived a *duty* of sincere cooperation.[53] The duty of sincere cooperation provides the EU with an additional constitutional remedy above and beyond ERTA pre-emption to sanction Member States that fail to 'facilitate the achievement of the Union's tasks' and fail to 'refrain from any measure which could jeopardise the attainment of the Union's objectives'.[54]

When applied to the vertical EU–Member State relationship, the duty of sincere cooperation is best understood as a form of 'pre-emption-light'. This characterization is adequate in light of the potentially significant restrictions the duty of sincere cooperation imposes on individual Member States, and its role as a means to resolve conflicts between EU and Member State external action. In addition to requiring the Member States to communicate with the EU institutions—in particular the Commission—whenever they undertake independent external action, in some instances the duty requires the Member States to abstain from undertaking action altogether.[55] When exactly is this the case, however? In its judgment in *PFOS*, the Court of Justice provided some clarifications.[56] To understand the origins, the meaning, and the effectiveness of the duty of sincere cooperation as a conflict resolution mechanism in EU foreign relations, it is helpful to discuss the *PFOS* case in more depth.[57]

[52] Robert Schütze, *Foreign Affairs and the EU Constitution: Selected Essays* (Cambridge University Press 2014) 334.

[53] See Case C–246/07 *Commission v Sweden ('PFOS')*, EU:C:2010:203, para 69, where the Court grounds the duty in (then) art 10 EC, current art 4(3) TEU. Before this decision, commentators disagreed on the constitutional foundation of the duty of sincere cooperation. See Christophe Hillion, 'Mixity and Coherence in EU External Relations: The Significance of the "Duty of Cooperation"' in Christophe Hillion and Panos Koutrakos (eds), *Mixed Agreements Revisited: the EU and its Member States in the World* (Hart 2010) 87–115, 89 and the references mentioned in fn 16 of that page. The 'requirement of unity in the international representation of the Community' represented one such alternative foundation. See Opinion 2/91 ('ILO Convention No 170'), EU:C:1993:106, para 36 ('This duty of cooperation, to which attention was drawn in the context of the EAEC Treaty, must also apply in the context of the EEC Treaty since it results from the requirement of unity in the international representation of the Community').

[54] TEU, art 4(3) third para.

[55] See Case C–433/03 *Commission v Germany ('Inland Waterways')*, EU:C:2005:462, and Case C–266/03 *Commission v Luxembourg ('Inland Waterways')*, EU:C:2005:341.

[56] Case C–246/07 *Commission v Sweden ('PFOS')*, EU:C:2010:203.

[57] For commentary on the decision, see Marise Cremona, 'Case C–246/07, Commission v. Sweden (PFOS), Judgment of the Court of Justice (Grand Chamber) of 20 April 2010' (2011) 48 Common

The controversy in *PFOS* arose from a unilateral decision by Sweden to submit a chemical substance 'perfluorooctanesulfonic acid' (PFOS) for inclusion on a list of hazardous substances maintained by an international body established by the Stockholm Convention on Persistent Organic Pollutants (the Stockholm Convention).[58] The Commission had initiated an infringement action against Sweden, arguing that by submitting the proposal Sweden had failed to fulfil its duty of sincere cooperation vis-à-vis the EU, which was also a party to the Stockholm Convention. Crucially, none of the parties before the Court contested that the subject matter of the controversy fell within the scope of EU shared competence, and that no common EU rules had pre-empted Sweden from acting. (It was significant, in that regard, that the Council had not adopted any formal decision on the issue of recommending PFOS for inclusion on the list of hazardous chemicals, and that thus no 'common rules' in the meaning of the ERTA pre-emption doctrine were present.) Despite these factors, the Commission considered that Sweden was not entitled to act in the way it had, and that, even in the sphere of shared EU competence, the EU Treaties did impose certain fetters on the freedom of action of Sweden.[59]

The Court of Justice agreed with the Commission. In its judgment in *PFOS*, and building on earlier case law on the subject, the Court further articulated the contours of a new doctrine, now commonly referred to as the 'duty of sincere cooperation'.[60] The Court started by emphasizing that this duty of sincere cooperation is of 'general application', which means it applies regardless of the nature of the EU's competence (exclusive or non-exclusive),[61] and even outside of the scope of EU competence altogether (ie when Member States are exercising their own powers).[62] It continued by emphasizing that it is 'essential to

Market Law Review 1639; Andres Delgado-Casteleiro and Joris Larik, 'The Duty to Remain Silent: Limitless Loyalty in EU External Relations?' (2011) 36 European Law Review 524; Geert De Baere, '"O, Where Is Faith? O, Where Is Loyalty?" Some Thoughts on the Duty of Loyal Co-operation and the Union's External Environmental Competences in the Light of the PFOS Case' (2011) 36 European Law Review 405.

[58] For more information on the Stockholm Convention, see <http://chm.pops.int/> accessed 29 November 2021.

[59] Case C-246/07 *Commission v Sweden ('PFOS')*, EU:C:2010:203, para 55.

[60] See in particular Case C-45/07 *Commission v Greece ('IMO')*, EU:C:2009:81; Case C-433/03, *Commission v Germany ('Inland Waterways')*, C-433/03, EU:C:2005:462; Case C-459/03, *Commission v Ireland ('Mox Plant')*, EU:C:2006:345. For an early discussion, see Christophe Hillion, 'Tous Pour Un, Un Pour Tous! Coherence in the External Relations of the European Union' in Marise Cremona (ed), *Developments in EU External Relations Law* (Oxford University Press 2008), in particular 29–30. The term 'duty of sincere cooperation' itself was first mentioned in a much earlier case: Case C-230/81 *Luxembourg v Parliament*, EU:C:1983:32.

[61] Case C-246/07 *Commission v Sweden ('PFOS')*, EU:C:2010:203, para 71.

[62] The scope of EU law does not necessarily correspond with the scope of the EU's competences. The Four Freedoms are the classical example. Koen Lenaerts speaks of the 'pervasive effects of EU law on the law of the Member States' to capture this phenomenon. See Koen Lenaerts, 'Federalism and the

ensure close cooperation between the Member States and the Community institutions, both in the process of negotiating and concluding of the agreement, and in the fulfilment of the commitments entered into';[63] and it added that 'Member States are subject to special duties of action and abstention in a situation in which the Commission has submitted to the Council proposals which, although they have not been adopted by the Council, represent the point of departure for concerted Community action'.[64] This means, in the particular context of external action, that:

> the adoption of a decision authorising the Commission to negotiate a multilateral agreement on behalf of the Community marks the start of a concerted Community action at international level and requires for that purpose, if not a duty of abstention on the part of the Member States, at the very least a duty of close cooperation between the latter and the Community institutions in order to facilitate the achievement of the Community tasks and to ensure the coherence and consistency of the action and its international representation.[65]

The thorny issue in *PFOS* was that the Council had not adopted a formal decision to *not* propose the contested substance for inclusion in the list of hazardous chemicals. This made recourse to ERTA pre-emption less of a possibility. Such a formal decision was not essential, the Court responded, as

> it does not appear to be indispensable that a common position take a specific form for it to exist and to be taken into consideration in an action for failure to fulfil the obligation of cooperation in good faith, provided that the content of that position can be established to the requisite legal standard.[66]

Rule of Law: Perspectives from the European Court of Justice' (2011) 33 Fordham International Law Journal 1338.

[63] Case C-246/07 *Commission v Sweden ('PFOS')*, EU:C:2010:203, para 73. In this sense, see also Opinion 2/91 ('ILO Convention N° 170'), EU:C:1993:106, para 36:

> [W]hen it appears that the subject-matter of an agreement or contract falls in part within the competence of the Community and in part within that of the Member States, it is important to ensure that there is a close association between the institutions of the Community and the Member States both in the process of negotiation and conclusion and in the fulfilment of the obligations entered into.

[64] Case C-246/07 *Commission v Sweden ('PFOS')*, EU:C:2010:203, para 74.

[65] ibid para 75.

[66] ibid para 77.

The Court of Justice concluded that '[i]t was at that time envisaged that PFOS would be nominated under that protocol as soon as the Commission had submitted a proposal for Community legislation on control measures in respect of that substance'.[67] The Court acknowledged that a decision to nominate PFOS had not yet been taken at the moment that Sweden made its unilateral proposal. Nonetheless, it considered that, 'in 2005, there was a common strategy not to propose, at that time, to list PFOS in Annex A to the Stockholm Convention'.[68] It followed that, by unilaterally proposing PFOS to be included in the list of hazardous substances, Sweden had 'dissociated itself from a concerted common strategy within the Council'.[69] This was particularly problematic in light of the fact that the outcome of the decision-making process within the international body would be binding upon the EU.[70] 'Such a situation,' the Court concluded, 'is likely to compromise the principle of unity in the international representation of the Union and its Member States and weaken their negotiating power with regard to the other parties to the Convention concerned.'[71] For this reason, the Court of Justice ruled that Sweden had violated its duty of sincere cooperation.

PFOS is a significant judgment due to the clarification it provides on a number of aspects of this 'emerging' duty of sincere cooperation.[72] A first clarification pertains to the material scope of the duty. In material terms, the Court affirmed that also outside of the scope of the EU's exclusive competence—be it a priori exclusive competence or the product of ERTA pre-emption—the Member States remain subject to restrictions and obligations derived from the principle of sincere cooperation.[73] A second clarification pertains to the duty's content. What exactly does the duty entail? One Advocate General had previously argued that the duty imposes only best effort obligations.[74] In *PFOS*, the Court affirmed that the duty is also one of results: the Member State at issue

[67] ibid para 85.

[68] ibid para 89.

[69] ibid para 91.

[70] ibid para 101.

[71] ibid para 104.

[72] The metaphor of 'emergence' is often used in law. I encountered it for example in the work of Canadian constitutionalists who speak of an 'emerging' doctrine of separation of powers in Canada. See eg Warren J Newman, 'The Constitutional Status of the Supreme Court of Canada' (2009) 47 Supreme Court Law Review 429, 437. For an example in the EU context, see the article by Robert Schütze, 'Supremacy Without Pre-Emption? The Very Slowly Emergent Doctrine of Community Pre-Emption' (2006) 43 Common Market Law Review 1023. Use of the term arguably has a normative undertone as the author who uses the term typically argues for the further emergence of the concept concerned.

[73] Prior to *PFOS*, this point remained contested, as the Court had never before recognized a duty to abstain outside of the context of the exclusive powers of the EU. See on this Case C-45/07 *Commission v Greece ('IMO')*, EU:C:2009:81, where the Court endorsed a duty to abstain in a context of EU exclusivity.

[74] See Opinion of AG Tesauro in Case C-53/96 *Hermès v FHT*, EU:C:1997:539, para 21 (emphasis added):

was required to abstain from acting. The Court made clear that the duty is not only procedural, but also—at least in some instances—substantive in nature: it would not have been enough for Sweden to communicate its intentions to the Commission; it was required to not act at all.

While *PFOS* clarifies certain aspects of the duty of sincere cooperation, questions nonetheless remain. Unclear, in particular, is the duty's temporal scope of application. From what moment onwards does the duty apply, and when exactly does it end? On the first issue, the Court in *PFOS* remained ambiguous. It reiterated language used in earlier decisions that suggests the duty comes into effect as soon as some form of 'concerted Community strategy' is initiated. In its earlier judgment in *IMO*, a Commission proposal was sufficient for the duty to apply.[75] At the same time, in *PFOS*, the Court also suggested that some form of common position must have been reached. While this position does not have to take the form of a formal Council decision, it must nonetheless be able to be established 'to the requisite legal standard.' In *PFOS*, the Court consulted Council minutes and found that an EU strategy not to propose PFOS for inclusion on the list of hazardous substances did exist. This holding can be contrasted with the *Inland Waterways* judgments, for example, in which the Court had held that procedural obligations to inform the Commission took effect as soon as steps had been undertaken towards concerted action, without this process having led to a common EU strategy, as was present in *PFOS*.[76]

On the second issue (ie until when exactly the duty applies), the Court of Justice had little to say in *PFOS*. If Sweden were to have been required to abstain from proposing PFOS for an indefinite amount of time, the difference between the effects of the duty of sincere cooperation on the one hand, and a pre-emptive effect on the other, would have become small indeed. Advocate General Poiares Maduro had proposed that Sweden be required to abstain

> To fulfil the obligation of cooperation and the requirement of unity in the international representation of the Community ... it is essential to ensure close cooperation between the Member States and the Community institutions, both in the process of negotiation and conclusion of the agreements on the subject and, even more important, in the fulfilment of the commitments entered into. In short, *they must endeavour to* adopt a common position.

[75] In *IMO*, the Commission had refused to respond to a request by Greece to discuss the possibility of having the EU submit a similar proposal to the one ultimately submitted by Greece. See Case C–45/07 *Commission v Greece ('IMO')*, EU:C:2009:81, para 25, where the Court of Justice mentions that the Commission's failure to discuss Greece's proposal could itself constitute a violation of the duty of sincere cooperation.

[76] See Case C–433/03 *Commission v Germany ('Inland Waterways')*, EU:C:2005:462, para 65, where the Court spoke of the 'point of departure for concerted Community action'. It should be noted that in this case the Council had nonetheless adopted a decision, which arguably reduces the precedential value of the Court's holding.

from acting for a 'reasonable period of time, until a conclusion to that process has been reached',[77] provided the decision-making process does not get caught in what he referred to as a 'never-ending process, in which a final decision by the Community is postponed to the point of inaction'.[78] In such a scenario, the Advocate General argued, a decision should be deemed to have been taken and Member States should be allowed to act.[79] The Court left the issue undecided.

Another question that remained unanswered pertains to the threshold that must be met for the duty to abstain to apply. In the above, I pointed out how, in its present form, the ERTA pre-emption doctrine precludes Member States from acting if an overlap exists between pre-existing common EU rules and a proposed international agreement. The requirement of a 'risk of affectation' is interpreted broadly; it is not necessary for a conflict to exist between the EU rules and the proposed agreement. By contrast, for the duty of sincere cooperation to preclude Member States from acting, arguably a higher threshold must be met. In particular, as the language of Article 4(3) TFEU suggests, for the duty of sincere cooperation to prohibit Member States from acting, their action must harm the common action of the EU.[80]

Despite this higher threshold, commentators have been critical about the potentially very broad scope of the duty of sincere cooperation.[81] Open-textured as it is—when does Member State action harm common EU action?—in many instances a case can be made that unilateral Member State initiatives harm the EU and its ability to undertake effective external action. To act united, with one voice, arguably serves the common EU interest better than to speak with many voices—regardless of what these voices have to say. (The American experience with pre-emption triggered by federal foreign policy is illustrative in this regard.) In this sense, the strictures of the duty of sincere cooperation could be considered to apply fairly quickly: once a 'common EU strategy' has been put in motion, without it having been established in detail, Member States are well advised not to undertake any unilateral action if they wish to avoid being subject to infringement proceedings before the Court of Justice.

In this sense, the duty of sincere cooperation can indeed be understood as a form of pre-emption, albeit a 'pre-emption-light'.[82] In contrast to ERTA-type

77 Opinion of AG Poiares Maduro in Case C-246/07 *Commission v Sweden ('PFOS')*, EU:C:2009:589, para 49.

78 ibid para 57.

79 ibid.

80 In this sense, see eg De Baere (n 57) 418.

81 Delgado-Casteleiro and Larik (n 57).

82 The close connection between the duty of sincere cooperation and ERTA-type pre-emption has been noted by commentators. See in particular Marise Cremona, 'Extending the Reach of the AETR Principle: Comment on Commission v Greece' (2009) 34 European Law Review 754, arguing that the

pre-emption, the Member States do not forever lose their ability to act.[83] Likewise, they do not lose their ability to act merely because the subject of their action overlaps with an action undertaken at EU level. By contrast, the duty of sincere cooperation does preclude Member States from acting independently in a fashion that does not contribute to the attainment of EU Treaty objectives. In this sense, the duty of sincere cooperation fulfils a similar conflict resolution function as does the pre-emption principle in the US. In US pre-emption cases, the federal government is pitted against a single state which has acted in a way the federal government considers contrary to the letter if not the spirit of federal law or policy. In comparison to ERTA pre-emption, however, the duty of sincere cooperation has more of an outward-looking, prospective role: it directly protects not only what has already been embedded in internal legislation, but also what is currently on the table in the EU's dealings with third country governments. Put differently, the duty of sincere cooperation strengthens the position of the EU as a distinct foreign policy actor, separate from the Member States, even within the framework of mixed external action.

3.3 The Limits of the Duty of Sincere Cooperation

Commentators have heralded the duty of sincere cooperation as an effective way to prevent conflicts from emerging between the EU and its Member States in the conduct of mixed external action.[84] While the duty of sincere cooperation is a helpful mechanism to ensure compliance by individual Member States with common EU external strategies, it is important also to be mindful of its limitations.

A first such limitation pertains to the duty's scope. As mentioned in the previous chapter, and as I discuss further Chapter 9 on intergovernmental relations, the duty of sincere cooperation cannot be interpreted as precluding

Court of Justice in *IMO* extends the scope of its *AETR* ruling to a unilateral act initiating a process which may lead to the adoption of new international rules, although those rules would not be directly binding on the Community. In contrast to this characterization, see however De Baere (n 57) 417, emphasizing that, in contrast to ERTA-type pre-emption, in order to judge whether the duty of cooperation has been complied with, a critical assessment of the specific circumstances of the case is indispensable.

[83] There is some discussion amongst commentators as to whether ERTA pre-emption is undone when the EU retracts the common rules that triggered a pre-emptive effect. See the references in Arena (n 27) 8. I argue that the characterization of ERTA pre-emption as a subcategory of exclusive competence in art 3(2) TFEU renders ERTA pre-emption permanent.

[84] See eg Hillion (n 55), praising the duty as a more appropriate means to ensure coherence and consistency in a pluralistic context.

individual Member States from participating in the decision-making process in the context of mixed external action altogether. In many circumstances, and certainly in the case of bilateral negotiations, mixity entails decision-making by unanimity amongst the Member States. As separate parties to the final agreement, each Member State has the freedom under international law to ratify (or not ratify) a mixed agreement,[85] and the duty of sincere cooperation cannot be stretched so as to compel Member States to ratify a mixed agreement.[86]

A second limitation pertains to the duty's reliance on judicial enforcement. The duty's strength—that is, its justiciable character and thus the possibility of enforcement by the Court—is also its main weakness, and this in two respects. First, the jurisdiction of the Court of Justice to enforce the duty of sincere cooperation vis-à-vis Member States does not extend to the Common Foreign and Security Policy (CFSP). This means that a case such as *PFOS* cannot be brought against a Member State if it were to act in conflict with a common EU strategy decided on in the Council on the EU's approach to the Taliban takeover of Afghanistan in the summer of 2021, to name an example that was fairly recent at the time of writing.[87] It means, also, that the Commission cannot bring infringement proceedings against Member States that fail to implement restrictive measures such as travel bans adopted by the Council on the basis of CFSP competence.[88] This lack of jurisdiction is likely to damage the credibility of the Union as a reliable partner in foreign policy matters.[89]

More fundamentally, however, it is important to be mindful of the inherent limitations of judicial conflict resolution mechanisms in a context in which both levels of governance have constitutional authority to act externally, including by incurring international legal commitments. Domestic courts have jurisdiction to enforce domestic constitutional rules and principles. As discussed, they can conclude that a member unit government or, for that matter, the federal/EU level of governance, has violated such a rule or principle. Often, however, the domestic court's options to provide relief are limited. The external action that gave rise to the violation of a constitutional rule or principle has been made. A fact on the ground has been created that cannot be undone through

[85] Sovereign states cannot be forced to express their consent to be bound. See VCLT, art 51.

[86] In this sense, see also Guillaume Van der Loo and Ramses A Wessel, 'The Non-Ratification of Mixed Agreements: Legal Consequences and Solutions' (2017) 54 Common Market Law Review 735, 745 ('[T]he duty of cooperation can be read as an obligation to initiate the national ratification procedure (e.g. parliamentary approval procedure), but without influencing the outcome of this procedure').

[87] See Council conclusions on Afghanistan, 15 September 2021, 11713/2/21 REV 2 <https://data.consilium.europa.eu/doc/document/ST-11713-2021-REV-2/en/pdf> accessed 6 December 2021.

[88] On the issue, see Konstanty Gebert, 'Shooting in the Dark? EU Sanctions Policies' (European Council on Foreign Relations 2013) Policy Brief 71.

[89] In this sense, see De Baere (n 30).

the intervention of a domestic court. If we take the example of *PFOS*: the Court of Justice concluded that Sweden had violated its duty of sincere cooperation by proposing PFOS for inclusion on a list of hazardous substances maintained by an international body established by the Stockholm Convention. Crucially, the Court could only provide declaratory relief; it could neither order Sweden to retract its unilateral proposal, nor order the international body to disregard Sweden's proposal. For the international body, Sweden's violation of its duty of sincere cooperation vis-à-vis the EU is immaterial.

Similar problems arise in the treaty-making context: if a Member State becomes a party to an international agreement covered by an ERTA pre-emptive effect or in violation of its procedural obligation under the duty of sincere cooperation to inform the Commission of its intention to become a party, as a general rule the validity under the international agreement or the Member State's ratification of the agreement is not affected and the Member State remains bound to perform its treaty obligations under the agreement.[90] An *ex post* judicial conflict resolution mechanism that declares one level of governance a 'winner' and the other a 'loser' is thus bound to remain somewhat unsatisfactory as the international legal consequences of the loser's actions cannot easily be undone. For this reason, it is worth considering whether additional institutional mechanisms should not be introduced to more proactively enforce the duty of sincere cooperation. To this end, I propose in Chapter 9 of the book that the Treaty framers introduce an 'EU Compact Clause'. Such a mechanism would provide the European Commission with an opportunity to screen international agreements Member States wish to conclude.

4. Conclusion

In this chapter and the previous chapter, I explored how conflicts between levels of governance are resolved in the conduct of foreign relations. We discovered how in Canada conflicts are resolved informally. Canada's foreign affairs constitution does not provide for formal mechanisms of conflict resolution. Instead, mutual accommodation is key to preventing and resolving tensions. In comparison to Canada's informal arrangements, Belgium's foreign affairs constitution provides for a more formalized set of political conflict resolution mechanisms. Designed to protect the 'coherence' of Belgium's foreign relations, these mechanisms allow the federal government to suspend

[90] In this sense, see VCLT, art 27.

member unit treaty negotiations and to substitute itself for the member units in the event they fail to comply with their international obligations. However, while these instruments appear far-reaching at first sight, the stringent conditions attached to their application have made their use not very attractive to Belgium's federal government. Since their introduction in 1993, neither instrument has been used at all. Instead, as in Canada, mutual accommodation is key to resolving conflicts between the federal and member unit governments in Belgium. On this point, Belgium and Canada differ from the US. In the US, conflict resolution through judicial mechanisms—primarily through the pre-emption doctrine—is a core feature of the US foreign affairs constitution. The Supremacy Clause ensures that state laws do not interfere with federal legislation, federal treaties, or even federal executive foreign policy.

When it comes to the topic of conflict resolution, the EU currently resembles more closely the US than it does either Canada or Belgium. In both the EU and the US, judicial conflict resolution mechanisms have been developed to ensure the effectiveness of federal/EU foreign relations. By contrast, political conflict resolution mechanisms are not a prominent feature of the EU's foreign affairs constitution, even though in recent years the EU legislature has been putting in place sector-specific mechanisms that endow the Commission with powers to screen Member State initiatives. However, no cross-sectoral mechanism exists that subjects draft Member State international agreements to *ex ante* screening by, for example, the European Commission—akin to the mechanism provided for in the EURATOM Treaty. Likewise, the Commission does not have any powers to either suspend Member State treaty negotiations akin to the Belgian suspension mechanism or to substitute itself for a Member State in case of non-compliance with treaty obligations.

Instead of relying on political conflict resolution mechanisms that operate *ex ante* (ie before the Member State has taken action), the Court of Justice has developed constitutional doctrines that aim to prevent conflicts between the EU and Member States from arising by imposing legal obligations to act or not to act on the Member States. EU law is distinctive from US pre-emption principles on this point in that these constitutional doctrines govern the *external* behaviour of the member units of the federation. (In the US, pre-emption typically affects *internal* state actions, even though there have been cases in which pre-emption principles have been invoked against state compacts.[91])

[91] See in particular *United States v California*, not reported in Fed Supp (2020), in which the Trump administration challenged on pre-emption grounds California's participation in the Quebec emissions trading scheme.

The application of pre-emption principles to the external actions of Member States raises enforcement challenges. In the US, a local federal district court can order state authorities to suspend the application of a contested state law pending judicial review. And while the Court of Justice possesses similar interim powers to US federal courts,[92] it is harder for courts to step in to stop Member States from taking actions in international bodies or from concluding international agreements that may have legal repercussions for the EU or other Member States. In particular, infringement actions provide only declaratory relief for the Commission, which, if successful, sees its legal position vindicated before the Court of Justice. The Court's ruling cannot however undo the steps taken by Sweden in the Stockholm Convention body, or order that body to ignore Sweden's actions. In this sense, the combination of far-reaching legal obligations to act and not to act that flow from the ERTA pre-emption doctrine and the duty of sincere cooperation, coupled with the exclusive reliance on judicial enforcement of those constitutional doctrines, creates a risk of underenforcement and, ultimately, non-compliance by the Member States who do not always act in a spirit of loyalty vis-à-vis the EU institutions.[93] From this vantagepoint, the Belgian suspension and substitution mechanisms—and, as we will see in Chapter 9, the US Compact Clause—are interesting avenues to explore also for the EU. Granting the European Commission a power to suspend Member State treaty negotiations before the agreement is concluded could make it easier for the Commission to assess whether the Member State concerned complies with ERTA pre-emption principles and with the duty of sincere cooperation, and, if necessary, block Member States from acting in violation of the EU Treaties.

[92] TFEU, art 279.

[93] There is evidence of such non-compliance. For example, the 2016 EU-Turkey Statement on the management of refugee flows from Turkey into Greece arguably fell at least in part under EU exclusive competence due to the existence of an important body of internal common rules in the field of migration policy. Yet the Member States were able, as a practical matter, to make the agreement with Turkey, without the EU as a party.

PART II
SHARED RULE

6

The Political Safeguards of Foreign Relations Federalism in the US, Canada, and Belgium

> Apart from the limitation on federal authority inherent in the delegated nature of Congress' Article I powers, the principal means chosen by the Framers to ensure the role of the States in the federal system lies in the structure of the Federal Government itself.
>
> Justice Harry Blackmun in *Garcia v San Antonio Metropolitan Transit Authority*[1]

1. Introduction

Federalism has two dimensions: self-rule and shared rule. Self-rule can in turn be pursued in two ways: through the allocation of powers to levels of government (see Chapters 2 and 3), and through the resolution of conflicts that arise when governments exercise powers allocated to them (see Chapters 4 and 5). In the following four chapters, I focus on the shared rule dimension of foreign relations federalism. Shared rule can be realized in two ways as well: either by granting the member units a voice in the federal decision-making process—a technique referred to by the term 'political safeguards of federalism'—or by engaging in direct government-to-government relations, in the comparative federalism literature referred to as 'intergovernmental relations'. I look at the former in this chapter and the next, and at the latter in Chapters 8 and 9.

Political safeguards of federalism are legal mechanisms that ensure that the federal level of government is mindful of member unit interests when it makes laws or takes decisions.[2] Such safeguards can be either formal or informal.

[1] *Garcia v San Antonio Metro. Transit Auth*, 469 US 528, 105 S Ct 1005, 83 L Ed 2d 1016 (1985) 550.

[2] The concept of political safeguards of federalism originated in the US. See generally Herbert Wechsler, 'The Political Safeguards of Federalism: The Role of the States in the Composition and Selection of the National Government' (1954) 54 Columbia Law Review 543; Jesse H Choper, *Judicial Review and the National Political Process: A Functional Reconsideration of the Role of the Supreme Court* (Quid

Foreign Relations Federalism. Thomas Verellen, Oxford University Press. © Thomas Verellen 2023.
DOI: 10.1093/oso/9780192844569.003.0006

Formal safeguards are those rules and institutional mechanisms that ensure member unit representation within federal institutions. An example of a formal safeguard is the representation of the EU Member State executives in the Council and the European Council in the EU, or the institutional role of US Senators when they were elected by the legislature of their state before the adoption of the Seventeenth Amendment in 1913. *Informal safeguards* include (i) the role of member unit governments in implementing federal policy, which may grant state governments indirect influence in the federal political process;[3] (ii) the role of political parties with ties to the member unit political space;[4] and (iii) the leverage that the fiscal capacity of the member units grants those member unit governments within the federal political process.[5] Taken together, the above four indicators—which are by no means exhaustive—give a sense of the role member unit governments can play, either directly or indirectly, within the federal foreign policy-making process. The table below (see Table 6.1) provides an overview of the different types of political federalism safeguards I look at in this book.

In this chapter and the next, I examine the political safeguards component of federalism's shared rule dimension as it plays out in the foreign relations context. I explore how, if at all, member units have a direct or an indirect voice within the federal foreign policy-making process. This chapter covers the US, Canada, and Belgium; the next chapter covers the EU. For each of the abovementioned categories of federalism safeguards, I will characterize the safeguard as 'strong', 'neutral', or 'weak'. The stronger the safeguard, the better

Pro Books 2013); D Bruce la Pierre, 'The Political Safeguards of Federalism Redux: Intergovernmental Immunity and the States as Agents of the Nation' (1982) 60 Washington University Law Quarterly 779. It has been used in the EU context as well; see eg Robert Schütze, 'Subsidiarity after Lisbon: Reinforcing the Safeguards of Federalism?' (2009) 68 The Cambridge Law Journal 525; Xavier Groussot and Sanja Bogojevic, 'Subsidiarity as a Procedural Safeguard of Federalism' in Loïc Azoulai (ed), *The Question of Competence in the European Union* (Oxford University Press 2014).

[3] See on this Larry Kramer, 'Understanding Federalism' (1994) 47 Vanderbilt Law Review 1485, 1544, writing in the US context that '[t]he federal government needs the states as much as the reverse, and this mutual dependency guarantees state officials a voice in the [federal political] process'. More recently, see also the work of Jessica Bulman-Pozen, who looks to the states in search of checks on federal executive power. See eg Jessica Bulman-Pozen, 'Administrative States: Beyond Presidential Administration' (2019) 98 Texas Law Review 265; Jessica Bulman-Pozen, 'Federalism as a Safeguard of the Separation of Powers' (2012) 112 Columbia Law Review 459.

[4] See again Kramer (n 3) 1522–24, arguing that the non-centralized and non-programmatic nature of political parties in the US protects state autonomy. And similarly Larry D Kramer, 'Putting the Politics Back into the Political Safeguards of Federalism' (2000) 100 Columbia Law Review 215.

[5] The government capable of levying taxes, borrowing on financial markets, and spending these resources in a discretionary manner, wields much influence within the federation. Conversely, if a government is not capable—formally or informally—to independently finance the policies it pursues, and instead depends on financial contributions of other governments, necessarily the latter governments will have a degree of influence within the political process of the former.

Table 6.1 A typology of political safeguards of foreign relations federalism

The political safeguards of foreign relations federalism			
Formal safeguards	*Informal safeguards*		
Direct representation within the federal foreign policy-making process	Political parties	Administrative capacity	Fiscal capacity

the autonomy of the member unit is protected. A *strong* safeguard means it endows the member unit government(s) with a voice in the federal foreign policy-making process. A *neutral* safeguard is a safeguard that does not affect the federal–member unit relationship and thus does not translate into a greater member unit voice in the federal foreign policy-making process. A *weak* safeguard is a safeguard that not only does not grant the member unit a voice in the federal foreign policy-making process, but one that actually weakens that voice because it strengthens the position of the federal government versus the member units.[6] Taken together, the analysis of this chapter and the next will show that, while the political safeguards of foreign relations federalism are not well developed in the two North American federations, they are an important feature of foreign relations federalism in Belgium as well as in the EU. In particular in the EU, member units have a strong voice in the EU foreign policy-making process.

2. United States: Weak Political Safeguards in a System of Dual Federalism

What political safeguards of foreign relations federalism can be identified in the US? Both formal and informal safeguards are weak in the US. In terms of *formal safeguards*, none of the political institutions involved in foreign policy-making at the federal level gives a meaningful voice to state interests. At the level of *informal safeguards*, neither political parties nor state governments through their role in administering federal law grant those state governments a voice in

[6] The political safeguards of federalism lens puts the member unit governments at the centre of the analysis and uses the extent to which safeguards protect member unit autonomy as a benchmark. The benchmark is however strictly analytical, not normative: the political safeguards of federalism lens is not used to suggest that federal governments *should* give voice to member unit interests within the federal foreign policy-making process. The question tackled in this chapter is, by contrast, an empirical one: *do* federal governments give a voice to member unit governments? And to what extent do the different safeguards we look at contribute (or not) to giving member units that voice?

the federal decision-making process. In short, when it comes to the protection of state interests and policy preferences in the federal foreign policy-making process, US states do not benefit from strong political safeguards. Instead, US foreign policy is articulated and implemented by the federal government—in particular the US President, but with significant involvement of Congress. As we will discover, the lack of voice within the federal foreign policy-making process gives individual US states an incentive to engage in diplomacy of their own.

2.1 Formal Political Safeguards: The Senate as a 'Federal Chamber'?

Neither of the two political institutions that play a central role in foreign policy-making in the US—that is, President and Congress—provides a direct voice to state governments. The Presidency is best understood as the antithesis of a body representing member unit interests: the President holds a directly elected office set up to provide leadership and unity of action within the federal government.[7] The House of Representatives, for its part, is a collective body. In contrast to the Senate, which represents regional interests within the federal political process, the House of Representatives represents individual US citizens.[8] This leaves the Senate as a potential 'federal chamber'—a function Justice Blackmun in the case of *Garcia*, quoted at the outset of this chapter, saw the Senate as fulfilling.

As mentioned earlier, prior to the adoption of the Seventeenth Amendment in 1913, state legislatures elected US Senators. In such a framework, it made sense to look at the US Senate as a channel for the representation of state interests in the federal political process.[9] However, since 1913, US Senators have been directly elected. This severed the direct link between US Senators and state governments. In Justice Blackmun's view, this did not detract from the

[7] In this sense, see eg Alexander Hamilton, James Madison, and John Jay, *The Federalist (The Gideon Edition), Edited with an Introduction, Reader's Guide, Constitutional Cross-Reference, Index, and Glossary by George W. Carey and James McClellan* (George W Carey and James McClellan eds, Liberty Fund 2001) No 70. Note that one of the main features of the 1787 Constitution with which the Anti-Federalists took issue was the office of the Presidency, which they regarded as an 'elected monarch'. See Antifederalist Paper No 67, <http://thefederalistpapers.org/antifederalist-paper-67> accessed 27 January 2022.

[8] For this reason, Congressional districts ought to be delineated on the basis of the principle of 'one person, one vote'. See seminally *Reynolds v Sims*, 377 US 533 (1964), holding that the Equal Protection Clause requires that state election systems be designed to give approximately equal weight to each vote cast.

[9] Highlighting how even before the Seventeenth Amendment the ability of state governments to exercise control over the Senators they sent to Washington was limited, see Kramer (n 3) 1508–10.

Senate's role as a representative of state interests in the federal political process. And to some extent, through the equal representation in the Senate of all fifty states, regardless of their population size, the Senate does still operate as a federal chamber in the sense that it represents geographically defined interests. However, the fact that the US Senate represents *geographically* defined interests does not necessarily imply that US Senators represent the interests of state *governments* in the federal political process. At most, they represent the interests of their state-wide constituencies. And as Larry Kramer has argued, these interests do not necessarily converge with those of state governments.[10]

However, if for the sake of the argument we do accept—as did Justice Blackmun in *Garcia*, and as Herbert Wechsler did in his 1954 article on the topic of political federalism safeguards[11]—that the US Senate continues to fulfil a 'federal' function within the constitutional architecture of the US federal government, then perhaps the Senate could be understood as protecting the interests of the member units through its role in the federal treaty-making procedure, its role in the legislative process, and through the practices of legislative oversight that come with delegations of Congressional authority to the President. I first examine the former and then turn to the latter.

2.2 The Senate's Role in Treaty-Making

As discussed, the US Senate must attach its 'advice and consent' to treaties negotiated by the President before the latter can proceed to ratification.[12] The constitutional text thus appears to grant the Senate a veto power over the exercise of the treaty-making power by the President. This position, in combination with its—albeit contested—role as a 'federal chamber' is sometimes regarded by commentators as a political safeguard of foreign relations federalism in the US. For example, as Oona Hathaway and her co-authors argued in a 2012 article on the treaty power in the US:

[10] Kramer (n 3) 1510:

> [A]llocating representation on this basis may enhance the power of geographically defined interests at the federal level. But it does so in a way that seems likely, if anything, to diminish the institutional role of state government. For if we assume that members of Congress elected on the basis of geography respond to state and local interests, doesn't this, in turn, give them an incentive to reduce or minimize the role of state and local government?

[11] Wechsler (n 2) 548, arguing that, even after the Seventeenth Amendment, 'the composition of the Senate is intrinsically calculated to prevent intrusion from the center on subjects that dominant state interests wish preserved for state control'.

[12] US Constitution, art II §2 cl 2.

> [A]lthough the Senate is now elected directly, senators are still of course representatives of their states; they are elected, after all, by a statewide electorate, and must be responsive to the desires of their constituency. It is far from clear that the proper federalism concern is with the interests of state legislatures than it is with state electorates. Moreover, the supermajority requirement in treaty making provides an additional level of protection for state interests. Any proposed treaty must convince two-thirds of the senators not only that it is substantively advantageous to the United States but also that it is an appropriate exercise of federal power. Treaties, moreover, are created by the Senate and President alone (the House of Representatives is excluded from the process)—hence, states each have equal representation in the treaty-making process. A minority of senators holding particularly strong views on states' rights, therefore, could derail a treaty, even one that enjoyed overwhelming majority support. Indeed, if anything, the process is too protective of state interests.[13]

Undermining Hathaway and her co-authors' argument, however, is the observation that the Article II procedure, which requires the President to obtain the advice and consent of the Senate to make a treaty, is not the only way for the US to conclude international agreements. In *Belmont* and *Pink*, both decided in the first half of the twentieth century, the Supreme Court recognized that the President can independently conclude international agreements on issues of claims settlement.[14] And, over time, an increasingly significant share of international agreements concluded by the US—over 93 per cent in the 1990–2012 period[15]—came to be adopted by other means than the Article II procedure. Such agreements, known as 'executive agreements', as mentioned earlier, are made by the President. If executive agreements require changes to domestic law, Congress can adopt the necessary implementing legislation on the basis of its Article I legislative powers. If this turns out to be necessary, the executive agreement is referred to as a 'Congressional executive agreement'. The North American Free Trade Agreement (NAFTA) was ratified and implemented

[13] Oona A Hathaway and others, 'The Treaty Power: Its History, Scope and Limits' (2012) 98 Cornell Law Review 239, 309.

[14] *US v Belmont*, 301 US 324 (1937) and *US v Pink*, 315 US 203 (1942).

[15] In the 1990–2012 period, only 6.2 per cent of US international agreements were adopted on the basis of the Article II process. See Curtis A Bradley and Jack L Goldsmith, 'Presidential Control over International Law' (2018) 131 Harvard Law Review 1201, 1210.

by the US in this way, as was its successor, the United States-Mexico-Canada Agreement (USMCA).[16]

While the constitutionality of the practice remains contested,[17] as a practical matter executive agreements have thus replaced Article II treaties as the preferred procedure through which the US concludes international agreements. This development has repercussions for the political safeguards of federalism in the foreign policy-making process in the US. While Article II treaties require the consent of two-thirds (or sixty-seven) of US Senators, and three Senators can thus derail a treaty, the President alone can conclude an executive agreement. If implementing legislation is required, an executive agreement can be adopted by means of the ordinary legislative process requiring majority support in both houses of Congress, or, if the Senate filibuster is taken into account, a majority of sixty-one out of 100 Senators.[18] While the filibuster slightly narrows the gap between the Article II treaty-making process and that of adopting Congressional-executive agreements in terms of the number of Senators required to derail a proposed agreement, Article II treaties still require a larger number of Senators to consent to the agreement compared to a Congressional-executive agreement (67 versus 60 or 51, depending on whether or not the filibuster applies). As such, treaty-making through executive agreements as

[16] See, respectively, HR3450—North American Free Trade Agreement Implementation Act, 103rd Congress (1993–94), and HR5430—United States-Mexico-Canada Agreement Implementation Act, 116th Congress (2019–20).

[17] The executive has defended the practice as constitutional. In this sense, see eg Office of Legal Counsel, Validity of Congressional-Executive Agreements that Substantially Modify the United States' Obligations Under An Existing Treaty, 25 November 1996, <www.justice.gov/file/19891/download> accessed 27 January 2022, in which the Office of Legal Counsel defends the authority of the President and Congress to modify treaty obligations by means of Congressional-executive agreement. Commentators have historically been divided over the issue. Some commentators have defended the 'interchangeability' thesis, according to which the President can choose freely between an Article II treaty and an executive agreement. In support of the thesis, see eg Myers S McDougal and Asher Lans, 'Treaties and Congressional-Executive or Presidential Agreements: Interchangeable Instruments of National Policy: I' (1945) 54 The Yale Law Journal 181. Other commentators such as Oona Hathaway assert that, whenever possible, the executive agreement route ought to be pursued. See Oona A Hathaway, 'Treaties' End: The Past, Present, and Future of International Lawmaking in the United States' (2008) 117 The Yale Law Journal 1236. Others, still, have attempted to articulate a criterion of distinction between Article II treaties and executive agreements. See eg John C Yoo, 'Laws as Treaties?: The Constitutionality of Congressional-Executive Agreements' (2001) 99 Michigan Law Review 757, arguing that Article II treaties should only be used to conclude international agreements on issues outside of the scope of Congress' legislative powers. And a final group, which includes Laurence Tribe, claims that all international agreements ought to be adopted via the Article II procedure. See Laurence H Tribe, 'Taking Text and Structure Seriously: Reflections on Free-Form Method in Constitutional Interpretation' (1995) 108 Harvard Law Review 1221.

[18] On the use of the filibuster when approving Congressional-executive agreements, see Oona Hathaway, *The Case for Replacing Article II Treaties With Ex Post Congressional-Executive Agreements* (American Constitution Society for Law and Policy 2008) 5–6, mentioning that while some Congressional-executive agreements can be approved by means of an ordinary majority in the Senate (in particular those subject to fast-track procedures such as trade agreements), many Congressional-executive agreements are subject to the filibuster.

opposed to Article II treaties means that the ability of the Senate to operate as a political safeguard of foreign relation federalism is weakened.

2.3 Congress as a Check on the President?

In addition to the Senate's role in the treaty-making process, Congress as a whole could make use of its Article I legislative powers to restrict the ability of the President to independently engage in foreign relations. Through its role in the bicameral legislative process, the Senate could perhaps still give voice to state interests.[19] Often, the President does not act on the basis of his own constitutional powers, but rather on the basis of Congressional delegations of authority. Congress could subject the exercise of such delegated powers to procedural checks. It could, for example, add a sunset clause to the delegation of authority. Doing so would require Congress to occasionally renew the delegation of authority to the President, which would require the approval of both houses of Congress, including the Senate. Similarly, Congress could make the exercise of delegated power subject to a legislative veto, which gives Congress the ability to oppose individual decisions by the President by means of legislation or a joint resolution adopted by both houses and presented to the President.[20] Here again, both houses, including the Senate, have a role to play. For Congress to terminate a measure taken by the President, a two-thirds majority in both houses is required, as the legislative veto must be insulated against the President's own veto power. Other, less 'hard', procedural checks can be imagined, such as report-and-wait requirements that require the President to report measures to Congress and let a set amount of time pass before the measure can enter into force so as to enable Congress to express its opposition, or consultation requirements that require the President to obtain the views of both houses of Congress before undertaking action.[21]

[19] See on this the argument that the federal separation of powers was in part designed to give voice to state interests in Bradford R Clark, 'Separation of Powers as a Safeguard of Federalism' (2000) 79 Texas Law Review 1321.

[20] Since the 1983 Supreme Court ruling in *INS v Chadha*, 462 US 919, 103 S Ct 2764, 77 L Ed 2d 317 (1983), a legislative veto can only be issued through a process that involves both houses and a presentment to the President. This means a veto can be issued by means of a joint resolution or through legislation, both of which are subject to the bicameralism and presentment requirements set out in art I § 7 cl 2 of the US Constitution.

[21] For an overview of the types of procedural checks Congress can attach to delegations of authority in the foreign policy sphere, see Curtis A Bradley, 'Reassessing the Legislative Veto: The Statutory President, Foreign Affairs, and Congressional Workarounds' [2021] Journal of Legal Analysis 439, 458–465.

However, it is not easy for Congress to effectively operate as a procedural check on the President as he engages in foreign policy-making. The President is a single individual whereas Congress is a collective body. The US President can create facts on the ground that Congress cannot easily undo. This is particularly clear in the military context where Congress holds important constitutional powers—including the power to declare war[22]—but has experienced difficulties in exercising control over the President's activities.[23] The events surrounding US involvement in the military campaign to topple the Khadhafi regime in Libya in 2011 offer a good example. The War Powers Resolution, a statute enacted in the final years of the Vietnam War, requires the President to report to Congress after deploying the US military.[24] The President must obtain Congress' approval of the deployment within a ninety-day period after the start of hostilities. Absent Congressional approval within that time limit, the President must withdraw all American military personnel.[25] When, in 2011, the ninety-day deadline had passed and Congress had not granted its approval, the Obama administration argued that the hostilities in Libya did not meet the threshold for being characterized as 'war' in the meaning of the War Power in Article I of the Constitution, and that the President therefore did not need Congress' approval under the War Powers Resolution to use military force.[26] Following that, Congress failed to take *any* measures that would have put an end to US involvement in the Libya campaign.[27]

The events surrounding US participation in the military intervention in Libya demonstrate how difficult it is for Congress to hold the President accountable in the conduct of his foreign policy. They highlight, first, the advantages

[22] US Constitution, art I §8 cl 11.

[23] The point has been made extensively in Harold H Koh, 'Why the President (Almost) Always Wins in Foreign Affairs: Lessons of the Iran-Contra Affair' (1988) 97 The Yale Law Journal 1255. Koh subsequently included his finding in his book *The National Security Constitution: Sharing Power After the Iran-Contra Affair* (Yale University Press 1990).

[24] War Powers Resolution, Pub L No 93-148, 87 Stat 555 (1973), 50 USC §§1541–48, s 4.

[25] ibid s 5.

[26] See Office of the Legal Counsel, 'Authority to Use Military Force in Libya' (Department of Justice 2011) 10 <www.justice.gov/olc/opinion/authority-use-military-force-libya> accessed 27 January 2022. The OLC's line of argumentation was developed further in early June 2011, when in a testimony before the Senate Foreign Relations Committee Harold Koh, at that time legal adviser of the State Department, argued that the intervention in Libya did not qualify as 'hostilities' in the meaning of the War Powers Resolution, and the sixty-day deadline thus did not apply. See US Senate, Hearing before the Committee on Foreign Relations, US Senate, 28 June 2011, 11, <https://fas.org/irp/congress/2011_hr/libya.pdf> accessed 27 January 2022. Criticizing this legal assessment, see Louis Fisher, 'The Law: Military Operations in Libya: No War? No Hostilities?' (2012) 42 Presidential Studies Quarterly 176.

[27] A resolution that would have directed the President to withdraw US armed forces from Libya failed to get adopted. See H CON RES 51 directing the President, pursuant to s 5(c) of the War Powers Resolution, to remove the United States Armed Forces from Libya, <www.congress.gov/bill/112th-congress/house-concurrent-resolution/51/text> accessed 27 January 2022.

the President enjoys in terms of his ability to act fast. (The President initiated the intervention a mere two days after the UN Security Council adopted the resolution authorizing the use of military force on 17 March 2011[28]). Secondly, the controversy illustrates the collective action problems Congress faces when attempting to stand up against the President. When the President failed to obtain Congressional approval before the ninety-day limit, different members of Congress pursued different strategies, and ultimately Congress as a whole failed to pursue *any* unified strategy vis-à-vis the President.

Issues such as these are not unique to the context of the use of military force. In other areas with a foreign affairs dimension, similar dynamics are at play. The reluctance of Congress to take action against President Trump's use of his delegated authority to impose import tariffs on national security grounds is an example in the trade policy sphere.[29] At the time of writing (January 2022), bills had been introduced in House and Senate to strengthen Congressional controls over the President in this area.[30] The lack of bipartisan support and the track record of similar bills introduced in the past suggest the bills will not become law.[31] The lack of a Congressional majority in support of stronger Congressional controls over the President's foreign policy activities may be caused by diverging opinions on the merits of specific initiatives, such as President Trump's tariffs on Chinese imports or President Obama's decision to participate in the 2011 Libya military campaign, or it may be due to differing opinions on the appropriate degree of Congressional oversight of the President as he engages in foreign policy-making. Regardless, it is difficult not to agree with Harold Koh, when he concluded in a 1988 article that the President '(almost) always wins in foreign affairs'.[32] This, in turn, means that Congress as a whole is not an effective political safeguard of foreign relations federalism in the US.

[28] Resolution 1973, adopted by the Security Council at its 6498th meeting, on 17 March 2011, <https://undocs.org/S/RES/1973(2011> accessed 28 January 2022.

[29] 19 US Code § 1862 (Trade Expansion Act).

[30] See eg S691—Global Trade Accountability Act, 117th Congress (2021–22), <www.congress.gov/bill/117th-congress/senate-bill/691?s=1&r=60> accessed 27 January 2022, and HR2618—Global Trade Accountability Act of 2021, 117th Congress (2021–22) <www.congress.gov/bill/117th-congress/house-bill/2618?s=2&r=47> accessed 27 January 2022, requiring Congressional approval of any proposed unilateral trade action that has the effect of increasing trade barriers.

[31] The Bill has three Republican cosponsors in addition to Republican Senator Lee who introduced the Bill. On earlier occasions, a similar bill failed to pass.

[32] Koh (n 23) 1255.

2.4 Informal Political Safeguards: Political Parties and Administrative Safeguards

Do informal political safeguards perhaps compensate for the absence of formal foreign relations federalism safeguards in the US? The answer must be in the negative. *Political parties* do not provide state governments with a meaningful say within the federal foreign policy-making process. Their ability to give voice to state interests is questionable. It is not clear, for example, why US political parties and the support they provide for federal officials would primarily protect regional interests. It appears equally possible—and perhaps more likely in an era of extremely polarized national politics[33]—for integrated political parties such as the Republican and Democratic Parties to operate as vehicles to nationalize state and local politics and pull state-level politics into the federal vortex.[34] The federal-state integration of political parties in the US in any case makes this type of scenario more likely to materialize than, for example, in Canada or Belgium, where political parties are less integrated (as in Canada) or not integrated at all (as in Belgium).

Can other informal political safeguards of foreign affairs federalism be identified? As for potential *fiscal safeguards* of federalism, states are not likely to obtain any influence in the federal political process by virtue of their fiscal resources as the bulk of fiscal capacity in the US is situated at the federal as opposed to the state level.[35] In marked contrast to the EU, the US federal government

[33] See generally Barbara F Walter, *How Civil Wars Start: And How to Stop Them* (Penguin 2022), arguing that polarization in the US has reached levels that risk leading the country into civil war.

[34] Emphasizing the integrative function of political parties in US federalism, see also Jessica Bulman-Pozen, 'Executive Federalism Comes to America' (2015) 102 Virginia Law Review 953, 975 ('In the United States ... the separation of powers and supermajority requirements impeded party government in Washington, but a national party system generates ties among state and federal actors'). In this sense, see also David Schleicher, 'The Seventeenth Amendment and Federalism in an Age of National Political Parties' (2014) 65 Hastings Law Journal 1043 and James A Gardner, 'The Myth of State Autonomy: Federalism, Political Parties, and the National Colonization of State Politics' (2013) 29 Journal of Law & Politics 1 ('[T]he growth of national political parties during and since the early nineteenth century created a two-way street'), and again in Larry M Bartels and Steven Rogers, 'National Forces in State Legislative Elections' (2016) 667 The ANNALS of the American Academy of Political and Social Science 207. ('[W]hile state legislatures wield considerable policymaking power, legislators' electoral fates appear to be largely out of their control'). For anecdotal evidence of this phenomenon, see eg Jonathan Martin and Alexander Burns, 'With Virginia, Voters Give Democrats First Big Wins of the Trump Era' *The New York Times* (New York City, 7 November 2017) <www.nytimes.com/2017/11/07/us/politics/virginia-election-democrats.html?_r=0> accessed 27 January 2022 ('Voters delivered their first forceful rebuke of President Trump and his party on Tuesday night, with Democrats exploiting Mr. Trump's deep unpopularity to capture the governorships in Virginia and New Jersey and make significant inroads into suburban communities that once favored the Republican Party').

[35] In 2009, federal revenues amounted to 3.3 trillion US dollars, whereas the combined revenue of all fifty states amounted to 2 trillion US dollars. See Walter Hellerstein, *Fiscal Federalism in the United States* (Turin 2011). Furthermore, the federal government's ability to borrow money dwarves that of any individual state.

never relies on state financial support for federal initiatives. Moving to *administrative safeguards*, as discussed, Larry Kramer argued that the state role in implementing federal law endows states with influence in the federal political process. Even if this still holds true in the domestic context—a point contested by Heather Gerken and Jessica Bulman-Pozen[36]—the hypothesis is likely to carry less weight in those areas of foreign policy-making, such as trade policy or defence policy, where state involvement in implementing federal law or policy is limited in the first place.

In other fields, such as immigration policy or environmental policy, the picture is different. In these policy areas, federal and state responsibilities overlap and state and federal officials must cooperate to effectively implement federal law. In such areas, one would expect state governments to have some degree of influence within the federal political process by virtue of the fact that states must implement the outcome of that process, and that the federal government cannot easily coerce states into enforcing federal law.[37] However, there is no empirical evidence available to corroborate such a hypothesis. If anything, there are signs that US governors who disagree with federal foreign policy choices interact with third countries independently of the US federal government.[38] This was visible, for example, in the wake of the US withdrawal from the Paris Agreement in 2017, which led governors of a number of US states to signal towards the international community that they remained committed to implementing the Agreement.[39] It would seem that some US governors, exasperated by a lack of voice within the federal foreign policy-making process, opted for an exit from parts of that process and instead branched out on their own, or together with like-minded governors, on issues on which they do not align with the federal government.[40] As the Trump administration made clear

[36] Jessica Bulman-Pozen and Heather K Gerken, 'Uncooperative Federalism' (2008) 118 Yale Law Journal 1256.

[37] States cannot be 'commandeered' into enforcing federal law in the US. See *Printz v United States*, 521 US 898 (1997). For a recent affirmation, see *Murphy v National Collegiate Athletic Ass'n*, 138 S Ct 1461 (2018), 1467 ('[T]he Constitution confers upon Congress the power to regulate individuals, not States'). However, the federal government can try to 'punish' for standing in the way of the effective implementation of federal law, eg by withholding grants. In this sense, see generally Greg Goelzhauser and David M Konisky, 'The State of American Federalism 2019–2020: Polarized and Punitive Intergovernmental Relations' (2020) 50 Publius: The Journal of Federalism 311.

[38] It should be emphasized, at the same time, that—despite extreme polarization on domestic issues—a bipartisan consensus continues to exist on many foreign policy issues. Highlighting this fact, see eg generally James D Bryan and Jordan Tama, 'The Prevalence of Bipartisanship in U.S. Foreign Policy: An Analysis of Important Congressional Votes' [2021] International Politics 874–97 <https://doi.org/10.1057/s41311-021-00348-7> accessed 20 September 2021.

[39] See eg Lisa Friedman and Brad Plumer, 'U.S. Governors at U.N. Assembly: "You Have Allies" on Climate Change' *The New York Times* (18 September 2017) <www.nytimes.com/2017/09/18/climate/climate-change-unga-governors.html> accessed 28 January 2022.

[40] On the connection between 'exit' and 'voice' in decision-making processes, see seminally Albert O Hirschman, *Exit, Voice, and Loyalty: Responses to Decline in Firms, Organizations, and States* (Harvard

when it challenged California's participation in the Quebec cap-and-trade emissions trading scheme,[41] in doing so they risk exposing their state(s) to pre-emption claims by the federal government, which may see in such initiatives an unconstitutional attempt at interfering with federal foreign policy. As there are no signs that state administrative capacity either strengthens or weakens the state voice in federal foreign policy-making, the state role in implementing federal law or policy is best understood as a neutral factor—one that does not operate as a political safeguard of federalism, but which does not weaken state autonomy either.

* * *

In summary, neither formal nor informal political safeguards of federalism are well developed in the US. In terms of *formal political safeguards*, the Senate is the main potential conduit for the representation of state interests in the federal foreign policy-making process. However, as discussed, the link between Senators and state governments is weak and the role of the Senate in the federal foreign policy process is small. Even in the treaty-making context, where the US Constitution grants the Senate a key role through its power to grant (or withhold) advice and consent, the Senate's role should not be overstated since over 90 per cent of international agreements concluded by the US take the form of executive agreements—often *sole* executive agreements that do not require Congressional legislation. The Senate can conceivably play a role in exercising oversight of the President as he engages in foreign policy-making. Yet, as discussed, it is difficult for Congress as a collective body to hold the President accountable. Finally, also in terms of *informal political safeguards*, the US offers a picture of relatively weak federalism safeguards. Political parties are nationalized in the US, states have limited fiscal capabilities, and the state role in implementing federal foreign policy (as eg in the implementation of the Paris Agreement) does not translate into a state voice in the federal political process. As we will see in the next section, similar observations can be made with regards to Canada, with one important exception: the informal safeguards of federalism are well developed north of the US–Canada border. The table below summarizes the findings (see Table 6.2).

University Press 1970). Hirschman's theory was put to a productive use by Joseph Weiler in his 'The Transformation of Europe' (1991) 100 Yale Law Journal 2403. On the rise of states and even cities as independent foreign policy actors in the US, see generally Rodrigo Tavares, *Paradiplomacy: Cities and States as Global Players* (Oxford University Press 2016).

[41] *US v California*, not reported in Fed Supp (2020), 2020 WL 4043034.

Table 6.2 Overview of the political safeguards of foreign relations federalism in the US

	The political safeguards of foreign relations federalism			
	Formal safeguards	*Informal safeguards*		
	Direct representation within the federal foreign policy-making process	Political parties	Administrative capacity	Fiscal capacity
United States	Weak	Weak	Neutral	Weak

3. Canada: Provinces as the Backbone of the Federation

Political scientist David Smith has argued that 'Canadian federalism is about jurisdiction rather than representation'.[42] Is he correct—in general? And in the specific context of foreign relations? Canada's federal institutions are modelled after the British example.[43] Referred to in Canada by the term 'responsible government', the Canadian federal government is structured along the lines of the Westminster model.[44] As discussed in the first chapter of this book, the power to engage in foreign relations, including the power to negotiate and make treaties and to ensure Canada's external representation in international bodies, falls within the scope of the prerogatives of the Crown.[45] Canada's federal executive advises the Crown on issues of foreign relations. In doing so, the federal executive in Canada is subject to the accountability mechanisms known to Westminster-style parliamentary democracies: the federal executive is to retain the confidence of the House of Commons and it is subject to parliamentary oversight by both the House of Commons and the Senate.[46] In addition, the federal executive relies on both the House of Commons and the Senate to enact legislation considered necessary in the conduct of Canada's foreign

[42] David E Smith, *Federalism and the Constitution of Canada* (University of Toronto Press 2013) 74.

[43] See the preamble to the Constitution Act, 1867: 'WHEREAS the Provinces of Canada, Nova Scotia, and New Brunswick have expressed their Desire to be federally united into One Dominion under the Crown of the United Kingdom of Great Britain and Ireland, *with a Constitution similar in Principle to that of the United Kingdom*' (emphasis added).

[44] See generally James R Mallory, *The Structure of Canadian Government* (Gage 1984).

[45] *Canada (Prime Minister) v Khadr*, [2010] 1 SCR 44, 2010 SCC 3 (CanLII) [35] ('The prerogative power over foreign affairs has not been displaced by s. 10 of the Department of Foreign Affairs and International Trade Act… and continues to be exercised by the federal government').

[46] For a classical articulation of Westminster-style parliamentary democracy, see Walter Bagehot, *The English Constitution*, vol 3 (1873) <http://socserv2.socsci.mcmaster.ca/econ/ugcm/3ll3/bagehot/constitution.pdf>accessed 28 January 2022. For an exploration of responsible government in Canada, see generally Mallory (n 44).

relations, including treaty-implementing legislation, the enactment of which is necessary for treaty obligations to become enforceable by Canadian courts.[47]

Does the Canadian Constitution provide for political safeguards of foreign relations federalism? As will be discussed, the constitutional and institutional arrangements in Canada are not altogether that different from those in the US—at least as far as the *formal* representation of member unit governments within the federal political process is concerned. In both North American federations, formal safeguards are weak. By contrast, the political environment within which the federal government of Canada operates is different from that in the US. Canadian provincial politics—primarily but not exclusively that of larger provinces—tends to trickle up and influence the federal political process (without going as far as to dominate it, however). As a result, despite the absence of formal safeguards, the federal political process—including on issues touching on foreign relations—is more mindful of the interests of provincial governments than that in the US, albeit that differences in size between individual Canadian provinces render provincial influence at the federal level unequal (the influence of Ontario, population 14.9 million, is greater than that of Prince Edward Island, population 166,000).[48]

3.1 Weak Formal Political Safeguards in a Westminster Parliamentary System

Within Canada's federal institutional framework, two institutions qualify as potential formal political safeguards of foreign relations federalism: the federal Senate and the federal Cabinet. On closer inspection, the effectiveness of either of these institutions in doing so reveals itself to be limited, however.

3.2 The Senate

The Constitution Act, 1867 requires the Canadian Senate to ensure a degree of regional representation. The Canadian Senate is divided into four divisions: one representing Western Canada, one Ontario, one Quebec, and one the Maritime provinces (New Brunswick, Nova Scotia, and Prince Edward Island).[49] Each

[47] On dualism in Canada, see eg Stéphane Beaulac, 'Arrêtons de dire que les tribunaux au Canada sont liés par le droit international' (2004) 38 Revue juridique Thémis 359.

[48] Statcan, Population estimates for Q4 2021, <www150.statcan.gc.ca/t1/tbl1/en/tv.action?pid=1710000901> accessed 28 January 2022.

[49] Constitution Act, 1867, s 22.

division mandatorily consists of four Senators to ensure that all Canadian regions have a minimum representation.[50] In addition, Newfoundland and Labrador, which joined Canada in 1949, are represented by six Senators, and each territory (Yukon, the Northwest Territories, and Nunavut) is represented by a single Senator.

Crucially, the Canadian Senate is an appointed chamber. The Governor General appoints Senators on the advice of the Prime Minister.[51] Provincial governments play no role in this process. As is the case for the US Senate, no direct institutional link thus exists between the 'federal chamber' and the member unit governments. As David Smith, mentioned earlier, suggested in his 2013 book *Federalism and the Constitution of Canada*, the Canadian Senate is best understood as an instrument to protect *regional* as opposed to *provincial* diversity within Canada, and in particular to grant a voice to the populations of the smaller Maritime provinces along Canada's Atlantic seaboard, which constitute a single economic and cultural but not a political unit within Canada.[52] In this sense, it is not entirely accurate to understand the Senate of Canada as a 'federal' chamber at all—a concept that evokes an institution which provides for a formal voice for the member unit governments within the federal political process.[53] And even by the standards of the US Senate, the Canadian Senate does not score well as a political safeguard of federalism as its members do not represent the geographically defined interests of Canada's provinces (the equivalent of US states), but rather those of larger 'regions' that encompass multiple provinces.

Furthermore, and crucially for our purposes, the Canadian Senate is not directly involved in Canada's foreign policy-making process. As is the case with its UK counterpart, the House of Lords, the Canadian federal Senate neither plays a role in the treaty-making procedure nor is it in a position to exercise political control over the federal executive. (The federal Cabinet is required only to retain the confidence of the directly elected House of Commons, not that of

[50] Pointing to this safeguard of regional representation: Smith (n 42) 63.

[51] Constitution Act, 1867, s 24.

[52] For a proposal to unite the Maritime provinces under a 'Maritime Union', see most recently Donald J Savoie, *Looking for Bootstraps: Economic Development in the Maritimes* (Nimbus Publishing Ltd 2017). The proposal is as old as confederation. The 1884 Charlottetown Conference, which became the first step towards confederation, was initially conceived as a meeting between the leaders of the Maritime provinces to discuss Maritime Union. Canadian mythology has it that the representatives of the Canadas (Upper and Lower) attended the meeting uninvited to persuade the Maritime Provinces to join in establishing a continent-wide Canadian confederation.

[53] In a similar sense, see also Wade K Wright, 'The Political Safeguards of Canadian Federalism: The Intergovernmental Safeguards' (2016) 36 National Journal of Constitutional Law 1, 18 ('[I]t is not clear that, as federal appointees and members of a federal institution, these senators would be inclined to vote to protect the jurisdiction of provincial institutions, as opposed to provincially-based interests').

the Senate.) Furthermore, in contrast to the US, where the President often acts on the basis of powers delegated to him by Congress, in Canada's parliamentary system the federal executive acts on the basis of its own constitutional prerogative powers, which leaves the legislature (including the Senate) in a weaker position compared to its US counterpart.

Likewise, in keeping with Canada's dualist approach to the reception of international treaty law,[54] treaties made by the federal Crown must be implemented via statute to have effect within Canada's domestic legal system—a process which involves both chambers of Canada's Parliament: the House of Commons and the Senate. But, as an appointed as opposed to a directly elected chamber, the Senate's legitimacy to vote down legislation is contested.[55] It follows that the Senate makes careful use of its powers. During the 1990s, for example, the Senate defeated only four bills, none of which have an obvious foreign policy dimension.[56] In the final analysis, the Canadian Senate's role in the Canadian foreign policy-making process is limited to that of drafting reports and conducting inquiries. In that context, the Senate Committee on Foreign Affairs and International Trade, and the Senate Committee on National Defence and Security are worth mentioning as they focus on issues pertaining to foreign relations.[57] If used well, these powers may enable the Canadian Senate to exercise some, albeit limited, oversight of Canada's federal executive as it engages in foreign relations.

3.3 The Federal Cabinet and the Prime Minister

Canada's federal Cabinet traditionally consists of representatives of all regions of Canada.[58] Yet here as well, as is the case for Canadian (and US) Senators, no

[54] See generally Beaulac (n 47) 359.

[55] In this sense, see also Wright (n 53) 17.

[56] The Bills were: Bill C-43 on abortion; Bill C-93 on the streaming of federal boards, agencies, commissions, and tribunals; Bill C-28 on the Lester B. Pearson International Airport in Toronto; and Bill C-220 on profiting from authorship with respect to a crime. See 'Canada's Senate: Sober Second Thought' *CBC News* (9 July 2010) <www.cbc.ca/news/canada/canada-s-senate-sober-second-thought-1.887861> accessed 28 January 2022. For a historical perspective on the Senate's legislative role, see John Lynch-Staunton, 'The Role of the Senate in the Legislative Process' [2000] Canadian Parliamentary Review 10.

[57] For an overview of the reports published during the 42nd Parliament (2015–19), see <https://sencanada.ca/en/Committees/aefa/Reports/42-1> accessed 1 February 2022.

[58] The practice of ensuring regional representation harks back to confederation in 1867. See in this sense Herman Bakvis, 'Regional Ministers, National Policies and the Administrative State in Canada: The Regional Dimension in Cabinet Decision-Making, 1980–1984' (1988) 21 Canadian Journal of Political Science/Revue canadienne de science politique 539, 542, who mentioned that '[f]rom [Canada's first Prime Minister] Macdonald's first ministry onward, the importance of regional

institutional link exists between the cabinet members and provincial governments. The Canadian Prime Minister appoints the members of his cabinet and he is under no constitutional obligation to ensure either regional or provincial representation.[59] Moreover, as cabinet meetings are confidential, it is difficult to assess to what extent individual members of the federal Cabinet in fact represent and defend the interests of their home province.[60] As Herman Bakvis and Brian Tanguay have pointed out, the extent to which cabinet ministers are able and willing to defend regional or provincial interests varies considerably from cabinet to cabinet, depending on the Prime Minister and ministers in question, and simply on the availability of elected MPs from the region in question.[61] A tradition did exist in Canada to include provincial chieftains in the federal Cabinet, who, once in office, played a role as the voice of their home province.[62] Nevertheless, just as common—and presumably more common in an era of increasing centralization of power within the Prime Minister's office—is the situation in which a cabinet member's loyalty lies first and foremost with the Prime Minister rather than with his or her home province.[63]

At a strictly institutional level, then—as is the case in the US—the architecture of Canada's federal government does not provide for strong federalism safeguards, let alone strong foreign relations federalism safeguards. This

considerations in the appointment of cabinet members has remained clear and can be ignored by prime ministers only at their peril.'

[59] Constitutional conventions are rules of political practice which are regarded as binding by those to whom they apply. While regional representation is a long-standing feature of Canadian federal cabinets, there is no evidence that the Prime Minister considers himself to be under an obligation to ensure regional representation. On constitutional conventions in Canada, see seminally *Re: Resolution to amend the Constitution*, [1981] 1 SCR 753, 1981 CanLII 25 (SCC), conforming the traditional understanding as articulated for example in Ivor Jennings, *The Law and the Constitution* (5th edition, 1959).

[60] SJR Noel, 'Consociational Democracy and Canadian Federalism' (1971) 4 Canadian Journal of Political Science/Revue canadienne de science politique 15, 17. ('The representative character of the cabinet, and particularly the emphasis placed on provincial representation, is well known. What is uncertain is the practical significance of this fact in the functioning of the political system').

[61] Herman Bakvis and A Brian Tanguay, 'Federalism, Political Parties, and the Burden of National Unity: Still Making Federalism Do the Heavy Lifting?' in Herman Bakvis and Grace Skogstad (eds), *Canadian Federalism: Performance, Effectiveness, and Legitimacy* (Oxford University Press 2012) 150.

[62] ibid 102–03. See, in a similar sense, Edwin R Black and Alan Cairns, 'A Different Perspective on Canadian Federalism' (1966) 9 Canadian Public Administration 27, 37–38, arguing that '[t]he institutional protection of the provinces at the federal capital, originally a task of the politically enfeebled Senate, has been assumed by the cabinet whose members not only are responsible for their government departments but are spokesmen as well for the interests of their home provinces'.

[63] In this sense, see Jean Leclair, 'Jane Austen and the Council of the Federation' (2006) 15 Constitutional Forum 51, 52 ('Party discipline, in particular, makes it impossible for individual members of the governing party to express the wishes and preferences of their region's constituents where these do not meet with the approval of Cabinet'). On the emergence of 'court government', understood here as a system of government in which power is increasingly centralized within the office of the Prime Minister, see generally Donald J Savoie, *Court Government and the Collapse of Accountability in Canada and the United Kingdom* (University of Toronto Press 2008).

conviction is widely shared in Canada where, as mentioned, commentators consider the absence of such safeguards one of the drivers of the process of 'province-building' that took place in the post-World War II period.[64] As in the US, and in keeping with the British monarchical tradition, the Canadian constitution centralizes foreign affairs powers within the (federal) executive. Unsurprisingly, it is the federal Cabinet—and increasingly the federal Prime Minister—which provides the necessary political leadership to Canadian foreign relations.[65] At least within the federal political process, Canadian member units do not have much influence. This raises the question: do provinces have alternative, less formal levers of influence at their disposal?

3.4 Informal Political Safeguards: Canada's Provinces

While formal political safeguards of foreign affairs federalism are thus as weak in Canada as they are in the US, informal safeguards are stronger in Canada compared to the US. Indeed, the constitutional picture characterized by weak formal safeguards in Canada must be read against a backdrop of a decentralized political landscape in which Canadian citizens turn as much to their provincial capitals as they do to Ottawa, the federal capital, in search of public services, and in which important bureaucracies have developed at both the federal *and* the provincial level of government in Canada. The strong position of Canada's provinces gives provincial governments at least an indirect voice within the federal political process, including on foreign relations questions.

How is this backdrop to be explained? With the important exception of the *Bloc québecois*, which participates in federal elections only in the province of Quebec, Canadian *political parties* do not play an important role in protecting the interests of provincial governments within the federal political process. In contrast to Belgium, where, as will be discussed, political parties are organized along regional lines, and member unit political parties thus operate at the federal and member unit levels, and in contrast also to the US, where political parties are organized nationally, in Canada twelve party systems co-exist: one

[64] Donald V Smiley, 'The Structural Problem of Canadian Federalism' (1971) 14 Canadian Public Administration/Administration publique du Canada 326 and Jean Leclair, 'The Securities Reference: The Ghost of Political Representation Comes Knocking at Federalism's Door' (Social Science Research Network 2012) SSRN Scholarly Paper ID 2189661 <http://papers.ssrn.com/abstract=2189661> accessed 1 February 2022.

[65] Nelson Michaud, 'The Prime Minister, PMO, and PCO: Makers of Canadian Foreign Policy?' in Patrick James, Nelson Michaud, and Marc J O'Reilly (eds), *Handbook of Canadian Foreign Policy* (Lexington Books 2006) 22 ('[T]he attention prime ministers have paid to international affairs—or lack thereof—has dictated in large part how Canada behaved on the international scene').

within each province, one within the Yukon territory, and one at the federal level.[66] (The territories of Nunavut and the Northwest Territories operate by consensus government and thus do not have political party systems.[67]) Mobility between federal and provincial political parties is not significant. Although movements do occur, politicians tend to build careers within either the federal or the provincial political arena.[68] While the influence of political parties in shaping Canadian federalism is an issue worth exploring in more detail, it is safe to conclude that political parties in Canada neither operate as channels to infuse provincial interests and policy preferences into the federal political process, as is the case in Belgium, nor as organizations that knit together the twelve provinces and territories into a single political community, as can be observed in the US, where national political parties draw state politics into the vortex of national politics.[69] Instead, the Canadian party system is best understood as a neutral factor in our analysis of political safeguards of foreign relations federalism.

A more promising place to look for an explanation of the significant voice provincial governments have within the federal political process in Canada is the role provincial governments have historically played in constructing the Canadian administrative state. In contrast with the US, which has seen the development—especially since the New Deal era—of an important federal administrative state active on a very broad range of issues, in Canada key elements of the administrative state have been spearheaded by Canada's provincial governments.[70] This was the case in part because the Constitution Act,

[66] See generally Kenneth Carty and William Cross, 'Political Parties and the Practice of Brokerage Politics' in John Courtney and David Smith (eds), *The Oxford Handbook of Canadian Politics* (Oxford University Press 2010).

[67] On government by consensus, and without political parties, in Nunavut see generally Graham White, 'Traditional Aboriginal Values in a Westminster Parliament: The Legislative Assembly of Nunavut' (2006) 12 The Journal of Legislative Studies 8.

[68] Former federal cabinet minister Jason Kenney for example has made the transfer from federal to Alberta politics. See J Gibson and D Bell, '"We Must Put Alberta First": Jason Kenney Launches PC Leadership Bid Urging Right to Unite' *CBC News* <www.cbc.ca/news/canada/calgary/jason-kenney-alberta-pc-wildrose-leadership-calgary-announcement-1.3666596> accessed 28 January 2022. Similarly, former Quebec Premier Jean Charest has been leader of both the federal Progressive Conservative Party and the Quebec Liberal Party. And in Conservative Prime Minister Stephen Harper's first minority government, seven out of twenty-seven cabinet ministers had previously served in provincial governments—a fact not seen since the founding of Canada, according to Bakvis and Tanguay (n 61) 148.

[69] See also Carty and Cross (n 66) 191 ('Canadian political parties are, by comparative standards, among the most organizationally weak and decentralized of parties in established democratic party systems').

[70] Discussing these contrasting developments, see generally J Milton Esman, 'Federalism and Modernization: Canada and the United States' (1984) 14 Publius 21. On the thesis that Canadian federalism is characterized by strong provincial governments which have engaged in projects of 'province-building', see eg Alan C Cairns, 'The Governments and Societies of Canadian Federalism' (1977) 10 Canadian Journal of Political Science 695, 699–700, mentioning that the Constitution Act, 1867 'created

1867 allocates exclusive responsibility over policy areas such as education, public health, and social policy to the provincial legislatures, not the federal Parliament, putting provincial governments in the driver's seat when it came to policy areas that became central tenets of the post-World War II welfare state.[71] This is of course a development that is not specific to the foreign relations context. However, the development of strong provincial governments spills over into the foreign relations sphere. As discussed in Chapter 2, unlike in the US, where the federal Congress possesses an implied power to implement federal treaty obligations that comes on top of Congress' already very broad concurrent legislative powers, in Canada *provincial* legislatures often have to implement treaty obligations incurred by the *federal* government.[72] This means that the presence of a foreign policy nexus does not *ipso facto* endow the federal government with the necessary powers to enact and implement policies. Instead, provinces retain important constitutional responsibilities.

Despite the lack of formal safeguards, these features of Canadian federalism grant Canada's provincial governments a greater voice in the federal foreign policy-making process than their US counterparts have. Simply put: because much of the constitutional authority, administrative capacity, and expertise to provide public goods and to address contemporary challenges such as climate change reside at the provincial level, provincial governments in Canada are in a comparatively strong position to influence the federal government when the latter engages in foreign relations on issues affecting those matters. These observations matter in particular because, as discussed in Chapter 2, only Canada's federal executive is empowered to make treaties. This means that Canada's federal government may find itself in a situation in which it negotiates international agreements on issues over which it does not have jurisdiction internally. Whenever that is the case, Canada's federal government has good reasons to consult provincial governments, which grants the latter a voice in the federal foreign policy-making process. It is for this reason, for example, that Canada's federal government closely involved provincial governments in

competitive political and bureaucratic elites at two levels of government endowed with an impressive array of jurisdictional, financial, administrative and political resources to deploy in the pursuit of their objectives'. For a recent reappraisal of the thesis, see generally Matt Wilder and Michael Howlett, 'Bringing the Provinces Back in: Re-Evaluating the Relevance of Province-Building to Theories of Canadian Federalism and Multi-Level Governance' (2015) 9 Canadian Political Science Review 1.

[71] See in particular s 92(7) of the Constitution Act, 1867 empowering the provincial legislatures to exclusively make laws in relation to '[t]he Establishment, Maintenance, and Management of Hospitals, Asylums, Charities, and Eleemosynary Institutions in and for the Province, other than Marine Hospitals'.

[72] *Attorney General for Canada v Attorney General for Ontario ('Labour Conventions')*, [1937] AC 326.

the negotiations with the EU on a free trade agreement—a topic to which I return in Chapter 8 on intergovernmental relations.[73]

The preceding conclusion—that is, that Canada's provincial governments have a voice within the federal foreign policy-making process by virtue of the fact that they hold the necessary administrative capacity and expertise to implement federal foreign policy—should be qualified to some extent by the lack of *fiscal* safeguards of federalism in Canada. The allocation of the powers to tax, borrow, and spend in Canada strengthens the position of the federal government vis-à-vis the provinces, including in areas over which provincial governments hold exclusive jurisdiction. It is constitutional in Canada for the federal government to spend federal monies on issues that fall outside of federal jurisdiction, and thus within provincial jurisdiction.[74] As a consequence, whenever the implementation of federal policies requires the spending of money, the federal government is in a stronger position compared to when such implementation can be achieved only by legislative or regulatory means. (In the former case, the federal government can take the necessary action; in the latter case, constitutional authority to act may lie with the provinces.[75]) This holds true also when federal foreign policy is involved. To return once again to the climate change file: one can imagine Canada's federal government mobilizing significant fiscal resources to reach Canada's Paris Agreement emission reduction targets, eg by directly subsidizing home renovations to make Canadian homes more energy efficient. It does not matter, in this regard, that the power to legislate on housing matters lies with the provincial legislatures.[76]

* * *

[73] In this sense, see Christopher Kukucha, 'Provincial Pitfalls—Canadian Provinces and the Canada-EU Trade Negotiations' in Kurt Hübner (ed), Europe, Canada and the Comprehensive Economic Partnership Agreement (Taylor & Francis 2011).

[74] In this sense, see eg *Reference Re Canada Assistance Plan (B.C.)*, [1991] 2 SCR 525, in which the Supreme Court of Canada confirmed that the Supreme Court does not supervise the federal government's exercise of its spending power in order to protect the autonomy of the provinces. In the same sense, see *Auton (Guardian ad litem of) v British Columbia (Attorney General)*, [2004] 3 SCR 657, 2004 SCC 78, appendix B: 'Under the Constitution Act, 1867, delivery of health care services lies primarily with the provinces. The federal government, however, has authority under its spending power to attach conditions to financial grants to the provinces that are used to pay for social programs.'

[75] Hoi Kong has argued that the Constitution Act, 1867, does impose substantive limits on the federal government's use of the spending power—limits that are not related to the division of powers between the federal and provincial governments. See generally Hoi L Kong, 'The Spending Power in Canada' in *The Oxford Handbook of the Canadian Constitution*, vol 1 (Oxford University Press 2017).

[76] Constitution Act, 1867, s 92(13), allocates exclusive legislative power over 'Property and Civil Rights in the Province' to the provincial legislatures. Housing policy is understood as falling within this category. This has not stopped the federal government, however, from playing an important role in this policy area through its use of the spending power. See eg the National Housing Strategy Act, SC 2019, c 29, s 313, which in its preamble indicates it aims to implement the right to housing contained in the International Covenant on Economic, Social and Cultural Rights, to which Canada is a party.

Table 6.3 Overview of the political safeguards of foreign relations federalism in Canada

	The political safeguards of foreign relations federalism			
	Formal safeguards	*Informal safeguards*		
	Direct representation within the federal foreign policy-making process	Political parties	Administrative capacity	Fiscal capacity
Canada	Weak	Neutral	Strong	Weak

In summary, Canadian provinces do not benefit from strong formal political safeguards of federalism—either in the domestic or in the foreign relations context. However, they do derive influence within the federal political process from their administrative capacities and expertise, as well as from the Labour Conventions principle, which requires the federal government to turn to the provinces to ensure full implementation of treaty obligations when such implementation requires legislative action on issues within provincial exclusive jurisdiction. These factors—coupled with the fact that Canada consists of merely thirteen provinces and territories (compared to the fifty US states), but counterbalanced to some extent by the fact that the federal government can spend money also outside of the scope of its legislative powers in Canada—mean that Canadian provinces and territories are strong political players within the Canadian federation, whose interests and values the federal government must take into account in the conduct of its foreign relations. The table below summarizes the findings (see Table 6.3).

4. Belgium: Political Parties as Informal Safeguards

Compared to the US and Canada, both formal and informal political safeguards of foreign relations federalism are well developed in Belgium. Before exploring these safeguards in greater depth, a note of caution: when exploring federalism safeguards in Belgium, it is important to be mindful of whom exactly the safeguards purport to protect. The Belgian federation is characterized by a juxtaposition of two conceptions of federalism: a '*fédéralisme à trois*' (Brussels, Flanders, Wallonia), and a '*fédéralisme à deux*' (French-speaking versus Dutch-speaking communities).[77] Most of the political safeguards of federalism in Belgium purport to protect the interests of the two main linguistic-cultural communities, while some protect the institutional interests of the various member unit governments.[78] With this distinction in mind, in this section I look at the political safeguards of foreign relations federalism in Belgium. Both formal and informal safeguards in Belgium are strong, including in the foreign policy-making process. This makes for a significant contrast with both North American federations and in particular with the US, where, as discussed, neither formal nor informal federalism safeguards are well developed. By contrast, it puts Belgium in the company of the EU. Both the EU and Belgium have strong informal and formal safeguards.

4.1 Formal Political Safeguards to Protect Belgium's Linguistic Communities

In all three of the main federal political institutions in Belgium—the federal Cabinet, the House of Representatives, and the Senate—mechanisms have been introduced to prevent one linguistic community from imposing its will on the other community. Importantly for our present purposes, these mechanisms apply internally as well as externally.

4.2 The Federal Cabinet

The Belgian federal Cabinet—*Conseil des ministres* in French, *Ministerraad* in Dutch—consists of an equal number of French- and Dutch-speaking ministers, excluding the Prime Minister and the secretaries of state.[79] Crucially, both of the main linguistic communities are represented in the 'Kern'. (The 'Kern'—a

[77] In this sense, see Johan Lievens and Karel Reybrouck, 'Reanimating Brussels—The Beating Heart of the Belgian Federation' in Ernst Hirsch Ballin and others (eds), *European Yearbook of Constitutional Law 2020: The City in Constitutional Law* (TMC Asser Press 2021) 55. For an introduction to Belgium's federal arrangements, see also Patricia Popelier, 'Intergovernmental Relations in Belgium: Obstacles to Effective Cooperation in Dyadic Federalism' in Yonatan T Fessha, Karl Kössler, and Francesco Palermo (eds), *Intergovernmental Relations in Divided Societies* (Springer International Publishing 2022) 65–68.

[78] Johanne Poirier, 'Les fédérations belge et canadienne: essai de comparaison synthétique et systématique' [2009] Revue du droit de l'ULB 13, 26 ('*De toute manière, in fine, la bi-polarisation entre francophones et néerlandophones domine le paysage tant constitutionnel que politique*').

[79] Belgian Constitution, art 99. For an inquiry, see Jan Velaers, 'De pariteit in de Ministerraad (Artikel 99, Tweede Lid van de Grondwet): Een vereiste met een louter taalkundige, een communautaire of ook een "taalgroep-Parlementaire" Betekenis?' [2015] Tijdschrift voor Bestuurswetenschappen en Publiekrecht 4.

Dutch term used by Dutch and French speakers in Belgium which translates into English as the 'core'—is the gathering of the Prime Minister and his deputy Prime Ministers which sets much of the Belgian federal government's policy.) As the 'Kern' operates on the basis of consensus, each linguistic community thus holds a veto power over federal government policy.[80] Considering the centrality of the Belgian federal Cabinet within the federal political process, the constitutionally mandated linguistic parity within the federal Cabinet is an important formal political safeguard of federalism in Belgium, at least if one accepts the characterization of Belgium as a dyadic—or bicommunal[81]—federation consisting of two linguistic-cultural communities (French- and Dutch-speaking), rather than as a federation consisting of a larger number of governments (Flanders, Wallonia, Brussels, and the German-speaking community). Noteworthy, in that regard, is that the function of the Prime Minister in Belgium is necessarily more closely aligned with the traditional conception of cabinet government in which the Prime Minister operates as a consensus-seeking *primus inter pares*, that is, a chairman responsible for facilitating the process of consensus-building amongst the different ministers and the political parties they represent.[82] This arrangement can be contrasted with that in Canada, where the Prime Minister has become a president-like figure with political power increasingly concentrated in the office of the Prime Minister.[83]

4.3 The Federal House of Representatives

In contrast to the federal Cabinet, the Belgian federal House of Representatives does not consist of an equal number of representatives of each linguistic-cultural community. Instead, the number of MPs depends on population numbers.[84] This makes the House the primary means of democratic representation of the Belgian citizenry. That being said, the framers of the Belgian Constitution also introduced mechanisms in the House of Representatives that

[80] Marc Hooghe, 'Wat een vicepremier moet doen' *De Standaard* (10 February 2015) <www.standaard.be/cnt/dmf20150209_01519905> accessed 3 February 2022.

[81] On the notion of dyadic federalism, see generally Ivo D Duchacek, 'Dyadic Federations and Confederations' (1988) 18 Publius 5.

[82] The phenomenon of 'court government' described by Donald Savoie in the Canadian context does not seem to manifest itself in the Belgian context. In this sense, see generally Jean-Luc Dehaene, 'De (on)macht van de Eerste Minister: Een a-wetenschappelijke ervaringsbenadering' (2001) 42 Res Publica 23, 25, discussing the power resources the Belgian Prime Minister has at his or her disposal. The impression left by this former Belgian PM is one of a role of the PM as *primus inter pares*, who, despite a weak formal position, can exercise significant influence if he or she is strategic and is a good team player.

[83] See generally Savoie (n 63).

[84] Belgian Constitution, art 63.

aim to protect the autonomy of the two main linguistic-cultural communities, and in particular the autonomy of the French-speaking minority, which otherwise would find itself at risk of being outvoted by the larger number of Dutch-speaking MPs. (By contrast, the small German-speaking community is not protected in the federal House.)

The mechanisms to protect the French-speaking minority in the federal House work as follows. Each federal MP is a member of a 'linguistic group' within the federal House.[85] As of 2021, the House consisted of eighty-eight Dutch-language MPs and sixty-two French-language MPs.[86] (There is no German linguistic group; the sole German MP is a member of the French linguistic group.[87]) Per a procedure colloquially referred to as the 'alarm bell' procedure, treatment of a Bill regarded by three-quarters of the members of one linguistic group as damaging to the interests of that group will be suspended, and the federal Cabinet will have to issue a reasoned opinion on the Bill.[88] This mechanism evacuates the contested issue from the House to the federal Cabinet, which, as mentioned, operates on the basis of equality between both linguistic groups.

The alarm bell procedure has only been put in motion twice, and most recently in the late 2000s, when a Dutch-speaking majority of members of the House voted in favour of splitting an electoral district in the suburbs surrounding Brussels inhabited by significant numbers of French- and Dutch-speaking citizens into two separate districts—one inhabited primarily by French-speakers, the other by Dutch-speakers.[89] Relevant for present purposes is that in the context of foreign relations—and in particular the specific context of treaty-making, where ratification requires parliamentary approval—the alarm bell procedure has never been used. It is moreover unlikely to be used in the future, considering the amount of international agreements that are concluded as mixed agreements in Belgium. If an agreement is mixed, each Belgian legislature can block the agreements ratification—no recourse to the alarm bell procedure needed. If an international agreement is federal-only, the alarm bell procedure could hypothetically be used by either of the two language groups to

[85] Two such groups exist: one French-speaking, and one Dutch-speaking, whereby the German-speaking member(s) of the House are grouped with the French-speaking members, and the members representing Brussels have the ability to choose to which group they wish to belong. See Belgian Constitution, art 43.

[86] Chambre des représentants de Belgique, Doc 55 000/015, 12 October 2021.

[87] House rules of procedure, art 10, available at <www.dekamer.be/kvvcr/pdf_sections/publications/reglement/reglementNL.pdf> accessed 1 February 2022.

[88] Belgian Constitution, art 54 and House rules of procedure, art 104.

[89] 'De Kwestie-BHV Verdwijnt in de Koelkast' (*deredactie.be*, 29 April 2010) <www.vrt.be/vrtnws/nl/2010/04/29/de_kwestie-bhv_verdwijntindekoelkast-1-769903/> accessed 1 February 2022.

block the ratification process. This would be a possibility since parliamentary approval to a treaty is granted by means of a statute,[90] and the alarm bell procedure applies indiscriminately to all Bills.[91]

Whereas the alarm bell procedure protects the interests of the two linguistic-cultural *communities* as represented in the federal House, the 'conflict of interests' procedure protects the interests of the regional and community *governments*.[92] Under this procedure, member unit governments (both their executive and legislative branches) also have the authority to suspend the federal legislative process when they consider a federal Bill to run counter the interests of their government. A conflict of interests procedure transfers the controversy to the Concertation Committee (*Comité de concertation* or *Overlegcomité*) rather than to the federal Cabinet, after the Senate has issued an opinion.[93] As with the alarm bell procedure, the conflict of interests procedure has never been used for treaty ratification Bills, even though the procedure could be used in this context as well.

4.4 The Federal Senate

The Senate is a third federal institution that could operate as a formal safeguard of foreign relations federalism in Belgium. In terms of its composition, the Senate clearly constitutes a 'federal' chamber: fifty out of its sixty members are also members of regional or community legislatures.[94] However, the Belgian Senate does not have significant responsibilities.[95] While Belgium used

[90] See eg Wet houdende instemming met het Verdrag tussen het Koninkrijk België en de Volksrepubliek China inzake de overbrenging van gevonniste personen, opgemaakt te Beijing op 31 oktober 2016, *BS* 31 May 2021.

[91] House rules of procedure, art 14 first para: 'Une motion peut être déposée prévoyant que les dispositions d'un projet ou d'une proposition de loi qu'elle désigne sont de nature à porter gravement atteinte aux relations entre les Communautés.'

[92] Belgian Constitution, art 143; and also, for the Federal House, House rules of procedure, arts 101–03, and Ordinary Law on Institutional Reform of 9 August 1980, *BS* 15 August 1980 ('OLIR'), arts 31–33*bis*.

[93] OLIR, art 32. The Concertation Committee consists of representatives of the executives of the different governments. It increasingly operates as the main forum for intergovernmental relations in Belgium. In this sense, see Emmanuel Vandenbossche, 'Het Overlegcomité: een instelling in opmars?' in Emmanuel Vandenbossche and Xavier Delgrange (eds), *Evoluties in het Belgisch cooperatief federalisme. Évolutions dans le fédéralisme coopératif belge* (Die Keure 2015). The Concertation Committee became the main decision-making body for the adoption of measures to tackle Covid-19 in Belgium. On the role of the Concertation Committee during Covid-19, see Dave Sinardet and Jade Pieters, 'Nationalism and COVID in Belgium: A Surprisingly United Response in a Divided Federal Country' (2021) 27 Nationalism and Ethnic Politics 311, 315–16.

[94] Belgian Constitution, art 67.

[95] Patricia Popelier, 'Bicameralism in Belgium: The Dismantlement of the Senate for the Sake of Multinational Confederalism' (2018) 10 Perspectives on Federalism 215, describing how the Belgian

to adhere to full bicameralism at the federal level, today the federal Senate has become a body with few constitutional responsibilities. Only rarely does it play a role in the legislative process, and it is never involved in the process of ratifying treaties.[96] Moreover, as is the case for the Canadian Senate, the federal executive does not have to maintain the confidence of a majority of the Belgian senators; this role is fulfilled exclusively by the federal House.[97]

One function the Belgian federal Senate continues to fulfil is that of issuing opinions in the abovementioned conflicts of interests procedure. When a conflict of interests is triggered by a member unit legislature, the federal legislative process is suspended.[98] This suspension serves to create the necessary time to reach a compromise. If no compromise can be found within sixty days, the Senate issues an opinion to the abovementioned Concertation Committee, which in turn has to find a solution within thirty days.[99] The gradual scaling down of the Senate's responsibilities that started in the early 1990s has led commentators to question the Senate's very existence. Some, including the current president of the Senate at the time of writing (February 2022),[100] argue for its abolition; others envisage a future as a think tank on constitutional questions.[101] In any case, it is clear that the Belgian Senate does not play a role in the conduct of Belgium's foreign relations. Telling, in that regard, is the lack of a Senate foreign relations committee.

4.5 Informal Safeguards: The Central Role of Political Parties in Belgian Federalism

Characteristic of Belgian federalism is the central role of political parties as federalism safeguards. It has become commonplace in Belgium to

Senate gradually turned into a House representative of the sub-states, while at the same time losing many of its responsibilities.

[96] But see arts 77 and 78 of the Belgian Constitution.

[97] Only the federal House can issue a motion to retract its confidence in the federal cabinet or vote down a motion of confidence in the federal cabinet. See art 46 of the Belgian Constitution.

[98] OLIR, art 32 §1*quater*. For an example, see 'Steven Vanackere: "Senaat heeft haar rol van bemiddelaar correct gespeeld"' <www.cdenv.be/wie-zijn-we/cdenv-als-politieke-partij/de-senaat/actua/steven-vanackere-senaat-heeft-haar-rol-van-bemiddelaar-correct-gespeeld/> accessed 1 February 2022.

[99] OLIR, art 32 §1*quater*.

[100] 'Senaatsvoorzitter Stephanie D'Hose (Open VLD) wil Senaat afschaffen' (*vrtnws.be*, 8 January 2022) <www.vrt.be/vrtnws/nl/2022/01/08/senaatsvoorzitter-wil-senaat-afschaffen/> accessed 1 February 2022.

[101] In this sense, see eg Jurgen Goossens and Pieter Cannoot, 'Belgian Federalism after the Sixth State Reform' (2015) 7 Perspectives on Federalism 40.

characterize the Belgian political system as a 'partitocracy', that is, a system of government in which political parties control different levers of the government apparatus and the political decision-making process.[102] The label fits Belgium well in light of the particularly pronounced form of party discipline, the relatively centralized structure of political parties in Belgium,[103] and, coupled with that, the existence of elaborate networks of political patronage within those parties.[104] When political parties began to split along linguistic-cultural lines from the 1970s onwards, they became torchbearers for their respective communities.[105] Unlike in the US or Canada, no national or even federal political parties exist in Belgium. The 'knitting together' function of parties visible in the US is absent in Belgium. To the contrary, the absence of national political parties, coupled with the presence in a single region of two large ethno-regionalist parties, further entrenches the autonomy of the two linguistic-cultural communities in Belgium and infuses federal decision-making with centrifugal dynamics.[106]

The role of political parties in managing federalism in Belgium is significant, especially when *congruent* coalitions are in power at the different levels of government. In such a constellation, party leaders can informally discuss issues with one another on a cross-jurisdictional basis. By contrast, when coalitions are *incongruent* (ie when different coalitions are in power in different governments), leader-to-leader discussions are more difficult, as at least in one government the leaders find themselves on different sides of the aisle. In such a context, the formal mechanisms of intergovernmental relations—and in particular the Concertation Committee—play a more outspoken role.[107]

[102] Lieven De Winter, Donatella Della Porta, and Kris Deschouwer, 'Partitocracies Between Crises and Reform: The Cases of Italy and Belgium' (1996) 2 Res publica: politiek-wetenschappelijk tijdschrift van de Lage Landen 215.

[103] Lieven De Winter and Patrick Dumont, 'Do Belgian Parties Undermine the Democratic Chain of Delegation?' (2006) 29 West European Politics 957, 964.

[104] Highlighting the role of patronage in the political party system in Belgium, see Patricia Popelier and Koen Lemmens, *The Constitution of Belgium: A Contextual Analysis* (Bloomsbury Publishing 2015) 108.

[105] Lieven De Winter, Marc Swyngedouw, and Patrick Dumont, 'Party System(s) and Electoral Behaviour in Belgium: From Stability to Balkanisation' (2006) 29 West European Politics 933, 934–38, describing the process of fragmentation of Belgium's political parties.

[106] The term 'ethno-regionalist' party is borrowed from Popelier and Lemmens (n 14) 108. On the role of regionalist parties as catalyst for the splitting up of Belgium's national political parties, see Emilie Van Haute and Jean-Benoit Pilet, 'Regionalist Parties in Belgium (VU, RW, FDF): Victims of Their Own Success?' (2006) 16 Regional & Federal Studies 297.

[107] For an example, see F Segers, 'Demotte dreigt met belangenconflict over onbelast bijverdienen' (*vrtnws.be*, 18 December 2017) <www.vrt.be/vrtnws/nl/2017/12/18/demotte-dreigt-met-belangenconflict-over-onbelast-bijverdienen/> accessed 1 February 2022.

The impact of the composition of coalitions within the different Belgian governments on Belgium's ability to conduct a coherent foreign policy is apparent, for example, in the context of climate policy.[108] In 2010, incongruent coalitions entered office at the federal and member unit levels. At that time, Belgium was called on by the EU to reach an intra-Belgium agreement on the division of emission reduction targets between the different Belgian governments. It took six years to reach an agreement. The presence of the French-speaking Green Party in the governing coalition in Wallonia (in favour of demanding targets), and the dominance of centre-right parties in Flanders (in favour of less demanding targets) complicated negotiations. After federal and regional elections took place in 2014, a centre-right coalition came into office at the federal level, while the French-speaking socialists retained control over the Brussels and Wallonia executives. This constellation further complicated discussions.[109] External pressure—in particular from the Paris Climate Conference, where Belgium was required to make a concrete commitment to reduce emissions—turned out to be needed to reach an agreement. In early December 2015, after the Paris Climate Conference had already started, an agreement was finally reached.[110]

The protracted negotiations that were needed to reach an intra-Belgian climate change agreement demonstrate the degree to which political parties in Belgium can facilitate or—as in this case—complicate policy-making, including on subjects with a significant external dimension such as climate policy. Complications such as those in the climate change file had not occurred prior to 2010 when congruent as opposed to incongruent coalitions were in office at both levels of government. It is noteworthy that it took so long for different governing coalitions to come to power at both levels of government in

[108] On this subject, see eg Sander Happaerts, Simon Schunz, and Hans Bruyninckx, 'Federalism and Intergovernmental Relations: The Multi-Level Politics of Climate Change Policy in Belgium' (2012) 20 Journal of Contemporary European Studies 441, 445–46, demonstrating how intergovernmental relations in Belgium are controlled by political parties and ministerial cabinets. The authors contend that this becomes problematic in a context of political asymmetry, where the distinct levels of government are ruled by different coalitions.

[109] In this sense, see Mathieu Dekleermaker, 'Une histoire belge: La coopération en matière environnementale et climatique et la COP21' (2019) 18 Fédéralisme Régionalisme 15 <https://popups.uliege.be/1374-3864/index.php?id=1792> accessed 17 July 2022.

[110] Dominique Fiers, 'Belgische klimaatakkoord eindelijk rond' (*deredactie.be*, 4 December 2015) <www.vrt.be/vrtnws/nl/2015/12/04/belgische_klimaatakkoordeindelijkrond-1-2514770/> accessed 1 February 2022.

Belgium, considering that the constitutional architecture that enabled different majorities to take power had been in place since 1993.[111]

The lack of national political parties thus operates as an important informal foreign relations federalism safeguard in Belgium. Can the same be said of the *administrative* and *fiscal* safeguards of federalism in Belgium? In keeping with the dual structure of Belgian federalism, the administrative capacity to implement laws and policies follows the allocation of legislative powers in Belgium. This distinguishes Belgium from the EU, where EU law is generally implemented by the Member State administrations,[112] and aligns it more closely to the Canadian and US models, where executive power follows legislative power and each level of government has at its disposal its own bureaucracy to implement policies. This means that, as is the case in Canada, both the federal and member unit governments in Belgium have significant administrative capacities. There is however a difference worth noting: in Canada, the federal government's exclusive power to conclude treaties makes for situations in which the federal government will negotiate treaties on issues over which it lacks domestic legislative competence, and thus administrative capacity and expertise. As discussed, this imbalance may give provincial governments an indirect voice in the federal decision-making process. Not so in Belgium, where—as discussed in Chapter 2—the member unit governments hold their own treaty-making powers over issues over which they have exclusive competence domestically. Member unit administrative capacity is thus more likely to be used to support the member unit government's own external actions than to be used to support the government's efforts to influence the federal decision-making process. In light of this feature of Belgium's foreign relations federalism, which distinguishes Belgium from Canada, I qualify the significant administrative capacity of Belgium's member units nonetheless as a neutral factor in the assessment of Belgium's political safeguards of foreign relations federalism.

Turning now to *fiscal* federalism safeguards: despite recent constitutional changes, the fiscal autonomy of the Belgian member units remains limited, and fiscal autonomy does not fully follow jurisdictional autonomy. The bulk of the

[111] See on this Wilfried Swenden, 'Asymmetric Federalism and Coalition-Making in Belgium' (2002) 32 Publius: The Journal of Federalism 67, pointing to the stabilizing role played by congruent coalitions in Belgium's asymmetric federal set-up.

[112] TFEU, art 291(1). See also Robert Schütze, 'From Rome to Lisbon: "Executive Federalism" in the European Union' (2010) 47 Common Market Law Review 1385.

funding of the Belgian member units consists of grants by the federal government, and the member units have limited authority to either borrow or tax.[113] However, the quasi-constitutional statute governing the distribution of federally levied taxes to the member units provides for a set of objective allocation factors. These objective factors ensure that in Belgium, in contrast to Canada as well as the US, the Belgian federal government cannot use its power to tax and spend to influence, let alone steer, member unit policy in areas outside of the federal government's exclusive jurisdiction (a federal power known in Canada as the federal spending power).[114] Rather, by embedding the rules on how federal government revenue is to be divided between Belgium's different governments in a quasi-constitutional statute, the issue has been evacuated from the arena of everyday politics. As a consequence, while the Belgian member units cannot make use of any autonomous fiscal capabilities to influence the federal foreign policy-making process, the converse is not possible either: the Belgian federal government cannot make use of its powers to tax, borrow, and spend to influence member unit policy choices. It follows that in Belgium the fiscal safeguards of foreign relations federalism are really not safeguards at all; they protect neither the autonomy of the federal government nor that of the member unit governments, and they certainly do not contribute to granting the member unit governments a voice in the federal foreign policy-making process.

* * *

In summary, Belgian foreign relations federalism is characterized by strong formal and informal safeguards. In particular, the role of political parties is key in ensuring that the Belgian member units have a say in federal decision-making processes. As political parties are organized along linguistic-cultural lines, they operate as champions of regional interests within the Belgian federation. As the case of the climate negotiations demonstrates, the strength of political parties in Belgium goes hand in hand with a comparatively weak federal executive, whose ability to exercise political leadership is dependent not

[113] For fiscal year 2022, 56 per cent of the revenue of the Flemish government is expected to consist of federal government grants. The amount of these grants is calculated as a fixed share of the federal income tax revenues. See Matthias Diependaele, 'Vlaamse begroting 2022' (Government of Flanders 2022) 8 <https://docs.vlaamsparlement.be/docs/begroting/bo2022/210927%20Begroting2022-centenboekje.pdf> accessed 4 February 2022.

[114] Special Law of 16 January 1989 Concerning the Financing of the Communities and the Regions, *BS* 17 January 1989.

Table 6.4 Overview of the political safeguards of foreign relations federalism in Belgium

	The political safeguards of foreign relations federalism			
	Formal safeguards	*Informal safeguards*		
	Direct representation within the federal foreign policy-making process	Political parties	Administrative capacity	Fiscal capacity
Belgium	Strong	Strong	Neutral	Neutral

only on the coalition of political parties that support the federal Cabinet in the House, but also (indirectly) on the governing coalitions at the member unit levels of government. By contrast, administrative and fiscal safeguards of federalism are neutral factors: they neither strengthen nor weaken the member unit voice in the federal foreign policy-making process. The table below summarizes the findings (see Table 6.4).

5. Conclusion

Weak political safeguards of foreign relations federalism in the two North American federations versus strong safeguards in Belgium: this is the picture that emerges from the analysis of the political safeguards of foreign relations federalism in the US, Canada, and Belgium undertaken in this chapter. Zooming in a bit closer, we observed how in the US neither formal nor informal safeguards are strong. In Canada, by contrast, weak formal safeguards are complemented with strong informal safeguards, endowing provincial governments with influence in the federal foreign policy-making process—in particular when issues that domestically fall within the exclusive jurisdiction of the provinces are involved. In Belgium, both formal and informal safeguards are strong, making Belgium a federation in which the autonomy of member units is particularly well protected. However, in contrast to Canada, in Belgium the strong informal federalism safeguards do not necessarily translate into a strong member unit voice in the federal foreign policy-making process. Rather, due to the fact that the Belgian member units have their own exclusive foreign relations powers, they are more likely to engage in government-to-government relations than is the case in Canada, where the federal government retains an

Table 6.5 Overview of the political safeguards of foreign relations federalism in the US, Canada, and Belgium

	The political safeguards of foreign relations federalism				**Overall assessment**
	Formal safeguards	*Informal safeguards*			
	Direct representation within the federal foreign policy-making process	Political parties	Administrative capacity	Fiscal capacity	
United States	Weak	Weak	Neutral	Weak	Weak
Canada	Weak	Neutral	Strong	Weak	Neutral
Belgium	Strong	Strong	Neutral	Neutral	Strong

exclusive power to make treaties. The table below shows how the different types of safeguards play out in the three federations explored in this chapter (see Table 6.5).

7

The Political Safeguards of EU Foreign Relations Federalism

> The European Council shall provide the Union with the necessary impetus for its development and shall define the general political directions and priorities thereof.
>
> Article 15(1) TEU

1. Introduction

Do the EU Treaties provide for effective political safeguards of foreign relations federalism in the EU? In this chapter, I argue that the EU Treaties provide for both strong formal and informal political safeguards. In so doing, the EU Treaties ensure that the Member States have a strong voice in the EU foreign policy-making process, and that—because of this voice—the EU institutions cannot unilaterally encroach on the autonomy of Member States. The purpose of the chapter is not to provide an exhaustive account of how the EU institutions conduct foreign relations. Rather, I aim to highlight and assess the ways in which the interests of the member units of the EU federation are given expression within the EU political process, both directly, through formal safeguards, and indirectly, through informal safeguards.

2. Formal Safeguards: The Two Councils at the Heart of EU Decision-Making

As an American observer once observed: 'Decision-making in the European Union is complex ... It is difficult for all but the most committed analysts of the EU to fully understand the formal process by which the EU makes decisions.'[1]

[1] Dorothee Heisenberg, 'The Institution of "Consensus" in the European Union: Formal versus Informal Decision-Making in the Council' (2005) 44 European Journal of Political Research 65, 65.

Foreign Relations Federalism. Thomas Verellen, Oxford University Press. © Thomas Verellen 2023.
DOI: 10.1093/oso/9780192844569.003.0007

There is truth to the statement. The institutional balance established by the EU Treaties does not fit easily within the *trias politica*: while it is possible to discern traces of the three functions identified by Montesquieu (legislative, executive, and judicial), the different functions are not neatly allocated to distinct institutions.[2] Instead, different EU institutions exercise different aspects of the three functions. This feature of the EU's institutional architecture, along with the compound structure of the EU, renders the institutional landscape opaque and difficult to understand for the outside observer. This is the case in particular with regard to the executive function, which in both its political and its administrative dimensions is fragmented, with Commission, Council, and European Council each exercising executive functions. This diffusion of executive authority between different EU institutions makes it difficult in the EU context to speak of an EU 'government' in the sense typically given to that term in common law jurisdictions such as Canada or the US.[3]

Four institutions and one office play a role in the articulation and implementation of EU foreign relations broadly considered—thus including both Common Foreign and Security Policy (CFSP) and non-CFSP issues: the European Council, the Council, the Commission, the European Parliament, and the High Representative.[4] In addition, the presidents of the European Council and the European Commission play roles of their own. The infographic below visualizes the institutional framework within which EU foreign relations are conducted (see Figure 7.1). The arrows represent lines of control whereby the direction of the arrow indicates who is in a position to issue instructions to whom. The two-way arrow between the Council and Parliament indicates that these two institutions operate on the basis of equality.

Do the above institutions provide for a member unit voice within the EU foreign policy-making process? Do they operate as formal political safeguards of foreign relations federalism? Undeniably so. The European Council and the

[2] For earlier explorations of the EU institutional framework from a separation of powers perspective, see Koen Lenaerts, 'Some Reflections on the Separation of Powers in the European Community' (1991) 28 Common Market Law Review 11; Gerard Conway, 'Recovering a Separation of Powers in the European Union' (2011) 17 European Law Journal 304. Much earlier, Emile Noel, then Secretary General of the European Commission, referred to the institutional framework of the EEC as constituting a 'separation of powers'. See Emile Noel, 'The Commission's Power of Initiative' (1973) 10 Common Market Law Review 123, 124 ('The Treaties set up a particular form of separation of powers').

[3] In this sense, see Deirdre Curtin, 'Democratic Accountability of EU Executive Power: A Reform Agenda for Parliaments' in Federico Fabbrini, EMH Hirsch Ballin, and Han Somsen (eds), *What Form of Government for the European Union and the Eurozone?* (Hart Publishing 2015) 175 ('[T]here is no single, comprehensive and unitary European executive institution or body that can, in a meaningful way, be described as an EU government in the sense that we know it from the national domain').

[4] I do not discuss the European External Action Service, which is best understood as operating at the bureaucratic-administrative level.

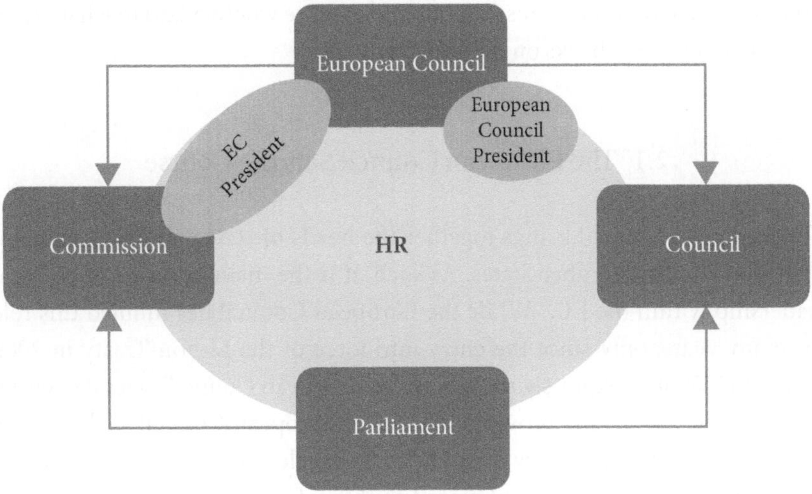

Figure 7.1 The institutional balance in EU foreign relations

Council consist of direct representatives of the executives of the twenty-seven Member States, either at the highest political level in the case of the European Council, or at the ministerial level in the case of the Council. The members of both Councils are thus double-hatted: they are *national* office-holders, who—when they meet in the two Councils—also exercise important *European* legislative and executive functions. Only in Belgium can similar double-hatting arrangements be found: most of the members of the Senate of Belgium simultaneously hold the office of MP at the regional or community level, and the Concertation Committee consists of federal and member unit executive office-holders. In Canada or the US, by contrast, member unit governments are not directly represented in the federal political process.

To get a full understanding of the effectiveness of the two Councils as political safeguards of foreign relations federalism in the EU, we must first acquire a clear understanding of their role within the EU foreign policy-making process, as well as their *modus operandi*.[5] Hence the following questions: What do the European Council and Council do? How do they do it? Once we have a clearer understanding of the role of the two Councils in the EU foreign policy-making

[5] While the European Council and the Council are distinct institutions, they nonetheless represent the same Member State interests. It is appropriate, then, to discuss them together. Making a similar point, see R Daniel Kelemen, 'Towards a New Constitutional Architecture in the EU?' in Federico Fabbrini, EMH Hirsch Ballin, and Han Somsen (eds), *What Form of Government for the European Union and the Eurozone?* (Hart Publishing 2015) 202.

process, I turn to the other institutions and explore whether and to what extent they can operate as checks on the two Councils.

2.1 The European Council Sets the Course

The European Council brings together the heads of state and government of the twenty-seven Member States. As such, it is the main provider of political leadership within the EU.[6] While the European Council has fulfilled this role for many years, only since the entry into force of the Lisbon Treaty in 2009 do the EU Treaties expressly recognize the European Council's agenda-setting role.[7] Article 15(1) TEU provides that '[t]he European Council shall provide the Union with the necessary impetus for its development and shall define the general political directions and priorities thereof'. In the narrower context of foreign relations, the European Council is responsible for articulating the EU's strategic interests on a cross-pillar basis.[8] Within the CFSP—the former second pillar—the European Council's strategy-devising task is emphasized further. Article 26(1) TEU holds: 'The European Council shall identify the Union's strategic interests, determine the objectives of and define general guidelines for the common foreign and security policy, including for matters with defence implications.' Similarly, within the Area of Freedom, Security and Justice policy area, which has an important external dimension, '[t]he European Council shall define the strategic guidelines for legislative and operational planning', the FEU Treaty provides.[9]

Soon after Herman Van Rompuy, the first permanent European Council President, entered into office in late 2009, the heads of state and government clarified what they understood to be the European Council's responsibility over foreign relations. The conclusions of the European Council meeting of 16 September 2010 stated that it was the European Council's responsibility to

[6] I define 'political leadership' as the ability to overcome collective action problems and to provide strategic guidance. In this sense, see Oran R Young, 'Political Leadership and Regime Formation: On the Development of Institutions in International Society' (1991) 45 International Organization 281, 281.

[7] On the genesis of the European Council, see eg Emmanuel Mourlon-Druol, 'Steering Europe: Explaining the Rise of the European Council, 1975–1986' (2016) 25 Contemporary European History 409, as well as Luuk van Middelaar, *The Passage to Europe: How a Continent Became a Union* (Yale University Press 2013).

[8] This task can be discerned from TEU, art 15(1), which is of general application, and thus applies to the CFSP and other areas of external action such as the CCP.

[9] TFEU, art 68.

> regularly discuss external relations in order to set strategic orientations in advance of key events, in particular with a view to determining key messages on our objectives and on the means to achieve them. This requires clear strategic guidance by the European Council on the basis of effective preparation by the High Representative and by the Council.[10]

The European Council has been able to do so with varying degrees of success. Despite the emphasis on staying ahead of current events, during the tenure of Van Rompuy from 2009 to 2014 the European Council arguably played more of a reactive than a proactive role in the context of foreign relations, preoccupied as it was with addressing the eurozone crisis.[11] This changed somewhat in subsequent years. For example, in 2016 the European Council endorsed an initiative by the High Representative to devise a 'Global Strategy' for EU external action;[12] and, that same year, it devised a strategy to address migratory pressures along Europe's southern shores.[13] This strategy had a significant external dimension, as it required the EU and its Member States to conclude agreements with countries of origin and to mobilize other EU and Member State foreign policy instruments, including development and trade instruments, to obtain leverage over these third countries. One aspect of the strategy consisted in increasing investment in the economies of sub-Saharan Africa, with the view of taking away the very reasons that motivate people to migrate to Europe.[14]

The role of the European Council as a collective body must be distinguished from the specific responsibilities of its President. The European Council President is elected by the members of the European Council by qualified majority vote.[15] His task is two-fold: first, he is to 'chair and drive forward' the work of the European Council, including by preparing and guaranteeing the continuity of its work, and by facilitating the consensus-building process amongst its members.[16] Secondly, the European Council President is to ensure the external representation of the EU on issues concerning the CFSP. He is to do so 'without prejudice to the powers of the High Representative of the Union

[10] European Council Meeting (16 September 2010)—Conclusions, EUCO 21/1/10 REV 1.

[11] In this sense, see also Nicole Koenig, 'Resetting EU External Action: Potential and Constraints' (Jacques Delors Institute 2015) 125, 13 ('Herman van Rompuy took a backstage role in foreign affairs, due also to his important focus on euro crisis management').

[12] European Council meeting (28 June 2016)—Conclusions, EUCO 26/16, 7.

[13] See eg ibid, 1–3 on migration and prior to that European Council meeting (18 and 19 February 2016)—Conclusions, EUCO 1/16, 3–5.

[14] For a critical assessment of this strategy, see the podcast series by *Foreign Policy*, a periodical on international affairs <http://foreignpolicy.com/2017/10/04/europe-slams-its-gates-part-one/> accessed 10 March 2022.

[15] TEU, art 15(5).

[16] TEU, art 15(6) first para.

for Foreign Affairs and Security Policy',[17] and he must be respectful also of the powers of the Commission President, who, as head of the Commission, plays a role in ensuring the external representation of the EU '[w]ith the exception of the [CFSP], and other cases provided for in the Treaties'.[18]

When a first permanent European Council President was to be selected after the coming into force of the Lisbon Treaty in 2009, the heads of state and government disagreed on the profile that would best fit the new office. These discussions revealed how different Member States had different conceptions of the institutional role of the permanent European Council presidency. Opinions ranged from a chairman-style conception to a conception of the office more akin to that of a high profile policy-entrepreneur.[19] The choice of Herman Van Rompuy as first President of the European Council suggests a qualified majority of Member States opted for the former conception.[20] As Van Rompuy argued in his 2014 book: 'I never claimed I would be a flashy "President of Europe", a peer of Obama, Putin or Xi; I did claim I would build bridges and make agreements between the Member States.'[21] That said, the scarcity of Treaty language on the institutional role of the European Council President also leaves room for different conceptions of the office's role to prevail in the future. Donald Tusk, Van Rompuy's successor, regularly expressed his own opinions and preferences. Crucially, if endowed with greater human and financial resources, the European Council President could conceivably develop technical expertise of their own and try to steer discussions within the European Council by setting the terms of discussions.[22]

[17] TEU, art 15(6) second para.

[18] TEU, art 17(1).

[19] Tony Blair circulated as a candidate for the office. For a discussion of his candidacy, see Charles Grant and Henry Porter, 'Is Tony Blair the Right Man to Be President of Europe?' *The Guardian* (24 October 2009) <www.theguardian.com/commentisfree/2009/oct/25/henry-porter-charles-grant> accessed 10 March 2022.

[20] Wolfgang Wessels, *The European Council* (1st edn, Palgrave 2015) 121, characterizing Van Rompuy as a 'highly attentive facilitating manager'. Similarly, see Ingeborg Tömmel, 'The Standing President of the European Council: Intergovernmental or Supranational Leadership?' (2017) 39 Journal of European Integration 175.

[21] Herman Van Rompuy, *Europa in de storm: lessen en uitdagingen* (Davidsfonds 2014) 113 (Translation TV. Original: *'Ik heb nooit beweerd dat ik een blitse "president van Europa" zou worden, een evenknie van Obama, Poetin of Xi, maar wel dat ik bruggen zou slaan en akkoorden tussen de lidstaten afsluiten'*).

[22] Interesting in that regard are calls to directly elect the permanent President of the European Council. In this sense, see Federico Fabbrini, 'Austerity, the European Council, and the Institutional Future of the European Union: A Proposal to Strengthen the Presidency of the European Council Symposium' (2015) 22 Indiana Journal of Global Legal Studies 269 and again in Federico Fabbrini, 'States' Equality v States' Power: The Euro-Crisis, Inter-State Relations and the Paradox of Domination' (2015) 17 Cambridge Yearbook of European Legal Studies 3.

The European Council President has played a role in the external representation of the EU. To avoid the Presidents of the Commission and the European Council from getting involved in interinstitutional controversies similar to those which have characterized the legislative and treaty-making process—a topic to which I return in Chapter 9 on intergovernmental relations—the Presidents of the Commission and European Council agreed during Van Rompuy's tenure to coordinate closely and jointly represent the EU at international fora such as the G7 and G20 and on bilateral visits.[23] Similar challenges arise in managing the relationship between the European Council President and the High Representative. The Treaties do not provide for a clear hierarchy between the two actors. Article 15(6) second paragraph TEU holds that '[t]he President of the European Council shall, at his level and in that capacity, ensure the external representation of the Union on issues concerning its common foreign and security policy' (suggesting a hierarchical relationship), but immediately adds that he shall do so 'without prejudice to the powers of the High Representative of the Union for Foreign Affairs and Security Policy' (suggesting a partnership of equals). Here again, coordination and regular contacts appear necessary if the EU is to project unity on the international stage. Whether such efforts are successful depends, to an important extent, on the personalities and political preferences of both individuals. The process does not always yield satisfactory results, as was apparent, for example, in the aftermath of Russia's annexation of Crimea in 2014, when European Council President Donald Tusk was perceived as pursuing a harder line than High Representative Federica Mogherini, who had proposed to gradually phase out sanctions.[24]

The European Council is a consensual body. The EU Treaty expressly provides that, exceptions notwithstanding, the European Council takes its decisions by consensus.[25] In the vast majority of its meetings, no votes are taken.[26] The expressly stated purpose of the European Council is to create an intimate environment within which trust can be built and heads of state and

[23] Van Rompuy (n 21) 116.

[24] Nicole Koenig, *Resetting EU External Action: Potential and Constraints* (Jacques Delors Institute 2015) 125, 13 and also Andrew Rettman, 'Mogherini Seen as Proposing "Business as Usual" with Russia' *EUObserver* (14 January 2015) <https://euobserver.com/foreign/127204> accessed 10 March 2022.

[25] TEU, art 15(4).

[26] It should be noted that, typically, in those cases in which the Treaties provide for decision-making by qualified majority vote (QMV), no actual vote takes place either. However, the lack of formal voting does not mean the dynamics of decision-making by QMV do not play out. Instead, members who expect to be outvoted will prefer not to express their opposition publicly. In the same sense in the Council, see Stéphanie Novak, 'The Silence of Ministers: Consensus and Blame Avoidance in the Council of the European Union' (2013) 51 Journal of Common Market Studies 1091.

government enjoy the necessary 'space to think'.[27] As is the case in Belgium, where federal Cabinet ministers must reach a consensus they can all live with, negotiations and conversations amongst Member State representatives typically continue until an agreement—a common accord—is reached amongst all parties around the table. Inevitably, a great deal of bargaining is involved in the decision-making process. Within the European Council, not all Member States are created equal, and smaller Member States must either form coalitions amongst themselves or side with larger Member States.[28] Larger Member States, and in particular Germany and France, often meet separately and prior to European Council meetings to develop a common position, which they subsequently defend within the European Council meeting.[29]

Within a small federation such as Belgium, decision-making by consensus between two communities roughly similar in size requires that both communities respect each other's interests and values to arrive at workable solutions. By contrast, within a European Union consisting of twenty-seven Member States of widely different sizes, decision-making in secret and by consensus provides no guarantees that an outcome is reached which all parties consider desirable or even acceptable. A risk of domination by larger Member States exists, given that smaller Member States would not likely want to risk the repercussions of expressing their disagreement to the outside world. Empirical studies on how the EU and its Member States tackled the eurozone crisis reveal hegemonic dynamics within the European Council in addressing the crisis.[30] Paul Craig observed:

> [T]he Euro crisis has ... impacted on the EU inter-institutional division of political power. It would be tempting to conclude that it has had a predictably

[27] On this 'space to think', see critically Maarten Hillebrandt and Stéphanie Novak, '"Integration without Transparency?" Reliance on the Space to Think in the European Council and Council' (2016) 38 Journal of European Integration 527.

[28] In this sense, see van Middelaar (n 7) 193 ('Germany bears more responsibility than ... Luxembourg ... the member states of the Union are unequal—large and small, rich and poor, with long or short external borders, with friendly and hostile neighbours inside or outside the Union').

[29] Commentators have referred to this phenomenon as the emergence of directories amongst the members of the European Council, after the French Directory, ie the five-member committee that governed revolutionary France after the Terror. Defending this practice as being 'occasionally inevitable' albeit 'uncomfortable', see L van Middelaar, *De nieuwe politiek van Europa* (Historische Uitgeverij Groningen bv 2017), 255. On strategies deployed by smaller Member States to increase their influence within the two Councils, see Diana Panke, 'Small States in the European Union: Structural Disadvantages in EU Policy-Making and Counter-Strategies' (2010) 17 Journal of European Public Policy 799.

[30] See eg Sergio Fabbrini, 'From Consensus to Domination: The Intergovernmental Union in a Crisis Situation' (2016) 38 Journal of European Integration 587 and Federico Fabbrini, 'States' Equality v States' Power: The Euro-Crisis, Inter-State Relations and the Paradox of Domination' (2015) 17 Cambridge Yearbook of European Legal Studies 3.

> Schmittian effect, with power being concentrated to an ever-greater extent in the EU executive, the rationale being that only it can respond with sufficient speed to the profound problems generated by the Euro crisis. [...] In terms of process, the lead on measures to address the Euro crisis has been taken by the European Council, and by Germany and France acting partly within the European Council and partly through bilateral discussion.[31]

While stakeholders such as Herman Van Rompuy highlight the exceptional circumstances within which the European Council had to operate during the eurozone crisis, there are few reasons to believe why similar intergovernmental dynamics would not play out in other contexts as well, including on non-CFSP foreign relations issues. As one privileged observer recently argued, what constitutes a *Chefsache*—and thus comes to be regarded as a matter of 'high politics'—depends on what the members of the European Council *themselves* regard as politically salient.[32] The category of *Chefsache* is not defined in the Treaties. It is not limited to policy areas considered inherently more prone to intergovernmental decision-making. There is no reason to believe, for example, that common commercial policy (CCP)-related matters cannot also be elevated to the level of the heads of state and government, if they consider doing so necessary.[33]

2.2 The Council as the EU's Main Decision-Making Body

The European Council is not the only EU institution representing the interests of the Member States. The Council of the EU does so as well. As is the

[31] Paul Craig, 'Economic Governance and the Euro Crisis: Constitutional Architecture and Constitutional Implications' in Maurice Adams, Federico Fabbrini, and Pierre Larouche (eds), *The Constitutionalization of European Budgetary Constraints* (Hart 2014) 36–37.

[32] On the notion of *Chefsache*, see van Middelaar (n 29) 212. Making a similar argument, see Petya Alexandrova, 'Institutional Issue Proclivity in the EU: The European Council vs the Commission' (2017) 24 Journal of European Public Policy 755, 770 ('The decision on whether to reshuffle attention lays with the European Council'). In more general terms, see also Stanley Hoffmann, 'Reflections on the Nation-State in Western Europe Today' (1982) 21 Journal of Common Market Studies 21, 29, defining matters of 'high politics' as those matters which states themselves regard as touching on the state's survival. For a constitutional analysis of the impact of the empowerment of the European Council in the wake of the eurozone crisis on the broader institutional balance within the EU, see also Mark Dawson and Floris de Witte, 'Constitutional Balance in the EU after the Euro-Crisis' (2013) 76 Modern Law Review 817.

[33] In this sense, see Edoardo Bressanelli and Nicola Chelotti, 'The Shadow of the European Council. Understanding Legislation on Economic Governance' (2016) 38 Journal of European Integration 511, arguing that the 'intergovernmental' mode of decision-making prevalent in the CFSP influences decision-making also in core areas of EU competence, including the CCP.

case for the European Council, the Council of the EU consists of direct representatives of the executives of the Member States: the representatives of the Member States are ministers or secretaries of state in their home countries. In contrast to the European Council, which consists of the heads of state and government, the representatives within the Council are of ministerial rank. The Council plays a central role in implementing the political directions set out by the European Council. The EU Treaty allocates to the Council the power to 'exercise legislative and budgetary functions' and to 'carry out policy-making and coordinating functions as laid down in the Treaties'.[34] In the context of foreign relations, '[t]he Foreign Affairs Council shall elaborate the Union's external action on the basis of strategic guidelines laid down by the European Council and ensure that the Union's action is consistent.'[35] (The Foreign Affairs Council consists of the foreign ministers of the twenty-seven Member States.)

In addition to the abovementioned executive functions, the Council plays a role in all types of legislative procedures. Furthermore, when the EU wishes to conclude an international agreement, several Council decisions are required: the Council must authorize the opening of negotiations, adopt negotiating directives, authorize the signing of agreements, and conclude them.[36] Also when the EU wishes to defend a position within an international body, 'when that body is called upon to adopt acts having legal effects', the Council must adopt the necessary decisions.[37] Within the context of the CFSP, '[t]he Council shall frame the common foreign and security policy and take the decisions necessary for defining and implementing it on the basis of the general guidelines and strategic lines defined by the European Council' and '[t]he Council and the High Representative of the Union for Foreign Affairs and Security Policy shall ensure the unity, consistency and effectiveness of action by the Union.'[38] Finally, if the EU wishes to undertake an action not provided for) by the Treaties, the Council must be involved if the action requires some form of policy determination.[39] As mentioned in an earlier

[34] TEU, art 16(1).

[35] TEU, art 16(6) third para.

[36] TFEU, art 218(2).

[37] TFEU, art 218(9). Note that a practice has emerged whereby the Council operates through more informal conclusions and decisions adopted by COREPER, the gathering of Member State ambassadors that prepares Council meetings. The practice was at issue in Joined Cases C-626/15 and 659/16 *Commission v Council ('Antarctica AMP')*. See in particular the opinion of AG Kokott, EU:C:2018:362, paras 47–67.

[38] TEU, art 26(2).

[39] TEU, art 16(1).

chapter, the scope for independent action by the Commission is narrow indeed.[40]

In contrast to the European Council, which, exceptions notwithstanding, decides by consensus, as a general rule the Council adopts decisions by means of a qualified majority vote (QMV).[41] A QMV can be understood as a form of supermajority.[42] A supermajority requirement means that decisions do not need unanimous approval and that, conversely, decisions can be adopted that run counter to the interests or preferences of individual Member States. Depending on one's perspective, this is a strong or a weak political safeguard. From the vantage point of the law of international organizations, the QMV vote mechanism is revolutionary in that it does not protect the sovereignty of individual Member States and states can thus be bound by decisions to which they did not attach their consent.[43] By contrast, from the perspective of comparative federalism, the arrangement is highly protective of Member State autonomy. The US Senate, discussed in the previous chapter, can decide by either sixty-one or fifty-one votes, out of a total number of 100 Senators, depending on whether or not the filibuster applies. In the Council, the threshold to adopt decisions is higher still, as a measure must garner support of 55 per cent of Member States representing at least 65 per cent of the Union population. In this sense, even when it can decide by QMV, the Council still strongly protects the autonomy of its members. It is, in this sense, a strong formal political safeguard of federalism, including in the foreign relations sphere. Furthermore, when the EU acts jointly with the Member States on the international stage—and it often does, as I explore further in Chapter 9—in practice the decision-making threshold in the Council is often higher still.

* * *

Taken together, the two Councils thus provide for a strong Member State voice in the EU foreign policy-making process. The Member State voice in EU decision-making is so strong that the political safeguards of federalism

[40] See for example Case C–660/13 *Council v Commission ('Swiss MoU')*, EU:C:2016:616, holding that the Commission did not have the authority to conclude a non-binding memorandum of understanding with Switzerland on the issue of the Swiss financial contribution to ensure access to the internal market.

[41] TEU, art 16(3).

[42] As explained in TEU, art 16(4), a qualified majority shall ordinarily be defined as at least 55 per cent of the members of the Council, comprising at least fifteen of them and representing Member States comprising at least 65 per cent of the population of the Union. Exceptionally, where the Council does not act on a proposal by the Commission or the High Representative, the qualified majority shall be defined as at least 72 per cent of the members of the Council, representing Member States comprising at least 65 per cent of the population of the EU. See TFEU, art 238(2).

[43] This runs counter to VCLT, art 51, according to which states cannot be forced to express their consent to a treaty.

question presents itself in a different way in the EU context as compared to the US, Canada, or Belgium. Herbert Wechsler, who coined the term, was concerned with the protection of member unit interests in the federal political process in the face of a powerful US President and Congress, both of which are directly elected. In the EU context, the opposite question arises: can the other EU institutions, which represent interests other than those of the Member States, stand up against the two Councils? I look at this question in the next section.

2.3 Looking for Checks on the Two Councils: The Commission, the Parliament, and the High Representative

The two Councils operate alongside the Commission, the Parliament, and the High Representative. Do the other EU institutions or offices operate as checks on the two Councils, with a view to ensuring that none of the EU institutions—and the interests they represent—come to dominate the others?

2.3.1 European Commission

The Commission cannot easily operate as a check against the European Council as the President of the Commission is herself a member of the European Council.[44] Membership of the European Council is a double-edged sword for the Commission President: European Council membership of the Commission President could allow her to influence the outcomes of European Council deliberations. Yet at the same time, the Commission President and, by extension, the Commission as a whole is politically bound by the outcomes of the European Council's deliberations.[45] Commentators are sceptical about the ability of the Commission President to influence the other members of the European Council in a meaningful way.[46] Their reasoning is straightforward: the Commission does not possess the same type of democratic legitimacy enjoyed by the heads of state or government of the Member States.[47]

[44] TEU, art 15(2).

[45] Referring to the presence of the Commission as a 'crucial yet often neglected fact', see van Middelaar (n 29) 222. On the centralization of authority within the office of the President of the Commission, see Neill Nugent and Mark Rhinard, *The European Commission* (2nd edn, Palgrave Macmillan 2015) 68 ('[F]ew scholars contest the basic fact that the role of Commission President has become increasingly more distinctive compared with the rest of the College of Commissioners').

[46] Discussing the issue: Wolfgang Wessels, *The European Council* (1st edn, Palgrave 2015) 95–101.

[47] Jean-Paul Jacqué, 'Lost in Transition: The European Commission between Intergovernmentalism and Integration' in Dominique Ritleng (ed), *Independence and Legitimacy in the Institutional System of the European Union* (Oxford University Press 2016) 23.

In addition, the establishment of a permanent President of the European Council has undercut the informational advantages previously enjoyed by the Commission: the Member States no longer rely on the Commission to provide expertise and continuity in the same way as they might have done during the tenure of Jacques Delors in the late 1980s and early 1990s.[48]

As Luuk van Middelaar argued in a 2017 book, the relationship between the Commission President and the European Council is complex. On the one hand, the Commission does continue to enjoy a degree of influence within the European Council: the Commission often assists the European Council President in drafting European Council conclusions. In this way, the Commission tries to write its own instructions.[49] There is, however, a limit to this practice: it is impossible for the Commission to launch and implement an initiative without full European Council support. Necessarily, the influence of the Commission is contingent on the particular context of each case, and in particular on the skilfulness of its President in shaping the views of the other members of the European Council. When the European Council is not on board, implementation will be difficult.[50]

Likewise, it is difficult for the Commission to operate as a check on the Council. Previously, the Commission derived a certain autonomy from the Council from its exclusive right to submit legislative proposals to the Council.[51] This autonomy has eroded, however.[52] The right of initiative is no longer exclusive to the Commission. In the context of the CFSP, the High Representative can also submit proposals,[53] and in the context of the Area of Freedom, Security and Justice a quarter of the Member States can in some instances do the same.[54]

[48] See Curtin (n 3) 176–77 ('[The tasks of power broker, agenda-setter and effective coordinator] belonged in the past to the Commission, but the latter has seen its position to some extent weakened over the years as bit-by-bit the European Council has progressively assumed steering and supervision roles'). Discussing the issue, see also Wessels (n 46) 95–101. Cf the thesis that the Commission is in decline: see also generally Neill Nugent and Mark Rhinard, 'Is the European Commission Really in Decline?' (2016) 54 Journal of Common Market Studies 1199.

[49] On this process, see eg Philipp Thaler, 'The European Commission and the European Council: Coordinated Agenda Setting in European Energy Policy' (2016) 38 Journal of European Integration 571.

[50] In this sense, see van Middelaar (n 29) 245–46. In a similar sense, pointing to the complexities of the Commission–European Council relationship, see Pierre Bocquillon and Mathias Dobbels, 'An Elephant on the 13th Floor of the Berlaymont? European Council and Commission Relations in Legislative Agenda Setting' (2014) 21 Journal of European Public Policy 20.

[51] The exclusive right of initiative is considered the core feature of the so-called 'Community method'. For a description of the Community method, see Emile Noel, 'The Commission's Power of Initiative' (1973) 10 Common Market Law Review 123.

[52] In this sense, see also generally Paolo Ponzano, Costanza Hermanin, and Daniela Corona, *The Power of Initiative of the European Commission: A Progressive Erosion?* (Notre Europe 2012) 89.

[53] TEU, art 27(1).

[54] TFEU, art 76.

Moreover, those proposals that the Commission does submit are often at the behest of other institutions, in particular the European Council, as discussed earlier.[55] And once a proposal is submitted, the Commission loses much of its leverage vis-à-vis the Council.

Institutional practice has come to diverge from the procedural rules set out in the Treaties in this area. Whereas the Treaties provide for a multi-step legislative process involving a back-and-forth between the Council and Parliament,[56] with the Commission having the possibility to oppose amendments that do not find unanimous support within the Council,[57] in practice most legislative acts are the product of so-called 'trilogue' negotiations between the Council, Parliament, and the Commission, whereby the formal procedure is limited to a first reading by Council and Parliament.[58] In this process, the power of the Commission to oppose Council amendments that fail to achieve unanimous support within the Council has fallen into desuetude.[59] In similar fashion, the Commission no longer makes use of its 'nuclear option', that is, the power to withdraw proposals and thus prevent any measures from being taken.[60] Instead, the Commission expresses its disagreements with the course taken by the Council in declarations, in the hope that its position will be taken up by the Parliament.[61] If the Parliament fails to do so, the Commission appears to have a preference for passing the hot potato to the Court of Justice by launching an action for annulment against Council decisions.

In the treaty-making context, the Commission plays a more central role throughout the decision-making process as compared to the internal legislative process. Article 218 TFEU sets out the treaty-making procedure. The Council appoints the EU negotiator.[62] Except in the context of trade agreements, where

[55] Jean-Paul Jacqué has estimated that 'truly innovative proposed directives' vary between two and four percent of the total number of proposals. See Jacqué (n 47) 18.

[56] TFEU, art 294.

[57] TFEU, art 294(9).

[58] During the 2014–19 legislative term, 1,185 trilogues took place at different stages of the legislative procedure (first, early second, and second reading) on 346 legislative proposals. See European Parliament, 'Activity Report. Development and Trends of the Ordinary Legislative Procedure. 1 July 2014–1 July 2019 (8th Parliamentary Term)' (2020) 8 <www.europarl.europa.eu/cmsdata/198024/activity-report-2014-2019_en.pdf> accessed 12 March 2022. On the informal institution of the 'trilogue', see the references to the literature in Christilla Roederer-Rynning and Justin Greenwood, 'The European Parliament as a Developing Legislature: Coming of Age in Trilogues?' (2017) 24 Journal of European Public Policy 735, 737–38.

[59] Jacqué (n 47) 18. Jacqué refers to the power of the Commission to oppose amendments proposed by the Council on the basis of TFEU, art 294(9), which holds that '[t]he Council shall act unanimously on the amendments on which the Commission has delivered a negative opinion'.

[60] Note that in 2015 the Court of Justice reaffirmed the existence of a right to withdraw legislative proposals. See Case C–409/13 *Council v Commission ('Macrofinancial assistance to third countries')*, EU:C:2015:217.

[61] Jacqué (n 47) 18.

[62] TFEU, art 218(1).

only the Commission can negotiate on behalf of the EU,[63] the Council can appoint anyone or anybody to conduct the negotiations. In practice, the Council usually appoints the Commission as the EU negotiator. When it does so, it also issues negotiating directives to the Commission.[64] The Court of Justice has made it clear that these directives are not binding on the Commission in so far as they contain substantive negotiating instructions, however.[65] The Commission thus enjoys a degree of flexibility and independence from the Council as it negotiates international agreements with third countries. That said, the Council supervises the Commission during negotiations, and the Council, not the Commission, will authorize the signature of the final agreement and decide on its conclusion.[66] The Commission can withdraw its initial recommendation to the Council to open negotiations, but once negotiations have started, the Commission loses this source of leverage.[67] In short, compared to the internal legislative process, the treaty-making procedure provides for a more balanced relationship between Commission and Council. The Council retains the final say, but the Commission plays a key role as the sole point of contact with the external parties with which the EU negotiates.

2.3.2 European Parliament

The Parliament cannot act as a check on the European Council, since the Treaty framers did not establish lines of accountability running from the European Council to the Parliament.[68] The President of the European Council must present a report to the European Parliament after each European Council meeting.[69] Herman Van Rompuy interpreted this provision narrowly by

[63] TFEU, art 207(3) third para.

[64] TFEU, art 218(4).

[65] Case C–425/13 *Commission v Council ('Greenhouse Gas Emissions Trading Scheme')*, EU:C:2015:483, para 88.

[66] See, respectively, TFEU art 218(4), (5), and (6).

[67] On such withdrawal, see Geert De Baere, 'Mercury Rising: The European Union and the International Negotiations for a Globally Binding Instrument on Mercury' (2012) 37 European Law Review 640. On the same subject, see also Pieter-Jan Kuijper, 'Post-CETA: How We Got There and How to Go On' (2017) 53 Revue trimestrielle de droit européen 181.

[68] In this sense, see Philipp Dann, 'European Parliament and Executive Federalism: Approaching a Parliament in a Semi-Parliamentary Democracy' (2003) 9 European Law Journal 549, 558 ('Quite obviously the position of the Council of Ministers and the European Council impedes the parliamentarization of the EU … The Council as a whole is generally beyond the reach of the European Parliament'). More recently, see also Sergio Fabbrini, *Which European Union?* (Cambridge University Press 2015) 144 ('[T]he European Council-based executive has developed without a significant check from the EP').

[69] TEU, art 15(6)(d), and Rules of Procedure of the European Council, art 5 second para <https://eur-lex.europa.eu/legal-content/EN/TXT/?uri=OJ%3AJOL_2009_315_R_0051_01> accessed 20 March 2022.

refusing to answer questions from MEPs.[70] Likewise, he did not allow the European Parliament President to attend meetings of the European Council. The European Council's rules of procedure, adopted at the start of Van Rompuy's tenure, provide that the Parliament President is invited at the start of the meeting, and has the opportunity to say a few words, but is then requested to leave the room.[71] In the same vein, the European Parliament cannot compel the European Council President to appear before the Parliament to answer questions—a power the Parliament does have vis-à-vis the Commission.[72] At the highest political level within the EU, then, the European Parliament remains a weak institutional player, unable to operate as a check on the European Council.

As far as political control by the Parliament over the Council is concerned, the picture is mixed. On the one hand, when legislation needs to be adopted or international agreements on subjects not exclusively related the CFSP need to be concluded, the Parliament often holds a veto power.[73] As it has demonstrated in the cases of the SWIFT and ACTA agreements, which the Parliament rejected respectively in 2010 and in 2012, the Parliament is not afraid to use these powers. And, as commentators have pointed out, the Parliament has succeeded to some extent in translating its veto power over the outcome of treaty negotiations into a continued influence throughout the treaty negotiating process.[74]

[70] Note that, in similar fashion, Van Rompuy barred the European Parliament President from participating in the meetings of the European Council 'because not in a single Member State does the legislature sit at the table of the executive'. See Van Rompuy (n 21) 126.

[71] Rules of Procedure of the European Council, art 4(2) <https://eur-lex.europa.eu/legal-content/EN/TXT/?uri=OJ%3AJOL_2009_315_R_0051_01> accessed 20 March 2022.

[72] See TFEU, art 230, which provides on the one hand that '[t]he Commission shall reply orally or in writing to questions put to it by the European Parliament or by its Members', and on the other that '[t]he European Council and the Council shall be heard by the European Parliament in accordance with the conditions laid down in the Rules of Procedure of the European Council and those of the Council'. The European Council thus has a right to be heard by the Parliament, but the Parliament does not have a right to compel the European Council to appear before it.

[73] In the framework of the ordinary legislative procedure, see TFEU, art 294. In the framework of treaty-making, see TFEU, art 218(6), providing for a series of cases in which Parliament must consent to the conclusion of an international agreements, including in cases when the proposed agreement covers a field to which the ordinary legislative procedure applies.

[74] See on this Maria Romaniello, 'The International Role of the European Parliament: The SWIFT Affair and the "Re-Assessed" European Institutional Balance of Power' (2013) 5 Perspectives on Federalism 97, and more recently also Katharina Meissner, 'Democratizing EU External Relations: The European Parliament's Informal Role in SWIFT, ACTA, and TTIP' (2016) 21 European Foreign Affairs Review 269, as well as Christina Eckes, 'How the European Parliament's Participation in International Relations Affects the Deep Tissue of the EU's Power Structures' (2014) 12 International Journal of Constitutional Law 904, 909–18; Wolfgang Weiss, 'The European Parliament's Role in the Operation of Trade Agreements: Parliamentary Control and Executive–Legislative Balance in External Action' in Diane Fromage and Anna Herranz-Surrallés (eds), *Executive–Legislative (Im)balance in the European Union* (Hart Publishing 2020) 210; and Magdalena Frennhoff Larsén, 'Parliamentary Influence Ten Years after Lisbon: EU Trade Negotiations with Japan' (2020) 58 Journal of Common Market Studies 1540.

As Philipp Dann argued in the early 2000s, vis-à-vis the Council the European Parliament takes up a position similar to that of the US Congress vis-à-vis the US President. As a 'working parliament'—as opposed to a Westminster-style 'debating parliament'—the European Parliament is not in a subservient position vis-à-vis the executive (in Dann's account, the Commission), but instead possesses its own powers, which it exercises independently.[75] The same arguably holds true with regards to the Council, which, in the treaty-making context, can be understood as exercising executive functions.

The Council exercises other executive functions of both a political and an administrative nature as well. The Foreign Affairs Council, in particular, regularly comments on recent events in the neighbourhood of the EU, and the Council's Political and Security Committee exercises 'political control' over EU crisis management operations and determines their 'strategic direction'.[76] Parliamentary oversight of these executive activities of the Council remains limited. The Parliament has some, albeit limited, influence over the conduct of the CFSP through its control over the EU budget, which includes the EU share of CFSP expenditures,[77] and the Council must keep the Parliament fully informed throughout the procedure to conclude international agreements on subjects pertaining to the CFSP.[78] Nowhere within the CFSP context does the Parliament hold a veto power, however. As is the case in many national settings, when it comes to 'high politics' foreign relations, the legislature does not play a central role.[79]

[75] Dann (n 68) 549. Similarly, see also Daniel Thym, 'Parliamentary Involvement in European International Relations' in Marise Cremona and Bruno de Witte (eds), *EU Foreign Relations Law: Constitutional Fundamentals* (Hart 2008) 210. But see more recently: Michael Shackleton, 'Transforming Representative Democracy in the EU? The Role of the European Parliament' (2017) 39 Journal of European Integration 191 and what the author refers to as an ongoing process of 'parliamentarization' of EU representative democracy.

[76] TEU, art 38 second para.

[77] In this sense, see Daniel Thym, 'Beyond Parliament's Reach? The Role of the European Parliament in the CFSP' (2006) 11 European Foreign Affairs Review 109, 126 ('Budgetary powers are the only instrument through which the EP may exercise any measurable influence [over the CFSP]'). On the ways in which the Parliament makes use of its limited budgetary powers to influence the conduct of the CFSP, see eg Andreas Maurer, Daniela Kietz, and Christian Volkel, 'Interinstitutional Agreements in the CFSP: Parliamentarization through the Back Door' (2005) 10 European Foreign Affairs Review 175.

[78] Case C-658/11 *Parliament v Council ('Tanzania')*, EU:C:2014:2025. On the subject, see also Ramses A Wessel, 'Legal Aspects of Parliamentary Oversight in EU Foreign and Security Policy' in Juan Santos Vara and Soledad Rodríguez Sánchez-Tabernero (eds), *The Democratisation of EU International Relations Through EU Law* (Routledge 2018).

[79] See again Thym (n 77) 126 ('Reflecting similar constitutional settings in the Member States, the formulation and articulation of individual foreign policy decisions will therefore largely remain an executive prerogative beyond the Parliament's reach'). But see Guri Rosén and Kolja Raube, 'Influence beyond Formal Powers: The Parliamentarisation of European Union Security Policy' (2018) 20 The British Journal of Politics and International Relations 69, highlighting how the Parliament exercises informal influence despite its lack of formal powers.

Finally, the European Parliament is not empowered to undertake legislative initiatives independently. In this sense, the Parliament differs from the US Congress, with which it otherwise shares some characteristics. While the US Congress can adopt legislation aimed at circumscribing the scope of action for the President or even changing the course of US foreign policy, the European Parliament's role is limited to co-deciding on the content of legislation proposed by the European Commission, or of approving (or rejecting) international agreements negotiated by the Commission. If the Parliament wishes to change the course of EU foreign policy as a whole, it will have to try to do so by means of non-binding resolutions (of which it adopts significant numbers) through which it expresses its differences in priorities with the other EU institutions.[80] Likewise, the Parliament can adopt so-called 'own initiative reports' in which it calls on the Commission to adopt a legislative proposal. The Commission is legally required to take such reports into account, even though it is not required to act on them.[81]

2.3.3 High Representative

The High Representative does not act as a countervailing power to the two Councils either. The High Representative is a vice-president of the Commission. In their capacity as Commission vice-president, the High Representative can persuade the Commission to submit proposals to undertake external actions. Within the context of the CFSP, the High Representative can even submit proposals independently.[82] Furthermore, they preside over the Foreign Affairs formation of the Council, except if it discusses CCP (ie trade)-related matters, in which case the rotating Presidency chairs the meeting.[83] Finally, in addition to this three-fold role, the High Representative shall also 'take part' in the work of the European Council, according to art 15(2) TEU. The underlying mission of the High Representative's office is to 'ensure the consistency of the Union's

[80] The Parliament makes ample use of its power to issue resolutions on foreign policy matters. See eg European Parliament resolution of 1 March 2022 on the Russian aggression against Ukraine (2022/2564(RSP)).

[81] Under the Framework Agreement on relations between the European Parliament and the European Commission, the Commission 'shall take into account the priorities expressed by Parliament' (art 35 of the Framework Agreement on relations between the European Parliament and the European Commission [2010] OJ L304/47).

[82] TEU, art 18(2).

[83] See TEU, art 18(3), and Rules of Procedure of the Council, art 2(5) second para, Council Decision of 1 December 2009 adopting the Council's Rules of Procedure (2009/937/EU) [2009] OJ L325/35, and the comment in fn 9: 'When the Foreign Affairs Council is convened to discuss common commercial policy issues, its President will ask to be replaced by the six-monthly Presidency as provided for in Article 2(5), second subparagraph.'

external action', in particular between the CFSP and non-CFSP aspects of the foreign relations of the EU.[84]

In none of these capacities does the High Representative take any decisions independently from the other institutions. As Carnegie Europe's Jan Techau observed, the office of the High Representative is best understood as that of Europe's 'coordinator-in-chief', linking the different EU institutions involved in EU foreign policy-making.[85] The office grants the High Representative many avenues to influence the other institutions. (We can think, for example, of the 2016 Global Strategy, which the High Representative prepared and subsequently presented to the European Council, which welcomed the document.[86]) In doing so, the High Representative can increase the 'coherence' and 'consistency' of EU foreign relations.[87] Nonetheless, influence derived from informational advantages, the possession of expertise, or, since the establishment of the European External Action Service, administrative capacity, arguably does not count as a meaningful counterweight to the executive powers at the disposal of the two Councils. Further empirical research on the issue would be welcomed, but it would appear that, as is the case for the Commission President within the European Council, the High Representative arguably can influence the two Councils (as Federica Mogherini tried, for example, through the Global Strategy), but they cannot undertake concrete actions at odds with the European Council's priorities.[88] In other words, if the High Representative possesses power, it is at most power of the softer type, consisting in an ability to attract and persuade, rather than power of the hard type, which would allow them to coerce others.[89]

[84] TEU, art 18(4).

[85] Jan Techau, 'Hoping for an Unexpectedly Strong EU Foreign Policy Chief' (*Carnegie Europe*, 26 August 2014) <http://carnegieeurope.eu/strategiceurope/56453> accessed 10 March 2022. See similarly van Middelaar (n 29) 241.

[86] On the process, see generally Pol Morillas, 'Autonomy in Intergovernmentalism: The Role of de Novo Bodies in External Action during the Making of the EU Global Strategy' (2020) 42 Journal of European Integration 231.

[87] On the need for increased 'consistency and coherence' in EU foreign relations, see eg Christophe Hillion, 'Tous Pour Un, Un Pour Tous! Coherence in the External Relations of the European Union' in Marise Cremona (ed), *Developments in EU External Relations Law* (Oxford University Press 2008) and Bart Van Vooren, *EU External Relations Law and the European Neighbourhood Policy: A Paradigm for Coherence* (Routledge 2012).

[88] For anecdotal evidence in this sense, see eg Giorgio Leali, 'EU's Borrell Makes Premature Pledge of €500M More Military Aid to Ukraine' *POLITICO* (12 March 2022) <www.politico.eu/article/eu-borrell-military-spend-momentum-false-step/>accessed 17 March 2022.

[89] Distinguishing between hard and soft power, see Joseph Nye, 'Get Smart' [2009] *Foreign Affairs* 160 <www.foreignaffairs.com/articles/2009-07-01/get-smart> accessed 18 January 2017.

2.4. The Member State Legislatures as an Alternative Check on the Two Councils?

Member State legislatures represent a final potential check on the power of the two Councils.[90] Commentators have looked at Member State legislatures as a potential remedy to address the democratic deficit in EU decision-making.[91] For intra-EU purposes, the Lisbon Treaty framers introduced a mechanism empowering Member State legislatures to suspend the EU legislative process if a sufficient number of them consider that a legislative proposal violates the principle of subsidiarity, and thus consider that the issue the Commission proposes to address at the EU level really ought to be addressed by the individual Member States.[92] The mechanism, set out in a protocol attached to the EU Treaties, applies only to legislative acts, however, and thus excludes international agreements.

Can Member State legislatures influence the EU foreign policy-making process? One obvious way in which Member State legislatures exercise meaningful influence is through their role in the ratification of mixed agreements. As the events surrounding the conclusion of CETA, the EU-Canada trade agreement, in late 2016 revealed, a regional legislature within a single Member State can in some instances stall the ratification of a multi-sectoral trade agreement between the EU and a third country.[93] By contrast, outside of the treaty-making context the role of Member State legislatures is limited. Commentators sometimes make the argument that the Council benefits from indirect democratic legitimacy as its members are accountable vis-à-vis their national legislatures. For this reason, as Andrew Moravscik has argued, criticisms of a democratic deficit at EU level are misguided.[94] There are reasons to question Moravscik's

[90] While not formally EU institutions, Member State legislatures do play a role in the EU foreign policy-making process as they are assumed to exercise political control over their executives, which are members of the two Councils. Moreover, they play a role in the EU treaty-making process as national legislatures must ratify mixed agreements.

[91] See for example Kalypso Nicolaïdis, 'European Demoicracy and Its Crisis' (2013) 51 Journal of Common Market Studies 351.

[92] See Protocol No 2 on the Application of the Principles of Subsidiarity and Proportionality.

[93] Cristina Fasone and Maria Romaniello, 'A Temporary Recalibration of Executive–Legislative Relations on EU Trade Agreements?: The Case of National and Regional Parliaments on CETA and TTIP' in Diane Fromage and Anna Herranz-Surrallés (eds), *Executive–Legislative (Im)balance in the European Union* (Hart Publishing 2020) 187–89. More recently, see also the efforts by the Cypriot Parliament to stall CETA's ratification, as discussed in Merijn Chamon and Thomas Verellen, 'Whittling Down the Collective Interest: CETA, Facultative Mixity, Democracy and Halloumi' (*Verfassungsblog*, 7 August 2020) <https://verfassungsblog.de/whittling-down-the-collective-interest/> accessed 7 August 2020.

[94] A Moravcsik, 'Reassessing Legitimacy in the European Union' (2002) 40 Journal of Common Market Studies 603.

assessment, however. National legislatures are often left in the dark about what happens within the two Councils, especially at the COREPER (ie ambassadorial) and working party (sub-ambassadorial) levels.[95] Some national legislatures are more interested in the EU political process than others. The Danish *Folketing*, for example, requires the responsible cabinet minister to report to Parliament before and after European Council and Council meetings.[96] In other Member States, such as Belgium, no such mechanisms exist, and it is often unbeknownst to the general public what position Belgium defends within the two Councils.

The lack of transparency of what happens within the Council makes it difficult for national legislatures as well as the media and, by extension, the broader public, to hold national executives to account for the positions they defend within the Councils. This, in turn, allows Member State executives to pursue policies unpopular with the general public.[97] And while national parliaments have been relatively successful in forcing national executives and the Council to share more information on the EU's treaty-making activities,[98] informational disadvantages continue to undermine the ability of national parliaments to operate as checks on the two Councils. Yet even if these disadvantages were to be remedied, national parliaments would still remain ineffective checks on the two Councils as their influence mirrors that of the Member State of which they are part. In this sense, national parliaments further entrench the power imbalances that exist within the Council. They operate as an additional political safeguard of foreign relations federalism, rather than as a check on the Member State executives meeting in the two Councils. To overcome this difficulty and for Member State parliaments to come to operate as a meaningful check on the two Councils, the national—and sub-national!—parliaments would have to act collectively in the same manner as the national executives within the

[95] Expressing concerns in this regard, see Deirdre Curtin and Päivi Leino, 'In Search of Transparency for EU Law-Making: Trilogues on the Cusp of Dawn' (2017) 54 Common Market Law Review 1673, 1675, referring to House of Commons European Scrutiny Committee, 'Transparency of Decision-Making in the Council of the European Union Second Report of Session 2016–17' (UK Parliament 2017) <https://publications.parliament.uk/pa/cm201617/cmselect/cmeuleg/128/128.pdf accessed 10 March 2022, in particular at 15.

[96] The effectiveness of the *Folketing* in exercising political control over the Danish executive's role in EU decision-making has nonetheless been questioned. See eg Mads Dagnis Jensen and Dorte Martinsen, 'Out of Time? National Parliaments and Early Decision-Making in the European Union' (2015) 50 Government and Opposition 240, pointing to the increased use of informal trilogues, which lead to interinstitutional agreements on legislation even before a formal proposal has been submitted to the Council.

[97] The phenomenon is well recorded. See eg Peter Mair, *Ruling the Void: The Hollowing of Western Democracy* (Verso 2013), criticizing the retrenchment of European politicians within institutions shielded from democratic pressures.

[98] On these successes, see Fasone and Romaniello (n 93) 191–93.

Council. Efforts to collaborate between parliaments have been undertaken.[99] Yet collective action problems make it very difficult for the around forty parliaments to constitute a genuine counterweight to the two Councils.

3. Informal Safeguards

The preceding section demonstrated how the formal political safeguards of foreign relations federalism in the EU are strong. The EU Treaties provide many opportunities for Member States to upload their interests and preferences to the EU political process. In marked contrast in particular to the US and Canada, where—in accordance with principles of dual sovereignty—each level of government derives its legitimacy directly from the citizenry, in the EU, democratic legitimation takes place primarily indirectly through the executives of the Member States as represented in the two Councils. The other institutions involved in the foreign policy-making process—Commission, Parliament, High Representative—face important hurdles as they try to hold the EU executive to account. As the previous section demonstrated, they are limited in their ability to act as a check on the Member States meeting in the two Councils.

This section further corroborates the overall picture of strong political federalism safeguards in EU foreign policy-making. For also at the level of *informal* safeguards, Member States are well protected. The lack of an EU-wide political party system akin to national political parties as they exist in both the US and Canada, the EU's reliance on Member States to enforce and implement EU policies, coupled with the small size of the EU budget and the absence of EU fiscal capacity further strengthen the hand of the Member States in the EU foreign policy-making process.

3.1 Looking for Europarties

Political parties play a small albeit not negligible role in EU foreign policy-making. As in Belgium, no genuine 'federal' (ie pan-EU) political parties exist at EU level, at least if one understands political parties as vehicles to lift individuals into elected office by supporting them with relevant resources.

[99] On the subject, see generally Nicola Lupo and Cristina Fasone (eds), *Interparliamentary Cooperation in the Composite European Constitution* (Hart 2016).

Member State representatives within the two Councils are members of the national (or sub-national) political parties that are in government. Member State political parties engage in contacts with one another based on ideological family linkages. These contacts have been formalized through the establishment of 'European political parties'. European political parties are interstitial in nature: they constitute alliances of (sub-)national political parties.[100] EU law recognizes such parties, grants them certain privileges as well as financial support, and imposes upon them certain transparency and accountability requirements.[101] As of March 2022, ten European political parties have been recognized, including the European People's Party, the Party of European Socialists, and the European Green Party. In addition, MEPs are organized in political groups in the European Parliament. Political groups are distinct from the abovementioned European political parties. They are provided with financial and logistical support by the European Parliament, in accordance with the Parliament's rules of procedure.[102] As of March 2022, there are seven political groups.[103]

Do European political parties or the political groups in the European Parliament act as informal political safeguards of foreign relations federalism, as political parties do in Belgium, or do they fulfil a 'knitting together' function, as they do in the US and Canada? It is important to distinguish between European political parties and the political groups in the European Parliament on this point. As Jonas Tallberg and Karl Magnus Johansson argued in a 2008 article, party politicization, including in the European Council, remains the exception rather than the rule as the conditions for party influence in that body are demanding.[104] In an article published in the same year, Sara Hagemann and Bjørn Høyland reached similar conclusions for the Council where they

[100] The relevant EU regulation defines a 'European political party' as a political 'alliance', ie a form of 'structured cooperation between political parties and/or citizens'. The regulation in turn defines the notion of 'political party' as 'an association of citizens, which pursues political objectives, and which is either recognised by, or established in accordance with, the legal order of at least one Member State'. At present, all of the European political parties are indeed 'alliances' of Member State political parties, rather than self-standing political parties organized at EU level with the possibility for individual EU citizens to purchase a membership card. See Regulation (EU, EURATOM) No 1141/2014 of the European Parliament and of the Council of 22 October 2014 on the statute and funding of European political parties and European political foundations [2014] OJ L317/1, art 2(1) and (2).

[101] See ibid.

[102] Rules of Procedure of the European Parliament, rule 34(1), 9th Parliamentary Term (2019–24) <www.europarl.europa.eu/doceo/document/RULES-9-2019-07-02_EN.pdf> accessed 18 March 2022.

[103] The Group of the European People's Party, the Group of the Progressive Alliance of Socialists and Democrats in the European Parliament, Renew Europe, Greens/European Free Alliance, Identity and Democracy, European Conservatives and Reformists, and the Left group in the European Parliament.

[104] Jonas Tallberg and Karl Magnus Johansson, 'Party Politics in the European Council' (2008) 15 Journal of European Public Policy 1222, 1223.

identified a 'clear, although weak, tendency of ideological coalition formation'.[105] These empirical inquiries suggest that contacts between political parties—including within the framework of the abovementioned European political parties—are real and meaningful. These contacts have not, however, transformed decision-making dynamics in the two Councils from a logic of diplomacy and intergovernmental bargaining towards one of ideology-based coalition-building. By contrast, political groups in the European Parliament do operate on the basis of political ideology rather than geographically defined interests. Empirical evidence suggests that it is difficult for Member State executives to control MEPs with shared political party affiliations.[106] This may be because MEPs derive a degree of independence from their national political parties by virtue of the fact that the activities of the European Parliament are not always well understood or even known in the national political arenas. Alternatively, Member State executives may not feel there is a need to control MEPs as they are already represented in the two Councils.

Regardless of the cause, the abovementioned empirical evidence suggests that loyalty amongst the Member State executives vis-à-vis European political parties is rather weak, whereas loyalty amongst MEPs to their political groups in the European Parliament is rather strong. This makes for a mixed picture in terms of the ability of political parties in the EU to operate as political safeguards of foreign relations federalism. Within the two Councils, *national* political parties may influence the behaviour of their Member State executive within the two Councils, whereas *European* political parties lack such influence. By contrast, within the European Parliament political groups do fulfil a 'knitting together' function as they socialize MEPs into a transnational community. In the final analysis, then, political parties as a force in EU foreign policy—and EU decision-making more generally—pull in opposite directions. On the one hand, European political parties and European Parliament groups Europeanize party politics and infuse decision-making—especially in the European Parliament, and to a much lesser degree in the two Councils—with a focus on pan-EU interests. On the other hand, the representatives of Member State executives in the two Councils are often loyal to their national political parties, which endows these national parties with an indirect voice in EU decision-making. The presence of factors pulling in opposite directions renders political parties a neutral political safeguard.

[105] Sara Hagemann and Bjørn Høyland, 'Parties in the Council?' (2008) 15 Journal of European Public Policy 1205, 1206.

[106] Monika Mühlböck, 'National versus European: Party Control over Members of the European Parliament' (2012) 35 West European Politics 607, 623.

3.2 The EU's Reliance on Member States to Implement and Enforce EU Policies

The EU's reliance on Member States to implement and enforce EU policies operates as a strong informal political safeguard of foreign relations federalism in the EU. As a general rule, Member States implement and enforce EU law.[107] Often, international agreements to which the EU is a party will be implemented in the EU legal order by means of directives. Directives require Member States to take the necessary measures to ensure that the result of the directive is attained.[108] Inevitably, the effectiveness of the directive is to a large extent dependent on the Member State's willingness and ability to implement it properly and in a timely fashion. And even if the EU proceeds by means of directly applicable regulations—as it does, for example, in the area of customs[109]—Member State administrative authorities are primarily responsible for the proper enforcement of those regulations. For example, Member State customs authorities are ultimately responsible for implementing the tariff-related provisions of EU trade agreements as they process customs declarations and levy the applicable duties.[110]

Also in the context of the CFSP, the EU depends on Member States to implement decisions taken by the Council. This is obvious in the context of the EU's defence-related activities: absent EU-owned military resources, the EU relies on Member State military assets to conduct a rule of law or police mission, as the EU has done, for example, in Kosovo or the Democratic Republic of the Congo.[111] Likewise, restrictive measures require Member State enforcement. This is most visibly the case for travel bans: Member State border officers must prevent targeted individuals from entering the EU. But it is also the case for asset freezes: Member State enforcement agents must take the necessary steps to ensure that targeted individuals can no longer make use of the frozen assets. This explains, for example, why it was the Italian *Guardia di Finanza* which sequestered the yacht of a Russian national targeted by EU restrictive measures

[107] TFEU, art 291(1).

[108] TFEU, art 288 third para.

[109] Regulation (EU) No 952/2013 of the European Parliament and of the Council of 9 October 2013 laying down the Union Customs Code [2013] OJ L269/1.

[110] On the subject, see generally Thomas Verellen, 'Common Commercial Policy and Customs Union' in Miroslava Scholten (ed), *Research Handbook on the Enforcement of European Union Law* (Routledge 2023).

[111] See, respectively, Council Joint Action 2008/124/CFSP of 4 February 2008 on the European Union Rule of Law Mission in Kosovo, EULEX KOSOVO [2008] OJ L42/92, and Council Joint Action 2004/847/CFSP of 9 December 2004 on the European Union Police Mission in Kinshasa (DRC) regarding the Integrated Police Unit (EUPOL 'Kinshasa') [2004] OJ L367/30.

imposed following the Russian invasion of Ukraine in 2022.[112] In both instances, the EU relies on enforcement by Member State authorities. This reliance by the EU on Member State enforcement authorities operates as a strong informal political safeguard.

3.3 The Lack of EU Budgetary and Fiscal Capacity

Member States control the purse strings in the compound EU polity. On the revenue side, the EU Treaties require the EU to finance its activities primarily through its 'own resources'.[113] Own resources are the main sources of revenue for the EU budget. The amounts and the sources of the EU's own resources are decided upon in a Council decision, which the Council adopts by unanimity after approval by all the Member States in accordance with their domestic constitutional requirements, and after consulting with the European Parliament.[114] On the expenditure side, the EU sets out a budgetary programme covering several years—typically five to seven years. This programme is known as the 'Multiannual Financial Framework' (MFF). The MFF is adopted by means of a Council decision, again adopted by unanimity.[115] In contrast to the 'own resources' decision, Member States are not required to ratify the decision independently and the role of the European Parliament is upgraded from a mere consultative role to that of a veto player. By embedding EU expenditure in a five- to seven-year cycle, the Treaty framers aimed at ensuring that 'Union expenditure develops in an orderly manner and within the limits of its own resources', as Article 312(1) TFEU provides. In addition to the multiannual MFF, the EU also adopts annual budgets. It does so by means of a Council decision, which can be adopted by QMV and which requires parliamentary approval.[116]

[112] 'Italy's Finance Police Seize Russian Oligarch's Mega Yacht' *CNN* (12 March 2022) <www.cnn.com/europe/live-news/ukraine-russia-putin-news-03-12-22/h_64c3a1fba253043a8a001a9d5c20b5af> accessed 12 March 2022.

[113] TFEU, art 311 para 2 ('Without prejudice to other revenue, the budget shall be financed wholly from own resources'). For an introduction to the system of EU budgetary rules, see Mario Monti and others, 'Future Financing of the EU. Final Report and Recommendations of the High Level Group on Own Resources December 2016' (2017), 18–35.

[114] TFEU, art 311 para 3. See most recently Council Decision (EU, EURATOM) 2020/2053 of 14 December 2020 on the system of own resources of the European Union and repealing Decision 2014/335/EU, EURATOM [2020] OJ L424/1.

[115] TFEU, art 312(2). See most recently Council Regulation (EU, EURATOM) 2020/2093 of 17 December 2020 laying down the multiannual financial framework for the years 2021 to 2027 [2020] OJ L433I/11.

[116] The procedure is complex. See TFEU, art 314. See fairly recently Council of the EU, Press release: Agreement reached on 2022 EU budget, 16 November 2021 <www.consilium.europa.eu/en/press/press-releases/2021/11/16/eu-budget-for-2022/> accessed 17 March 2022.

The annual budget has to respect the budgetary ceilings set out in the MFF decision.

It is important to bear in mind the interplay between expenditures and financial resources. The system is set up in such a way that, as the Council decides to increase expenditures, the EU's financial resources must increase in parallel. Article 311 first paragraph TFEU makes this point where it provides that '[t]he Union shall provide itself with the means necessary to attain its objectives and carry through its policies'. EU budgets must, in other words, be balanced. As a large component of the EU's 'own resources' consists of Member State financial contributions calculated as a percentage of Member State Gross National Income (GNI),[117] the absolute amount of Member State contributions must increase or decrease in keeping with the ceilings set out in the MFF and the actual allocations in the EU's annual budgets. Through their role in the adoption of the Own Resources Decision, the MFF, and the annual EU budgets, Member States determine what the EU can and cannot do in the five to seven years following the MFF's adoption.

In addition to the procedural rules governing the allocation and expenditure of financial resources, the overall scale of the EU budget also speaks to how Member States, through their fiscal resources, can indirectly influence EU decision-making. In 2022, the EU's annual expenditures hovered around 170 billion euros, of which approximately 18.95 billion euros was earmarked for foreign relations under the headings of 'security and defence' and 'neighbourhood and the world'.[118] The total EU budget represented around 1.14 per cent of nominal EU GDP.[119] While significant in absolute terms, the amounts pale in comparison with the annual budget of the federal government of Canada, which in fiscal year 2021–22 equated to around 355.19 billion euros (497.6 billion Canadian dollars),[120] with Canada having a nominal GDP equating to only 8.8 per cent of that of the twenty-seven EU Member States.[121] If we compare the annual EU expenditures of 170 billion euros in fiscal year 2022 to those of

[117] Council Decision (EU, EURATOM) 2020/2053 of 14 December 2020 on the system of own resources of the European Union and repealing Decision 2014/335/EU, EURATOM [2020] OJ L424/1, art 2(1)(a).

[118] Council of the EU, Press release: Agreement reached on 2022 EU budget, 16 November 2021 <www.consilium.europa.eu/en/press/press-releases/2021/11/16/eu-budget-for-2022/> accessed 17 March 2022.

[119] Ibid.

[120] See the budget for the 2021–22 fiscal year <www.budget.gc.ca/2021/pdf/budget-2021-en.pdf> accessed 17 March 2022. I used the 17 March 2022 exchange rate of 0.71 euro/Canadian dollar.

[121] In 2021, Canada's nominal GDP amounted to 1.74 trillion euros or 1.93 trillion US dollars, compared to an EU nominal GDP of 19.73 trillion euros or 21.89 trillion US dollars. For GDP figures, see <https://data.oecd.org/gdp/nominal-gdp-forecast.htm> accessed 17 March 2022. I used the 17 March 2022 exchange rate of 0.90 euro/US dollar.

the US federal government, the difference is overwhelming: under the 2022 federal government budget, US federal expenditures amounted to 5.41 trillion euros,[122] with US nominal GDP representing 95 per cent of EU nominal GDP.[123] Clearly, the EU has at its disposal a very small budget in comparison to the federal governments of both Canada and the US—a budget which, moreover, decreased in size following the exit of the UK from the EU.

Given the limited size of the EU budget, it is not surprising that Member States often directly contribute to EU actions outside of the EU budgetary framework. EU external action is regularly financed through both EU and Member State resources.[124] In the context of the CFSP, the need for Member State financial contributions is even constitutionally mandated. Article 26(3) TEU, in particular, sets out that '[t]he common foreign and security policy shall be put into effect by the High Representative and by the Member States, *using national and Union* resources'.[125] Article 41 TEU puts further flesh on the bones of this provision. The provision distinguishes between *administrative* and *operational* expenditure. The former is to be borne by the EU budget (over which the European Parliament has a say). The latter is also borne by the EU budget, except if the expenditure arises from 'operations having military or defence implications', or if the Council by unanimity decides that the expenditure shall be borne by the Member States.[126] The Member States thus have the possibility to keep 'operating' expenditures outside of the EU budget, even if the expenditures do not pertain to 'operations having military or defence implications' in the meaning of Article 41 TEU. This ability demonstrates the extent to which Member States control CFSP-related expenditures. Whenever EU action in the framework of the CFSP has military or defence implications, it must be financed through off-budget instruments over which Member States retain control. The European Peace Facility, established in 2021, offers an example. The Facility, which came to prominence during the Russian invasion

[122] 6 trillion US dollars. See Table 1 of the budget for the 2022 fiscal year <www.whitehouse.gov/wp-content/uploads/2021/05/budget_fy22.pdf> accessed 17 March 2022.

[123] According to the abovementioned OECD data, in 2021, US nominal GDP amounted to 18.83 trillion euros or 20.89 trillion US dollars.

[124] For an old example, see the facts leading up to Opinion 1/78 on the International Agreement on Rubber in which the Court of Justice held that if the finances of the Member States would be involved in the execution of the agreement, the agreement had to be concluded as a mixed agreement. See Opinion 1/78 ('International Agreement on Rubber'), EU:C:1979:224, para 62: 'If ... the financing is to be by the Member States that will imply the participation of those States in the decision-making machinery or, at least, their agreement with regard to the arrangements for financing envisaged and consequently their participation in the agreement together with the Community.'

[125] Emphasis added.

[126] In 2021, the EU established the European Peace Facility, to fund EU actions with military and defence implications. See the Council Decision (CFSP) 2021/509 of 22 March 2021 establishing a European Peace Facility, and repealing Decision (CFSP) 2015/528 [2021] OJ L102/14.

of Ukraine in 2022,[127] has a budget of 5 billion euros for the 2021–27 period. It is managed by a Facility Committee, which consists of a representative of each Member State.[128] The Committee takes decisions by unanimity.[129]

Outside of the CFSP context, direct Member State contributions outside of the EU budget also continue to play an important role. The Emergency Trust Fund for Africa is a good example. The objective of the Fund is to finance investments in sub-Saharan Africa, with a view to tackling the 'root causes of migration'.[130] The projects undertaken in this framework are financed in part by the EU budget, by re-channelling development policy resources to the Fund, but in part also by direct Member State contributions.[131] Similarly, until 2018 the European Development Fund, which represented 30 per cent of EU spending on development aid, was financed by Member State contributions outside of the EU budget.[132] The Fund was negotiated by the EU and its Member States for six-year periods.

The small size of the EU budget, coupled with the lack of EU powers to increase resources without unanimous Member State approval, the Multiannual Framework within which annual budgets have to fit, as well as the constitutional prohibition against funding key aspects of the CFSP with EU 'own resources': these arrangements ensure that Member States keep control over the EU political process. As Member States control the purse strings, they have a determinative say over the outcomes of that process. Ultimately, by restricting the size of the EU budget and locking in these amounts for years to come, Member States limit the types of policies that can be pursued within the EU framework. This, in turn, requires Member States to supplement EU action

[127] See Maïa de la Baume and Jacopo Barigazzi, 'EU Agrees to Give €500M in Arms, Aid to Ukrainian Military in "Watershed" Move' *POLITICO* (27 February 2022) <www.politico.eu/article/eu-ukraine-russia-funding-weapons-budget-military-aid/> accessed 12 March 2022.

[128] Council Decision (CFSP) 2021/509 of 22 March 2021 establishing a European Peace Facility, and repealing Decision (CFSP) 2015/528 [2021] OJ L102/14, art 11(1).

[129] ibid art 11(14).

[130] See the political declaration issued after the Valletta Summit of 11–12 November 2015 <www.consilium.europa.eu/media/21841/political_decl_en.pdf> accessed 12 March 2022, which led to the establishment of the European Trust Fund for Africa: 'We commit to address the root causes of irregular migration and forced displacement resulting from state fragility and insecurity, as well as from demographic, economic and environmental trends.'

[131] See art 3.1 of the Constitutive Agreement Establishing the European Union European Union Emergency Trust Fund for Stability and Addressing Root Causes of Irregular Migration and Displaced Persons in Africa, and its Internal Rules <https://ec.europa.eu/trustfundforafrica/sites/default/files/original_constitutive_agreement_en_with_signatures.pdf> accessed 7 June 2022.

[132] See most recently Council Regulation (EU) 2018/1877 of 26 November 2018 on the financial regulation applicable to the 11th European Development Fund, and repealing Regulation (EU) 2015/323 [2018] OJ L307/1. On the incorporation of the Fund into the EU's Multiannual Financial Framework, see generally Alexandra Pouwels, 'The Integration of the European Development Funds into the MFF 2021–2027' (European Parliament 2021) Briefing.

in intergovernmental fashion. In this way, control over the purse constitutes a strong informal political safeguard of foreign relations federalism in the EU.

4. Conclusion

The political safeguards of foreign relations federalism in the EU are strong. When compared to the US, Canada, and Belgium, they are in fact the strongest. *Formal safeguards* are very strong: within the EU institutional framework, the Member States—represented in the two Councils—take centre stage. Through their membership of the two Councils, Member States set the strategic course of the EU; they make legislation, along with the European Parliament; they authorize the signature of international agreements and decide on their conclusion; and they are involved in executive decision-making. Formal safeguards are so strong in the EU that it becomes more salient to query whether *other* interests than those of the Member States have a meaningful voice in the EU's foreign policy-making process. In this regard, the EU differs strongly from the two North American federations. As discussed in the previous chapter, both Canada and the US are characterized by comparatively weak formal political safeguards of foreign relations federalism. By contrast, the EU shares some features with Belgium. There, too, member units play a direct role within the federal executive. However, unlike at EU level, member unit representation in Belgium is more reactive than it is proactive: linguistic groups and member unit governments can block federal initiatives, whereas at EU level member unit executives make EU foreign policy by virtue of their membership of the two Councils.

Informal safeguards of foreign relations federalism are strong in the EU as well. Political parties are a neutral factor, but the limited administrative and fiscal capabilities of the EU do further strengthen the position of the Member States in the EU foreign policy-making process. As far as fiscal capabilities are concerned, the EU offers a mirror image of the US and Canada. In both North American federations, federal fiscal resources are an important lever of federal power. By contrast, in the EU the opposite is the case. Dependent as they are on Member State fiscal resources, EU institutions are not in a position to tax and spend to pursue foreign policy objectives. In particular on CFSP issues, a lack of autonomous EU fiscal resources buttresses the influence of Member States in the foreign policy-making process. A similar point can be made with regards to administrative capacity: while the administrative capacity of the European Commission in core areas such as the CCP is significant, many aspects of

Table 7.1 Overview of the political safeguards of foreign relations federalism in the US, Canada, Belgium, and the EU

	The political safeguards of foreign relations federalism				**Overall assessment**
	Formal safeguards	*Informal safeguards*			
	Direct representation within the federal foreign policy-making process	**Political parties**	**Administrative capacity**	**Fiscal capacity**	
United States	Weak	Weak	Neutral	Weak	Weak
Canada	Weak	Neutral	Strong	Weak	Neutral
Belgium	Strong	Strong	Neutral	Neutral	Strong
European Union	Strong	Neutral	Strong	Strong	Strong

EU foreign relations require Member State implementation. (And even CCP measures ultimately require Member State administrative action to be implemented on the ground.) In this respect, and despite the dualist philosophy undergirding Canadian federalism more generally, the EU and Canada share features as both federal unions rely on member unit administrative capacity to implement federal foreign policy.

Taken together, the combination of strong formal and informal safeguards demonstrates how foreign relations federalism in the EU is, to an important extent, a federalism of shared rule rather than self-rule. As discussed in the previous chapters, a balance between unity and diversity is not achieved through the allocation of exclusive powers or through the resolution of conflicts between levels of governance through the application of primacy or pre-emption principles. Rather, it is pursued through institutional design and, as will be discussed in the following chapters on intergovernmental relations, through mixed external action whereby the EU and the Member States act jointly on the international stage. The table below summarizes the findings of this chapter (see Table 7.1).

8

Intergovernmental Relations in the US, Canada, and Belgium

> Canadian federalism is not simply a matter of legalisms. The Constitution, though a legal document, serves as a framework for life and for political action within a federal state, in which the courts have rightly observed the importance of co-operation among government actors to ensure that federalism operates flexibly.
>
> A unanimous Supreme Court of Canada in
> *Canadian Western Bank v Alberta*[1]

1. Introduction

Intergovernmental relations represent the second dimension of shared rule as defined in Chapter 1 to this book. Characterized by commentators as the 'lifeblood of federalism in practice', intergovernmental relations are a central feature of many contemporary federal systems.[2] For this reason, the phenomenon is discussed in two separate chapters—one on the US, Canada, and Belgium, and another on the EU. For the purpose of this chapter, I define intergovernmental relations broadly as the variety of ways in which governments enter into direct relations with one another.[3] It is important to have a clear understanding of which phenomena fall within the scope of this definition and which do not. 'Intergovernmental relations' is a term commonly used in the North American federations, and in particular in Canada, where formal and informal government-to-government interactions are a key feature of federalism.[4] These

[1] *Canadian Western Bank v Alberta*, [2007] 2 SCR 3, 2007 SCC 22 [42].

[2] Johanne Poirier and Cheryl Saunders, 'Comparing Intergovernmental Relations in Federal Systems: an Introduction' in John Kincaid, Johanne Poirier, and Cheryl Saunders (eds), *Intergovernmental Relations in Federal Systems* (Oxford University Press 2015) 4.

[3] ibid 5.

[4] Commentators often characterize Canada as a form of 'interstate' or 'executive' federalism. See eg Alan Cairns, 'From Interstate to Intrastate Federalism in Canada' (1978) 2 Bulletin of Canadian Studies 13 and J Stefan Dupré, 'Reflections on the Workability of Executive Federalism' in Barbara Carroll,

Foreign Relations Federalism. Thomas Verellen, Oxford University Press. © Thomas Verellen 2023.
DOI: 10.1093/oso/9780192844569.003.0008

interactions can be *vertical* (federal-to-state/province) or *horizontal* (state/province-to-state/province); they can be *bilateral* (involving two governments) or *multilateral* (involving some or even all governments).[5] In European federations, including Belgium, the more normatively laden term 'cooperative federalism' is often used to refer to the same phenomenon, implicitly suggesting that cooperation between governments is a desirable thing within a federation and that, more often than not, governments in fact cooperate, rather than enter into conflict with one another.[6]

In the EU context, 'intergovernmentalism' is best known as a theory to describe the nature of the European integration process.[7] It is contrasted with 'supranational' theories of integration that focus on the autonomy of some EU institutions from the Member States—in particular the Commission, the European Parliament, and, since the establishment of the European Monetary Union (EMU), also the European Central Bank.[8] Horizontal relations between Member States are typically not understood as inter*governmental* relations, but rather as inter*national* relations, and the agreements that governments make in that context constitute inter*national* agreements (think, for example, of the bilateral investment agreements Member States have concluded with each other over the years) as opposed to inter*governmental* agreements, which is a term used in Canada and the US.[9]

It is well established today that the EU Treaties did not fully integrate the Member States into a single, unified EU legal order. As the Court of Justice held, for example, in the *Wightman* judgment in the context of the UK's withdrawal from the EU, the EU and Member State legal orders are *both* autonomous from

David Siegel, and Mark Sproule-Jones (eds), *Classic Readings in Canadian Public Administration* (Oxford University Press 2005).

[5] On these distinctions, see also Robert Schertzer, 'Intergovernmental Relations in Canada's Immigration System: From Bilateralism towards Multilateral Collaboration' (2015) 48 Canadian Journal of Political Science/Revue canadienne de science politique 383.

[6] See eg Emmanuel Vandenbossche and Xavier Delgrange (eds), *Evoluties in het Belgisch cooperatief federalisme. Évolutions dans le fédéralisme coopératif belge* (Die Keure 2015). The term has its origins in German federalism. See eg Fritz Wilhelm Scharpf, Bernd Reissert, and Fritz Schnabel, *Politikverflechtung: Theorie und Empirie des kooperativen Föderalismus in der Bundesrepublik* (Hain 1976).

[7] See seminally Andrew Moravcsik, 'Preference and Power in the European Community: A Liberal Intergovernmentalist Approach' in Simon Bulmer (ed), *Economic and Political Integration in Europe: Internal Dynamics and Global Context* (Blackwell Publishers 1994), and more recently Christopher J Bickerton, Dermot Hodson, and Uwe Puetter, *The New Intergovernmentalism: States and Supranational Actors in the Post-Maastricht Era* (Oxford University Press 2015).

[8] See generally Ernst B Haas, *The Uniting of Europe: Political, Social, and Economic Forces, 1950–1957* (University of Notre Dame Press 1958).

[9] Pointing to this difference, see Poirier and Saunders (n 2) 6.

one another.[10] (*Wightman* can be contrasted to earlier pronouncements of the Court in which it regarded EU law as having become an 'integral part of the legal system of the Member States'.[11]) This implies that Member States on some occasions act *within* the scope of EU law and, on others, *outside* of the scope of EU law. This is visible, for example, in the recognition that the scope of the Charter of Fundamental Rights of the EU is limited to instances in which the Member States are 'implementing' EU law.[12] Outside of those instances, the Charter does not apply. Likewise, the EU's free movement provisions do not apply to strictly internal situations without a cross-border element.[13] That said, the fact that the EU and Member State legal orders are, in contrast to the three other federations explored in this book, legally not fully integrated, does not detract from the usefulness of comparing how governments interact with one another in areas in which their competences either overlap or are intertwined with one another. In functional terms, as Ingolf Pernice has argued, the EU institutions and EU Member States act as 'a unity in substance and as a coherent institutional system, within which competence for action, public authority or, as one may also say, the power to exercise sovereign rights is divided among two or more levels'.[14] This explains, also, why comparative legal scholars have included the EU in studies on intergovernmental relations in recent years.[15]

This chapter examines the intergovernmental relations landscape in the US, Canada, and Belgium. In the next and final substantive chapter of the book I turn to the EU. In the EU, intergovernmental relations play a significant role in the management of mixed external action as well as in the development of asymmetrical forms of cooperation between Member States as have been established, for example, in the context of EMU. The former constitute a form of *vertical* intergovernmental relations, whereas the latter are a form of horizontal intergovernmental cooperation. I look at both issues in turn. For each federation, I start by briefly describing patterns of intergovernmental relations. In a second step, I look at the constitutional rules and principles governing those

[10] Case C–621/18 *Andy Wightman v Secretary of State for Exiting the European Union*, EU:C:2018:999, para 45, speaking of the autonomy of EU law with respect to *both* the law of the Member States and to international law.

[11] See in particular Case 6/64, *Flaminio Costa v ENEL*, EU:C:1964:66, 593.

[12] Charter, art 51(1).

[13] See eg Case C–268/15 *Fernand Ullens de Schooten v État belge*, EU:C:2016:874, in particular para 55, holding that 'it is for the referring court to indicate to the Court . . . in what way the dispute pending before it, despite its purely domestic character, has a connecting factor with the provisions of EU law'.

[14] Ingolf Pernice, 'Multilevel Constitutionalism and the Treaty of Amsterdam: European Constitution-Making Revisited?' (1999) 36 Common Market Law Review 703, 703.

[15] See eg Nicolas Levrat, 'The European Union: From International Relations to Intergovernmental Relations' in Johanne Poirier, Cheryl Saunders, and John Kincaid (eds), *Intergovernmental Relations in Federal Systems* (Oxford University Press 2015).

patterns. As will quickly become apparent, intergovernmental relations are particularly significant in areas of 'low politics' such as environmental policy or international trade, and—with the important exception of the EU—not so much in areas of 'high politics' touching on the federation's internal or external security. This should not be surprising: intergovernmental relations are most relevant in areas in which powers overlap. As mentioned in Chapter 3, in the US, Canada, and Belgium, national defence remains an exclusively federal matter, whereas international trade, environmental policy, or even immigration policy involve elements of both federal and member unit powers.

2. United States: Intergovernmental Relations in a System of Dual Sovereignty

Do governments in the US engage in intergovernmental relations? If yes, what is the format of such relations (vertical-horizontal, bilateral-multilateral)? And if governments in the US do engage in intergovernmental relations, what constitutional rules and principles govern these relations?

2.1 Patterns of Intergovernmental Relations in the US

For a long period of time, intergovernmental relations were not considered an important feature of federalism in the US. This changed in the New Deal era as federal and state governments increasingly came to rely on one another to achieve shared policy objectives.[16] In terms of *vertical* intergovernmental relations, federal decisions have created space for state governments to undertake initiatives. As discussed also in Chapter 4, in climate policy, for example, the federal government has granted waivers to allow states to impose higher emission reduction standards on tailpipe emissions.[17] In so doing, the US federal government, acting through the Environmental Protection Agency (EPA), built state efforts into the federal scheme. More conventional forms of vertical intergovernmental relations can also be found in the US. There have, for example, been intergovernmental agreements to which both state governments

[16] For a historical account, see Jessica Bulman-Pozen, 'Our Regionalism' (2017) 166 University of Pennsylvania Law Review 377, 394–414.

[17] John M Broder and Peter Baker, 'Obama Putting Quick Stamp on Environmental Policy' *The New York Times* (6 February 2009) <www.nytimes.com/2009/01/26/world/americas/26iht-calif.3.19685095.html> accessed 2 March 2022.

and the federal government have been party. The Delaware River Basin Commission is an example.[18] It is comprised of federal and state officials and is charged with the responsibility of planning, conserving, and allocating water resources in the Delaware River Basin.

Practices of *horizontal* intergovernmental relations can also be identified. By means of interstate compacts states collaborate with one another on issues of shared interest without the involvement of the federal government. For example, in 1921 the Port Authority of New York and New Jersey was established by means of an interstate compact concluded between the states of New York and New Jersey.[19] In an article published in 2017, Jessica Bulman-Pozen estimated that around 150 such agreements were in effect in that year.[20] Less formal agreements concluded by means of memorandums of understanding are also common practice, as is the simultaneous adoption of legislation without any prior written agreement between state governments.[21] The Regional Greenhouse Gas Initiative is a good example of this more informal type of intergovernmental collaboration. After the US federal government decided to withdraw from the Kyoto Protocol in the early 2000s, a group of New England states jointly concluded a memorandum of understanding to reduce greenhouse gas emissions.[22] They did so independently from the federal government. At the time of writing, in the spring of 2022, ten states are involved in the initiative (Connecticut, Delaware, Maine, Maryland, Massachusetts, New Hampshire, New York, New Jersey, Rhode Island, and Vermont). In terms of the number of parties involved, the vast majority of these more or less formal agreements are either bilateral (involving two states) or plurilateral (involving more than two states). By contrast, there have been very few agreements concluded by all fifty states.[23]

Horizontal collaboration between state governments can take other forms as well. In particular, in recent years like-minded state governments have on several occasions jointly brought suits against the federal government to challenge federal initiatives through litigation. For example, in 2015, twenty-four states brought suit against the EPA's Clean Power Plan, which was an important component of the Obama administration's efforts to meet the Paris Agreement's

[18] The Commission is mentioned in Bulman-Pozen (n 16) 392.

[19] The Authority is mentioned in Bulman-Pozen (n 16) 385.

[20] See Bulman-Pozen (n 16) 385.

[21] On these practices, see Bulman-Pozen (n 16) 386.

[22] The memorandum is available at <www.rggi.org/sites/default/files/Uploads/Design-Archive/MOU/MOU_12_20_05.pdf> accessed 2 March 2022.

[23] Bulman-Pozen refers to the Interstate Compact for Adult Offender Supervision, the Interstate Compact on the Placement of Children, and the Emergency Management Assistance Compact as examples of interstate compacts that involve all fifty states. See Bulman-Pozen (n 16) fn 25.

emission reduction targets. On 30 June 2022, the Supreme Court ruled in favour of the twenty-four states and restricted the authority of the EPA to regulate carbon dioxide emissions.[24] This litigation comes on the back of a case brought ten years earlier by twelve other states against the EPA's *failure* to undertake any action under the Clean Air Act to tackle climate change under the Bush administration.[25] Here we see states engaging in intergovernmental collaboration to oppose federal initiatives via judicial means.[26]

Horizontal intergovernmental relations in the US sometimes involve third country governments as well. Canadian provinces are obvious partners for US states, given the long border between the US and Canada. It is no surprise, then, that many agreements have been concluded between Canadian provinces and US state governments on issues related to the shared border. The Great Lakes-Saint Lawrence River Basin Sustainable Water Resources Agreement is a well-known example of this type of agreement;[27] the Pacific Northwest Economic Region, which comprises the US states of Alaska, Idaho, Oregon, Montana, and Washington, and the Canadian provinces of Alberta, British Columbia, and Saskatchewan and the Canadian territories of the Northwest Territories and the Yukon, is another.[28] But there has also been collaboration outside of that context. Perhaps most famously, California joined the Quebec cap-and-trade programme in 2013.[29]

Both vertical and horizontal intergovernmental relations have thus become a prominent feature of US federalism, including in areas with an external dimension such as climate change policy, where efforts to reduce emissions are closely connected with diplomatic efforts to negotiate a global agreement. By contrast, *vertical-multilateral intergovernmental relations* involving all states and the federal government do not take place very often in the US. No forum brings together representatives of all fifty states and the federal government, and no initiatives have been undertaken to engage in forms of collective

[24] *West Virginia v Environmental Protection Agency*, 597 US ___ (2022).

[25] *Massachusetts v EPA*, 549 US 497, 127 S Ct 1438, 167 L Ed 2d 248 (2007).

[26] Commentators have argued such initiatives represent an additional safeguard of federalism. See in particular Daniel Francis, 'Litigation as a Political Safeguard of Federalism' (2017) 49 Arizona State Law Journal 1. In the same spirit, see Jessica Bulman-Pozen, 'Partisan Federalism' (2014) 127 Harvard Law Review 1077, 1097.

[27] Bulman-Pozen also mentions the Northeastern Forest Fire Protection Compact and the International Emergency Management Assistance Compact. See Bulman-Pozen (n 16) 386.

[28] The Pacific Northwest Economic Region is an example of horizontal intergovernmental relations that occurs through the simultaneous adoption of legislation in all of the member units concerned. The statutes are available on the Region's website: <www.pnwer.org/governance-structure.html> accessed 2 March 2022.

[29] Agreement Between the California Air Resources Board and the Gouvernement du Québec Concerning the Harmonization and Integration of Cap-and-Trade Programs for Reducing Greenhouse Gas Emissions (2013).

law-making by bodies established through intergovernmental collaboration.[30] In the same spirit, no formal institutional framework has been set up to involve state governments in the conduct of US foreign relations, as exists for example in Belgium (to which I turn later in the chapter). The US federal government informs state governments of ongoing developments, as the US Trade Representative does, for example, through the Intergovernmental Policy Advisory Committee. Yet overall, state involvement in this area remains informal and fairly limited.[31]

Similarly, *horizontal-multilateral intergovernmental relations* involving all states but not the federal government are not very prominent in the US. All fifty state governments are represented in the National Governors Association. The National Governors Association is best understood as a lobbying organization: it tries to influence federal policy-making but does not adopt any form of legally binding norms of its own. Arguably, the large number of US states make it more difficult in the US than it is, for example, in Canada or even the EU to undertake joint action involving all fifty state governments, either on their own or with the federal government.

2.2 Intergovernmental Relations in a System of Dual Sovereignty

What constitutional rules and principles govern intergovernmental relations in the US? Two principles play a key role: pre-emption and the non-commandeering principle. First, as discussed in Chapter 4 on conflict resolution, *pre-emption* is the principle by which, under the Supremacy Clause,

[30] Note that the President occasionally addresses meetings of the National Governors' Association. Yet these meetings are irregular. President Biden addressed the Association most recently in January 2022. See 'Remarks by President Biden at Meeting With the National Governors Association' (*The White House*, 31 January 2022) <www.whitehouse.gov/briefing-room/speeches-remarks/2022/01/31/remarks-by-president-biden-at-meeting-with-the-national-governors-association/> accessed 2 March 2022.

[31] It is telling that in a seventy-three-page article discussing the governance of trade policy-making in the US, no reference is made to state governments at all. See Kathleen Claussen, 'Trade Administration' (2021) 107 Virginia Law Review 845. Similarly, in a 2019 article Timothy Meyer and Ganesh Sitaraman drew attention to the tension between the federal government's international commitments, including under the WTO agreements, on the one hand, and state interests and policy preferences, on the other. They highlight how the latter may enter into conflict with the former. As a remedy, the authors seem to favour a broader power for the federal government to pre-empt conflicting state law, rather than a greater involvement of state governments in federal trade policy-making. See Timothy Meyer and Ganesh Sitaraman, 'Trade and the Separation of Powers' (2019) 107 California Law Review 583, 666–71 and in particular 670 ('[W]hat Congress has not done is give the executive the authority to preempt WTO-inconsistent state laws through regulation').

state law yields to federal law in case of conflict. The ability of the US federal government to pre-empt state law allows the federal government to unilaterally decide how much policy space states enjoy to engage in intergovernmental relations. If the federal government has not acted, the 'field' is clear, and state governments may act on the basis of their own constitutional powers. Conversely, the federal government may have covered the field entirely. In such an event, states are no longer in a position to act independently. It may also mean, however, that federal law expressly allows state governments to act, despite the federal government's exhaustive regulation of an area.

Secondly, under the *non-commandeering principle*, the federal government cannot issue instructions to the states.[32] This approach—based on an underlying philosophy the late Justice Scalia in the *Printz* case referred to as one of 'dual sovereignty'[33]—can be contrasted, as Justice Breyer noted in the same case,[34] with the EU's system of executive federalism wherein Member States are constitutionally obliged to implement EU law.[35] The non-commandeering principle also prevents a framework from emerging wherein the US federal government would be constitutionally obliged under a principle of 'federal loyalty', 'sincere cooperation', or 'cooperative federalism' to involve states in the federal foreign policy decision-making process, or to take into account state interests in that process. Instead, as discussed in Chapter 4, US states are to stay clear of whatever the federal government undertakes on the international stage. And if they interfere, for example by adopting legislation that affects US foreign policy, they risk having that legislation pre-empted on the basis of the dormant foreign affairs pre-emption doctrine.[36] Indeed, the combination of the pre-emption and non-commandeering principles leads to a constitutional landscape in which state governments simultaneously find themselves in a *weak position*, as their ability to act independently depends on the preferences of the federal government, and in a relatively *strong position*, since the federal government, when it does act, cannot coerce state governments into following federal orders.

[32] *Printz v United States*, 521 US 898, 117 S Ct 2365, 138 L Ed 2d 914 (1997), 925 ('[T]he Federal Government may not compel the States to enact or administer a federal regulatory program').

[33] ibid 918.

[34] ibid 976 ('The federal systems of Switzerland, Germany, and the European Union, for example, all provide that constituent states, not federal bureaucracies, will themselves implement many of the laws, rules, regulations, or decrees enacted by the central "federal" body').

[35] TEU, art 4(3).

[36] *Am Ins Ass'n v Garamendi*, 539 US 396, 123 S Ct 2374, 156 L Ed 2d 376 (2003).

To this picture consisting of the pre-emption and non-commandeering principles should be added the *Compact Clause*, which empowers state governments to conclude compacts—some without Congressional approval, some subject to such approval. In Chapter 2, I discussed how compacts that do not affect the 'just supremacy' of the US fall in the former category; those that do so fall in the latter. And in the US State Department's view, agreements that purport *not* to be binding do not affect the just supremacy of the US and thus do not require prior Congressional approval. To this rough sketch I now add some further nuance in an effort to explain why it is that intergovernmental collaboration in the US remains relatively informal—in marked contrast to the arrangements in Belgium and the EU, as will be discussed.

In its 1978 decision in *US Steel Corporation v Multistate Tax Commission*, the US Supreme Court provided some indicia to determine whether a state compact risks reaching the 'just supremacy' threshold.[37] A number of corporations had challenged the constitutionality under the Compact Clause of the agreement establishing the Multistate Tax Commission, a horizontal intergovernmental body that aims to support uniformity among state tax laws. The corporations, including the US Steel Corporation, argued that the agreement constituted a 'compact' in the meaning of the Compact Clause and thus required Congressional approval for it to be enacted. Such approval had of course neither been granted nor requested. The Supreme Court sided with the Multistate Tax Commission. It held that, while the agreement did constitute a compact, it was nonetheless not subject to the requirement of Congressional approval. In support of that conclusion, Justice Powell mentioned that (i) the pact '[did] not purport to authorize the member States to exercise any powers they could not exercise in its absence'; (ii) '[n]or [was] there any delegation of sovereign power to the Commission'; (iii) 'each State retain[ed] complete freedom to adopt or reject the rules and regulations of the Commission'; and, finally, (iv) 'each State [was] free to withdraw at any time'.[38]

Important in the Supreme Court's assessment was the absence of a central body with authority to adopt binding norms. *Some* degree of institutionalization appears to be permitted—and in *US Steel Corp* a multi-state body had in fact been established, but the institutional structure should not be granted rule-making authority. If the intergovernmental body is allocated such authority,

[37] *US Steel Corp v Multistate Tax Comm'n*, 434 US 452 (1978).
[38] ibid 473.

Congressional approval is required prior to the body's establishment. If Congress approves the agreement establishing the body, the agreement itself becomes part of federal law.[39] This means that the agreement pre-empts conflicting state law, but also that Congress has authority to repeal the agreement by means of a later statute in pursuance of the later-in-time rule. Consequently, in no scenario can state governments prevent the federal Congress from pre-empting state law by teaming up in order to establish collective institutions. As will be discussed later in the chapter, this arrangement differs substantially from that found within the EU, where relatively few restrictions exist on Member States engaging in horizontal intergovernmental relations and, in doing so, concluding IGAs.

* * *

In summary, the constitutional framework within which such collaboration is to take place in the US remains hierarchical and, to paraphrase Justice Scalia, distinctly 'dualist' in its orientation: the federal government has at its disposal the constitutional means to determine the extent to which state governments can engage in intergovernmental relations, be it with the federal government, or amongst themselves. And contrary to arrangements in federations such as the EU and Belgium, the US Constitution does not recognize a constitutional obligation to cooperate and respect the interests of the federation as a whole. Instead, intergovernmental relations in the US take place on the basis of what Daniel Halberstam has referred to as entitlements to power, not on the basis of considerations of federal loyalty or comity.[40] As state governments hold few such entitlements in the sphere of foreign relations, and as the federal government holds particularly broad authority to pre-empt state law within that sphere, it is perhaps not surprising that intergovernmental relations—despite being increasingly significant in practice—do not benefit from any form of constitutional protection in the US.

[39] See eg *Joint Resolution Expressing the consent and approval of Congress to an interstate compact regarding water resources in the Great Lakes—St Lawrence River Basin*, Public Law No: 110-342 <www.gpo.gov/fdsys/pkg/PLAW-110publ342/pdf/PLAW-110publ342.pdf> accessed 2 March 2022.

[40] Daniel Halberstam, 'Of Power and Responsibility: The Political Morality of Federal Systems' (2004) 90 Virginia Law Review 731.

3. Canada: Intergovernmental Relations Caught between Cooperative Federalism and Parliamentary Sovereignty

3.1 Patterns of Intergovernmental Relations in Canada

Intergovernmental relations—both vertical and horizontal—are an important feature of Canadian federalism.[41] At the political and the administrative levels, representatives of the federal and member unit governments meet regularly, both to determine strategic objectives and to implement policies. Also in the context of foreign relations governments often engage with one another. International trade policy is a case in point. In the first half of the twentieth century, Canada became more and more involved in international negotiations on subject matters under provincial jurisdiction. As a consequence, it became increasingly important for Canada's federal government to engage with provincial governments. Provinces can provide the federal government with valuable expertise and, in pursuance of the *Labour Conventions* ruling discussed in Chapter 2, their support might be crucial in ensuring the compliance of Canada with the outcome of negotiations.

In terms of *vertical* intergovernmental relations, over time mechanisms for federal–provincial consultations on foreign relations issues have developed.[42] At the political level, federal and provincial premiers occasionally organize summit-like meetings, referred to as First Ministers Meetings.[43] At the administrative level, contacts between federal and provincial officials are organized along sectoral lines.[44] For example, in the framework of international trade policy, Canada's federal government regularly—typically four

[41] Marc-Antoine Adam, Josée Bergeron, and Marianne Bonnard, 'Intergovernmental Relations in Canada: Competing Visions and Diverse Dynamics' in Johanne Poirier, Cheryl Saunders, and John Kincaid (eds), *Intergovernmental Relations in Federal Systems (*Oxford University Press Canada 2015) 135, 140, speaking of 'a very rich web of intergovernmental relations'.

[42] Describing this machinery, see eg Christopher J Kukucha, 'Federalism Matters: Evaluating the Impact of Sub-Federal Governments in Canadian and American Foreign Trade Policy' (2015) 21 Canadian Foreign Policy Journal 224.

[43] First Ministers Meetings bring together the premiers of Canada's provinces and territories and Canada's Prime Minister. They are to be distinguished from the Council of the Federation, a body that brings together only the former but not the latter. On the Council of the Federation, see generally Julie M Simmons, 'Canadian Multilateral Intergovernmental Institutions and the Limits of Institutional Innovation' (2017) 27 Regional & Federal Studies 573.

[44] André Lecours, 'Balancing Self-Rule and Shared-Rule: Sources of Tensions and Political Responses in Contemporary Political Systems', in Alberto López Basaguren and Leire Escajedo San Epifanio, *The Ways of Federalism in Western Countries and the Horizons of Territorial A utonomy in Spain* (Springer 2013) 109 ('Consultation surrounding the implementation of treaties or the definition of Canadian positions on matters of provincial jurisdiction takes place within sectoral intergovernmental forums').

times a year—consults with the provinces within the Committee for North American Free Trade Negotiations (CTRADE).[45] Moreover, in the context of the CETA negotiations with the EU in the 2010–14 period, Canadian provincial governments were, for the first time, directly involved in negotiations with the European Commission.[46] By contrast, during the negotiations with South Korea and India, provincial involvement was limited to the CTRADE committee.[47]

Crucially, the machinery and processes of consultation between the federal and provincial governments in Canada remain, as they are in the US, informal. No vertical-multilateral intergovernmental agreements have been concluded between the federal and provincial governments in Canada, even though provincial governments have called for such agreements.[48] The machinery operates on the basis of mutual trust between the federal and provincial governments, and thus only performs as well as the participants allow it to function.[49] This is true not only for international trade. In the framework of environmental policy—another policy area of international concern over which the division of legislative power between the federal and provincial levels of government is contested[50]—the federal and provincial governments

[45] Yulia Minaeva, 'Canadian Federalism Uncovered: The Assumed, the Forgotten and the Unexamined in Collaborative Federalism' (PhD thesis, University of Ottawa 2012) 168.

[46] On this topic, see generally Christopher J Kukucha, 'Canadian Sub-Federal Governments and CETA: Overarching Themes and Future Trends' (2013) 68 International Journal: Canada's Journal of Global Policy Analysis 528. For a positive assessment of the influence of the provinces on the CETA negotiations, see Pierre-Marc Johnson, Patrick Muzzi, and Véronique Bastien, 'The Voice of Quebec in the CETA Negotiations' (2013) 68 International Journal: Canada's Journal of Global Policy Analysis 560. Pierre-Marc Johnson is a former premier of Quebec. He represented Quebec during the CETA negotiations.

[47] Christopher J Kukucha, 'Federalism and Liberalization: Evaluating the Impact of American and Canadian Sub-Federal Governments on the Negotiation of International Trade Agreements' (2017) 22 International Negotiation 259, 266. Kukucha emphasized that provincial governments did not protest against this return to previous patterns of provincial involvement. He regarded the strong trust-ties as an explanation for this lack of protest. The positive CETA experience arguably further strengthened these ties.

[48] See Carl Meyer, 'Provinces Want Trade Role Outlined in Writing' *Embassy* (August 2011) <http://canada-europe.org/en/pdf/Provinces%20Want%20Trade%20Role%20Outlined%20in%20Writing%20-%20August%202011.pdf> accessed 2 March 2022. See further Gregory J Inwood, Carolyn Johns, and Patricia O'Reilly, *Intergovernmental Policy Capacity in Canada: Inside the Worlds of Finance, Environment, Trade, and Health* (McGill-Queen's Press 2011) 224.

[49] It should be added that trust levels between federal and provincial governments is typically high. In this sense, see eg the comments by the representative of Quebec during the CETA negotiations, speaking of 'a solid and enriching working relationship' (Johnson, Muzzi, and Bastien (n 46) 561). This does not mean conflicts never arise, however. During the CETA negotiations, the province of Newfoundland and Labrador occasionally picked fights with the federal government. See eg 'CETA Negotiations with Ottawa Suspended over Fisheries Fund, N.L. Says' *CBC News* (19 January 2015) <www.cbc.ca/1.2917699> accessed 2 March 2022.

[50] See recently *References re Greenhouse Gas Pollution Pricing Act*, 2021 SCC 11 on the constitutionality of a federal 'carbon tax'. The Supreme Court of Canada upheld the Act, considering the issue to be of 'national concern' under the federal Parliament's power to legislate with regard to the 'peace, order and good government' of Canada.

in 2017 'adopted' a 'Pan-Canadian Framework on Clean Growth and Climate Change'. The plan of action aimed to ensure that Canada would meet its emission reduction targets under the Paris Agreement.[51] The Framework is not clothed in legal language. It is best understood not as a multilateral intergovernmental agreement, but rather as a shared political commitment by most of Canada's first ministers. This is an effective approach as long as a sufficient number of governments participate and are committed to the plan's success.[52] Saskatchewan—one of the few Canadian governments led by a conservative government in late 2017[53]—refused to 'adopt' the plan,[54] and the Progressive Conservative Ontario government which entered into office in June 2017 decided not to implement a provincial carbon tax, which was one of the plan's core components.[55]

It is not hard to imagine more provincial governments, led by political parties of a different ideological persuasion than the party in power in Ottawa, Canada's federal capital, opposing federal-led intergovernmental initiatives. When this happens, one can expect the federal government to try to revert to coercion—for example through the use of its power to spend or tax. This is what happened following the disavowal of the abovementioned Pan-Canadian Framework on Clean Growth and Climate Change by several provincial governments. The plan required all Canadian provinces to put in place a carbon pricing mechanism. For those provinces who refused to do so, the federal government decided to impose a federal carbon tax. Several provincial governments challenged the constitutionality of the federal carbon tax. The Supreme Court of Canada rejected the challenge in September 2021.[56] Dynamics such as these point to the degree to which intergovernmental relations in Canada are contingent on political ideology and partisan affiliations, as well as on the personality of the different stakeholders.

[51] The plan is available at <www.canada.ca/en/services/environment/weather/climatechange/pan-canadian-framework.html> accessed 2 March 2022.

[52] On the plan, see Hélène Trudeau and Charles Codère, 'À la recherche d'une tarification pancanadienne du carbone: les enjeux juridiques de la coopération intergouvernementale pour protéger le climat' (2018) 18 Fédéralisme Régionalisme 3–4.

[53] In mid-2018, five governments were led by liberal premiers; two governments by New Democratic Party premiers, while Saskatchewan was led by the conservative-leaning Saskatchewan Party and both Manitoba and Ontario by a Progressive Conservative premier.

[54] John P Tasker, 'Trudeau Announces "pan-Canadian Framework" on Climate—but Sask., Manitoba Hold Off' *CBC News* (10 December 2016) <www.cbc.ca/news/politics/trudeau-premiers-climate-deal-1.3888244> accessed 2 March 2022.

[55] 'Cap-and-Trade Is over, Ontario PCs Say as New Legislation Unveiled' *CBC News* (25 July 2018) <www.cbc.ca/news/canada/toronto/ontario-pc-legislation-kills-cap-and-trade-1.4761398> accessed 2 March 2022.

[56] *References re Greenhouse Gas Pollution Pricing Act*, 2021 SCC 11.

While vertical and horizontal *multilateral* intergovernmental relations in Canada remain informal in nature, the federal government does sometimes conclude more formal *bilateral* intergovernmental agreements with provinces. For example, in 2006, the governments of Canada and Quebec concluded an agreement granting the Quebec government a right of representation within the Canadian delegation to UNESCO.[57] Similarly, the federal government has concluded separate agreements on immigration policy with Quebec, Manitoba, and British Columbia, making it possible for these provinces to play a role in selecting immigrants applying for settlement in Canada. Similarly, provincial governments can conclude horizontal intergovernmental agreements with one another. They have done so, for example, in the context of climate change policy, where Ontario in September 2017 announced that it would join the Quebec-California cap-and-trade system mentioned earlier—a decision which the subsequent Progressive Conservative government reversed.[58]

3.2 Intergovernmental Relations in Canada: Caught between Cooperative Federalism and Parliamentary Sovereignty

What is the constitutional status of these intergovernmental agreements? And what would be the status of an agreement that aims to formalize existing consultation processes between all federal and provincial governments in the context of treaty negotiations? As a matter of Canadian constitutional theory, both the federal and provincial legislatures remain supreme (or 'sovereign') within their sphere of jurisdiction.[59] In this way, the principle of parliamentary sovereignty, which Canada inherited from the UK, remains applicable, albeit adapted to Canada's federal architecture. According to this understanding, it is not possible for governments to incur legally binding commitments with one another, at least not commitments that are protected against later legislative

[57] Agreement between the Government of Canada and the Government of Quebec concerning the United Nations Educational, Scientific, and Cultural Organization (UNESCO) <www.mrif.gouv.qc.ca/content/documents/en/accord-unesco.pdf> accessed 30 November 2017.

[58] 'Ontario Signs Formal Agreement to Join Quebec-California Carbon Market in 2018' *The Toronto Star* (22 September 2017) <www.thestar.com/news/canada/2017/09/22/ontario-signs-formal-agreement-to-join-quebec-california-carbon-market-in-2018.html> accessed 2 March 2022.

[59] On the 'classical' conception of Canadian federalism, see Bruce Ryder, 'The Demise and Rise of the Classical Paradigm in Canadian Federalism: Promoting Autonomy for the Provinces and First Nations' (1990) 36 McGill Law Journal 308, 310.

measures. As is the case in the UK, apart from so-called 'manner and form' requirements, Canadian legislatures cannot bind their successors.[60]

The Supreme Court of Canada has provided guidance on what the principle of parliamentary sovereignty means for the legal status of intergovernmental agreements.[61] In its 1991 decision in *Canada Assistance Plan*, the Court held that the federal executive could lawfully table a Bill in the federal Parliament that aimed to unilaterally reduce the contribution of the federal government to the Canada Assistance Plan, even though, in doing so, the federal government would violate financial commitments towards provincial governments.[62] These commitments were formalized in a series of agreements concluded with the provinces. In response to the unilateral decision by the federal government to reduce its contribution, British Columbia had launched a constitutional challenge. It argued that by concluding an intergovernmental agreement with British Columbia when the Canada Assistance Plan was first established, the federal government had created 'legitimate expectations' that it would maintain its financial contributions to the federal-provincial scheme over time.[63] The Supreme Court rejected the legitimate expectations argument. It held that British Columbia's argument ran counter the principle of parliamentary sovereignty. By preventing the federal executive from proposing a Bill, Parliament itself would be prevented from exercising its powers.[64] In short, in *Canada Assistance Plan*, the Supreme Court of Canada affirmed that within the scope of each province's exclusive legislative powers the principle of parliamentary sovereignty retains its full force. As a consequence, both federal and provincial legislatures can at all times override an intergovernmental agreement to which

[60] The debate between those supportive of the possibility of placing legal fetters on the sovereignty of Parliament, and those that oppose this possibility on the basis of the argument that the will of Parliament is the *Grundnorm* of the British constitution, is of long standing. For a defence of the latter conception, see seminally the work of AV Dicey, in particular Albert V Dicey, *Introduction to the Study of the Law of the Constitution* (Reprint. Originally published 8th edn, Macmillan 1915, Liberty Classics 1982). For a defence of the former conception, see Sir Ivor Jennings, *The Law and the Constitution* (University of London Press 1963), in particular ch 4.

[61] For a brief exploration of the issue, see also J Anthony VanDuzer, 'Could an Intergovernmental Agreement Increase the Credibility of Canadian Treaty Commitments in Areas of Provincial Jurisdiction?' (2012) 68 International Journal 536, and more elaborately: J Anthony VanDuzer and Melanie J Mallet, 'Compliance with Canada's Trade and Investment Treaty Obligations: Addressing the Gap Between Provincial Action and Federal Responsibility' (2016) 54 Alberta Law Review 89, 124–37.

[62] *Reference Re Canada Assistance Plan (BC)*, [1991] 2 SCR 525, 1991 CanLII 74 (SCC).

[63] The doctrine of legitimate expectations is well known in Canadian administrative law and in common law more generally. On this topic in the former context, see generally David Wright, 'Rethinking the Doctrine of Legitimate Expectations in Canadian Administrative Law' (1997) 35 Osgoode Hall Law Journal 139.

[64] *Reference Re Canada Assistance Plan (BC)*, [1991] 2 SCR 525, 1991 CanLII 74 (SCC) ('A restraint on the executive in the introduction of legislation would place a fetter on the sovereignty of Parliament itself').

its executive is a party. This is possible, even if the legislature had previously confirmed the intergovernmental agreement by means of a legislative act.

Canada Assistance Plan was decided in 1991. In its 1998 *Quebec Secession Reference*, the Supreme Court of Canada recognized the existence of unwritten constitutional principles in Canada, the purpose of which was to steer the interpretation of the constitutional text.[65] The principle of federalism was recognized as such a principle; the principle of parliamentary sovereignty, curiously enough, was not. More recently still, in a series of judgments on the division of legislative powers between the federal and provincial governments, the Supreme Court of Canada has recognized a principle of 'cooperative federalism'.[66] This principle influences the division of powers analysis in the sense that it steers Canadian courts towards a more 'flexible' approach grounded in a recognition that it is impossible to maintain a strict ('watertight compartments') separation between the federal and provincial legislative powers. As policy challenges cut across areas of jurisdiction, it is important that Canadian governments can work together effectively, the argument ran. To facilitate this process, the Supreme Court has been willing to uphold 'interlocking' federal-provincial legislative and administrative frameworks.[67]

The emphasis on 'cooperative federalism' led some commentators to wonder whether a duty of sincere cooperation akin to the German principle of *Bundestreue*—or the EU's duty of sincere cooperation—might be in the process of emerging in Canada. In a 2014 article, Jean-François Gaudréault-DesBiens, for example, made the case for a Canadian principle of 'federal loyalty'.[68] In support, he relied on the abovementioned *Quebec Secession Reference*, in which Canada's Supreme Court had derived a duty incumbent on the federal and Quebec governments to engage in discussions if Quebec were to vote in

[65] *Reference re Secession of Quebec*, [1998] 2 SCR 217, 1998 CanLII 793 (SCC). On the role of unwritten constitutional principles in Canada, see generally Mark D Walters, 'Written Constitutions and Unwritten Constitutionalism' in Grant Huscroft (ed), *Expounding the Constitution: Essays in Constitutional Theory* (Cambridge University Press 2008). On the significance of the *Quebec Secession Reference* in the development of Canadian constitutional theory, see generally Sujit Choudhry and Robert Howse, 'Constitutional Theory and The Quebec Secession Reference' (2000) 13 Canadian Journal of Law & Jurisprudence 143, 151ff.

[66] See eg *Canadian Western Bank v Alberta*, [2007] 2 SCR 3, 2007 SCC 22 (CanLII).

[67] The clearest example of this willingness to uphold cooperative legislative schemes can be found in *Fédération des producteurs de volailles du Québec v Pelland*, [2005] 1 SCR 292, 2005 SCC 20 (CanLII). But see also *Reference re Securities Act*, [2011] 3 SCR 837, 2011 SCC 66 (CanLII), in which the court invalidated a federal statute to establish a national securities regulator. The court held at [62] that, 'notwithstanding the Court's promotion of cooperative and flexible federalism, the constitutional boundaries that underlie the division of powers must be respected. The "dominant tide" of flexible federalism, however strong its pull may be, cannot sweep designated powers out to sea, nor erode the constitutional balance inherent in the Canadian federal state.'

[68] Jean-François Gaudreault-DesBiens, 'Cooperative Federalism in Search of a Normative Justification: Considering the Principle of Federal Loyalty' (2014) 23 Constitutional Forum 1.

favour of seceding from Canada. If such a duty exists in the event of a constitutional crisis of this type, should it not also exist in the everyday management of Canadian federalism, Gaudréault-DesBiens wondered. In the same vein, an argument could perhaps be made that the federal government is under a constitutional obligation to consult and involve provincial governments in treaty negotiations that touch on subject matters within their legislative jurisdiction, and that intergovernmental agreements are protected against legislative override by later legislatures by virtue of a principle of federal loyalty.

In the 2015 decision in the case of *Firearms Registry II*, the Supreme Court rejected arguments of this type and reaffirmed the principle of parliamentary sovereignty.[69] The province of Quebec had argued that, by refusing to transfer to the Quebec authorities the data contained in a soon-to-be-destroyed firearms registry, the federal government had violated the principle of cooperative federalism. In response to the decision by the federal government to repeal the national registry, the Quebec government wished to establish its own registry. To do so, it wanted to make use of the data held by the federal government. The Quebec Superior Court had accepted the argument of the Quebec government. The Quebec Court of Appeals overturned and reaffirmed the primacy of the principle of parliamentary sovereignty within the constitutional order of Canada. The majority of the members of the Supreme Court took the same position as the Court of Appeals. They held that:

> [n]either this Court's jurisprudence nor the text of the Constitution Act, 1867 supports using [the principle of cooperative federalism] to limit the scope of legislative authority or to impose a positive obligation to facilitate cooperation where the constitutional division of powers authorizes unilateral action. To hold otherwise would undermine parliamentary sovereignty and create legal uncertainty whenever one order of government adopted legislation having some impact on the policy objectives of another. Paradoxically, such an approach could discourage the practice of cooperative federalism for fear that cooperative measures could risk diminishing a government's legislative authority to act alone.[70]

[69] *Quebec (Attorney General) v. Canada (Attorney General) ('Firearms Registry II')*, [2015] 1 SCR 693, 2015 SCC 14 (CanLII) [20].

[70] ibid [20].

The Supreme Court in *Firearms Registry II* reaffirmed the classic 'diceyan' position, albeit modified to Canada's federal framework.[71] This means, firstly, that Canadian governments cannot rely on an unwritten cooperative federalism principle to challenge the constitutionality of what is otherwise a lawful exercise of legislative authority. Secondly, the ruling in *Firearms Registry II* reaffirms *Canada Assistance Plan*, in the sense that intergovernmental agreements remain legally fragile in Canada.[72] As in the US, even if an agreement—for example a hypothetical agreement in which the federal government commits itself to involving the provincial governments in all treaty negotiations on subject matters within provincial legislative jurisdiction—were to be embedded in federal legislation, it remains possible for a future federal parliament to override the terms of the agreement, or even to repeal the agreement in its entirety, provided it does so clearly and unambiguously.

Whether a Canadian *executive* could repeal an intergovernmental agreement independently from the *legislature* is an open question. Johanne Poirier highlighted how the Supreme Court in *Canada Assistance Plan* rejected the argument based on the legitimate expectations doctrine in so far as that doctrine could not restrict parliamentary sovereignty.[73] This does not necessarily mean that the executive, absent any legislative initiative, would be equally free to withdraw from or amend intergovernmental agreements concluded with other Canadian governments. However, even if the doctrine of legitimate expectations does indeed restrict the *executive* in its ability to amend or withdraw from agreements, the executive retains its ability to do so by involving the *legislature*, provided the executive has the confidence of a majority of MPs. (In Canada's Westminster parliamentary system characterized by executive control over the legislature, this would not be a hypothetical scenario.)

***

In summary, intergovernmental relations in Canada occur both horizontally, between provincial governments, and vertically, between federal and provincial governments in Canada. They can be bilateral, plurilateral, or multilateral,

[71] Albert Venn Dicey defined parliamentary sovereignty as the principle 'that Parliament has the right to make or un-make any law whatever; and further, that no person or body is recognised by the law of England as having a right to override or set aside the legislation of Parliament'. See Dicey (n 60) xxxvi.

[72] *Quebec (Attorney General) v Canada (Attorney General) ('Firearms Registry II')*, [2015] 1 SCR 693, 2015 SCC 14 (CanLII) [25].

[73] Johanne Poirier, 'Souveraineté parlementaire et armes à feu: le fédéralisme coopératif dans la ligne de mire? (Parliamentary Sovereignty and Firearms: Cooperative Federalism on the Line)' (2015) 45 Revue de droit de l'Université de Sherbrooke 47, 93.

and they touch on Canada's foreign relations as well as on strictly domestic issues. In the daily functioning of Canadian federalism, intergovernmental relations are crucial as they compensate, to some extent, for the comparatively weak political safeguards of Canadian federalism discussed in Chapter 6. Or as Jean Leclair put it: 'Federalism having deserted for all intents and purposes the Senate, the House of Commons and the Cabinet, it made its nest in intergovernmental relations.'[74] However, in constitutional terms, the status of these intergovernmental relations is fragile. Intergovernmental agreements concluded between Canadian governments, be they provincial or federal, can be legally binding. However, they cannot bind future parliaments, in accordance with what in the US is known as the 'later-in-time rule'. A constitutional principle of cooperative federalism exists in Canada, but it cannot restrict governments in their ability to legislate. At most, the principle serves as an aid in the interpretation of the scope of the powers allocated to Canada's governments: to facilitate cooperation between governments, courts should interpret the heads of power broadly so as to protect interlocking schemes of federal-provincial collaboration.

4. Belgium: A Constitutional Obligation to Build Consensus

4.1 Patterns of Intergovernmental Relations in Belgium

As is the case with foreign relations federalism in Canada, intergovernmental relations are a central feature of Belgian foreign relations federalism. In contrast to Canada as well as the US, intergovernmental relations are highly formalized in Belgium: intergovernmental agreements between Belgian governments are abundant.[75] They are concluded between the federal and member unit governments (vertical agreements) and between member unit governments (horizontal

[74] Jean Leclair, 'Tolstoï et les juges Beetz et Laskin: à la recherche du citoyen dans le discours judiciaire relatif au fédéralisme' in Alain-G Gagnon, Pierre Noreau, and José Woehrling (eds), *Constitutionnalisme, droits et diversité: mélanges en l'honneur de José Woehrling* (Les éditions Thémis 2017) 135 (Translation TV. Original: *'Le fédéralisme ayant, à toutes fins utiles, déserté le Sénat, la Chambre de communes et le Cabinet, il a fait son nid dans les relations intergouvernementales'*).

[75] Writing in 2006, Johanne Poirier mentioned that between 200 and 300 intergovernmental agreements had been concluded on the basis of Article 92*bis* SLIR. See Johanne Poirier, 'Le droit public survivra-t-il à sa contractualisation?' (2006) 33 Revue de droit de l'ULB 261, 267. In 2022, Patricia Popelier mentioned that over 500 agreements had been concluded, of which 417 were still in force at the time of writing. See Patricia Popelier, 'Intergovernmental Relations in Belgium: Obstacles to Effective Cooperation in Dyadic Federalism' in Yonatan T Fessha, Karl Kössler, and Francesco Palermo (eds), *Intergovernmental Relations in Divided Societies* (Springer International Publishing 2022) 77.

agreements).[76] Some agreements are multilateral, involving several or all governments, others are bilateral.[77] Relevant for present purposes is that Belgian governments have concluded vertical-multilateral intergovernmental agreements which allow for member unit involvement in the exercise of federal foreign relations powers, including the power to ensure the external representation of Belgium within international organizations or in third countries.[78] In addition, intergovernmental agreements are key instruments to facilitate the negotiation and conclusion of mixed agreements in Belgium.[79]

Intergovernmental agreements have contributed to the emergence of an infrastructure for vertical government-to-government cooperation in foreign relations in Belgium. The rules and principles set out in these agreements are premised on the fundamental equality of the different Belgian governments. In the treaty-making context, for example, the Cooperation Agreement Mixed Agreements requires the different governments involved in the process of negotiating mixed agreements to share information and jointly decide on a negotiation strategy. They must do so 'on an equal footing', the agreement provides.[80] Unanimous approval is required also in the subsequent phases of the treaty-making process: all governments must agree to the signing of the treaty,[81] the legislatures of the different governments must grant their consent,[82] and all governments must agree on a potential termination of the agreement.[83]

Similarly, the Cooperation Agreement International Organizations requires the Belgian federal government to share information with the member unit governments on issues that are of importance to them,[84] and it grants member unit governments the possibility of designating a representative within the

[76] See eg *Samenwerkingsakkoord van 10 december 2014 tussen de Vlaamse Gemeenschap, de Franse Gemeenschap en de Duitstalige Gemeenschap betreffende het beheer van het elektronisch toezicht*, *BS* 2 March 2015.

[77] See eg *Accord de coopération entre la Région wallonne et la Communauté germanophone du 28 novembre 1998*, *BS* 21 March 1998. <http://environnement.wallonie.be/legis/accords_de_cooperation/rw_cgerm.htm> accessed 2 March 2022.

[78] *Samenwerkingsakkoord van 18 mei 1995 tussen de federale staat, de gemeenschappen en de gewesten betreffende het statuut van de vertegenwoordigers van de gemeenschappen en de gewesten in de diplomatieke en consulaire posten* (*BS* 16 October 2014, err. 21 October 2014)) ('Cooperation Agreement Diplomatic Representatives').

[79] *Samenwerkingsakkoord van 8 maart 1994 tussen de federale overheid, de gemeenschappen en de gewesten over de nadere regelen voor het sluiten van gemengde verdragen*, *BS* 17 December 1996 ('Cooperation Agreement Mixed Agreements').

[80] Cooperation Agreement Mixed Agreements, art 5 para 1.

[81] Johanne Poirier, 'Formal Mechanisms of Intergovernmental Relations in Belgium' (2002) 12 Regional & Federal Studies 24, 36.

[82] 1831 Belgian Constitution, art 167 §3.

[83] Cooperation Agreement Mixed Agreements, art 17.

[84] *Kaderakkoord van 30 juni 1994 tot samenwerking tussen de federale staat, de gemeenschappen en de gewesten over de vertegenwoordiging van het Koninkrijk België bij de internationale organisaties waarvan de werkzaamheden betrekking hebben op gemengde bevoegdheden*, *BS* 19 November 1994 ('Cooperation Agreement International Organizations'), art 2.

Belgian delegation. This delegate is to receive instructions directly from the member unit government.[85] As is the case in the context of mixed treaty negotiations, the Belgian position to be defended within the international organization at issue is to be determined on a consensual basis by the different governments. The different governments meet within a working group consisting of civil servants. If an agreement fails to be reached at the administrative level, the matter is transferred to the Interministerial Conference on Foreign Policy (ICFP).[86] If no agreement can be reached in this forum, the matter can ultimately be discussed within the Concertation Committee, which consists of the heads of government—although it should immediately be added that this is a rare occurrence.

The involvement of Belgium in the workings of the EU is structured along similar lines as well.[87] Here, too, the different Belgian governments jointly determine the position Belgium will defend during the meetings of the Council, the body representing the interests of the Member States within the EU political process. Before each meeting of the Council, representatives of the Belgian governments coordinate to decide on a common position.[88] Without a common position determined beforehand, Belgium has no position, and it cannot vote in the Council.[89] Furthermore, when the Council discusses topics that primarily fall within the scope of the powers of the Belgian member units, member unit ministers will represent Belgium. To this end, the Cooperation Agreement European Union provides for a rotation system whereby ministers of the different member unit governments decide on who is to represent Belgium on which occasion.[90] Also, in the preparatory meetings of the Council at the ambassadorial and technical levels, the abovementioned cooperation agreement includes arrangements to ensure that the different Belgian governments have an equal say in the decision-making process.[91]

[85] ibid art 4.

[86] ibid art 7.

[87] See the *Samenwerkingsakkoord van 8 maart 1994 tussen de federale staat, de gemeenschappen en de gewesten, met betrekking tot de vertegenwoordiging van het Koninkrijk België in de Ministerraad van de Europese Unie, BS* 17 November 1994 ('Cooperation Agreement European Union').

[88] ibid art 2(2).

[89] ibid art 2(5), which states that without prior coordination Belgium cannot vote. In the same spirit, the equal position of all governments in the coordination process implies that Belgium cannot vote absent a position all governments agreed upon during the coordination process. In this sense, see also Popelier (n 75) 74, who for further support refers to Bart Kerremans, 'Determining a European Policy in a Multi-level Setting: The Case of Specialized Co-ordination in Belgium' (2000) 10 Regional & Federal Studies 36.

[90] Cooperation Agreement European Union, art 7.

[91] The unofficial explanatory annex to the Cooperation Agreement European Union provides that Belgium's permanent representative to the EU will represent Belgium in the meetings of COREPER, the meeting of the Member State ambassadors which prepares Council meetings. He will be assisted by sectoral working groups, which include representatives of the member unit governments.

In short, intergovernmental agreements have transposed to the external sphere the domestic practices of consensus-based decision-making that characterize domestic Belgian federalism as a result of the fragmented division of exclusive competences.[92] As will be discussed in the next chapter, the express recognition of federal-member unit equality in the context of mixed external action can be contrasted with the state of affairs at EU level, where no comprehensive provisions have been made to manage mixity.

4.2 Intergovernmental Relations in Belgium: A Constitutional Obligation to Build Consensus

What is the legal status of intergovernmental agreements between Belgian governments? Taking into account the choice of the framers of the Belgian constitution to divide powers on an exclusive basis, one might have expected an answer similar to that articulated in Canada, where the Supreme Court clarified that the cooperative federalism principle cannot preclude governments from exercising the competences allocated to them by the constitution. This is not the course taken in Belgium, however. As Johanne Poirier mentioned in a 2002 contribution, most Belgian commentators have displayed a visceral desire to portray cooperative agreements as binding legal instruments.[93] Furthermore, there is an understanding that the agreements are binding also on future governments, in the sense that a government cannot, be it through executive action or through legislation, override or amend an intergovernmental agreement.[94] Intergovernmental agreements are thus ranked above legislation adopted by the various Belgian legislatures.

Different theories have been articulated to identify a normative basis for the primacy of intergovernmental agreements over secondary legislation. Some have relied on international law, where the *pacta sunt servanda* principle requires states to respect their international obligations regardless of later changes to their domestic law.[95] Others—and most notably the Belgian Constitutional

[92] In this sense, see also Geert Craenen, 'België en het buitenland. De nieuwe regeling van de buitenlandse betrekkingen' in André Alen and LP Suetens (eds), *Het federale België na de vierde staatshervorming. Een commentaar op de Nieuwe Grondwet en haar uitvoeringswetten* (die Keure 1993) 100–01.

[93] Poirier (n 81) 41. By contrast, early commentators questioned the very constitutionality of intergovernmental agreements. See eg Craenen (n 92) 102.

[94] See on this Constitutional Court Nr 62/2016 of 28 April 2016, at B.3.4, where the Belgian Constitutional Court held that, taking into account the principle of federal loyalty, the terms of a cooperative agreement cannot be amended unilaterally.

[95] Vienna Convention on the Law of Treaties (VCLT), art 27. See on this Marc Uyttendaele, *Trente leçons de droit constitutionnel* (2nd edn, Anthémis Editions 2014) 959–60, identifying a *'parallelisme des*

Court—have turned to a principle of federal loyalty as a normative foundation for the binding character and primacy of cooperation agreements.[96] Yet others have argued—perhaps inspired by Hans Kelsen's three circle theory of federalism[97]—that they are governed by a 'third level' of law that encompasses the federal and member unit legal orders.[98] While overarching principles of constitutional and international law may very well lend additional support to the proposition that Belgian governments cannot unilaterally override the provisions of cooperation agreements, a textual argument may however be sufficient to make the point, at least for those agreements we have looked at in this chapter. Article 39 of the Belgian Constitution holds:

> The law assigns to the regional bodies that it creates and that are composed of elected representatives the power to manage the matters that it determines, with the exception of those referred to in Articles 30 and 127 to 129, within the scope and according to the manner laid down by a law. This law must be passed by a majority as described in Article 4, last paragraph.

This constitutional provision empowers the federal Parliament, by means of a 'special law' adopted by a supermajority (ie the 'majority as described in Article 4, last paragraph'), to both allocate powers to the member units (the 'regional bodies') and impose restrictions on the scope of those powers as well as the way in which those powers can be exercised by those regional bodies ('within the scope and according to the manner laid down by a law'). In the federal 'special law' adopted in pursuance of this constitutional provision, the federal supermajority *mandated* the different Belgian governments to conclude cooperation agreements with one another. This is the case for the Cooperation Agreement

formes' between international agreements and IGAs. For an earlier argument in this sense, see Pierre Klein, *Un aspect du fédéralisme coopératif horizontal: les accords de coopération entre entités fédérées* (ULB Centre d'études du fédéralisme 1990), 9 (*'Il reste que, dans de très nombreuses situations, ce sont ces règles tirées du droit des traités qui fournissent les réponses les plus appropriées à des problèmes qui, s'ils se situent dans un ordre juridique différent, n'en sont pas moins fondamentalement de même nature*'). The legislative division of the Belgian Council of State has made a similar application by analogy with the principle to support the holding that intergovernmental agreements in Belgium cannot be amended unilaterally. See the reference to the opinion in Frank Judo, 'De zesde staatshervorming en het confederalisme' in Instituut voor Constitutioneel Recht Colloquium (ed), *Het federale België na de Zesde Staatshervorming* (die Keure 2014) 630. For further arguments in this sense, see the Council of State opinions mentioned in Dries Van Eeckhoutte and others, 'Behoorlijke wetgeving in de adviespraktijk van de afdeling wetgeving van de Raad van State' [2009] Tijdschrift voor Wetgeving 100, 116–17.

[96] See the reference in n 86.

[97] See generally Hans Kelsen, *General Theory of Law and State* (The Lawbook Exchange Ltd 1999).

[98] Yannick Peeters, *De plaats van samenwerkingsakkoorden in het constitutioneel kader* (Die Keure 2016) 164. In the Belgian context, the Kelsenian model has also been discussed in Raf Geenens and Helder De Schutter, 'A Tripartite Model of Federalism' [2022] Philosophy & Social Criticism 1, 12.

International Organizations, the Cooperation Agreement Mixed Agreements, and the Cooperation Agreement European Union.[99] The supermajority statute here delegates the legislature's authority to regulate how the different governments are to exercise their powers to those governments, and expressly empowers them to do so by means of an intergovernmental agreement. This delegation of authority by the supermajority legislator explains why the agreements themselves override later federal or member unit legislation: they have the same quasi-constitutional status as the supermajority statute from which they derive their authority. Hence, while *pacta sunt servanda* or federal loyalty may lend further support to the proposition that the agreements are binding and cannot be overridden by later legislation, the direct legal basis in the supermajority law, which in turn finds its legal basis directly in the Belgian Constitution, is sufficient in and of itself at least for the abovementioned intergovernmental agreements that are mandated by the SLIR.

Regardless of its precise normative foundations, the proposition is the same: the contractual nature of cooperation agreements in Belgium is understood to require that these agreements be binding not only today, but in the future as well.[100] This observation demonstrates how Belgian foreign relations federalism is ultimately, and despite its emphasis on exclusive powers, a federalism of shared as opposed to self-rule. Ironically, considering the framers' choice for exclusive treaty-making powers, Belgian foreign relations are to an important extent *mixed* foreign relations whereby the different member units must collaborate jointly to achieve policy objectives. This necessity of collaboration has translated into a web of intergovernmental agreements that aim to give a voice to the different Belgian governments in the 'mixed' political process. As we will see in the next chapter, these intergovernmental agreements differ in one important respect from the intergovernmental arrangements that exist between the EU and the Member States. Whereas intergovernmental agreements in Belgium are binding on all parties, in the EU they bind the Member States, but are not capable of overriding the autonomy of the EU.

[99] Art 92*bis*, §4*bis* and §4*ter* of the Special Law on Institutional Reform ('SLIR'), *BS* 8 August 1980.

[100] Emphasizing the linkages between the domestic constitutional principle of federal loyalty and the international legal principle of *pacta sunt servanda*, see Geert De Baere and Timothy Roes, 'EU Loyalty as Good Faith' (2015) 64 International & Comparative Law Quarterly 829.

5. Conclusion

The comparative overview of intergovernmental relations in the foreign relations sphere offered in this chapter once again puts into relief the different weight each of the federations explored in this book attaches to self-rule and shared rule. In both the US and Canada, self-rule carries greater weight than shared rule. In the US, governments work together, including on foreign relations issues, but they do so on the basis of what Daniel Halberstam calls entitlements rather than considerations of federal loyalty or comity.[101] The same can be said about Canada. While a constitutional principle of cooperative federalism has found its way into the case law of Canada's Supreme Court, the Supreme Court has already had the opportunity to clarify the principle's limits: it is, at most, an interpretative device which helps governments and courts to determine whether governments act within the limits of the legislative powers allocated to them by Canada's Constitution Act, 1867. The principle does not restrict their ability to exercise those powers.

By contrast, in Belgium, shared rule carries greater weight than self-rule in foreign relations. In Chapter 4, I explored the mechanisms that exist in Belgium to resolve conflicts between the federal and member unit governments. However, as discussed, these mechanisms are only seldom used and have in fact *never* been used in the context of Belgium's foreign relations. Instead, the Belgian foreign affairs constitution aims to facilitate shared rule. It does so, first, through the establishment of multiple political safeguards of foreign relations federalism, as discussed in Chapter 6. And it does so, secondly, by obliging governments to conclude what Yvan Peeters has referred to as 'intrafederal treaties', that is, intergovernmental agreements that are binding and have primacy over later secondary law.[102] Taken together, the Belgian foreign affairs constitution reveals itself as a consensus-building framework based on the fundamental proposition that absent consensus, nothing gets done.

[101] Daniel Halberstam, 'Of Power and Responsibility: The Political Morality of Federal Systems' (2004) 90 Virginia Law Review 731.
[102] Peeters (n 98) 177.

9
Intergovernmental Relations in EU Foreign Policy-Making

> Mixed agreements remain a fundamental characteristic of the [Union]'s external relations; and ... they are to be regarded as a pragmatically justified way of solving the problem of international representation in a multi-layered constitutional order such as the [European Union].
>
> Geert De Baere, member of the EU General Court[1]

1. Introduction

What practices of intergovernmental relations can be observed in EU foreign relations? How does EU law govern those practices? And how does the EU compare to the three federations examined in the previous chapter? In addressing these questions, I will look at both vertical and horizontal intergovernmental relations.

As mentioned in the introduction to the previous chapter, in the EU context *vertical intergovernmental relations* refers to relations between the EU institutions and the Member States outside of the framework of the two Councils in which the Member States are represented. Vertical intergovernmental relations are an important feature of EU foreign relations. Whenever the EU engages in mixed external action—and, as discussed in Chapter 3, it does so quite often—conceptually speaking the EU and its Member States are acting jointly on the international stage. How EU law manages the interactions between EU institutions and Member States on the international stage, as opposed to the role of Member States within the two Councils, is an evergreen question in the study of EU foreign relations law.[2]

[1] Geert De Baere, *Constitutional Principles of EU External Relations* (Oxford University Press 2008) 264.

[2] See eg David O'Keeffe and Henry G Schermers (eds), *Mixed Agreements* (Kluwer Law and Taxation Publishers 1983).

Foreign Relations Federalism. Thomas Verellen, Oxford University Press. © Thomas Verellen 2023.
DOI: 10.1093/oso/9780192844569.003.0009

By *horizontal intergovernmental relations*, I mean the interactions between Member States (intra-EU Member State agreements) and interactions between Member States and third countries (extra-EU Member State agreements). As international legal subjects in their own right, EU Member States have ample opportunity to engage in both types of interactions. Here as well, questions arise as to what limits, if any, EU law places on the ability of Member States to engage in either type of horizontal intergovernmental relations. For each subcategory of intergovernmental relations, I will look at patterns of institutional practice and at how EU law governs those patterns.

2. Vertical Intergovernmental Relations: Managing Mixity

I first look at vertical intergovernmental relations. As discussed in Chapter 3, in fields such as the common commercial policy (CCP), the EU holds exclusive competences to act externally. In these fields, EU law precludes Member States from acting. In other fields, the EU has no external competence at all. In such fields, only Member States can act externally. And in yet other fields, the EU has a shared competence to act externally. In such fields, both the EU and the Member States have a competence to act externally. However, when the EU acts, the Member States are precluded from acting. Whether or not the EU acts is a political decision that only the Council—which represents the Member States—can make.[3] When the Council determines that the EU should not exercise EU shared competence, the Member States can still act externally. This feature of the EU's foreign affairs constitution is relevant in particular when the EU considers concluding an international agreement that in whole or in part falls within the scope of the EU's shared competence. If the Council chooses not to exercise all of the shared EU competence needed to conclude the agreement, Member States must 'supplement' EU action to enable the EU to conclude the agreement. In such a scenario, the agreement becomes a mixed agreement.

The same principles apply to the implementation of international agreements. If an agreement establishes a body that can adopt decisions, and that body is called upon to take decisions which, as a matter of EU law, fall within the scope of the EU's shared competences, the Council is again at liberty to enable or not enable the EU to exercise its shared competence. Here, too, if the Council chooses to not exercise shared EU competence, Member States can act themselves, in their own capacity as parties to the mixed agreement.

[3] Case C-600/14 *Germany v Council ('COTIF')*, EU:C:2017:935, paras 65–68.

In practice, Member States will often choose to be represented by a single institution or office—often the Commission, sometimes the rotating Council Presidency—but legally speaking, any statements by that representative will be made not on behalf of the EU, but on behalf of the Member States collectively.[4]

The preceding paragraphs demonstrate how in the conduct of EU foreign relations Member States wear two hats. They are, on the one hand, decision-makers within the Council. They are, on the other, actors in their own right, outside of the EU framework. The EU and the Member States are often both present in international forums. This raises questions of shared rule: how do Member States work together to ensure that their respective interests—that is, those of the individual Member States *and* those of the EU—are properly safeguarded?

2.1 Revisiting the Duty of Sincere Cooperation

In Chapter 5 on conflict resolution, I looked at how the duty of sincere cooperation provides part of the answer to the above question. In *PFOS*, the Court held that, in some instances, individual Member States are precluded from acting in so far as their actions run counter a concerted Union action.[5] I discussed, however, how the duty of sincere cooperation has important limitations. It is a relatively abstract principle. Absent further determination, Member States do not know exactly what it requires of them. The remedies available to the Court of Justice to enforce the duty of sincere cooperation are also limited. By its very nature, a Court of Justice judgment establishing that a Member State has violated its duty of sincere cooperation comes too late: the Member State may have incurred international legal commitments which a declaration by the Court of Justice cannot undo.

Because of these uncertainties, it is useful to explore what other options are available to put in place a system of shared rule in this space in which both the EU and its Member States have powers to act. What attempts have been undertaken in the past to translate the abovementioned, fairly abstract, duty of sincere cooperation into a more concrete set of rules of engagement? And how do these efforts compare with those undertaken in Belgium and Canada—two federations in which courts have recognized the existence of a principle of

[4] Confirming that Member States are free to decide on a case-by-case basis on the modalities of their own external representation, including when acting jointly in the interest of the EU, see Case C-161/20 *Commission v Council ('IMO')*, EU:C:2022:260.

[5] Case C-246/07 *Commission v Sweden ('PFOS')*, EU:C:2010:203, para 74.

'federal loyalty'? The US does not figure prominently in the comparative analysis I conduct in this section because, as discussed in the previous chapter, vertical intergovernmental relations are not an important feature of US foreign relations.

2.2 Further Determining the Duty of Sincere Cooperation: Towards an 'EU Mixity Act'?

EU Member States and the EU have to coordinate with one another to make external action work when such action cuts across areas of exclusive and non-exclusive EU competence, as well as areas that fall outside of the scope of EU competence altogether. However, such coordination takes a different shape compared to the other federations considered in this book due to the strong formal political safeguards of foreign relations federalism in the EU which I discussed in Chapter 7. Possibly because Member State executives themselves heavily influence EU decision-making through their representation in the two Councils, there is less need for individual Member States to be present during the negotiations of international agreements that are likely to be concluded as mixed agreements, or during negotiations within international bodies in which the EU is represented. Even when EU external action extends beyond the sphere of EU exclusive competence—which it often does given the relatively limited scope of the EU's exclusive competence—EU Member States less often feel the need to be individually present throughout the decision-making process compared to their Canadian or Belgian counterparts.

To return to the example of the Comprehensive Economic and Trade Agreement (CETA): during the CETA negotiations, Canadian provinces were directly involved in negotiations with the European Commission on topics that fall under provincial jurisdiction within Canada.[6] From the perspective of those provinces, this approach made much sense. As they are not represented within the federal decision-making process, they had an interest in being involved directly as Canada's federal government negotiated a free trade agreement that touches on issues which, domestically, fall under provincial jurisdiction. In marked contrast to the Canadian delegation, which consisted of federal and provincial negotiators, only the Commission negotiated on behalf

[6] See eg Stéphane Paquin, 'Trade Paradiplomacy and the Politics of International Economic Law: The Inclusion of Quebec and the Exclusion of Wallonia in the CETA Negotiations' [2021] New Political Economy 1.

of the EU. This, too, is understandable as EU Member States exercise internal oversight over the Commission. The Council issues negotiation instructions to the Commission; the Commission reports to the responsible Council working party (the so-called 'Article 133 Committee'); and the Council needs to adopt the necessary decisions to carry the treaty-making process forward. Moreover, if the agreement is to be concluded as a mixed agreement, each Member State must ratify the agreement in accordance with its own constitutional requirements. This further increases the weight of the Member States in the EU treaty-making process, and makes it less of a priority for Member States to be directly represented at the negotiating table with Canada or whichever other country with which the EU is negotiating an international agreement.

That said, there are instances in which additional EU-Member State coordination efforts are needed. This is the case, in particular, for instances of parallel membership of international bodies, mentioned earlier in Chapter 3. In such bodies, the question arises as to who is entitled to take the floor and how voting rights are to be exercised. (EU Member States are potentially overrepresented in such bodies as they can both participate directly as members of the body and indirectly through their role in the intra-EU decision-making process.)[7] Coordination is needed even more urgently when the EU is not a member of the international body, but the body's activities fall in whole or in part within the scope of the EU's exclusive competence. In such cases, the Member States are precluded from acting independently as a matter of EU law. They must instead act collectively as trustees of the EU, and it is up to the Council to issue instructions to the Member States on the position(s) to be defended and the vote(s) to be cast.[8] The Council may mandate the Commission to represent them, but it may also ask the Council Presidency, or any other Member State, to do so.[9]

Such coordination typically takes place on an ad hoc basis through the adoption of Council decisions, or—less formally—through the adoption of Council conclusions or even COREPER decisions.[10] (COREPER, or the *Comité des représentants permanents*, is the Council preparatory body consisting of Member State ambassadors.) Only on rare occasions have efforts

[7] For an example of how the presence of EU institutions and the Member States may lead to difficulties, see generally Geert De Baere, 'Mercury Rising: The European Union and the International Negotiations for a Globally Binding Instrument on Mercury' (2012) 37 European Law Review 640. More recently, see also Jed Odermatt, *International Law and the European Union* (Cambridge University Press 2021) 249–59.

[8] See eg Case C-45/07 *Commission v Greece ('IMO')*, EU:C:2009:81, paras 30–31.

[9] In this sense, see Case C-261/20 *Commission v Council ('IMO')*, EU:C:2022:33.

[10] See ibid, where the Commission challenged the validity of a COREPER decision mandating the Council Presidency to submit a proposal to the International Maritime Organization.

been undertaken to put EU-Member State coordination on a more structured footing. One example of such efforts is PROBA 20. In the early 1980s, COREPER endorsed 'arrangements' on the joint representation of the EU and the Member States during the negotiation of commodity agreements. (Commodity agreements are agreements to stabilize trade, supplies, and prices of a commodity for the benefit of participating parties.) The 'PROBA 20' arrangements—named after the Council working party covering commodity agreements—encouraged the EU and its Member States to articulate common positions and to have the Commission represent those positions as often as possible.[11] However, the arrangements did not preclude the Council Presidency, or even individual Member States, from taking the floor if they considered doing so to be beneficial for political or tactical reasons. Furthermore, the arrangements did not provide for a procedure to be followed in the event no common position could be arrived at. In such an event, Member States could defend their own positions.[12]

A second example: in the early 2010s the UK pursued a policy of systematically blocking statements by the EU which it considered to fall outside of the scope of EU competence.[13] In response to this UK strategy, the Council endorsed 'general arrangements' to govern the joint representation of the EU and its Member States within multilateral organizations.[14] In contrast to the PROBA 20 arrangements, which applied only to the negotiation of commodity agreements, the 2011 general arrangements are, as their name suggests, applicable on a cross-sectoral basis. The arrangements provide that, within the sphere of EU shared competence, the EU and its Member States must endeavour to articulate common positions and, if necessary, coordinate their actions within

[11] The arrangements are printed in full in Panos Koutrakos, *EU International Relations Law* (2nd edn, Hart Publishing 2015) 171–72.

[12] See the declaration made by a number of Member States, added in attachment to the PROBA 20 arrangements, mentioned in ibid 173. The declaration stated:

> These delegations start from the principle that the Arrangement between the Council and the Commission provides for the effective participation of the Community and its Member States in the negotiations, the preparatory work and the institutions of international commodity agreements and equally, takes into account their national interests regarding commodity policy. If, in the light of essential interests in wholly exceptional cases, the above objective is not met, it should be possible to make national declarations. This should be the case provided that every effort has been made in a persistent manner in order to find a common position and that the interests of the Community are respected.

[13] 'Blocking Tactics: UK Infuriating Partners by Obstructing EU Foreign Policy' *Spiegel Online* (5 December 2011) <www.spiegel.de/international/europe/blocking-tactics-uk-infuriating-partners-by-obstructing-eu-foreign-policy-a-801756.html> accessed 16 April 2022.

[14] Council of the European Union, *EU Statements in Multilateral Organisations—General Arrangements*, Doc No 15901/11, 24 October 2011 ('General Arrangements'), available at <http://register.consilium.europa.eu/doc/srv?l=EN&f=ST%2015901%202011%20INIT> accessed 16 April 2022.

the organizations involved. Member States 'will seek to ensure and promote possibilities for the EU actors to deliver statements on behalf of the EU', the arrangements hold, without Member States losing their own authority to address the gathering. In contrast to the PROBA 20 arrangements, the 2011 general arrangements do provide for a form of dispute resolution mechanism: when a problem arises in the application of the arrangements, the 'Head of the EU delegation will refer the matter to the EEAS which will, in close consultation with the Commission, submit when appropriate the matter to COREPER for decision'. In other words, disputes are resolved by the Member States meeting within COREPER. While Commission representatives do attend COREPER meetings, they do not hold decision-making powers in that forum.

PROBA 20 was 'endorsed' by COREPER; it was not included in a formal Council decision. Likewise, the 2011 general arrangements were attached to Council conclusions and were thus not included in a legally binding Council decision. That said, and despite the fact that neither arrangement was included in a Council decision, arrangements of this type may nonetheless be binding on the Commission and the Council as well as the Member States as they can be considered concrete expressions of the duty of sincere cooperation. In the *FAO* case, the Court of Justice held that an 'arrangement' between Council and Commission setting up a coordination procedure between the Commission and the Member States to decide on the exercise of responsibilities or on statements on a particular point within the Food and Agriculture Organization (FAO) of the United Nations constituted a 'fulfilment' of the duty of sincere cooperation between the EU and its Member States within the FAO, and that the two EU institutions thus intended to enter into a 'binding commitment' towards each other.[15]

The *FAO* case was an annulment action brought by the Commission against a Council decision. However, since the arrangement was a fulfilment of the duty of sincere cooperation, and the duty of sincere cooperation applies both between EU institutions and between the EU and its Member States, it would be conceivable for the Commission to bring an infringement action against a Member State acting in violation of the arrangement—and thus of its duty of sincere cooperation—as well. The same arguably applies to other arrangements such as PROBA 20 and the 2011 general arrangements. It is thus possible for Council and Commission—two EU institutions—to regulate *vertical* intergovernmental relations in EU foreign relations. While in and by themselves the arrangements may not be legally binding—and even if they were, they could

[15] Case C-25/94 *Commission v Council ('FAO')*, EU:C:1996:114, para 49.

only be binding between the parties that agreed to them since agreements are *res inter alios acta*—the duty of sincere cooperation extends their normative reach to include also the Member States, including when they are exercising their own competences.[16] To the extent that informal arrangements further determine the duty of sincere cooperation, such arrangements are binding on the Commission and the Council as well as the Member States. Since the duty of sincere cooperation is reviewable by the Court of Justice, the arrangements, which give concrete expression to that duty, are reviewable as well.

The EU Treaties thus provide a legal basis for a comprehensive regulation of the interactions between the EU institutions and the Member States as they engage in 'joint' or 'mixed' external action. The EU could thus adopt what could be called an 'EU Mixity Act', that is, an interinstitutional agreement—not unlike the intergovernmental agreements that govern mixed external action in Belgium—that regulates the necessary cooperation between the EU and the Member States as they engage in mixed external action.[17] Adopting an EU Mixity Act would bring benefits. An EU Mixity Act could, for example, make provisions for Member State parliaments to be involved earlier in the treaty-making process so as to avoid a national or regional legislature vetoing an agreement that has been a decade in the making, as nearly occurred with CETA when the Walloon region of Belgium threatened to block the signature of CETA by the EU in the autumn of 2016.[18] Conversely, Member State parliaments can signal earlier on in the negotiating process that they do not support the agreement, which could lead negotiators to change the course of negotiations or even abandon negotiations altogether. Regardless of the legislatures' position on specific agreements, by involving Member State parliaments—and the European Parliament—earlier in the process, the democratic legitimacy of international agreements would be strengthened. An EU Mixity Act could also foreclose interinstitutional disputes on who gets to represent the Member States when they exercise their own competences in international bodies (The Commission? The Council Presidency? Another Member State?) by introducing arrangements that apply regardless of issue area. To streamline

[16] On the point that the scope of the duty of sincere cooperation extends beyond the scope of the EU's competences, see eg Eleftheria Neframi, 'The Duty of Loyalty: Rethinking Its Scope through Its Application in the Field of EU External Relations' (2010) 47 Common Market Law Review 323, 342.

[17] For such a proposal in the narrower context of trade policy, see Thomas Cottier, 'Front-Loading Trade Policy-Making in the European Union: Towards a Trade Act' in Marc Bungenberg and others (eds), *European Yearbook of International Economic Law 2017*, vol 8 (Springer International Publishing 2017).

[18] Janyce McGregor, '"I Am Very Sad": Freeland Walks as Last-Ditch Canada-EU Trade Talks Collapse' *CBC News* (21 October 2016) <www.cbc.ca/news/politics/canada-eu-ceta-brussels-friday-1.3815332> accessed 12 March 2022.

practices of external representation would benefit the EU as well as the EU's international partners, who would have a better sense of who to deal with when the EU and the Member States are both at the table.

2.3 Sincere Cooperation versus the Autonomy of EU Law

The *FAO* case demonstrates that it is possible under current EU law to regulate vertical intergovernmental relations in the EU foreign policy-making context—even in the absence of a specific legal basis in the Treaties empowering the EU to adopt legislative acts to do so. That said, important questions remain. In particular, to what extent, if any, does the duty of sincere cooperation restrict the ability of the EU, rather than that of individual Member States, to exercise its competences? We have seen in Chapter 8 how in Canada the Supreme Court in *Canada Pension Plan* ruled, albeit in a strictly intra-Canadian context, that Canadian legislatures remain capable of overriding intergovernmental agreements concluded between Canadian governments. Conversely, we have seen how in Belgium the Constitution itself requires governments to operate on the basis of consensus when different governments act jointly. And we have seen how in Belgium a quasi-constitutional statute imposes an obligation on the different Belgian governments to conclude intergovernmental agreements that further determine the obligation to act on the basis of consensus. Where does the EU stand on this issue? Are the EU and its Member States constitutionally obligated to act on the basis of consensus or unanimity as is the case for the Belgian federal and member unit governments? Or does the EU's foreign affairs constitution align more closely to the Canadian model and does the duty of sincere cooperation not reach as far as to restrict the EU in its ability to exercise its own competences?

In two cases, *US Air Transport Agreement* and Opinion 1/19, the Court of Justice made clear that the EU blends the Belgian and Canadian models: while Member States cannot override their loyalty obligations vis-à-vis the EU on the basis of their national sovereignty, the constitutional principle of the autonomy of EU law does seem to enable the EU to override its own loyalty obligations vis-à-vis the Member States. Before discussing both cases, a reminder: as mentioned, in *PFOS* the Court of Justice made clear that in some instances individual Member States are precluded from acting externally when their actions run counter to a concerted Union strategy.[19] This was an important decision

[19] See n 5.

as it confirmed that the duty of sincere cooperation is not merely a best efforts obligation (try to work together!), but that in some instances it also imposes an obligation of result on Member States (don't act!). The question now becomes: does the duty of sincere cooperation restrict the autonomy of the *EU* to the same extent as it restricts that of the *Member States*? Or put more succinctly: is the duty of sincere cooperation a one-way or a two-way street?

In *US Air Transport Agreement*, an annulment action decided in 2015, the Court of Justice held that formal Council decisions cannot be merged with decisions adopted by the Member States acting qua sovereign states but meeting within the Council premises.[20] By participating in the adoption of such 'hybrid acts', the Court considered, the Council had violated the decision-making rules set out in the EU Treaties. These rules required the Council to operate by qualified majority, not consensus.[21] As a consequence, the 'hybrid' EU-Member State decision violated EU law, and its EU component was thus annulled by the Court. On the subject of the duty of sincere cooperation, the Court expressly mentioned that this duty is 'essential to ensure close cooperation between the Member States and the EU institutions, both in the process of negotiation and conclusion and in the fulfilment of the commitments entered into'.[22] But, the Court continued, the duty 'cannot justify the Council setting itself free from compliance with the procedural rules and voting arrangements laid down in Article 218 TFEU [on the procedure to negotiate international agreements]'.[23]

Following *US Air Transport Agreement*, the Council (and the Member States meeting in the Council) stopped adopting 'hybrid acts'. Instead, the Council reverted to its earlier practice of adopting the Council decision to conclude an international agreement on behalf of the EU only in the presence of a 'common accord' amongst—read: unanimous approval of—all Member States. Perhaps unsurprisingly, the practice of waiting for a 'common accord' became controversial as well. In 2019, the Commission requested the Court to issue an opinion on the legality of the Council decision concluding the Istanbul Convention, an international agreement that aims to tackle violence against women and domestic violence.[24] In its request for an opinion, the Commission asked the Court to clarify whether or not the abovementioned 'common accord' practice

[20] Case C–28/12 *Commission v Council ('US Air Transport Agreement')*, EU:C:2015:282. I discussed the case in Thomas Verellen, 'On Hybrid Decisions, Mixed Agreements and the Limits of the New Legal Order: Commission v Council ('US Air Transport Agreement')' (2016) 53 Common Market Law Review 741.

[21] Case C–28/12 *Commission v Council ('US Air Transport Agreement')*, EU:C:2015:282, para 52.

[22] ibid para 54.

[23] ibid para 55.

[24] The text of the Istanbul Convention is available at <www.coe.int/en/web/istanbul-convention/text-of-the-convention> accessed 14 September 2022.

was compatible with the EU rules that require the Council to act by qualified majority as well as, more generally, the principle of institutional balance laid down in Article 13(2) TEU. The Court answered that a requirement that the Council proceed by unanimity is not a legal obligation. However, the Court added that

> nothing precludes the Council from extending its discussions in order to achieve, inter alia, the greatest possible majority with a view to concluding an international agreement, the majority required for a broader exercise of the external competences of the European Union or, in the case of mixed agreements, closer cooperation between the Member States and the EU institutions in the process of concluding that agreement, which may involve waiting for the 'common accord' of the Member States.[25]

In other words, the Court explained that, while the Council does not have to proceed by common accord, it is not precluded from doing so if a qualified majority of its members considers that doing so is politically desirable. Yet, to bring home the crucial point that decision-making by common accord cannot be imposed on the abovementioned qualified majority, the Court went on to point out that nothing stops a majority of Member States in the Council from demanding that the Council Presidency put the decision to conclude an agreement to a vote. (The Council voting rules provide that '[t]he [Council] President shall ... be required to open a voting procedure on the initiative of a member of the Council or of the Commission, provided that a majority of the Council's members so decides'.)[26]

By making it clear that a qualified majority of Member States in the Council can adopt the decision to conclude the agreement on behalf of the EU, the Court of Justice thus sticks to the course taken previously in *US Air Transport Agreement*: the full effectiveness of the EU's decision-making rules carries greater weight than the duty of sincere cooperation, which requires Member States to ensure 'close cooperation' as they negotiate and conclude mixed agreements.[27] In the future, there may thus be instances in which one or several Member States do not become a party to a mixed agreement—a situation

[25] Opinion 1/19, para 253.

[26] Council voting rules, art 11(1) second subpara.

[27] For a narrower reading of what the Court had to say on the duty of sincere cooperation in *US Air Transport Agreement* focused on judicial economy, see Panos Koutrakos, 'Institutional Balance and Sincere Cooperation in Treaty-Making under EU Law' (2019) 68 International & Comparative Law Quarterly 1, 15.

which in the literature has been described as one of 'incomplete' mixity.[28] In such a scenario, the EU may be exposed to liability risks, as it may become bound by international obligations that it cannot enforce internally due to a lack of internal competence.[29]

In both of the above cases, *US Air Transport Agreement* and Opinion 1/19, the Court of Justice thus took a different tack from the one taken by the framers of the Belgian foreign affairs constitution. The Belgian framers embraced the proposition that mixity entails decision-making by consensus amongst the federal and member unit governments. Instead, the EU approach resembles an application in the external sphere of the approach followed by Canada's Supreme Court in *Canada Pension Plan*, discussed in the previous chapter. In that case, the Supreme Court confirmed that in Canada's constitutional framework a principle of 'cooperative federalism' does not limit the sovereignty of Canada's federal Parliament, and that it remains possible at all times for future parliaments to override earlier intergovernmental agreements. Similarly, in the EU context, the duty of sincere cooperation, whether or not further determined in 'arrangements' or interinstitutional agreements, cannot prevent the Council—and thus the EU—from exercising its competences on the basis of the decision-making rules set out in the EU Treaties.

A combined reading of *US Air Transport Agreement* and Opinion 1/19 suggests that in EU law the balance between sincere cooperation and autonomy tilts in favour of the latter. As discussed, in Belgium federal loyalty requires the different governments to act jointly, on the basis of consensus. By contrast, in Canada parliamentary sovereignty requires that Canadian legislatures and, by extension, Canadian executives, cannot bind themselves into the future, and future legislatures remain able to override earlier agreements. The EU positions itself in between both extremes and thus blends the Belgian and Canadian models: the duty of sincere cooperation does restrict the autonomy of the Member States as they engage in external action. Yet, at the same time, EU law requires that the Council remain capable of taking decisions on the basis of qualified majority vote whenever the Treaties empower the Council to do so. When we read *FAO*, discussed earlier, in light of *US Air Transport Agreement* and, most recently, Opinion 1/19, a picture thus emerges whereby the EU and its Member States are under a justiciable constitutional obligation to cooperate closely, but this obligation does not go as far as it does in Belgium

[28] See generally Guillaume Van der Loo and Ramses A Wessel, 'The Non-Ratification of Mixed Agreements: Legal Consequences and Solutions' (2017) 54 Common Market Law Review 735.

[29] The risk is discussed in Panos Koutrakos, 'Confronting the Complexities of Mixed Agreements—Opinion 1/19 on the Istanbul Convention' (2022) 47 European Law Review 247, 259.

Table 9.1 Loyalty versus autonomy in in the US, Canada, Belgium, and the EU

	US	Canada	EU	Belgium
Principle of 'federal loyalty' recognized	No	Yes	Yes	Yes
Justiciable	No	No	Yes	Yes
Further determined through acts of rule-making	No	No	Yes	Yes
Restricts autonomy of member units acting unilaterally	No	No	Yes	Yes
Restricts autonomy of the federal level of governance	No	No	No	Yes

as the Council cannot be barred from acting without a prior 'common accord' amongst the Member States, whereas in Belgium the federal government cannot act without a common accord amongst all Belgian governments. This makes for a picture in the EU in which self-rule at EU level prevails over shared rule: the duty of sincere cooperation can restrict the autonomy of individual Member States, but not that of the EU. The table below summarizes this picture (see Table 9.1).

3. Horizontal Intergovernmental Relations: Managing Member State Agreements

Horizontal intergovernmental relations are relations between the member units of a federal union. EU Member States engage directly with one another in a myriad of ways, both within and outside of the EU institutional framework. Outside of that framework, relations can be more or less formal. Relevant for our purposes is that EU Member States often conclude agreements with one another on a wealth of issues, ranging from the management of shared borders to human rights treaties such as the European Convention on Human Rights (ECHR). Such Member State agreements can be bilateral (eg double taxation treaties between individual EU Member States or with third countries), plurilateral (eg the Treaty establishing the European Stability Mechanism to which nineteen EU Member States are a party), or multilateral in the sense that all Member States are a party to them (eg the ECHR). Agreements can be intra-EU, involving only EU Member States (eg the abovementioned tax treaties), or they can also include non-EU Member States (eg the ECHR). Agreements can be binding under international law or they can be informal, non-binding agreements.[30]

In this section, I look at the landscape of Member State agreements; I look at how EU law treats such agreements; and I look at a unique feature of the EU's constitutional framework, that is, the ability of Member States to assign tasks to EU institutions through the conclusion of agreements between Member States to which the EU itself is not a party. I conclude on a comparative note with the suggestion that, given the many opportunities EU Member States have to conclude agreements with third countries, an 'EU Compact Clause' should be considered as a means to more effectively enforce the duty of sincere cooperation on those Member States, to prevent conflicts between EU Member State agreements and EU law from arising, and to provide the EU institutions with an instrument to prevent Member States from making agreements that run counter to the collective Union interest.

3.1 Horizontal Intergovernmental Agreements and EU Law

The thick web of intra- and extra-EU agreements amongst Member States is a reflection of the history of the European integration process as a process of integrating pre-existing sovereign states. The Rome Treaty, which established the (then) EEC, extinguished neither the international legal personality of Member States nor the international commitments Member States had incurred prior to the entry into force of the Rome Treaty. Thus, for example, EU Member States were already party to the ECHR and also remained a party after concluding the Rome Treaty. EU law acknowledges and accommodates this fact. It does so by suspending the primacy of EU law for agreements between EU Member States and third countries that predate the Rome Treaty or the accession of a Member State to the EU, as the case may be.[31] At the same time, the EU Treaties impose on Member States an obligation to resolve conflicts between pre-existing commitments and the EU Treaties, for example by renegotiating or terminating the agreements that contain such commitments.[32]

[30] For an example of a non-binding agreement between two Member States, see memorandum of understanding entitled *Grensoverschrijdende samenwerking inzake digitale geo-informatie tussen België, Nederland en Luxemburg*, signed on 1 June 2012, <www.fdfa.be/nl/memorandum-of-understanding-grensoverschrijdende-samenwerking-inzake-digitale-geo-informatie-tussen> accessed 27 April 2022.

[31] TFEU, art 351. On the provision, see eg Allan Rosas, 'The Status in EU Law of International Agreements Concluded by EU Member States' (2010) 34 Fordham International Law Journal 1304, 1321–23.

[32] This rule only applies to agreements with third countries, not to agreements between EU Member States. In this sense, see also ibid 1320. This is relevant, for example, for intra-EU bilateral investment

As discussed in Chapter 5, for agreements with third countries that post-date the Rome Treaty or accession, EU law provides for a number of conflict resolution mechanisms as well. First, the EU Treaties grant the EU an exclusive competence to the extent that a proposed agreement risks affecting pre-existing secondary internal EU rules in order to prevent conflicts from materializing in the first place. Secondly, the duty of sincere cooperation imposes procedural, and in some instances substantive, limits on what individual Member States can do once the EU has articulated a common strategy to tackle a given issue. In particular, as the Court of Justice made clear in *PFOS*, once a 'concerted Union strategy' has been initiated, for example after the Commission has submitted a proposal to the Council, Member States must closely cooperate with the EU institutions and may in some instances be under a 'duty of abstention'.[33] And thirdly, the primacy principle extends to intra- and extra-EU Member State agreements, in the sense that such agreements must yield to EU law norms with direct effect. This means, for example, that Member State courts are obliged to disregard—and thus refuse to enforce—awards granted by arbitration panels established under intra-EU BITs, because, as the Court made clear in *Achmea*, the provisions of such BITs establishing the panels are incompatible with EU law.[34]

Within the abovementioned limits, however, Member States are free to conclude agreements as they see fit. The legal basis for their ability to do so can be found in international law, not EU law, as Member States have an inherent authority to conclude international agreements which they derive from their status as sovereign states. As the Court of Justice made clear, for example in *Wightman*, on the UK's departure from the EU, accession to the EU in no way extinguished Member States' sovereignty.[35] On this point, EU Member States differ from their North American and Belgian counterparts, none of which had international legal personality before the establishment of the federation of which they are part today.[36] That said, the EU does share with

treaties (BITs)—a category of agreements which has been in the spotlight following the Court of Justice's judgment in the *Achmea* case. The primacy of EU law over such agreements is not suspended.

[33] Case C-246/07 *Commission v Sweden ('PFOS')*, EU:C:2010:203, paras 74–75.

[34] See on this Case C-3/91 *Exportur SA*, EU:C:1992:420, para 8: '[T]he provisions of a convention concluded after 1 January 1958 by a Member State with another State could not, from the accession of the latter State to the Community, apply in the relations between those States if they were found to be contrary to the rules of the Treaty.'

[35] Case C-621/18 *Wightman ea v Secretary of State for Exiting the European Union*, EU:C:2018:999, para 56, speaking of the 'sovereign right' of a Member State to withdraw from the EU.

[36] Whether US states had external sovereignty prior to the 1776 revolution is an interesting historical question—one which Justice Sutherland in the Supreme Court in *Curtiss-Wright* answered in the negative. See *US v Curtiss-Wright Export Corporation*, 299 US 304 (1936), 317: 'Sovereignty is never held in suspense. When, therefore, the external sovereignty of Great Britain in respect of the colonies ceased,

Belgium the constitutional feature that both orders of governance—'federal' and member unit—have treaty-making powers, albeit that the freedom of EU Member States to make use of these powers is more significant compared to their Belgian counterparts. As discussed, the fragmented division of exclusive powers makes mixed federal-member unit action often a constitutional necessity in Belgium. By contrast, the fields of EU shared competence that the EU has not yet 'occupied' and the fields of EU exclusive competence are, respectively, larger and smaller compared to the areas of exclusive competence at the disposal of Belgian member unit governments. This offers EU Member States greater opportunities to conclude horizontal agreements, including international agreements, both with each other and with third countries.

3.2 Member States Assigning Tasks to EU Institutions

From a comparative perspective, a unique feature of horizontal intergovernmental relations in the EU is the Member State practice of assigning tasks to EU institutions by means of agreements they conclude with one another without the EU being a party to such agreements. This occurred, for example, with the European Stability Mechanism (ESM) Treaty.[37] Under this agreement, the Commission plays a role in assessing requests for financial assistance, in negotiating memoranda of understanding with Member States in need of financial assistance, and in reviewing whether Member States benefiting from financial assistance respect the 'conditionalities' imposed upon them. A similar assigning of tasks by the Member States to EU institutions occurred also in 2016, when the 'EU-Turkey Statement' was concluded in an effort to stem refugee flows from Turkey into Greece. Under this agreement, the Commission plays a role in setting up the refugee exchange system. Relevant for our purposes is that the EU-Turkey Statement was an agreement between the EU Member States and a third country, Turkey.[38] The practice of assigning tasks to

it immediately passed to the Union.' But criticizing Sutherland's theory on historical grounds, see generally David M Levitan, 'The Foreign Relations Power: An Analysis of Mr. Justice Sutherland's Theory' (1946) 55 Yale Law Journal 467.

[37] See Treaty Establishing the European Stability Mechanism, signed on 2 February 2012, T/ESM 2012-LT/en 1, <www.esm.europa.eu/sites/default/files/20150203_-_esm_treaty_-_en.pdf> accessed 26 April 2022.

[38] Exploring the nature and the normative implications of the EU-Turkey Statement—Was it an international agreement? Was the EU bound by the agreement?—see Carmelo Danisi, 'Taking the "Union" out of "EU": The EU-Turkey Statement on the Syrian Refugee Crisis as an Agreement Between States under International Law' (*EJIL:Talk!*, 20 April 2017) <www.ejiltalk.org/tak

EU institutions by concluding agreements amongst Member States is thus not limited to intra-EU agreements; it extends also to extra-EU agreements.

The practice of assigning responsibilities to EU institutions is a reverse form of cooperative federalism whereby the *EU institutions* play a role in implementing and ensuring compliance with policies determined by the *Member States*. (In cooperative federalism schemes prevalent in the other federations looked at in this book, the member units of the federation play a role in the implementation of federal law, not the other way around.) EU practice also goes further than cooperative federalism practices in the two North American federations. In the US and Canada, the federal government must reach an agreement with the member unit governments to have them play a role in the implementation of federal policy. By contrast, within the EU the assignment is imposed on the EU institutions, which themselves are not in a position to refuse to participate. The legal basis of the EU's obligation to comply with the agreement is, however, unclear. The agreement between the Member States being a *res inter alios acta*, it cannot impose obligations on the EU.[39] Moreover, a similar reasoning as the one at work in the *FAO* judgment, discussed earlier, cannot apply in this context: the duty of sincere cooperation, which also applies to the EU institutions, only requires those institutions to assist the Member States in carrying out tasks that flow from the Treaties.[40] In so far as the tasks Member States assign to the EU institutions do not 'flow from the Treaties', the duty of sincere cooperation does not apply and thus cannot be relied upon to compel those institutions—in particular the Commission—to comply with instructions contained in agreements made amongst the Member States.

EU law thus does not provide for a legal basis empowering the Member States to assign tasks to the EU institutions. That said, do the Treaties at the very least not preclude the Member States from assigning tasks to the EU institutions by means of horizontal intergovernmental agreements? In the 2014 case of *Pringle*, the Court of Justice reaffirmed that EU law does not preclude

ing-the-union-out-of-eu-the-eu-turkey-statement-on-the-syrian-refugee-crisis-as-an-agreement-between-states-under-international-law/> accessed 28 April 2022.

[39] One theory could be that the EU, through the implementation actions undertaken by the Commission, unilaterally expressed an intention to be bound by the agreement to which it was not a party. This theory would find support in the International Court of Justice's *Nuclear Tests Cases (Australia & New Zealand v France)*, 1974 ICJ 253, 457.

[40] TEU, art 4(3) first para.

Member States from assigning certain tasks to EU institutions.[41] In particular, the Court held that:

> the Member States are entitled, in areas which do not fall under the exclusive competence of the Union, to entrust tasks to the institutions, outside the framework of the Union, such as the task of coordinating a collective action undertaken by the Member States or managing financial assistance ... *provided that those tasks do not alter the essential character of the powers conferred on those institutions by the EU and FEU Treaties.*[42]

And the Court went on to hold that the involvement of both the Commission and the European Central Bank (ECB) in the management of financial assistance under the ESM Treaty would not alter the 'essential characteristics' of the powers conferred on them.[43] The Commission's powers as guardian of the Treaties were safeguarded because, through its involvement in the programme, the Commission could make sure that EU law is complied with. And the ECB's mission to 'support the general economic policies in the Union', laid down in Article 282(2) TFEU, would be preserved as the ECB would be consulted when Member States ask for financial assistance on the need for such assistance, it would be involved in the negotiations of memoranda of understanding, and it would be involved in monitoring compliance with those memoranda. In *Pringle*, the Court of Justice thus made clear that the EU Treaties are remarkably tolerant towards Member States 'borrowing' EU institutional capacity to pursue their own aims, outside of the EU Treaty framework.[44] The requirement the EU Treaties impose is a negative one: the tasks assigned to the EU institutions should not undermine their 'essential tasks'. In addition, it is clear also

[41] In earlier case law, the Court of Justice had already clarified that it is permissible for Member States to informally meet in the premises of EU institutions. See Joined Cases C-181/91 and 248/91 *Parliament v Council ('Bangladesh')*, EU:C:1993:271, para 16: '[I]t should be pointed out that the Community does not have exclusive competence in the field of humanitarian aid, and that consequently the Member States are not precluded from exercising their competence in that regard collectively in the Council or outside it.'

[42] Case C-370/12 *Pringle*, EU:C:2012:756, para 158 (emphasis added).

[43] ibid paras 159–69.

[44] The CJEU's approach was criticized in the literature. Commentators questioned whether the introduction in the EU Treaties of a mechanism of enhanced cooperation, which is designed to enable EU action when the ordinary decision-making thresholds in the Council cannot be met, should not be understood as precluding Member States from acting outside of the framework of the EU Treaties altogether to pursue aims they could also pursue through enhanced cooperation. In this sense, see eg Paul Craig, 'Pringle and Use of EU Institutions Outside the EU Legal Framework: Foundations, Procedure and Substance' (2013) 9 European Constitutional Law Review 263, 272–73. Cf, see the view of AG Kokott in C-370/12 *Pringle*, EU:C:2012:675, para 174, as well as Steve Peers, 'Towards a New Form of EU Law?: The Use of EU Institutions Outside the EU Legal Framework' (2013) 9 European Constitutional Law Review 37, 47–48.

that any agreement the Member States conclude amongst themselves has to comply with EU law more generally, and any provision of such an agreement will have to be disapplied to the extent that it conflicts with EU law, in accordance with the primacy principle.

An arrangement of this type, whereby member unit governments assign tasks to federal institutions, would be inconceivable in any of the other three federations I look at in this book. In the US, Canada, and Belgium, member units cannot issue instructions to the federal government. In the US, doing so would undermine the supremacy of federal law. In Canada and Belgium, the full spectrum of government action is covered by the division of exclusive powers. This means that any given issue will fall either within the exclusive responsibility of the federal government or that of the member units. *Tertium non datur*, and governments cannot be assigned tasks that fall outside of the scope of their own competence. By contrast, in the EU compound polity Member States remain capable of acting in areas of shared competence and in areas in which the EU does not have any competence. And in doing so, they can assign tasks to EU institutions, provided that the core of those institutions' responsibilities under the EU Treaties is not compromised.

3.3 *De lege ferenda*: An 'EU Compact Clause'?

EU Member States thus have much space to conclude intergovernmental agreements with one another as well as with third countries. Such agreements can be non-binding, but they can also constitute binding international agreements. The EU shares this feature with Belgium. Under Belgium's foreign affairs constitution, member units can also conclude binding international agreements without federal involvement. As discussed, the fact that EU Member States can continue to conclude binding international agreements is not surprising in light of the history of the European integration project as a project of integration within limited fields that left the sovereign statehood of its Member States intact. On this point, the EU arrangement is different from the US and Canadian constitutional arrangements. In both of the North American federations, the member units lost the authority—if they ever had it—of concluding binding international agreements when the federal constitution entered into force. In this sense, in comparative terms, the EU is a very *open* federation.[45]

[45] Distinguishing between 'open' and 'closed' federations, see generally Bardo Fassbender, *Der offene Bundesstaat: Studien zur auswärtigen Gewalt und zur Völkerrechtssubjektivität bundesstaatlicher Teilstaaten in Europa* (Mohr Siebeck 2007).

Not only can EU Member States act jointly with the EU, they can also independently make agreements with third countries.

In light of the abovementioned openness of the EU towards the international legal order, it is worth considering whether the EU should not be endowed with additional institutional tools to prevent Member States from concluding agreements with third countries that risk violating EU law, including the duty of sincere cooperation. In a similar spirit, it is also worth exploring whether tools should be introduced to enable EU institutions to review Member State agreements on *policy* grounds (Is the agreement desirable? Is it in the Union interest?) in addition to *legal* grounds (Is the agreement compatible with EU law? Does it comply with the duty of sincere cooperation?).

As I discussed in Chapter 5, the EURATOM Treaty provides for an *ex ante* control mechanism for international agreements that Member States wish to conclude and which fall within the scope of the EURATOM Treaty. Under this mechanism, Member States must inform the Commission of planned agreements. The Commission and ultimately the Court of Justice can stop the Member State from concluding the agreement if it violates the EURATOM Treaty. The EU Treaties do not provide for a similar mechanism. By contrast, as discussed in Chapter 4, the US Constitution precludes states from making agreements that increase the political power of the states and affect the just supremacy of the US. A proper application of the Compact Clause involves all three branches of the US government: the federal courts have interpreted the Compact Clause to exclude certain agreements; the State Department expresses its view on the compatibility of individual agreements with the Compact Clause, and if necessary recommends the agreements to be subjected to Congressional approval, Congress approves (or rejects) those agreements that otherwise would undermine the just supremacy of the federal government. It remains possible for states to apply for judicial review of the State Department's assessment if the state considers the agreement to not reach the thresholds for Congressional approval.

De lege ferenda, it is worth considering introducing a similar mechanism—an 'EU Compact Clause'—in the EU context.[46] EU law could require Member States to inform the European Commission of any and all agreements they consider concluding with each other and with third countries. The Commission could, in turn, be asked to issue an opinion on the compatibility of the

[46] For a proposal in this sense, see Robert Schütze, 'EC Law and International Agreements of the Member States—An Ambivalent Relationship?' (2006) 9 Cambridge Yearbook of European Legal Studies 387, 437.

proposed agreement with EU law—including the Member State's duty of sincere cooperation—and, I suggest, express its opinion on whether the proposed agreement aligns with the Union interest. If the Commission identifies a possible incompatibility with existing EU law, it could refer the matter to the Court of Justice—as is the case today under Article 103 of the EURATOM Treaty. If the Commission considers the agreement to run counter to the Union interest, it could refer the matter to the Council, which, following a debate, could oppose the agreement by qualified majority. Such a mechanism could also cover binding and non-binding agreements alike. (Bringing non-binding memoranda of understanding within the mechanism's scope would be necessary to avoid a flight into informality.) Moreover, to further reduce the risk of circumvention, the Commission could be endowed with investigative powers enabling it to compel Member States to provide the Commission with the necessary information to enable it to issue an informed opinion.

An EU Compact Clause would bring a number of advantages. First, it would reduce the risk that Member States conclude international agreements in conflict with EU law. In so doing, it avoids the *Achmea* scenario, mentioned earlier, in which Member States find themselves caught between conflicting international commitments. Secondly, it would (further) increase awareness in Member State capitals that the bilateral relations a Member State entertains with a given third country are likely to affect other Member States and, in some instances, the EU as a whole. The mechanism would encourage Member States to pay greater attention not only to the national interest, but also to the Union interest in their treaty-making practices. Thirdly, an *ex ante* control mechanism covering agreements between Member States and third country governments would complement existing and upcoming autonomous trade instruments.

As discussed in Chapter 5, at the time of writing (July 2022) EU law already encourages Member States to screen foreign direct investments on security grounds and provides for a Commission role in that process.[47] In the same spirit, EU law will soon empower the Commission to investigate and sanction companies that have received subsidies from third countries and which distort the internal market.[48] And it will soon also empower the Commission to restrict access to EU procurement markets for third country companies in the

[47] On the subject, see generally Thomas Verellen, 'When Integration by Stealth Meets Public Security: The EU Foreign Direct Investment Screening Regulation' (2021) 48 Legal Issues of Economic Integration 19.

[48] Proposal for a regulation of the European Parliament and of the Council on foreign subsidies distorting the internal market, COM/2021/223 final.

absence of reciprocal access.[49] These instruments enable the Commission to tackle unfair trade practices and to protect the integrity of the EU's internal market. The foreign direct investment screening regulation, moreover, protects the security of the Member States and that of the EU as a whole. In a similar spirit, an *ex ante* control mechanism of Member State agreements regardless of issue area could enable the Commission and the Council to flag and, if the requisite majority in the Council can be found, veto agreements that run counter to the Union interest—an open-textured notion that can be understood as including public security. To put in place a truly comprehensive mechanism that cuts across areas of competence, an amendment of the EU Treaties would be necessary.

4. Conclusion

In this chapter I explored what intergovernmental relations look like in the EU, and how EU law governs such relations. This analysis concludes the second part of the book, which focused on the shared rule dimension of foreign relations federalism. Both dimensions—the political safeguards of foreign relations federalism and intergovernmental relations—are closely connected to each other. In federations in which political safeguards are weak, as in the US and Canada, intergovernmental relations are an important technique to manage shared rule. Belgium is an interesting case in this regard: formal political safeguards are already strong in Belgium. Yet, because the Belgian Constitution allocates treaty-making powers to both levels of government, the need was felt to further supplement existing political safeguards with a highly formalized system of intergovernmental relations through which decision-making by consensus is imposed on all governments.

The situation is different in the EU. Member States have much leverage over the EU decision-making process. This leverage makes government-to-government intergovernmental relations less of a necessity in the EU framework. Often, Member States are happy to let the European Commission represent both the EU and the Member States in international bodies or during treaty negotiations. Yet, in the EU as well, intergovernmental relations do matter. They matter, first, because mixed external action inevitably requires Member States to undertake action. At the very least, they must each

[49] European Commission, 'EU Acts to Improve Access to International Procurement' (14 March 2022) <https://ec.europa.eu/commission/presscorner/detail/en/ip_22_1728> accessed 2 June 2022.

individually ratify proposed mixed agreements for the agreements to enter into force. They matter, secondly, because Member States are often represented in international bodies, possibly alongside the EU. This combined presence inevitably requires coordination. And they matter, thirdly, because Member States retain important capabilities to conclude agreements with each other and with third countries. As explored, they can even assign tasks to EU institutions by concluding agreements amongst themselves.

EU law regulates both vertical and horizontal intergovernmental regulations involving the Member States and the EU. *Vertically*, we have seen how the EU Treaties, as interpreted by the Court of Justice, prioritize the autonomy of EU law and the full effectiveness of the decision-making rules within the Council over the duty which EU law imposes on the EU and its Member States to cooperate closely when they act jointly on the international stage. EU law here is reminiscent more of Canadian and American 'dualist' conceptions of federalism than it is of the 'cooperative federalism' approach we can see at work in Belgium and which privileges consensus-building over preserving the autonomy of any one government. *Horizontally*, the EU Treaties are accommodating towards the practice of Member States concluding agreements with each other and with third countries. The main restriction lies in the division of competences: when EU exclusive competence is involved, the EU must become a party to any agreement Member States envisage concluding. In addition, the duty of sincere cooperation does impose constitutional constraints on Member States. Yet, these constraints would benefit from a more effective institutional enforcement mechanism. An 'EU Compact Clause' could provide the EU institutions with additional opportunities to enforce the duty of sincere cooperation. By subjecting proposed Member State agreements to a 'Union interest' test in addition to a review on legality grounds, an EU Compact Clause would also endow the EU institutions with an additional instrument to prevent Member States from concluding agreements that may not reach the required threshold to be considered contrary to the duty of sincere cooperation, but which nonetheless are not desirable in light of the EU's foreign policy agenda.

10
General Conclusion

> The functioning of the Union shall be founded on representative democracy.
>
> Article 10 TFEU

1. Introduction

In the introduction to this book, I defined federalism as a combination of self-rule and shared rule. Federalism thus understood has four components: power allocation, conflict resolution, political safeguards of federalism, and intergovernmental relations. Bringing together the findings with regard to these four components, in this concluding chapter I identify four approaches to the quintessentially federal objective of striking a balance between unity and diversity in the foreign relations context. I refer to the US approach as a 'unity +' approach, the Canadian approach as an 'external unity, internal diversity' approach, and the Belgian approach as a 'diversity +' approach. Compared with these three federations, the EU's brand of foreign relations federalism represents a 'diversity ++' approach, characterized as it is by a balance between unity and diversity that tilts quite strongly—and arguably altogether too strongly—towards the pole of diversity. This negative assessment of the emphasis of the EU's foreign affairs constitution on diversity is justified due to the democratic deficit that it entails. Diversity as it is understood in the EU foreign affairs constitution has a cost: the strong political safeguards of foreign relations federalism, and the concomitantly weak checks on the two Councils, shield EU foreign policy-making from the constraints imposed by representative democracy. In the final section of this concluding chapter, I put forward three proposals for reform that aim to put EU foreign relations on a firmer democratic footing.

Foreign Relations Federalism. Thomas Verellen, Oxford University Press. © Thomas Verellen 2023.
DOI: 10.1093/oso/9780192844569.003.0010

2. Findings: Different Approaches to Foreign Relations Federalism

2.1 United States: Unity +

The US represents a first approach to foreign relations federalism. The US Constitution allocates broad powers to the federal level of government, including a de facto exclusive power to incur international legal commitments. Moreover, mindful of the fact that most federal powers—not least the power to adopt legislation—are concurrent rather than exclusive in nature, the US Constitution provides for conflict resolution mechanisms that benefit the federal government. These mechanisms aim to ensure that state governments cannot negatively affect the conduct of foreign policy by the federal government. This combination of broad federal powers with federal enforcement mechanisms does much to ensure that the US speaks with one voice on the international stage and is capable of living up to the commitments it makes with third countries.

The emphasis on the ability to speak with one voice and to effectively enforce federal foreign policy in the US goes hand in hand with a relatively weak member unit voice within the federal political process. In keeping with the Whearian understanding of federalism as a method of dividing powers between levels of government—a splitting of the 'atom of sovereignty', as Justice Kennedy once put it[1]—the US Constitution does not provide for institutional avenues for member unit voice. Only when the federal government needs state assistance to implement federal policies can states occasionally exercise some influence over the federal government. But, as discussed, even then, such influence remains limited. Finally, within a hierarchical framework characterized by broad federal powers and powerful enforcement mechanisms, horizontal cooperation between states, and cooperation between states and the federal government is not constitutionally protected. Collaboration can occur, both horizontally and vertically, and both bilaterally and multilaterally, but the federal Constitution endows the federal government with a set of tools to exercise control over these collaborative enterprises.

[1] *US Term Limits, Inc v Thornton*, 514 US 779 (1995) (Kennedy J, concurring), 838:

> Federalism was our Nation's own discovery. The Framers split the atom of sovereignty. It was the genius of their idea that our citizens would have two political capacities, one state and one federal, each protected from incursion by the other. The resulting Constitution created a legal system unprecedented in form and design, establishing two orders of government, each with its own direct relationship, its own privity, its own set of mutual rights and obligations to the people who sustain it and are governed by it.

In summary, the US foreign affairs constitution puts greater emphasis on protecting unity than it does on safeguarding diversity. It does so by protecting the capacity for self-rule at the federal level: the federal government can make decisions independently from the states and it has the constitutional tools at its disposal to enforce these decisions vis-à-vis the states. This does not mean that states have no role to play in foreign relations in the US. States can play a useful role as amplifiers of federal policy: they can undertake actions broadly in line with federal foreign policy as long as the federal government has not expressed objections against those actions, or has not articulated a policy or adopted a statute at odds with those state actions.[2] Crucially, however, it is the federal government—either Congress or the President, or when the political institutions do not take a clear stance, the federal courts—who have the final say on the breadth of the margin for state independent foreign relations action. It is in this sense that the US approach to foreign relations federalism is best understood as a 'unity +' approach: the US Constitution places a premium on protecting the unity of the polity as it engages in foreign relations.

2.2 Canada: External Unity, Internal Diversity

The American 'unity +' approach can be contrasted with the Canadian 'external unity, internal diversity' approach. In Canada, as in the US, the federal government holds the bulk of the powers to engage in foreign relations. In keeping with the monarchical tradition Canada inherited from the UK, the traditional powers associated with sovereign statehood are allocated exclusively to the federal government, and in particular to the federal executive. As a consequence, only the federal executive can incur international legal commitments in Canada. By contrast, provincial governments do not have access to the international legal order. Their foreign relations activities, while often significant in political terms, remain outside of the realm of international law. In Canada as well, then, the constitution attaches great importance to protecting the unity of the federation as it engages in foreign relations.

That being said, the emphasis on unity and federal exclusivity when it comes to Canada's participation in international law transactions should be seen in conjunction with the exclusive nature of the legislative powers of Canada's provincial governments. In contrast to the US, the Canadian constitution does

[2] See eg Daniel Halberstam, 'The Foreign Affairs of Federal Systems: A National Perspective on the Benefits of State Participation' [2001] Villanova Law Review 1015.

not provide for a *Missouri*-style federal treaty-implementing power. For international treaty commitments to be enforced within Canada, they must first be implemented by means of legislation. The power to adopt such legislation remains divided in accordance with the division of legislative powers set out in sections 91 and 92 of the Constitution Act, 1867. While the theory of 'cooperative federalism' articulated by the Supreme Court of Canada in recent division of power cases arguably makes it less likely for federal legislation to be declared invalid for encroaching on exclusive provincial legislative powers, such a possibility can nonetheless not be entirely excluded.

The lack of a federal treaty-implementing power, coupled with the historically strong role of provincial governments in the delivery of services to Canadian citizens, translates into a federal-provincial relationship characterized by greater equality between both orders of governance than can be observed in the federal-state relationship in the US. Domestically, both vertical and horizontal intergovernmental relations have in recent decades become the lifeblood of Canadian federalism as they make it possible for governments to attain policy objectives that cut across areas of exclusive federal and provincial jurisdiction. Increasingly, intergovernmental relations take place also in areas with external dimensions. In areas such as environmental and trade policy, the boundary between the internal and the external breaks down: domestic policy initiatives are linked with bilateral and multilateral initiatives. It is not surprising, then, that in these areas as well, provincial governments play an increasingly significant role, as they have done for example during the EU-Canada Comprehensive Economic and Trade Agreement (CETA) negotiations. Due to the combination of formally exclusive federal powers to engage in foreign relations with comparatively strong provincial entitlements, it is appropriate to characterize Canada's approach to foreign relations federalism as one of 'external unity, internal diversity'.

2.3 Belgium: Diversity +

Belgium finds itself at the opposite end of the spectrum from the US. Whereas the US Constitution represents a 'unity +' approach to foreign relations federalism, the Belgian Constitution represents a 'diversity +' approach. As a former premier of Flanders, one of Belgium's member units, once pointed out: Belgium is unique amongst federal states in the extent to which it projects its internal diversity onto the international arena.[3] It is not surprising that, together with

[3] Luc Van den Brande, 'The International Legal Position of Flanders: Some Considerations' in Karel Wellens (ed), *International Law: Theory and Practice. Essays in Honour of Eric Suy* (Kluwer Law

the recognition of member unit treaty-making powers on subject matters over which the member units hold internal legislative powers, Belgium also extended its domestic practices of consensus-based decision-making to the external sphere. As the discussions in Chapter 4 on conflict resolution in Belgium demonstrated, there is no alternative to consensus and compromise in Belgian foreign relations federalism. The substitution mechanism, which allows the federal government to suspend the negotiation or application of member unit agreements, has never been used. When conflicts do erupt, as they did in late 2016 when Belgium was unable to authorize the Council to sign CETA, negotiations are the only viable approach.

Given the need for negotiations between governments—a need the framers of the Belgian Constitution themselves recognized by mandating the conclusion of vertical-multilateral intergovernmental agreements—intergovernmental relations play a central role in Belgian foreign relations federalism. In contrast to Canada, where collaboration between the federal and member unit governments is necessary to implement international legal commitments, and only indirectly necessary to strengthen the federal government's external negotiation positions, in Belgium such collaboration is necessary at all stages of the decision-making process, including in the process of articulating a Belgian position within international organizations. In contexts such as these, the federal government increasingly has to involve the member unit governments as ever fewer policy areas are under exclusive federal control. It is in this sense that Belgium is best understood as an example of a 'diversity + ' approach to foreign relations federalism. In comparison with the US in particular, the Belgian foreign affairs constitution places little emphasis on unity. The ability of Belgium to speak with one voice is achieved by coercing the different Belgian governments to decide jointly on the course of Belgian foreign policy. In contrast to the US, no single government in Belgium can determine that course unilaterally. (This is despite the fact that the federal government retains a formal exclusive authority to represent Belgium within multilateral organizations and in foreign capitals.)

2.4 European Union: Diversity ++

How does the EU's brand of foreign relations federalism compare to the approach taken in the three other federations explored in this book? For each

International 1998) 146.

of the four components of federalism identified in the introduction, the EU foreign affairs constitution tilts towards the pole of diversity. Taken together, they justify characterizing the EU's brand of foreign relations federalism as a 'diversity ++' approach.

First, in terms of power allocation, it is noteworthy that despite the EU's origins as an inward-looking project of market integration, the EU Treaties allocate broad foreign relations powers to the EU. This is a remarkable observation considering that the 1958 Rome Treaty provided for few express legal bases for the EU to conclude international agreements. Today, Article 216(1) TFEU makes it clear that the EU's external competence is broad. While the EU Treaties do not put in place a parallelism between internal and external competence as exists in Belgium, the doctrine of implied external competences, according to which the EU may conclude international agreements 'where the conclusion of an agreement is necessary in order to achieve, within the framework of the Union's policies, one of the objectives referred to in the Treaties', leaves few issues outside of the scope of the EU's treaty-making competences. That said, the bulk of the EU's external competence is shared, not exclusive. This implies that the Council may opt to not exercise EU competence, thereby enabling Member States to act outside of the EU framework. This means Member States may continue to conclude international agreements in many areas. And it also means Member States are in a position to ensure that international agreements the EU aims to conclude will take the form of mixed as opposed to EU-only agreements.

Secondly, the Court of Justice takes centre stage in resolving conflicts between Member States and the EU institutions. Through the development of constitutional principles—the ERTA principle, the duty of sincere cooperation—the Court gradually developed a constitutional framework that both protects the ability of the EU to act externally and limits the ability of Member States to do so if and in so far as Member State actions risk negatively affecting EU external action. An important development can be discerned in this corner of the EU's foreign affairs constitution. Whereas in the decades following the *ERTA* judgment the Court of Justice aimed to prevent conflicts from arising by interpreting broadly the scope of the EU's exclusive external competences, in more recent decades emphasis shifted towards the duty of sincere cooperation, which operates as a conflict prevention tool in a paradigm of shared competences.[4] Common to both approaches, however, is a reliance

[4] On this development, see generally Thomas Verellen, 'Convergence and Divergence in EU External Action: The Very Slowly Emerging Doctrine of Shared Competence' in Marjan Kos, Jaka Kukavica, and

on the Court of Justice to resolve conflicts between the EU institutions on the one hand, and between EU institutions and the Member States, on the other. Lacking in the EU's foreign affairs constitution are political mechanisms that allow for conflicts to be prevented before they materialize. This lack of *ex ante* political mechanisms raises enforcement questions.

Thirdly, political safeguards of foreign relations federalism in the EU are particularly well developed. In marked contrast to the two North American federations, but not unlike the arrangements in Belgium, the member units are at the heart of EU decision-making. Their centrality to the EU political process is such that the salient question when it comes to institutional design at EU level is not how member units can be granted sufficient voice in the EU political process, but rather how other interests—and in particular the interests of individual citizens in a Union constitutionally committed to representative democracy—can be adequately represented. (I return to this issue further later in the chapter as I put forward proposals for reform.) Moreover, the direct representation of Member States within the EU institutional framework should be understood in conjunction with the significant informal safeguards that are in place. In particular, Member States control most fiscal, administrative, and military resources. They can leverage these resources to control the political process at EU level. This is particularly pronounced in the Common Foreign and Security Policy (CFSP), but dynamics of this type are visible in all areas of EU foreign relations.

Fourthly, when it comes to intergovernmental relations, the EU is the odd one out when compared to the other three federations looked at in this book. Intergovernmental relations occur both vertically and horizontally. Vertically, EU institutions and Member States engage with one another in the framework of mixed external action, as well as when the EU holds the necessary external competence to act but is precluded from doing so for reasons derived from international law (eg because the EU is not a member of the international body at issue). Vertical intergovernmental relations are to an important extent informal. There have been no meaningful efforts to codify practices or to further determine what the duty of sincere cooperation requires of the Member States and the EU. Such informality is reminiscent of intergovernmental relations in the two North American federations, whereas the constitutional obligation to cooperate, which finds its normative foundation in the principle of sincere cooperation, is reminiscent more of the Belgian foreign affairs constitution.

Maja Sahadžić (eds), *The Dialectics in Multilevel Systems—Mechanisms of Divergence and Convergence* (Hart 2023).

(There, too, the constitution requires governments to cooperate to enable the federation as a whole to function.)

Yet, in contrast to Belgium, the duty to cooperate between levels of governance in the EU does not prevail over the autonomy of the federal/EU level of governance to exercise its own competences in accordance with the decision-making rules set out in the EU Treaties. In this sense, sincere cooperation as understood in EU law is of a weaker form as compared to its Belgian counterpart. The limits on the duty of sincere cooperation based on the autonomy of EU law echo the pronouncements by the Canadian Supreme Court on the significance of parliamentary sovereignty in Canadian federalism: as the Supreme Court made clear in *Canada Assistance Plan*, Canada's constitution encourages cooperation between governments, but such cooperation cannot put limits on the sovereignty of each parliament to exercise its own powers. Similarly, as the Court of Justice made clear in *US Air Transport Agreement* and again in Opinion 1/19, the duty of sincere cooperation cannot preclude the Council from exercising its competences if a political majority to do so has been found. That said, the parallel does seem to be only partial. In the EU this autonomy-based—or rather, sovereignty-based[5]—reasoning runs one way only: it protects the autonomy of the EU to act, but not that of the Member States, who are bound by loyalty obligations to act and not to act.

Horizontal intergovernmental relations are a prominent feature of foreign relations federalism in the EU as well. While such relations are typically governed by international law, Member States must at all times comply with their obligations under EU law as they engage with one another. This means, in particular, that they cannot act in areas of EU exclusive competence; that, in the exercise of their own competence, they must comply with their loyalty obligations vis-à-vis the EU; and that they should not incur international legal obligations that conflict with EU law. These obligations significantly restrict the Member States' autonomy to engage in horizontal intergovernmental relations. That said, the EU Treaties provide for few institutional tools to monitor and, if necessary, proactively block Member States from acting in violation of their EU law obligations. Considering how difficult it is to resolve conflicts once they have arisen—the *Achmea* controversy, mentioned in Chapter 9, is a case in point—an 'EU Compact Clause' should be considered. I touched on this proposal in the previous chapter. I return to it further shortly.

[5] On the parallels between both concepts, see Thomas Verellen, 'European Sovereignty Now? A Reflection on What It Means to Speak of "European Sovereignty"' (2020) 5 European Papers 307, 310–13.

The allocation of broad but shared external competence to the EU, the lack of *ex ante* conflict prevention mechanisms, the strong political safeguards of federalism, and the prevalence of intergovernmental relations that fall outside of the scope of EU law altogether: these features justify characterizing the EU's approach to foreign relations federalism as a 'diversity ++' approach. To be clear, as mentioned, the EU foreign affairs constitution imposes significant legal limits on the ability of Member States to act on the international stage. The constitutional principles that govern EU foreign relations—primacy, pre-emption, exclusivity—are reminiscent of those we encountered in the US, a federation with a 'unity +' approach to foreign relations federalism. Yet when we add to the equation the other components of federalism as understood in this book—in particular the political safeguards of foreign relations federalism—the picture changes. In the US, the supremacy of federal law (and executive policy) goes hand in hand with comparatively weak political safeguards—a lack of member unit voice in the federal political process coupled with significant federal fiscal, administrative, and military capabilities. Conversely, the constitutional principles that govern EU foreign relations exist alongside an institutional framework in which Member States take central stage.[6] The scarcity of checks on the two Councils, the ability of Member States to exit the EU framework, coupled with the strong informal safeguards of foreign relations federalism, ensure that Member States exert a significant amount of control over EU foreign relations. Due to a lack of institutional machinery to enforce the constitutional principles mentioned earlier, the Court of Justice plays an important—and perhaps too important—role in maintaining the balance between unity and diversity put in place by the Treaty framers. For these reasons, the EU is best understood as a 'diversity ++' approach to foreign relations federalism.

3. Moving Forward: Democratizing EU Foreign Relations

3.1 The Issue: A Democratic Deficit in EU Foreign Relations

Federalism and democracy are no easy bedfellows.[7] The constitutional limits that a federal covenant places on the exercise of public authority at each level of

[6] The point is reminiscent of Joseph Weiler's thesis in 'The Transformation of Europe' (1991) 100 Yale Law Journal 2403.

[7] Discussing whether democracy and federalism are compatible, see generally Robert A Dahl, 'Federalism and the Democratic Process Part II: Federalism: Section 3' (1983) 25 NOMOS: American Society for Political and Legal Philosophy 95. And in reply to Dahl: David Braybrooke, 'Can

governance inevitably constrain the ability of the political communities which together constitute the federation to govern themselves. This is the case in all four of the federations explored in this book. In the US, self-government within the fifty states is constrained by the ability of the federal Congress to adopt laws that have supremacy over state law. Conversely, the powers of the federal Congress have constitutional limits that flow from the Tenth Amendment. In Canada, both federal and provincial legislatures are supreme, but only within the spheres allocated to them by Canada's Constitution Act, 1867. The same holds true in Belgium, where each government is empowered to act within the confines of its exclusive competences, both internally and externally. And it is true also within the EU. EU law has primacy over Member State law, even if the latter has been democratically enacted by a national (or sub-national) parliament. And conversely, the central role of Member States in the EU political process ensures that that process is controlled by the member units. Each of these constitutional restrictions constrains the ability of the 'people'—or, more accurately: the different 'peoples' which together constitute the federal union—to govern themselves. To be sure, to some extent such constraints are inherent in constitutional government. However, in federal unions constraints on the scope and exercise of constitutional powers flow not only from fundamental rights and from a horizontal separation of powers between the different branches of government, but also from a vertical division of powers between levels of governance. There are thus, simply put, *more* constraints in federal unions as compared to unitary constitutional systems. As a consequence, while democracy is always imperfect in a system of constitutional government—assuming, for the sake of the argument, that 'perfect' democracy can ever be realized—it is likely to be *even more* imperfect in federal unions.

In addition to internal constraints that flow from the federal architecture of the polity, constraints on the process of democratic will-formation also find their origins in the international sphere.[8] In foreign relations, policy outcomes are often the product of negotiations between actors. As such, they are not likely to correspond to the democratic preferences of any one single actor.[9] This feature of international law-making further weakens the connection between

Democracy Be Combined with Federalism or with Liberalism? Part II: Federalism: Section 4' (1983) 25 NOMOS: American Society for Political and Legal Philosophy 109.

[8] I make abstraction of other forces that constrain democracy within the confines of the nation-state, such as economic globalization that enabled free movement of capital. On this topic, see David Held, 'Democracy and Globalization' (1997) 3 Global Governance 251.

[9] See on this Jan Wouters, Bart De Meester, and Cedric Ryngaert, 'Democracy and International Law' (2003) 34 Netherlands Yearbook of International Law 139, 179.

a given people's policy preferences as expressed in the domestic process of democratic will-formation on the one hand, and the policy outcomes as they are reflected in international agreements or decisions of international bodies on the other. In federal unions, when it comes to the foreign policy-making, the connection between the people's preferences and policy outcomes is thus weakened at two levels: both within the federation, where it is subject to constitutional constraints that flow from the federal architecture of the polity, and at the international level, where it is subject to the wheeling and dealing that is part and parcel of international law-making.

The above two-fold weakening of the connection between democratic preferences and policy outcomes—what democratic theorists have called 'input legitimacy'[10]—is particularly pronounced within the EU. As discussed in Chapter 7, and as mentioned earlier in this conclusion, both formal and informal political safeguards of foreign relation federalism are well developed in the EU: checks on the two Councils are weak, and the role of the European Parliament—a direct source of democratic legitimation—remains limited in many corners of EU foreign relations, in particular within the CFSP. Moreover, Member States often act jointly with the EU as sovereign states under international law. Such joint or mixed action further strengthens Member States' position vis-à-vis the EU institutions. As discussed in Chapter 9, mixity often makes decision-making by common accord a practical necessity even when the Treaties call for decision-making by qualified majority in the Council, and it blurs accountability lines as it is not clear which level of governance is responsible for each of the elements of a proposed agreement or decision.[11] As a result, the democratic deficit that is inherent in international law-making is thus further exacerbated by the constitutional and institutional set-up of the EU. To be clear, an uneasy relationship between federalism and democracy is not unique to the EU. In Belgium as well, federalism and democracy are no easy bedfellows. Belgium's federal architecture empowers the federal and member unit executives—and the political parties that constitute the governing majority—without concomitantly empowering the respective legislatures.[12]

[10] See generally Vivien A Schmidt, 'Democracy and Legitimacy in the European Union Revisited: Input, Output and "Throughput"' (2013) 61 Political Studies 2. The distinction between input and output legitimacy was first introduced by Fritz Scharpf in his *Demokratietheorie zwischen Utopie und Anpassung* (Druckerei und Verlagsanstalt Universitätsverlag 1970).

[11] A blurring of accountability lines empowers the bureaucracy and thus undermines democratic accountability. See on this Stefan Oeter, 'Federalism and Democracy' in Armin von Bogdandy and Jürgen Bast (eds), *Principles of European Constitutional Law* (Bloomsbury Publishing 2009) 78.

[12] The phenomenon is captured by the term 'executive federalism.' See eg Petra Meier and Peter Bursens, 'Belgium: The Democratic State of the Federation' in Jared Sonnicksen and Arthur Benz (eds), *Federal Democracies at Work* (University of Toronto Press 2021) 190.

Yet in contrast to the two Councils, the Belgian federal executive is itself democratically legitimized through the organization of federal elections. Within the two Councils, a similar channel of direct democratic legitimacy is lacking as the members of the two Councils are accountable only to the Member State legislatures, not to the European Parliament, as discussed in Chapter 7.

How, then, to remedy the democratic deficit that afflicts EU foreign policy-making? The question is complex and it is impossible to put forward fully fleshed out proposals in this concluding chapter. That said, three avenues are worth pursuing—none of them novel, each of them worth reiterating. First, constitutional limits should be recognized on the authority of the Member States in the Council to not exercise EU shared competence with the sole aim of rendering an international agreement mixed. Fewer opportunities for mixed action means that Member States more often act entirely within the EU framework, where they are fully subject to the accountability mechanisms set up by the EU Treaties. Secondly, the CFSP should be fully normalized. The 'special rules and procedures' to which the CFSP is subject should be abolished.[13] Instead, decision-making on CFSP issues—for example the adoption of economic sanctions, or the setting up of a police mission outside of EU territory—should involve the Commission and the Parliament, and CFSP decisions should be subject to full judicial review. Normalizing the CFSP means strengthening checks on the Council by bringing this corner of EU foreign relations within the scope of existing accountability mechanisms. Thirdly, the offices of the European Council and European Commission presidencies should be merged and the democratic credentials of the merged presidency should be enhanced. A merged presidency that is fully under democratic control will operate as a more meaningful check on the two Councils, which will continue to play a central role in EU foreign relations. I discuss each proposal in turn.

3.2 First Proposal: Limiting Facultative Mixity

In the previous chapter, I proposed an 'EU Mixity Act' as a means to further determine the duty of sincere cooperation as it plays out in the framework of mixed external action. By spelling out in greater detail and on a cross-sectoral basis how the EU institutions and the Member States are to collaborate in international bodies and during treaty negotiations, all stakeholders will have a better understanding of how to engage with one another in the different phases

[13] TEU, art 24(1) second para.

of the decision-making process. That said, an EU Mixity Act can only do so much to remedy the abovementioned democratic deficit. Needed, also, are constitutional limits on the authority of Member States in the Council to not exercise EU shared competence with the sole purpose of rendering a proposed agreement mixed.

As discussed in Chapter 3, in many instances mixity is compulsory. In others it is facultative. 'Facultative' should, however, not be understood to mean that the Council's choice to exercise or not exercise EU shared competence is not subject to any constitutional limits. In a framework of EU shared competence, a proposed agreement becomes a mixed agreement when the Council opts not to exercise part of the EU competence necessary to conclude the agreement and the Member States step in to 'supplement' the competence not exercised at EU level. When Member States exercise their own competence with the sole purpose of rendering an international agreement mixed, they may be violating their duty of sincere cooperation vis-à-vis the EU by precluding the latter from exercising its competence. This would be the case, for example, when an agreement, if it is to be ratified at all, should be ratified quickly—an unlikely prospect if all Member States must ratify the agreement before it can enter into force.[14] This decision by the Member States should not be considered a non-justiciable political question. Member States are subject to general principles of EU law, including the duty of sincere cooperation, when they exercise their own competences. As a consequence, provided admissibility requirements are met, the Court of Justice can review Member State actions in light of the duty of sincere cooperation.

The constitutional limits the EU Treaties impose on Member States as they exercise their own competences in areas covered by EU shared competence limit the number of agreements that can be concluded as mixed agreements. If enforced, this would have an important advantage: if the EU acts independently rather than jointly with the Member States, existing mechanisms of democratic legitimation work as intended by the Treaty framers. The Parliament is the only legislature to approve (or reject) international agreements, and the Council can decide by qualified majority vote whenever the Treaties provide for qualified majority voting rather than unanimity. From the vantage point of voters, it will be clear that the political conversation on the merits and pitfalls of an agreement is to be had at EU level amongst MEPs and amongst the Member State

[14] See on this Opinion of AG Wahl in Opinion 3/15 ('Marrakech Convention'), EU:C:2016:657, para 121. See also, somewhat more sceptically, Merijn Chamon, 'Constitutional Limits to the Political Choice for Mixity' in Eleftheria Neframi and Mauro Gatti (eds), *Constitutional Issues of EU External Relations Law* (Nomos 2018) 160–61.

executives meeting in the Council.[15] Public attention will shift from the national to the EU arena.

Such a shift from a national to an EU-level conversation is to be welcomed considering that the agreement would affect all EU citizens. Assuming that all citizens who are affected by a measure should have a right to participate in approving or rejecting it,[16] and assuming that in that process each citizen should carry equal weight,[17] the European Parliament is the preferred venue to ensure that international agreements to which the EU is a party are democratically legitimized. Conversely, national parliaments are sub-optimal venues: national MPs represent only a party of the constituency that will be affected by an agreement, which grants individual Member State MPs an excessive weight in the decision-making process. Moreover, to the extent that Member State MPs vote on issues that fall within the exclusive competence of the EU—as occurs when Member State executives submit the entirety of a mixed agreement to their respective parliaments for an up or down vote without distinguishing between issues that fall within and outside of EU exclusive competence—those MPs can be understood to be circumventing the EU's exclusive competence.[18]

3.3 Second Proposal: Normalizing the Common Foreign and Security Policy

The Maastricht Treaty put in place a Common Foreign and Security Policy. The CFSP was, as a UK foreign secretary once put it, 'ring-fenced' as a distinct area of external action, equal to other areas such as trade or development policy.[19] Until this day, the CFSP continues to operate on the basis of a distinct set of rules and procedures.[20] As discussed in Chapter 7, the powers of the

[15] See on this Merijn Chamon and Thomas Verellen, 'Whittling Down the Collective Interest: CETA, Facultative Mixity, Democracy and Halloumi' (*Verfassungsblog*, 7 August 2020) <https://verfassungsblog.de/whittling-down-the-collective-interest/> accessed 7 August 2020.

[16] Althusius' adage '[w]hat touches all ought to be approved by all' can be extended to the sphere of the individual: the relevant unit for democratic will-formation should, ideally, be the unit of individuals that are affected by the measures (to be) taken. For a critical assessment of the 'all-affected principle', see Eerik Lagerspetz, 'Democracy and the All-Affected Principle' (2015) 10 Res Cogitans 6.

[17] David Held, 'The Possibilities of Democracy' (1991) 20 Theory and Society 875, 876.

[18] In this sense, see eg Freya Baetens and others, 'Why The Netherlands Should Ratify CETA' (*EJIL:Talk!*, 30 June 2020) <www.ejiltalk.org/why-the-netherlands-should-ratify-ceta/> accessed 2 July 2020.

[19] David Miliband as quoted in Paul James Cardwell, 'On Ring-Fencing the Common Foreign and Security Policy in the Legal Order of the European Union' (2013) 64 Northern Ireland Legal Quarterly 443, 443.

[20] See generally Graham Butler, *Constitutional Law of the EU's Common Foreign and Security Policy: Competence and Institutions in External Relations* (Hart 2019).

Commission and Parliament are limited, as is the jurisdiction of the Court of Justice. By carving out the CFSP from the scope of application of the accountability mechanisms set up by the EU Treaties, the CFSP is an area in which checks on the Council are particularly weak. As a result, to a greater extent than is the case in other areas of EU external action, the CFSP is an area of EU policy-making insulated against democratic accountability pressures. Democratic legitimation in this area is at most indirect: it is to be provided by the Member State executives that sit in the Council and who are themselves democratically controlled by Member State parliaments.[21] However, on issues of security policy Member State parliaments tend to defer to the executive.[22] And even if in some Member States meaningful legislative oversight does exist, it certainly does not exist in all Member States. As a result, existing indirect democratic controls are not up to the task of ensuring that the Council's actions are under adequate democratic control.

Normalizing the CFSP by involving the European Commission and the European Parliament in CFSP decision-making, and by fully extending the jurisdiction of the Court of Justice to all corners of the CFSP, would be an obvious way of strengthening democratic controls over EU foreign policy-making. The European Parliament would infuse an element of direct democratic legitimacy into the decision-making process, and the Court of Justice could more easily ensure that the institutional balance is maintained and that individuals are protected.[23] Normalizing the CFSP would, moreover, enhance the effectiveness of the CFSP. Council and Commission would lose incentives to engage in interinstitutional turf wars over whether an issue falls within or outside of the scope of the CFSP,[24] and the threshold for EU action would be lowered as decision-making by unanimity would be replaced by decision-making by

[21] But see Guri Rosén and Kolja Raube, 'Influence beyond Formal Powers: The Parliamentarisation of European Union Security Policy' (2018) 20 British Journal of Politics and International Relations 69, highlighting how the European Parliament is able to exert influence despite its lack of formal powers.

[22] Also in the North American federations, security policy is controlled to an important degree by the executive. In the Canadian constitutional tradition, the prerogative was long considered non-justiciable. See on this Jennifer A Klinck, 'Modernizing Judicial Review of the Exercise of Prerogative Powers in Canada' [2017] Alberta Law Review 997, pointing out that Canadian courts respond much more tentatively when asked to review exercises of prerogative powers than exercises of statutory powers. And in the US, Thomas Franck famously wondered whether the rule of law applies to foreign affairs. See his *Political Questions Judicial Answers: Does the Rule of Law Apply to Foreign Affairs?* (Princeton University Press 1992).

[23] See in this regard Case C–658/11 *Parliament v Council ('Mauritius')*, EU:C:2014:2025, in which the Court interpreted broadly the Council's obligation to share information with the Parliament in the process of negotiating and concluding international agreements on CFSP issues.

[24] For a recent example, see Case C–244/17 *Commission v Council ('Agreement with Kazakhstan')*, EU:C:2018:662.

qualified majority, as is the general rule in other areas of EU external action such as trade or development policy.

3.4 Third Proposal: Merging and Democratizing the Offices of European Council and European Commission President

Chapter 7 demonstrated how difficult it is for other EU institutions to operate as a check on the two Councils, which represent the Member States. To further strengthen the checks on the two Councils and to further reinforce the democratic legitimacy of EU foreign policy-making—and EU decision-making more generally—the offices of the European Council and European Commission Presidents should be merged and the democratic credentials of the resulting unified presidency should be enhanced. Merging the two offices would transform the existing bifurcated presidency into a meaningful counterweight against the twenty-seven Member States within the EU institutional framework. The merged presidency would preside over the Commission bureaucracy, which brings to the table expertise and administrative capacity, and they would chair European Council meetings, which would enable them to more effectively shape the EU policy-making agenda. (Moreover, a merger would simplify the EU's external representation—an issue which in recent years has led to a number of diplomatic controversies.[25])

The position of the merged European Council/European Commission President vis-à-vis the Member States in the European Council would be strengthened further if they could tap into a direct source of democratic legitimacy. Two options present themselves, both of which have been explored in the literature. First, a *parliamentarization* of the Commission as a whole, whereby the Commission—and thus the merged European Council/Commission President—operates on the basis of a democratic mandate issued by the European Parliament and whereby the President needs to retain the confidence of the Parliament to stay in office.[26] Secondly, a *presidentialization* of the office of the merged European Council/Commission President, whereby the holder of the office would be directly elected, in an election organized

[25] See eg Andrew Gray, 'Charles Michel on Sofagate: Not My Fault' (*POLITICO*, 7 April 2021) <www.politico.eu/article/charles-michel-on-sofagate-not-my-fault-ursula-von-der-leyen-recep-tayyip-erdogan/> accessed 12 April 2021. Or Benjamin Fox, 'Barroso and Van Rompuy Win Battle for Nobel Limelight' *EUObserver* (19 October 2012) <https://euobserver.com/news/117926> accessed 16 January 2018.

[26] For a critical assessment, see Sergio Fabbrini, 'The European Union and the Puzzle of Parliamentary Government' [2015] Journal of European Integration 1.

separately from the European Parliament elections.[27] Which of these models is implemented is of secondary importance for the purpose of this book. Whichever model is retained, its aim should be to further strengthen the ability of EU citizens to hold the EU democratically accountable for its actions and to have a say in the policy choices the EU makes. In so doing, citizens would operate as a check on the European Council—the body which, according to Article 15(1) TEU, provides the EU with 'the necessary impetus for its development and shall define the general political directions and priorities thereof'.

4. Conclusion

The three suggestions for reform proposed in this concluding chapter would pull the EU from a 'diversity ++' approach to a 'diversity +' approach. By strengthening the offices and institutions that infuse the EU political process with direct democratic legitimacy, they will be able to more effectively operate as a check on the two Councils. Such a rebalancing is needed not because more unity is inherently desirable. Rather, it is needed because the EU foreign affairs constitution currently imposes significant limits on the authority of Member States to act unilaterally without simultaneously ensuring that actions at EU level are fully under democratic control. By ensuring that collective Member State action takes place within the EU legal framework, and by strengthening democratic safeguards at EU level, EU foreign relations will be more in keeping with the preferences of the aggregate EU citizenry. As such, these reforms help to realize the Treaty requirement mentioned at the head of this chapter: that the EU's functioning shall be founded on representative democracy.

[27] Proposing that the European Council President be directly elected, see Walter Van Gerven, *The European Union: A Polity of States and Peoples* (Stanford University Press 2005) 367. And also Federico Fabbrini, 'Austerity, the European Council, and the Institutional Future of the European Union: A Proposal to Strengthen the Presidency of the European Council Symposium' (2015) 22 Indiana Journal of Global Legal Studies 269. Proposing that the Commission President be directly elected, see Simon Hix, 'Elections, Parties and Institutional Design: A Comparative Perspective on European Union Democracy' (1998) 21 West European Politics 19. For a more recent reassessment, see Frank Decker and Jared Sonnicksen, 'An Alternative Approach to European Union Democratization: Re-Examining the Direct Election of the Commission President' (2011) 46 Government and Opposition 168.

Bibliography

Abrams K, 'Plenary Power Preemption' (2013) 99 Virginia Law Review 601

Adam MA, Bergeron J, Bonnard M, 'Intergovernmental Relations in Canada: Competing Visions and Diverse Dynamics' in J Prior, C Saunders, and J Kincaid (eds), *Intergovernmental* Relations *in Federal Systems* (OUP 2015)

Adler E, 'Constructivism in International Relations: Sources, Contributions, and Debates' in W Carlsnaes, T Risse, and B Simmons (eds), *Handbook of International Relations* (SAGE Publications Ltd 2013)

Albert R, 'The Difficulty of Constitutional Amendment in Canada' (2016) 53 Alberta Law Review 85

Alexandra P, 'The Integration of the European Development Funds into the MFF 2021–2027' (European Parliament 2021) Briefing

Alexandrova P, 'Institutional Issue Proclivity in the EU: The European Council vs the Commission' (2017) 24 Journal of European Public Policy 755

American Law Institute, 'Restatement (Third) of Foreign Relations Law of the United States' (1987)

American Law Institute, 'Restatement (Fourth) of Foreign Relations Law' (2018)

Arena A, 'Exercise of EU Competences and Pre-Emption of Member States' Powers in the Internal and the External Sphere: Towards "Grand Unification"?' [2016] Yearbook of European Law 1

Atkey RG, 'The Role of the Provinces in International Affairs' (1971) 26 International Journal 261

Baetens F and others, 'Why The Netherlands Should Ratify CETA' (EJIL: Talk!, 30 June 2020) <www.ejiltalk.org/why-the-netherlands-should-ratify-ceta/> accessed 2 July 2020

Bagehot W, *The English Constitution*, vol 3 (1873) <http://socserv2.socsci.mcmaster.ca/econ/ugcm/3ll3/bagehot/constitution.pdf> accessed 7 March 2023

Bakvis H, 'Regional Ministers, National Policies and the Administrative State in Canada: The Regional Dimension in Cabinet Decision-Making, 1980-1984' (1988) 21 Canadian Journal of Political Science / Revue canadienne de science politique 539

—— and Tanguay AB, 'Federalism, Political Parties, and the Burden of National Unity: Still Making Federalism Do the Heavy Lifting?' in Herman Bakvis and Grace Skogstad (eds), *Canadian Federalism: Performance, Effectiveness, and Legitimacy* (Oxford University Press 2012)

Baraton E, *De Gaulle ou l'hypothèque française sur le Canada* (L'Harmattan 2013)

Barnett RE, 'Foreword: The Power of Presumptions' (1994) 17 Harvard Journal of Law & Public Policy 613

Bartels LM and Rogers S, 'National Forces in State Legislative Elections' (2016) 667 The ANNALS of the American Academy of Political and Social Science 207

BBC News, 'Brexit: UK Signs First US State-Level Trade Agreement with Indiana', 27 May 2022 <www.bbc.com/news/uk-politics-61604784> accessed 2 June 2022

Beaud O, *Théorie de la fédération* (Presses Universitaires de France—PUF 2007)

Beaulac S, 'Arrêtons de dire que les tribunaux au Canada sont liés par le droit international' (2004) 38 Revue juridique Thémis 359

—— 'Myth of Js Tractatus in La Belle Province: Quebec's Gerin-Lajoie Statement' (2012) 35 Dalhousie Law Journal 237

—— and Currie JH, 'Canada' in D Shelton (ed), *International Law and Domestic Legal Systems: Incorporation, Transformation, and Persuasion* (Oxford University Press 2011)

Bebr G, 'The European Defence Community and the Western European Union: An Agonizing Dilemma' (1955) 7 Stanford Law Review 169

Bélanger L, 'The Domestic Politics of Quebec's Quest for External Distinctiveness' (2002) 32(2) *The American Review of Canadian Studies* 195

Bickerton CJ, Hodson D, and Puetter U, *The New Intergovernmentalism: States and Supranational Actors in the Post-Maastricht Era* (Oxford University Press 2015)

Black ER, Cairns A, 'A Different Perspective on Canadian Federalism' (1966) 9 Canadian Public Administration 27

Bocquillon P, Dobbels M, 'An Elephant on the 13th Floor of the Berlaymont? European Council and Commission Relations in Legislative Agenda Setting' (2014) 21(1) Journal of European Public Policy 20

Boffey D, 'Nine EU States Sign off on Joint Military Intervention Force.' *The Guardian* (25 June 2018) sec. World news. <www.theguardian.com/world/2018/jun/25/nine-eu-states-to-sign-off-on-joint-military-intervention-force> accessed 7 March 2023

—— 'EU-UK Inaugural Meeting "postponed" after Bloc Ambassador's Status Downgrade' *The Guardian* (28 January 2021) <www.theguardian.com/world/2021/jan/28/eu-uk-inaugural-meeting-postponed-after-bloc-ambassadors-status-downgrade> accessed 16 November 2021

Bolt A and Lagassé P, 'Beyond Dicey: Executive Authorities in Canada' (2021) 3 Journal of Commonwealth Law 1

Bossuyt MJ and Wouters J, *Grondlijnen van internationaal recht* (Intersentia 2005)

Bradley CA, 'The Treaty Power and American Federalism' (1998) 97 Michigan Law Review 390

—— 'A New American Foreign Relations Law?' (1999) 70 Colorado Law Review 1090

—— 'Reassessing the Legislative Veto: The Statutory President, Foreign Affairs, and Congressional Workarounds' [2021] Journal of Legal Analysis 439

—— and Goldsmith JL, 'Presidential Control over International Law' (2018) 131 Harvard Law Review 1201

Braybrooke D, 'Can Democracy Be Combined with Federalism or with Liberalism? Part II: Federalism: Section 4' (1983) 25 NOMOS: American Society for Political and Legal Philosophy 109

Bressanelli E and Chelotti N, 'The Shadow of the European Council. Understanding Legislation on Economic Governance' (2016) 38 Journal of European Integration 511

Broder JM and Baker P, 'Obama Putting Quick Stamp on Environmental Policy' *The New York Times* (6 February 2009) <www.nytimes.com/2009/01/26/world/americas/26iht-calif.3.19685095.html> accessed 2 March 2022

Bryan JD and Tama J, 'The Prevalence of Bipartisanship in U.S. Foreign Policy: An Analysis of Important Congressional Votes' [2021] International Politics <https://doi.org/10.1057/s41311-021-00348-7> accessed 20 September 2021

Bulman-Pozen J, 'Federalism as a Safeguard of the Separation of Powers' (2012) 112 Columbia Law Review 459

—— 'Partisan Federalism' (2014) 127 Harvard Law Review 1077

—— 'Executive Federalism Comes to America' (2015) 102 Virginia Law Review 953

—— 'Our Regionalism' (2017) 166 University of Pennsylvania Law Review 377

—— 'Administrative States: Beyond Presidential Administration' (2019) 98 Texas Law Review 265

—— and Gerken HK, 'Uncooperative Federalism' (2008) 118 Yale Law Journal 1256

Burgess M, 'Daniel J. Elazar and Federalism as Covenant' in M Burgess, *In Search of the Federal Spirit: New Theoretical and Empirical Perspectives in Comparative Federalism* (Oxford University Press 2012)

—— *In Search of the Federal Spirit: New Theoretical and Empirical Perspectives in Comparative Federalism* (Oxford University Press 2012)

Butler G, *Constitutional Law of the EU's Common Foreign and Security Policy: Competence and Institutions in External Relations* (Hart 2019)

Buzbee WW (ed), *Preemption Choice: The Theory, Law, and Reality of Federalism's Core Question* (Cambridge University Press 2009)

Cairns AC, 'The Governments and Societies of Canadian Federalism' (1977) 10 Canadian Journal of Political Science 695

—— 'From Interstate to Intrastate Federalism in Canada' (1978) 2 Bulletin of Canadian Studies 13

Cappelletti M, Seccombe M, and Weiler J, *Integration Through Law: Europe and the American Federal Experience* (Walter de Gruyter 1985)

Cardwell PJ, 'On Ring-Fencing the Common Foreign and Security Policy in the Legal Order of the European Union' (2013) 64 Northern Ireland Legal Quarterly 443

Carty K and Cross W, 'Political Parties and the Practice of Brokerage Politics' in J Courtney and D Smith (eds), *The Oxford Handbook of Canadian Politics* (Oxford University Press 2010)

CBC News, 'Canada's Senate: Sober Second Thought', 9 July 2010 <www.cbc.ca/news/canada/canada-s-senate-sober-second-thought-1.887861> accessed 7 March 2023

CBC News, 'CETA Negotiations with Ottawa Suspended over Fisheries Fund, N.L. Says', 19 January 2015 <www.cbc.ca/1.2917699> accessed 7 March 2023

CBC News, 'Cap-and-Trade Is over, Ontario PCs Say as New Legislation Unveiled', 25 July 2018 <www.cbc.ca/news/canada/toronto/ontario-pc-legislation-kills-cap-and-trade-1.4761398> accessed 7 March 2023

CD&V, 'Steven Vanackere: 'Senaat Heeft Haar Rol van Bemiddelaar Correct Gespeeld' <www.cdenv.be/wie-zijn-we/cdenv-als-politieke-partij/de-senaat/actua/steven-vanackere-senaat-heeft-haar-rol-van-bemiddelaar-correct-gespeeld/> accessed 27 September 2017

Chamon M, 'Constitutional Limits to the Political Choice for Mixity' in Eleftheria Neframi and Mauro Gatti (eds), *Constitutional Issues of EU External Relations Law* (Nomos 2018)

—— 'Implied Exclusive Powers in the ECJ'S Post-Lisbon Jurisprudence: The Continued Development of the ERTA Doctrine' (2018) 55 Common Market Law Review 1101

—— and Govaere I (eds), *EU External Relations Post-Lisbon: The Law and Practice of Facultative Mixity* (Brill Nijhoff 2020)

—— and Verellen T, 'Whittling Down the Collective Interest: CETA, Facultative Mixity, Democracy and Halloumi' (*Verfassungsblog*, 7 August 2020) <https://verfassungsblog.de/whittling-down-the-collective-interest/> accessed 7 August 2020

—— and Cremona M, 'The Representation of the EU and Its Member States in Multilateral Fora' in N Levrat and others (eds), *The EU and its Member States' Joint Participation in International Agreements* (Hart Publishing 2022)

Chernow R, *Alexander Hamilton* (Penguin 2005)

Choper JH, *Judicial Review and the National Political Process: A Functional Reconsideration of the Role of the Supreme Court* (Quid Pro Books 2013)

Choudhry S and Howse R, 'Constitutional Theory and The Quebec Secession Reference' (2000) 12 Canadian Journal of Law & Jurisprudence 143

Clark BR, 'Separation of Powers as a Safeguard of Federalism' (2000) 79 Texas Law Review 1321

Claussen K, 'Trade Administration' (2021) 107 Virginia Law Review 845

Cleveland SH, 'Crosby and the One-Voice Myth in US Foreign Relations' (2001) 46 Villanova Law Review 975

—— 'Powers Inherent in Sovereignty: Indians, Aliens, Territories, and the Nineteenth Century Origins of Plenary Power over Foreign Affairs' (2002) 81 Texas Law Review 1

Clinton G, 'Antifederalist Paper No 67' <http://thefederalistpapers.org/antifederalist-paper-67> accessed 27 January 2022

CNN, 'Italy's Finance Police Seize Russian Oligarch's Mega Yacht', 12 March 2022 <www.cnn.com/europe/live-news/ukraine-russia-putin-news-03-12-22/h_64c3a1fba253043a8a001a9d5c20b5af> accessed 12 March 2022

Condorelli O, '«Quod omnestangit, debet ab omnibus approbari». Note sull'origine e sull'utilizzazione del principio tra medioevo e prima età moderna' (2013) 53 Ius Canonicum 101

Conway G, 'Recovering a Separation of Powers in the European Union' (2011) 17 European Law Journal 304

Cottier T, 'Front-Loading Trade Policy-Making in the European Union: Towards a Trade Act' in M Bungenberg and others (eds), *European Yearbook of International Economic Law 2017*, vol 8 (Springer International Publishing 2017)

Craenen G, 'België En Het Buitenland. De Nieuwe Regeling van de Buitenlandse Betrekkingen' In A Alen and LP Suetens (eds), *Het Federale België Na de Vierde Staatshervorming. Een Commentaar Op de Nieuwe Grondwet En Haar Uitvoeringswetten* (die Keure 1993)

Craig P, 'Pringle and Use of EU Institutions Outside the EU Legal Framework: Foundations, Procedure and Substance' (2013) 9 European Constitutional Law Review (EuConst) 263

—— 'Economic Governance and the Euro Crisis: Constitutional Architecture and Constitutional Implications' in M Adams, F Fabbrini, and P Larouche (eds), *The Constitutionalization of European Budgetary Constraints* (Hart 2014)

Cremona M, 'The Doctrine of Exclusivity and the Position of Mixed Agreements in the External Relations of the European Community' (1982) 2 Oxford Journal of Legal Studies 393

—— 'Extending the Reach of the AETR Principle: Comment on Commission v Greece' (2009) 34 European Law Review 754

—— 'Case C-246/07, Commission v. Sweden (PFOS), Judgment of the Court of Justice (Grand Chamber) of 20 April 2010' (2011) 48 Common Market Law Review 1639

—— 'EU External Relations: Unity and Conferral of Powers' in L Azoulai (eds), *The Question of Competence in the European Union* (Oxford University Press 2014)

—— 'Structural Principles and Their Role in EU External Relations Law' (2016) 69 Current Legal Problems 35

—— 'EU External Competence—Rationales for Exclusivity' in S Garben and I Govaere (eds), *The Division of Competences between the EU and the Member States: Reflections on the Past, the Present and the Future* (Hart 2017)

—— 'External Competences and the Principle of Conferral' in R Schütze and T Tridimas (eds), *Oxford Principles of European Union Law: The European Union Legal Order: Volume I* (Oxford University Press 2018)

—— 'Shaping EU Trade Policy Post-Lisbon: Opinion 2/15 of 16 May 2017: ECJ, 16 May 2017, Opinion 2/15 Free Trade Agreement with Singapore' (2018) 14 European Constitutional Law Review 231

Criekemans D, 'The Foreign Policy and Diplomatic Representation of the Belgian Regions: Flanders and Wallonia Compared' In F Requejo Coll and D Criekemans (eds), *Foreign Policy of Constituents Units at the Beginning of the 21st Century* (Inst d'Estudis Autonòmics 2010)

Cross DE, 'Pre-Emption of Member State Law in the European Economic Community: A Framework for Analysis' (1992) 29 Common Market Law Review 447

Curtin D, 'The Constitutional Structure of the Union: A Europe of Bits and Pieces' (1993) 30 Common Market Law Review 17

—— 'Democratic Accountability of EU Executive Power: A Reform Agenda for Parliaments' in F Fabbrini, EMH Hirsch Ballin, and H Somsen (eds), *What Form of Government for the European Union and the Eurozone?* (Hart Publishing 2015)

—— and Leino P, 'In Search of Transparency for EU Law-Making: Trilogues on the Cusp of Dawn' (2017) 54 Common Market Law Review 1673

Cyr H, *Canadian Federalism and Treaty Powers: Organic Constitutionalism at Work* (Peter Lang 2009)

Cyr H and de Mestral A, 'International Treaty-Making and Treaty Implementation' in P Oliver, P Macklem and N des Rosiers (eds), *The Oxford Handbook of the Canadian Constitution* (Oxford University Press 2017)

Dahl RA, 'Federalism and the Democratic Process Part II: Federalism: Section 3' (1983) 25 NOMOS: American Society for Political and Legal Philosophy 95

Danisi C, 'Taking the "Union" out of "EU": The EU-Turkey Statement on the Syrian Refugee Crisis as an Agreement Between States under International Law' (*EJIL: Talk!*, 20 April 2017) <www.ejiltalk.org/taking-the-union-out-of-eu-the-eu-turkey-statement-on-the-syrian-refugee-crisis-as-an-agreement-between-states-under-international-law/> accessed 28 April 2022

Dann P, 'European Parliament and Executive Federalism: Approaching a Parliament in a Semi-Parliamentary Democracy' (2003) 5 European Law Journal 549

Dashwood A, 'The Attribution of External Relations Competence' in A Dashwood and C Hillion (eds), *The General Law of E.C. External Relations* (Sweet & Maxwell 2000)

—— 'The Relationship between the Member States and the European Union/European Community' (2004) 41 Common Market Law Review 355

—— 'The Continuing Bipolarity of EU External Action' in I Govare and others (eds), *The European Union in the World: Essays in Honour of Marc Maresceau* (Brill 2014)

Davis MJ, 'Unmasking the Presumption in Favor of Preemption' (2001) 53 South Carolina Law Review 967

Davis SR, *The Federal Principle: A Journey Through Time in Quest of a Meaning* (University of California Press 1978)

Dawson M and de Witte F, 'Constitutional Balance in the EU after the Euro-Crisis.' (2013) 76(5) The Modern Law Review 817

De Baere G, *Constitutional Principles of EU External Relations* (Oxford University Press 2008)

—— '"O, Where Is Faith? O, Where Is Loyalty?" Some Thoughts on the Duty of Loyal Co-Operation and the Union's External Environmental Competences in the Light of the PFOS Case.' (2011) 36(3) European Law Review 405

—— 'Mercury Rising: The European Union and the International Negotiations for a Globally Binding Instrument on Mercury' (2012) 37 European Law Review 640

—— 'EU Status in Other International Organizations' in R Schütze and T Tridimas (eds), *Oxford Principles of European Union Law - Volume I: The European Union Legal Order* (Oxford University Press 2018)

—— and Gutman K, 'Federalism and International Relations in the European Union and the United States: A Comparative Outlook' in E Cloots, G De Baere, and S Sottiaux (eds), *Federalism in the European Union* (Hart 2012)

de la Baume M and Barigazzi J, 'EU Agrees to Give €500M in Arms, Aid to Ukrainian Military in "Watershed" Move' *POLITICO* (27 February 2022) <www.politico.eu/article/eu-ukraine-russia-funding-weapons-budget-military-aid/> accessed 12 March 2022

De Winter L, Della Porta D, and Deschouwer K, 'Partitocracies Between Crises and Reform: The Cases of Italy and Belgium.' (1996) 2 Res Publica: Politiek-Wetenschappelijk Tijdschrift van de Lage Landen 215

—— and Dumont P, 'Do Belgian Parties Undermine the Democratic Chain of Delegation?' (2006) 29(5) West European Politics 957

Decker F and Sonnicksen J, 'An Alternative Approach to European Union Democratization: Re-Examining the Direct Election of the Commission President' (2011) 46 Government and Opposition 168

Dehaene JL, 'De (on)macht van de Eerste Minister: Een a-wetenschappelijke ervarings-benadering' (2001) 42 Res Publica 23

Dekleermaker M, 'Une histoire belge: La coopération en matière environnementale et climatique et la COP21' (2019) 18 Fédéralisme Régionalisme <https://popups.uliege.be/1374-3864/index.php?id=1792> accessed 17 July 2022

Delgado-Casteleiro A, *The International Responsibility of the European Union From Competence to Normative Control* (Cambridge University Press 2016)

—— and Larik J, 'The Duty to Remain Silent: Limitless Loyalty in EU External Relations?' (2011) 36(4) European Law Review 524

Demedts V and Chamon M, 'The Commission Back on the Leash: No Autonomy to Sign Non-Binding Agreements on Behalf of the EU: Council v. Commission' (2017) 54 Common Market Law Review 245

den Heijer M and Spijkerboer T, 'Is the EU-Turkey Refugee and Migration Deal a Treaty?' (*EU Law Analysis*, 7 April 2016) <http://eulawanalysis.blogspot.be/2016/04/is-eu-turkey-refugee-and-migration-deal.html> accessed 29 July 2016

Denza E, *The Intergovernmental Pillars of the European Union* (Oxford University Press 2002)

deredactie.be, 'De Kwestie-BHV Verdwijnt in de Koelkast' 29 April 2010 <http://deredactie.be/cm/vrtnieuws/politiek/1.769903> accessed 7 March 2023

—— 'Kris Dierckx Mag Blijven in Flanders House' 20 July 2010 <http://deredactie.be/cm/vrtnieuws/binnenland/1.829218> accessed 7 March 2023

Dicey AV, *Introduction to the Study of the Law of the Constitution* (8th edn, first published Macmillan 1915, Liberty Classics, 1982)

Droesse G, *Membership in International Organizations: Paradigms of Membership Structures, Legal Implications of Membership and the Concept of International Organization* (Asser Press, Springer 2020)

Duchacek ID, 'Dyadic Federations and Confederations' (1988) 18 Publius 5

Dupré JS, 'Reflections on the Workability of Executive Federalism' in B Caroll, D Siegel, and M Sproule Jones (eds), *Classic Readings in Canadian Public Administration* (Oxford University Press 2005)

Duquet S and Wouters J, 'The EU and International Diplomatic Law: New Horizons?' (2012) 7(1) The Hague Journal of Diplomacy 31

Durán GM, 'Sustainable Development Chapters in EU Free Trade Agreements: Emerging Compliance Issues' (2020) 57 Common Market Law Review 1031

Eckes C, 'How the European Parliament's Participation in International Relations Affects the Deep Tissue of the EU's Power Structures' (2014) 12(4) International Journal of Constitutional Law 904

Eeckhout P, 'Bold Constitutionalism and Beyond' in M Maduro and L Azoulai (eds), *The Past and Future of EU Law: The Classics of EU Law Revisited on the 50th Anniversary of the Rome Treaty* (Hart 2010)

—— 'Exclusive External Competences: Constructing the EU as an International Actor' in Court of Justice of the European Union (ed), *The Court of Justice and the Construction of Europe: Analyses and Perspectives on Sixty Years of Case-law* (TMC Asser Press 2013)

Ehlermann CD, 'Mixed Agreements—A Set of Problems' in D O'Keefe and HG Schermers (eds), *Mixed Agreements* (Kluwer Law and Taxation Publishers 1983)

Elazar D, *Exploring Federalism* (University of Alabama Press 1987)

Emiliou N, 'The Death of Exclusive Competence?' (1996) 21 European Law Review 294

Emmott R, 'EU to Aim for Rapid Deployment Force without U.S. Assets by 2025, Document Says' (16 November 2021) <www.reuters.com/business/aerospace-defense/eu-aim-rapid-deployment-force-without-us-assets-by-2025-document-says-2021-11-16/> accessed 16 November 2021

English J, *Just Watch Me: The Life of Pierre Elliott Trudeau* (1st edn, Alfred A. Knopf Canada 2006)

Erlanger S, 'U.S. Downgraded E.U.'s Diplomatic Status (but Didn't Say Anything)' *The New York Times* (8 January 2019) <www.nytimes.com/2019/01/08/world/europe/eu-us-diplomatic-status.html> accessed 16 November 2021

Esman MJ, 'Federalism and Modernization: Canada and the United States' (1984) 14 Publius 21

Estreicher S, 'Taking Treaty-Implementing Statutes Seriously' in PB Stephan and SH Cleveland (eds), *The Restatement and Beyond* (Oxford University Press 2020)

Fabbrini F, 'Austerity, the European Council, and the Institutional Future of the European Union: A Proposal to Strengthen the Presidency of the European Council Symposium' (2015) 22 Indiana Journal of Global Legal Studies 269

—— 'States' Equality v States' Power: The Euro-Crisis, Inter-State Relations and the Paradox of Domination' (2015) 17 Cambridge Yearbook of European Legal Studies 3

Fabbrini S, *Compound Democracies: Why the United States and Europe Are Becoming Similar* (Oxford University Press 2010)

—— 'The European Union and the Puzzle of Parliamentary Government' [2015] Journal of European Integration 1

—— *Which European Union?* (Cambridge University Press 2015)

—— 'From Consensus to Domination: The Intergovernmental Union in a Crisis Situation' (2016) 38(5) Journal of European Integration 587

Fasone C and Romaniello M, 'A Temporary Recalibration of Executive–Legislative Relations on EU Trade Agreements?: The Case of National and Regional Parliaments on CETA and TTIP' in D Fromage and A Herranz-Surrallés (eds), *Executive–Legislative (Im)balance in the European Union* (Hart Publishing 2020)

Fassbender B, *Der offene Bundesstaat: Studien zur auswärtigen Gewalt und zur Völkerrechtssubjektivität bundesstaatlicher Teilstaaten in Europa* (Mohr Siebeck 2007)

Federale Overheidsdienst Volksgezondheid, Veiligheid van de Voedselketen en Leefmilieu (Dienst Klimaatverandering), 'Syntheserapport Belgisch "Klimaat-Governance"' (2018) <https://klimaat.be/doc/KlimGov_Synth_NL.pdf> accessed 3 June 2022

Feyt A, 'Les Communautés et les régions peuvent-elles se doter d'une diplomatie propre?' [2002] Chroniques de Droit Public—Publiekrechtelijke Kronieken (CDPK) 25

Fiers D, 'Belgische Klimaatakkoord Eindelijk Rond' (*Deredactie.Be*, 4 December 2015) <http://deredactie.be/cm/vrtnieuws/politiek/1.2514770> accessed 7 March 2023

Fisher L, 'The Law: Military Operations in Libya: No War? No Hostilities?' (2012) 42 Presidential Studies Quarterly 176

—— *The Law of the Executive Branch: Presidential Power* (Oxford University Press 2014)

Forcese C, 'The Executive, the Royal Prerogative, and the Constitution' in P Oliver, P Macklem, and N des Rosiers (eds), *The Oxford Handbook of the Canadian Constitution*, vol 1 (Oxford University Press 2017)

Foreign Policy, 'Europe Slams Its Gates. Part One' accessed 10 March 2022 <http://foreignpolicy.com/2017/10/04/europe-slams-its-gates-part-one>

Fox B, 'Barroso and Van Rompuy Win Battle for Nobel Limelight' *EUObserver* (19 October 2012) <https://euobserver.com/news/117926> accessed 16 January 2018

Francis D, 'Litigation as a Political Safeguard of Federalism' (2017) 49 Arizona State Law Journal 1

Franck T, *Political Questions Judicial Answers: Does the Rule of Law Apply to Foreign Affairs?* (Princeton University Press 1992)

Freeman M, 'Canadian Federalism and Treaty Powers: Organic Constitutionalism at Work' (2011) 37(1) Commonwealth Law Bulletin 210

Freeman Engstrom D and Weinstein JM, 'What If California Had a Foreign Policy? The New Frontier of States' Rights' [2018] The Washington Quarterly 27

Friedman L and Plumer B, 'U.S. Governors at U.N. Assembly: "You Have Allies" on Climate Change' *The New York Times* (18 September 2017) <www.nytimes.com/2017/09/18/climate/climate-change-unga-governors.html> accessed 28 January 2022

Gardbaum SA, 'Nature of Preemption' (1994) 79 Cornell Law Review 767

Gardner JA, 'The Myth of State Autonomy: Federalism, Political Parties, and the National Colonization of State Politics' (2014) 29(1) Journal of Law & Politics 1

Gaudreault-DesBiens JF, 'Cooperative Federalism in Search of a Normative Justification: Considering the Principle of Federal Loyalty' (2014) 23 Constitutional Forum 1

—— 'From Dualism to Cooperative Federalism and Back?: Evolving and Competing Conceptions of Canadian Federalism' in P Oliver, P Macklem, and N des Rosiers (eds), *The Oxford Handbook of the Canadian Constitution*, vol 1 (Oxford University Press 2017)

Gayard G, 'Projection internationale des entités fédérées: les politiques internationales du climat du Québec et de la Région wallonne' [2020] Études canadiennes/Canadian Studies 301

Gebert K, 'Shooting in the Dark? EU Sanctions Policies.' Policy Brief. Warsaw: European Council on Foreign Relations, January 2013

Geenens R and others, 'Walen Blokkeren Continent? Naast de Kwestie' *De Standaard* (21 October 2016) <www.standaard.be/cnt/dmf20161020_02531035> accessed 7 March 2023

Geenens R and De Schutter H, 'A Tripartite Model of Federalism' [2022] Philosophy & Social Criticism 1

Gendron RS and Tabachnik DE, 'The Libreville Conference and Federalism in Canadian Foreign Relations' in MK Hawes, AC Holman, and C Kirkey (eds), *1968 in Canada: A Year and Its Legacies* (University of Ottawa Press 2021)

Gérin-Lajoie P, 'Allocution du ministre de l'Éducation, M. Paul Gérin-Lajoie, aux membres du Corps consulaire de Montréal, lundi, le 12 avril à 12h30 de l'après-midi, à l'hôtel Windsor' 1965 <https://www.persee.fr/doc/rqdi_0828-9999_2016_hos_2_1_2224> accessed 7 March 2023

Gerken H, 'Slipping the Bonds of Federalism' (2016) 128 Harvard Law Review 85

Gibson J and Bell D, '"We Must Put Alberta First": Jason Kenney Launches PC Leadership Bid Urging Right to Unite' *CBC News*, accessed 24 August 2017 <www.cbc.ca/news/canada/calgary/jason-kenney-alberta-pc-wildrose-leadership-calgary-announcement-1.3666596> accessed 7 March 2023

Glennon MJ and Sloane RD, *Foreign Affairs Federalism: The Myth of National Exclusivity* (Oxford University Press 2016)

—— and Sloane RD, 'The Sad, Quiet Death of Missouri v. Holland: How Bond Hobbled the Treaty Power' (2016) 41(1) Yale *Journal of International Law* 51

Goelzhauser G and Konisky DM, 'The State of American Federalism 2019–2020: Polarized and Punitive Intergovernmental Relations' (2020) 50 Publius: The Journal of Federalism 311

Goldsmith J, 'Statutory Foreign Affairs Preemption' (2000) 2000 The Supreme Court Review 175

—— 'Zivotofsky II as Precedent in the Executive Branch' (2015) 129 Harvard Law Review 112

Goossens J and Cannoot P, 'Belgian Federalism after the Sixth State Reform' (2015) 7(2) Perspectives on Federalism 29

Gottlieb A, *Canadian Treaty-Making* (Butterworths 1968)

Grant C and Porter H, 'Is Tony Blair the Right Man to Be President of Europe?' *The Guardian* (24 October 2009) sec. Opinion <www.theguardian.com/commentisfree/2009/oct/25/henry-porter-charles-grant> accessed 7 March 2023

Gray A, 'Charles Michel on Sofagate: Not My Fault' *POLITICO* (7 April 2021) <www.politico.eu/article/charles-michel-on-sofagate-not-my-fault-ursula-von-der-leyen-recep-tayyip-erdogan/> accessed 12 April 2021

Groussot X and Bogojevic S, 'Subsidiarity as a Procedural Safeguard of Federalism' in L Azoulai (ed), *The Question of Competence in the European Union* (Oxford University Press 2014)

Gutierrez-Fonz JA, 'Transatlantic Adjudication Techniques. The Commerce Clause and the EU's Internal Market Harmonization Clause in Perspective' in E Fahey and D Curtin (eds), *A Transatlantic Community of Law: Legal Perspectives on the Relationship between the EU and US Legal Orders* (Cambridge University Press 2014)

Haas EB, *The Uniting of Europe: Political, Social, and Economic Forces, 1950–1957* (University of Notre Dame Press 1958)

Hagemann S and Hoyland B, 'Parties in the Council?' (2008) 15 Journal of European Public Policy 1205

Hahn M and Van der Loo G (eds), *Law and Practice of the Common Commercial Policy: The First 10 Years after the Treaty of Lisbon* (Brill Nijhoff 2020)

Hakimi M, 'The Bond Court's Institutional Truce' (2014) 108 American Journal of International Law 89

Halberstam D, 'The Foreign Affairs of Federal Systems: A National Perspective on the Benefits of State Participation' [2001] Villanova Law Review 1015

—— 'Of Power and Responsibility: The Political Morality of Federal Systems' (2004) 90 Virginia Law Review 731

Hamilton A, Madison J, and Jay J, *The Federalist (The Gideon Edition), Edited with an Introduction, Reader's Guide, Constitutional Cross-Reference, Index, and Glossary by George W. Carey and James McClellan* (GW Carey and J McClellan, eds, Liberty Fund 2001)

Happaerts S, Schunz S, and Bruyninckx H, 'Federalism and Intergovernmental Relations: The Multi-Level Politics of Climate Change Policy in Belgium' (2012) 20(4) Journal of Contemporary European Studies 441

Hathaway OA, 'The Case for Replacing Article II Treaties With Ex Post Congressional-Executive Agreements' (American Constitution Society for Law and Policy 2008)

—— 'Treaties' End: The Past, Present, and Future of International Lawmaking in the United States' (2008) 117(7) Yale Law Journal 1236

—— and others, 'The Treaty Power: Its History, Scope and Limits' (2012) 98 Cornell Law Review 239

Healy T, 'Is "Missouri v. Holland" Still Good Law? Federalism and the Treaty Power' (1998) 98 Columbia Law Review 1726

Heisenberg D, 'The Institution of "Consensus" in the European Union: Formal versus Informal Decision-Making in the Council' (2005) 44 European Journal of Political Research 65

Held D, 'The Possibilities of Democracy' (1991) 20 Theory and Society 875

—— 'Democracy and Globalization' (1997) 3 Global Governance 251

Hellerstein W, 'Fiscal Federalism in the United States' (Turin 2011)

Henkin L, *Foreign Affairs and the United States Constitution* (2nd edn, Oxford University Press 1996)

Hillebrandt M and Stéphanie N, '"Integration without Transparency?" Reliance on the Space to Think in the European Council and Council' (2016) 38(5) Journal of European Integration 527

Hillion C, 'Tous Pour Un, Un Pour Tous! Coherence in the External Relations of the European Union' in M Cremona (ed), *Developments in EU External Relations Law* (Oxford University Press 2008)

—— 'Mixity and Coherence in EU External Relations: The Significance of the "Duty of Cooperation"' in C Hillion and P Koutrakos (eds), *Mixed Agreements Revisited: the EU and its Member States in the World* (Hart 2010)

—— and Koutrakos P (eds), *Mixed Agreements Revisited: The EU and Its Member States in the World. Modern Studies in European Law*, vol 21 (Hart 2010)

Hirschman AO, *Exit, Voice, and Loyalty: Responses to Decline in Firms, Organizations, and States* (Harvard University Press 1970)

Hix S, 'Elections, Parties and Institutional Design: A Comparative Perspective on European Union Democracy' (1998) 21 West European Politics 19

Hoffmann S, 'Reflections on the Nation-State in Western Europe Today' (1982) 21(1) Journal of Common Market Studies 21

Hoffmeister F, 'Of Presidents, High Representatives and European Commissioners—the External Representation of the European Union Seven Years after Lisbon' (2017) 1 Europe and the World: A Law Review 1

Hogg PW, *Constitutional Law of Canada* (5th edn, Thomson/Carswell 2007)

Holmes OW, *Collected Legal Papers* (Harcourt, Brace and Company 1920)

Hooghe M, 'Wat Een Vicepremier Moet Doen', *De Standaard*, 10 February 2015 <www.standaard.be/cnt/dmf20150209_01519905> accessed 4 November 2022

Hueglin TO, 'Johannes Althusius: Medieval Constitutionalist or Modern Federalist?' (1979) 9 Publius: The Journal of Federalism 9

—— 'Federalism at the Crossroads: Old Meanings, New Significance' (2003) 36 Canadian Journal of Political Science/Revue canadienne de science politique 275

—— *Early Modern Concepts for a Late Modern World: Althusius on Community and Federalism* (Wilfrid Laurier University Press 2006)

—— and Fenna A, *Comparative Federalism: A Systematic Inquiry, Second Edition* (University of Toronto Press 2015)

Ingelaere F, 'De nieuwe wetgeving inzake de internationale betrekkingen van de Gemeenschappen en de Gewesten' [1993] Tijdschrift voor Bestuurswetenschappen & Publiekrecht 807

Inwood GJ, Johns C, and O'Reilly P, *Intergovernmental Policy Capacity in Canada: Inside the Worlds of Finance, Environment, Trade, and Health* (McGill-Queen's Press—MQUP 2011)

Jacomy-Millette AM, *Treaty Law in Canada. Monographies Juridiques, No 8* (University of Ottawa Press 1975)

Jacqué JP, 'Lost in Transition: The European Commission between Intergovernmentalism and Integration' in D Ritleng (ed), *Independence and Legitimacy in the Institutional System of the European Union* (Oxford University Press 2016)

Jennings I, *The Law and the Constitution* (University of London Press 1963)

Jensen MD and Martinsen D, 'Out of Time? National Parliaments and Early Decision-Making in the European Union' (2015) 50(2) Government and Opposition 240

Johnson PM, Muzzi P, and Bastien V, 'The Voice of Quebec in the CETA Negotiations' (2013) 68(4) International Journal: Canada's Journal of Global Policy Analysis 560

Judo F, 'De zesde staatshervorming en het confederalisme' in Instituut voor Constitutioneel Recht Colloquium (eds), *Het federale België na de Zesde Staatshervorming* (die Keure 2014)

Kelemen RD, 'Towards a New Constitutional Architecture in the EU?' in F Fabbrini, EMH Hirsch Ballin, and H Somsen (eds), *What Form of Government for the European Union and the Eurozone?* (Hart Publishing 2015)

Kelsen H, *General Theory of Law and State* (The Lawbook Exchange Ltd 1999)

Kennedy D, *The Rise and Fall of Classical Legal Thought* (Beard Books 2006)

Kerremans B, 'Determining a European Policy in a Multi-level Setting: The Case of Specialized Co-ordination in Belgium' (2000) 10 Regional & Federal Studies 36

Keukeleire S and Delreux T, *The Foreign Policy of the European Union* (Palgrave Macmillan 2014)

Klamert M, *The Principle of Loyalty in EU Law* (Oxford University Press 2014)

Klein P, *Un aspect du fédéralisme coopératif horizontal: les accords de coopération entre entités fédérées* (ULB Centre d'études du fédéralisme 1990)

Klinck JA, 'Modernizing Judicial Review of the Exercise of Prerogative Powers in Canada' [2017] Alberta Law Review 997

Koenig N, 'Resetting EU External Action: Potential and Constraints', Policy Paper, Jacques Delors Institute, 3 February 2015

Koh HH, *The National Security Constitution: Sharing Power After the Iran-Contra Affair* (Yale University Press 1990)

—— 'Why the President (Almost) Always Wins in Foreign Affairs: Lessons of the Iran-Contra Affair' (1998) 97(7) Yale Law Journal 1255

Kong HL, 'The Spending Power in Canada' in P Oliver, P Macklem, and N des Rosiers (eds), *The Oxford Handbook of the Canadian Constitution*, vol 1 (Oxford University Press 2017)

Koutrakos P, *The EU Common Security and Defence Policy* (Oxford University Press 2013)

—— *EU International Relations Law* (2nd edn, Hart Publishing 2015)
—— 'Institutional Balance and Sincere Cooperation in Treaty-Making under EU Law' (2019) 68 International & Comparative Law Quarterly 1
—— 'Confronting the Complexities of Mixed Agreements—Opinion 1/19 on the Istanbul Convention' (2022) 47 European Law Review 247
Kramer LD, 'Understanding Federalism' (1994) 47 Vanderbilt Law Review 1485
—— 'Putting the Politics Back into the Political Safeguards of Federalism' (2000) 100 Columbia Law Review 215
Kübek G, 'The Non-Ratification Scenario: Legal and Practical Responses to Mixed Treaty Rejection by Member States' (2018) 23(1) European Foreign Affairs Review 21
Kuijper PJ, 'Post-CETA: How We Got There and How to Go On' (2017) 53 Revue trimestrielle de droit européen 181
Kuisma M and Larik J, 'The Continuing Contestation of ERTA' in N Levrat and others (eds), *The EU and its Member States' Joint Participation in International Agreements* (Hart 2022)
Kukucha CJ, 'Provincial Pitfalls—Canadian Provinces and the Canada-EU Trade Negotiations' in Kurt Hübner (ed), *Europe, Canada and the Comprehensive Economic Partnership Agreement* (Taylor & Francis 2011)
—— 'Canadian Sub-Federal Governments and CETA: Overarching Themes and Future Trends' (2013) 68(4) International Journal: Canada's Journal of Global Policy Analysis 528
—— 'Federalism Matters: Evaluating the Impact of Sub-Federal Governments in Canadian and American Foreign Trade Policy' (2015) 21(3) Canadian Foreign Policy Journal 224
—— 'Federalism and Liberalization: Evaluating the Impact of American and Canadian Sub-Federal Governments on the Negotiation of International Trade Agreements' (2017) 22(2) International Negotiation 259
Kumm M, 'How Does European Union Law Fit into the World of Public Law? Costa, Kadi and Three Conceptions of Public Law' in J Neyer and A Wiener (eds), *Political Theory of the European Union* (Oxford University Press 2011)
La Libre Belgique, 'CETA: Les Détails de l'accord Intrabelge', 28 October 2016 <www.lalibre.be/actu/politique-belge/ceta-les-details-de-l-accord-intrabelge-5812577ccd70958a9d5906be> accessed 7 March 2023
la Pierre DB, 'The Political Safeguards of Federalism Redux: Intergovernmental Immunity and the States as Agents of the Nation' (1982) 60 Washington University Law Quarterly 779
Lagerspetz E, 'Democracy and the All-Affected Principle' (2015) 10 Res Cogitans 6
Larsén MF, 'Parliamentary Influence Ten Years after Lisbon: EU Trade Negotiations with Japan' (2020) 58(6) Journal of Common Market Studies 1540
Lavenex S and Schimmelfennig F, 'EU Rules beyond EU Borders: Theorizing External Governance in European Politics' (2009) 16(6) Journal of European Public Policy 791
Leali G, 'EU's Borrell Makes Premature Pledge of €500M More Military Aid to Ukraine' *POLITICO* (12 March 2022) <www.politico.eu/article/eu-borrell-military-spend-momentum-false-step/> accessed 17 March 2022
Leclair J, 'Jane Austen and the Council of the Federation' (2006) 15 Constitutional Forum 51
—— 'The Securities Reference: The Ghost of Political Representation Comes Knocking at Federalism's Door' SSRN Scholarly Paper. Rochester, NY: Social Science Research Network, 2012 <http://papers.ssrn.com/abstract=2189661> accessed 4 November 2022
—— 'Tolstoï et les juges Beetz et Laskin: à la recherche du citoyen dans le discours judiciaire relatif au fédéralisme' in A-G Gagnon, P Noreau, and J Woehrling (eds), *Constitutionnalisme, droits et diversité: mélanges en l'honneur de José Woehrling* (Les éditions Thémis 2017)

Lecours A, 'Balancing Self-Rule and Shared-Rule: Sources of Tensions and Political Responses in Contemporary Political Systems' in *The Ways of Federalism in Western Countries and the Horizons of Territorial Autonomy in Spain* (Springer 2013)

Leider R, 'Federalism and the Military Power of the United States' (Social Science Research Network 2013) SSRN Scholarly Paper ID 2330648 <https://papers.ssrn.com/abstract=2330648> accessed 3 October 2017

Lenaerts K, 'Les répercussions des compétences de la Communauté Européenne sur les compétences externes des États Membres et la question de « preemption »' in P Demaret (ed), *Relations extérieures de la Communauté Européenne et marché intérieur: aspects juridiques et fonctionnels: Colloque 1986* (Story-Scientia, 1988)

—— 'Some Reflections on the Separation of Powers in the European Community' (1991) 28 Common Market Law Review 11

—— 'Federalism and the Rule of Law: Perspectives from the European Court of Justice' (2011) 33 Fordham International Law Journal 1338

—— and Verhoeven A, 'Institutional Balance as a Guarantee for Democracy in EU Governance' in *Good Governance in Europe's Integrated Market* (Oxford University Press 2002)

—— and others, *EU Procedural Law* (Oxford University Press 2014)

Levitan DM, 'The Foreign Relations Power: An Analysis of Mr. Justice Sutherland's Theory' (1946) 55 Yale Law Journal 467

Levrat N, 'The European Union: From International Relations to Intergovernmental Relations' in J Poirier, C Saunders, and J Kincaid (eds), *Intergovernmental Relations in Federal Systems* (Oxford University Press 2015)

Lievens J and Reybrouck K, 'Reanimating Brussels—The Beating Heart of the Belgian Federation' in E Hirsch Ballin and others (eds), *European Yearbook of Constitutional Law 2020: The City in Constitutional Law* (TMC Asser Press 2021)

Lonardo L, 'Integration in European Defence: Some Legal Considerations' (2017) 2 European Papers—A Journal on Law and Integration 887903

Loughlin M, *Foundations of Public Law* (Oxford University Press 2010)

Lupo N and Fasone C (eds), *Interparliamentary Cooperation in the Composite European Constitution* (Hart 2016)

Lynch-Staunton J, 'The Role of the Senate in the Legislative Process' [2000] Canadian Parliamentary Review 10

Mair P, 'Popular Democracy and the European Union Polity' (EUROGOV 2005) C-05-03

—— *Ruling the Void: The Hollowing of Western Democracy* (Verso 2013)

Major C and Mölling C, 'France Moves From EU Defense to European Defense' *Carnegie Europe* (7 December 2017) <http://carnegieeurope.eu/strategiceurope/74944?lang=en> accessed 7 March 2023

Mallory JR, *The Structure of Canadian Government* (Gage 1984)

Maresceau M, 'Belgium' in FG Jacobs, S Roberts, and United Kingdom National Committee of Comparative Law (eds), *The Effect of Treaties in Domestic Law* (Sweet & Maxwell 1987)

Martin J and Burns A, 'With Virginia, Voters Give Democrats First Big Wins of the Trump Era' *The New York Times* (7 November 2017) <www.nytimes.com/2017/11/07/us/politics/virginia-election-democrats.html?_r=0> accessed 7 March 2023

Martin P, *Federalism and International Relations*. Sessional Papers 265 (The Queen's Printer 1968)

McDougal MS and Asher L, 'Treaties and Congressional-Executive or Presidential Agreements: Interchangeable Instruments of National Policy: I' (1945) 54(2) Yale Law Journal 181

McGregor J, '"I Am Very Sad": Freeland Walks as Last-Ditch Canada-EU Trade Talks Collapse' *CBC News* (21 October 2016) <www.cbc.ca/news/politics/canada-eu-ceta-brussels-friday-1.3815332> accessed 4 November 2022

McHugh JT, 'Paradiplomacy, Protodiplomacy and the Foreign Policy Aspirations of Quebec and Other Canadian Provinces' (2015) 21(3) Canadian Foreign Policy Journal 238

McLachlan C, *Foreign Relations Law* (Cambridge University Press 2014)

McWhinney E, 'Canadian Federalism, and the Foreign Affairs and Treaty Power. The Impact of Quebec's 'Quiet Revolution' " [1969] The Canadian Yearbook of International Law 3

Meier P and Bursens P, 'Belgium: The Democratic State of the Federation' in J Sonnicksen and A Benz (eds), *Federal Democracies at Work* (University of Toronto Press 2021)

Meissner K, 'Democratizing EU External Relations: The European Parliament's Informal Role in SWIFT, ACTA, and TTIP' (2016) 21(2) European Foreign Affairs Review 269

Mendez M, *The Legal Effects of EU Agreements* (OUP 2013)

—— 'The Application of International Law by the Court of Justice of the European Union' in CA Bradley (ed), *The Oxford Handbook of Comparative Foreign Relations Law* (Oxford University Press 2019)

Meunier S and Nicolaïdis K, 'The Geopoliticization of European Trade and Investment Policy' (2019) 57 Journal of Common Market Studies 103

Meyer C, 'Provinces Want Trade Role Outlined in Writing' *Embassy* (August 2011) <http://canada-europe.org/en/pdf/Provinces%20Want%20Trade%20Role%20Outlined%20in%20Writing%20-%20August%202011.pdf> accessed 4 November 2022

Meyer T and Sitaraman G, 'Trade and the Separation of Powers' (2019) 107 California Law Review 583

Michaud N, 'The Prime Minister, PMO, and PCO: Makers of Canadian Foreign Policy?' in P James, N Michaud, and MJ O'Reilly, *Handbook of Canadian Foreign Policy* (Lexington Books 2006)

Minaeva Y, 'Canadian Federalism Uncovered: The Assumed, the Forgotten and the Unexamined in Collaborative Federalism' (University of Ottawa 2012)

Molinari C, 'The EU and Its Perilous Journey Through the Migration Crisis: Informalisation of the EU Return Policy and Rule of Law Concerns' (2019) 44 European Law Review 824

Monti M and others, 'Future Financing of the EU. Final Report and Recommendations of the High Level Group on Own Resources December 2016' (Brussels, 4 January 2017)

Moore DH, 'Beyond One Voice' (2014) 98 *Minnesota Law Review* 953

Moravcsik A, 'Preference and Power in the European Community: A Liberal Intergovernmentalist Approach' in S Bulmer (ed), *Economic and Political Integration in Europe: Internal Dynamics and Global Context* (Blackwell Publishers 1994)

—— 'Reassessing Legitimacy in the European Union' (2002) 40(4) Journal of Common Market Studies 603

Morillas P, 'Autonomy in Intergovernmentalism: The Role of de Novo Bodies in External Action during the Making of the EU Global Strategy' (2020) 42 Journal of European Integration 231

Morin JY, 'La personnalité internationale du Québec' (1984) 1 Revue Québécoise de droit international 163

Mourlon-Druol E, 'Filling the EEC Leadership Vacuum? The Creation of the European Council in 1974' (2010) 10(3) Cold War History 315

Mühlböck M, 'National versus European: Party Control over Members of the European Parliament' (2012) 35 West European Politics 607

Murer A, Kietz D, and Volkel C, 'Interinstitutional Agreements in the CFSP: Parliamentarization through the Back Door' (2005) 10 European Foreign Affairs Review 175

Neframi E, 'The Duty of Loyalty: Rethinking Its Scope through Its Application in the Field of EU External Relations' (2010) 47 Common Market Law Review 323

Neuwahl N, 'Joint Participation in International Treaties and the Exercise of Power by the EEC and Its Member States: Mixed Agreements' (1991) 28(4) Common Market Law Review 717

Newman WJ, 'The Constitutional Status of the Supreme Court of Canada' (2009) 47 Supreme Court Law Review 429

Nicolaïdis K, 'European Demoicracy and Its Crisis' (2013) 51(2) Journal of Common Market Studies 351

Noel E, 'The Commission's Power of Initiative' (1973) 10 Common Market Law Review 123

Noel SJR, 'Consociational Democracy and Canadian Federalism' (1971) 4(1) Canadian Journal of Political Science/Revue Canadienne de Science Politique 15

Nollkaemper A, 'The Duality of Direct Effect of International Law' (2014) 25(1) European Journal of International Law 105

Novak S, 'The Silence of Ministers: Consensus and Blame Avoidance in the Council of the European Union' (2013) 51(6) Journal of Common Market Studies 1091

Nugent N and Rhinard M, *The European Commission* (2nd edn, Palgrave Macmillan 2015)

——— and Rhinard M, 'Is the European Commission Really in Decline?' (2016) 54 Journal of Common Market Studies 1199

Nye J, 'Get Smart' [2009] *Foreign Affairs* <www.foreignaffairs.com/articles/2009-07-01/get-smart> accessed 18 January 2017

O'Keeffe D and Schermers HG (eds), *Mixed Agreements* (Kluwer Law and Taxation Publishers 1983)

Odermatt J, *International Law and the European Union* (Cambridge University Press 2021)

Oeter S, 'Federalism and Democracy' in A von Bogdandy and J Bast (eds), *Principles of European Constitutional Law* (Bloomsbury Publishing 2009)

Ohlin JD, *The Assault on International Law* (Oxford University Press USA 2015)

Oliver P, 'The Busy Harbours of Canadian Federalism: The Division of Powers and Its Doctrines in the McLachlin Court' in DA Wright and AM Dodek (eds), *Public Law at the McLachlin Court: The First Decade* (Irwin Law 2011)

Olson P, 'Mixity from the Outside: The Perspective of a Treaty Partner' in C Hillion and P Koutrakos (eds), *Mixed Agreements Revisited: The EU and its Member States in the World* (Hart 2010)

Ott A, 'Informalization of EU Bilateral Instruments: Categorization, Contestation, and Challenges' (2021) 39 Yearbook of European Law 569

Panke D, 'Small States in the European Union: Structural Disadvantages in EU Policy-Making and Counter-Strategies' (2010) 17(6) Journal of European Public Policy 799

Paquin S, *Les relations internationales du Québec depuis la doctrine Gérin-Lajoie (1965–2005): le prolongement externe des compétences internes* (Presses Université Laval 2006)

—— 'Identity Paradiplomacy in Québec' (2018) 66 Quebec Studies 3

—— 'Trade Paradiplomacy and the Politics of International Economic Law: The Inclusion of Quebec and the Exclusion of Wallonia in the CETA Negotiations' [2021] New Political Economy 1

Patel KK, *Project Europe: A History* (Cambridge University Press 2020)

Peers S, 'Towards a New Form of EU Law?: The Use of EU Institutions Outside the EU Legal Framework' (2013) 9 European Constitutional Law Review 37

Peeters Y, *De plaats van samenwerkingsakkoorden in het constitutioneel kader* (Die Keure 2016)

Pelletier R, 'La Révolution Tranquille' in G Daigle (ed), *Le Québec en jeu. comprendre les grands défis* (Les Presses de l'Université de Montréal 1992)

Pernice I, 'Multilevel Constitutionalism and the Treaty of Amsterdam: European Constitution-Making Revisited?' (1999) 36 Common Market Law Review 703

Pescatore P, 'External Relations in the Case-Law of the Court of Justice of the European Communities' (1979) 16 Common Market Law Review 615

—— 'Preface' in T Sandalow and E Stein (eds), *Courts and Free Markets*, vol II (Clarendon Press 1982)

—— 'Opinion 1/94 on "Conclusion" of the WTO Agreement: Is There an Escape from a Programmed Disaster?' (1999) 36 Common Market Law Review 387

Poirier J, 'Formal Mechanisms of Intergovernmental Relations in Belgium' (2002) 12(3) Regional & Federal Studies 24

—— 'Le droit public survivra-t-il à sa contractualisation?' (2006) 33(1) Revue de Droit de l'ULB 261

—— 'Les Fédérations Belge et Canadienne: essai de comparaison synthétique et systématique' (2009) 1 Revue de Droit de l'ULB 13

—— 'Souveraineté parlementaire et armes à feu: le fédéralisme coopératif dans la ligne de mire? (Parliamentary Sovereignty and Firearms: Cooperative Federalism on the Line)' (2015) 45 Revue de droit de l'Université de Sherbrooke 47

—— and Saunders C, 'Comparing Intergovernmental Relations in Federal Systems: an Introduction' in J Kincaid, J Poirier, and C Saunders (eds), *Intergovernmental Relations in Federal Systems* (OUP Canada 2015)

Ponzano P, Hermanin C, and Corona D, 'The Power of Initiative of the European Commission: A Progressive Erosion?' (2012) Notre Europe 1

Popelier P, 'Bicameralism in Belgium: The Dismantlement of the Senate for the Sake of Multinational Confederalism' (2018) 10 Perspectives on Federalism 215

—— 'Intergovernmental Relations in Belgium: Obstacles to Effective Cooperation in Dyadic Federalism' in YT Fessha, K Kössler, and F Palermo (eds), *Intergovernmental Relations in Divided Societies* (Springer International Publishing 2022)

—— and Lemmens K, *The Constitution of Belgium: A Contextual Analysis* (Bloomsbury Publishing 2015)

Post R, 'Constructing the European Polity: ERTA and the Open Skies Judgments' in M Maduro and L Azoulai (eds), *The Past and Future of EU Law: The Classics of EU Law Revisited on the 50th Anniversary of the Rome Treaty* (Bloomsbury Publishing 2010)

Rankin J, 'EU-Canada Trade Deal in Crisis as Canadian Minister Walks Out' *The Guardian* (22 October 2016) <www.theguardian.com/world/2016/oct/21/eu-canada-ceta-trade-deal-meltdown-canadian-minister-walks-out> accessed 4 November 2022

Read JH, 'Constitutionalizing the Dispute: Federalism in Hyper-Partisan Times' (2016) 46(3) Publius: The Journal of Federalism 337

Regan DH, 'The Supreme Court and State Protectionism: Making Sense of the Dormant Commerce Clause' (1986) 84 Michigan Law Review 1091

Resnik J, 'Categorical Federalism: Jurisdiction, Gender, and the Globe' (2001) 111 Yale Law Journal 619

Rettman A, 'Mogherini Seen as Proposing 'Business as Usual' with Russia' *EUObserver* (14 January 2015) <https://euobserver.com/foreign/127204> accessed 7 March 2023

Reybrouck K and Sottiaux S, *De federale bevoegdheden* (Intersentia 2019)

Rodrigo CM, 'Trump Administration Officially Revokes California Tailpipe Emissions Waiver' *TheHill* (19 September 2019) <https://thehill.com/policy/energy-environment/462142-trump-administration-officially-revokes-california-tailpipe> accessed 12 October 2021

Roederer-Rynning C and Greenwood J, 'The European Parliament as a Developing Legislature: Coming of Age in Trilogues?' (2017) 24(5) Journal of European Public Policy 735

Roes T and De Baere G, 'EU Loyalty as Good Faith' (2015) 64(4) International and Comparative Law Quarterly 829

Romaniello M, 'The International Role of the European Parliament: The SWIFT Affair and the "Re-Assessed" European Institutional Balance of Power' (2013) 5(1) Perspectives on Federalism 97

Rosas A, 'The European Union and Mixed Agreements' in A Dashwood and C Hillion (eds), *The General Law of E.C. External Relations* (Sweet & Maxwell 2000)

—— 'The Status in EU Law of International Agreements Concluded by EU Member States' (2010) 34 Fordham International Law Journal 1304

—— 'Exclusive, Shared and National Competence in the Context of EU External Relations: Do Such Distinctions Matter?' in I Govaere and others (eds), *The European Union in the World: Essays in Honour of Marc Maresceau* (Brill 2014)

—— 'Mixity and the Common Commercial Policy after Opinion 2/15: An Overview' in M Hahn and G Van der Loo (eds), *Law and Practice of the Common Commercial Policy: The First 10 Years after the Treaty of Lisbon* (Brill Nijhoff 2020)

Rosén G and Raube K, 'Influence beyond Formal Powers: The Parliamentarisation of European Union Security Policy' (2018) 20 The British Journal of Politics and International Relations 69

Rosenkranz NQ, 'Executing the Treaty Power' (2005) 118 Harvard Law Review 1867

Ryder B, 'Demise and Rise of the Classical Paradigm in Canadian Federalism: Promoting Autonomy for the Provinces and First Nations' (1990) 36 McGill Law Journal 308

Savoie DJ, *Court Government and the Collapse of Accountability in Canada and the United Kingdom* (University of Toronto Press 2008)

—— *Looking for Bootstraps: Economic Development in the Maritimes* (Nimbus Publishing 2017)

Saxi HL, 'British and German Initiatives for Defence Cooperation: The Joint Expeditionary Force and the Framework Nations Concept' (2017) 17(2) Defence Studies 171

Scharpf FW, *Demokratietheorie zwischen Utopie und Anpassung* (Druckerei u Verlagsanst Universitätsverlag 1970)

—— Reissert B, and Schnabel F, *Politikverflechtung: Theorie und Empirie des kooperativen Föderalismus in der Bundesrepublik* (Hain 1976)

Schertzer R, 'Intergovernmental Relations in Canada's Immigration System: From Bilateralism towards Multilateral Collaboration' (2015) 48(2) Canadian Journal of Political Science/Revue Canadienne de Science Politique 38

Schleicher D, 'The Seventeenth Amendment and Federalism in an Age of National Political Parties' (2014) 65 Hastings Law Journal 1043

Schmidt VA, 'Democracy and Legitimacy in the European Union Revisited: Input, Output and "Throughput"' (2013) 61 Political Studies 2

Schütze R, 'EC Law and International Agreements of the Member States—An Ambivalent Relationship?' (2006) 9 Cambridge Yearbook of European Legal Studies 387

—— 'Supremacy Without Pre-Emption? The Very Slowly Emergent Doctrine of Community Pre-Emption' (2006) 43 Common Market Law Review 1023

—— *From Dual to Cooperative Federalism: The Changing Structure of European Law* (Oxford University Press 2009)

—— 'Subsidiarity after Lisbon: Reinforcing the Safeguards of Federalism?' (2009) 68 The Cambridge Law Journal 525

—— 'Federalism and Foreign Affairs: Mixity as a (Inter)National Phenomenon' in C Hillion and P Koutrakos (eds), *Mixed Agreements Revisited: the EU and its Member States in the World* (Hart 2010)

—— 'From Rome to Lisbon: "Executive Federalism" in the European Union' (2010) 47 Common Market Law Review 1385

—— *Foreign Affairs and the EU Constitution: Selected Essays* (Cambridge University Press 2014)

—— *European Union Law* (Cambridge University Press 2015)

Scott FR, 'The Consequences of the Privy Council Decisions' (1937) XV Canadian Bar Review 485

Scoville RM, 'The International Commitments of the Fifty States' [2022] UCLA Law Review 51

Segers F, 'Demotte Dreigt Met Belangenconflict over Onbelast Bijverdienen' (*Vrtnws.Be*, 18 December 2017) <www.vrt.be/vrtnws/nl/2017/12/18/demotte-dreigt-met-belangenconflict-over-onbelast-bijverdienen/> accessed 4 November 2022

Senden LAJ, 'Soft Law and Its Implications for Institutional Balance in the EC' (2005) 1 Utrecht Law Review 79

Shackleton M, 'Transforming Representative Democracy in the EU? The Role of the European Parliament' (2017) 39(2) Journal of European Integration 191

Simmons JM, 'Canadian Multilateral Intergovernmental Institutions and the Limits of Institutional Innovation' (2017) 27 Regional & Federal Studies 573

Sinardet D and Pieters J, 'Nationalism and COVID in Belgium: A Surprisingly United Response in a Divided Federal Country' (2021) 27 Nationalism and Ethnic Politics 311

Sitaraman G and Wuerth I, 'The Normalization of Foreign Relations Law' (2015) 128 Harvard Law Review 1897

Smiley DV, 'The Structural Problem of Canadian Federalism' (1971) 14(3) Canadian Public Administration/Administration Publique du Canada 326

Smith DE, *The Invisible Crown: The First Principle of Canadian Government* (University of Toronto Press 1995)

—— *Federalism and the Constitution of Canada* (University of Toronto Press 2013)

—— *Europe's Common Security and Defence Policy: Capacity-Building, Experiential Learning, and Institutional Change* (Cambridge University Press 2017)

Sottiaux S, *Grondwettelijk Recht* (Intersentia 2016)

Sparrow A, 'Jean-Claude Juncker Calls for EU Army' *The Guardian* (8 March 2015) <www.theguardian.com/world/2015/mar/08/jean-claude-juncker-calls-for-eu-army-european-commission-miltary> accessed 4 November 2022

Spiegel J, 'Embracing Foreign Affairs Federalism in a Post-Trump Era' (*Lawfare*, 3 March 2021) <www.lawfareblog.com/embracing-foreign-affairs-federalism-post-trump-era> accessed 27 October 2021

Spiegel Online, 'Blocking Tactics: UK Infuriating Partners by Obstructing EU Foreign Policy', 5 December 2011 <www.spiegel.de/international/europe/blocking-tactics-uk-infuriating-partners-by-obstructing-eu-foreign-policy-a-801756.html> accessed 4 November 2022

Stephan PB and Cleveland SH (eds), *The Restatement and Beyond: The Past, Present, and Future of U.S. Foreign Relations Law* (Oxford University Press 2020)

St-Pierre C, 'La Doctrine Gérin-Lajoie, Un Socle Solide' *Le Devoir* (14 April 2015) <www.ledevoir.com/politique/quebec/437068/la-doctrine-gerin-lajoie-un-socle-solide> accessed 7 March 2023

Sutherland G, *Constitutional Power and World Affairs* (1st edn 1919 HardPress Publishing 2013)

Swenden W, 'Asymmetric Federalism and Coalition-Making in Belgium' (2002) 32 Publius: The Journal of Federalism 67

Sykes JB and Vanatko N, 'Federal Preemption: A Legal Primer' (Congressional Research Service 2019) CRS Report R45825

Tallberg J and Johansson KM, 'Party Politics in the European Council' (2008) 15 Journal of European Public Policy 1222

Tasker JP, 'Trudeau Announces 'pan-Canadian Framework' on Climate—but Sask., Manitoba Hold Off' *CBC News* (10 December 2016) <www.cbc.ca/news/politics/trudeau-premiers-climate-deal-1.3888244> accessed 4 November 2022

Tavares R, *Paradiplomacy: Cities and States as Global Players* (Oxford University Press 2016)

Techau J, 'Hoping for an Unexpectedly Strong EU Foreign Policy Chief' *Carnegie Europe* (26 August 2014) <http://carnegieeurope.eu/strategiceurope/56453> accessed 10 March 2022

Thaler P, 'The European Commission and the European Council: Coordinated Agenda Setting in European Energy Policy' (2016) 38(5) Journal of European Integration 571

Thaler P and Pakalkaite V, 'Governance through Real-Time Compliance: The Supranationalisation of European External Energy Policy' (2021) 28 Journal of European Public Policy 208

The Toronto Star, 'Ontario Signs Formal Agreement to Join Quebec-California Carbon Market in 2018', 22 September 2017 <www.thestar.com/news/canada/2017/09/22/ontario-signs-formal-agreement-to-join-quebec-california-carbon-market-in-2018.html> accessed 4 November 2022

Thym D, 'Beyond Parliament's Reach? The Role of the European Parliament in the CFSP' (2006) 11(1) European Foreign Affairs Review 109

—— 'Parliamentary Involvement in European International Relations' in M Cremona and B de Witte (eds), *EU Foreign Relations Law: Constitutional Fundamentals* (Hart Publishing 2008)

Tömmel I, 'The Standing President of the European Council: Intergovernmental or Supranational Leadership?' (2017) 39(2) Journal of European Integration 175

Tribe LH, 'Taking Text and Structure Seriously: Reflections on Free-Form Method in Constitutional Interpretation' (1995) 108(6) Harvard Law Review 1221

Trudeau H and Codère C, 'À la recherche d'une tarification pancanadienne du carbone: les enjeux juridiques de la coopération intergouvernementale pour protéger le climat' (2018) 18 Fédéralisme Régionalisme 1

Turp D, 'L'arrêt Bazylo c. Collins et la nature juridique des ententes internationales du Québec' (1985) 1-1984 Revue Québécoise de droit international 345 <www.sqdi.org/fr/larret-bazylo-c-collins-et-la-nature-juridique-des-ententes-internationales-du-quebec/> accessed 7 March 2023

Tushnet M, 'The Possibilities of Comparative Constitutional Law' (1999) 108 Yale Law Journal 1225

—— 'Enforcement of National Law against Subnational Units in the US' in A Jakab and D Kochenov (eds), *The Enforcement of EU Law and Values: Ensuring Member States' Compliance* (Oxford University Press 2017)

Twomey A, 'Responsible Government and the Divisibility of the Crown' (2008) Public Law 742

Uyttendaele M, *Trente leçons de droit constitutionnel* (2nd edn, Anthémis Editions 2014)

Van den Brande L, 'The International Legal Position of Flanders: Some Considerations' in K Wellens (ed), *International Law: Theory and Practice. Essays in Honour of Eric Suy* (Kluwer Law International 1998)

Van den Sanden T, 'Between Constitutional Strictures and Policy Objectives: An Examination of the Legal Framework of EU Development Cooperation' (PhD thesis, Leuven University 2018)

Van der Loo G, 'The Court's Opinion on the EU-Singapore FTA: Throwing off the Shackles of Mixity?' (CEPS Policy Insights 2017)

—— and Wessel RA, 'The Non-Ratification of Mixed Agreements: Legal Consequences and Solutions' (2017) 54 Common Market Law Review 735

Van Eeckhoutte D and Vandaele A, 'Doorwerking van internationale normen in de Belgische rechtsorde' (Instituut voor Internationaal Recht, KU Leuven 2002) Working Paper 33 <www.law.kuleuven.be/iir/nl/onderzoek/working-papers/WP33n.pdf> accessed 4 November 2022

—— and others, 'Behoorlijke Wetgeving in de Adviespraktijk van de Afdeling Wetgeving van de Raad van State' (2009) 2 Tijdschrift Voor Wetgeving 100

van Ert G, 'The Legal Character of Provincial Arrangements with Foreign Governments' (2001) 42(4) Les Cahiers de Droit 1093

—— *Using International Law in Canadian Courts* (Irwin Law Incorporated 2008)

—— 'The Domestic Application of International Law in Canada' in CA Bradley (ed), *The Oxford Handbook of Comparative Foreign Relations Law* (Oxford University Press 2019)

Van Gerven W, *The European Union: A Polity of States and Peoples* (Stanford University Press 2005)

Van Ginneken S and Winckelmans W, 'Het Geduld van Rutten Is Op' *De Standaard* (20 October 2016) <www.standaard.be/cnt/dmf20161019_02528737> accessed 4 November 2022

Van Haute E and Pilet JB, 'Regionalist Parties in Belgium (VU, RW, FDF): Victims of Their Own Success?' (2006) 16 Regional & Federal Studies 297

Van Middelaar L, *The Passage to Europe: How a Continent Became a Union* (Yale University Press 2013)

—— *De nieuwe politiek van Europa* (Historische Uitgeverij Groningen 2017)

Van Nieuwenhove J, 'Bevoegdheidsverdeling En Verdragen' in G Geudens and F Judo (eds), *Internationale Betrekkingen En Federalisme: Staatsrechtconferentie 2005—Vlaamse Juristenvereniging* (Uitgeverij Larcier 2006)

Van Rompuy H, *Europa in de storm: lessen en uitdagingen* (Davidsfonds 2014)

Van Vooren B, *EU External Relations Law and the European Neighbourhood Policy: A Paradigm for Coherence* (Routledge 2012)

Vandenbossche E, 'Het Overlegcomité: Een Instelling in Opmars?' in E Vandenbossche and X Delgrange, *Evoluties in Het Belgisch Cooperatief Federalisme =: Évolutions dans le fédéralisme coopératif Belge* (Die Keure 2015)

Vandenbossche E and Delgrange X (eds), *Evoluties in Het Belgisch Cooperatief Federalisme. Évolutions dans le fédéralisme coopératif Belge* (Die Keure 2015)

VanDuzer JA, 'Could an Intergovernmental Agreement Increase the Credibility of Canadian Treaty Commitments in Areas within Provincial Jurisdiction?' (2013) 68(4) International Journal: Canada's Journal of Global Policy Analysis 536

—— and Mallet MJ, 'Compliance with Canada's Trade and Investment Treaty Obligations: Addressing the Gap Between Provincial Action and Federal Responsibility' (2016) 54(1) Alberta Law Review 89

Vanpraet J and Peeters Y, 'Autonomie En Samenwerking in Het Federale België' in E Vandenbossche and X Delgrange, *Evoluties in Het Belgisch Cooperatief Federalisme = : Évolutions dans le fédéralisme coopératif Belge* (Die Keure 2015)

Vázquez CM, 'Treaties as Law of the Land: The Supremacy Clause and the Judicial Enforcement of Treaties' (2008) 122(2) Harvard Law Review 599

Velaers J, *De Grondwet en de Raad van State, afdeling Wetgeving: vijftig jaar adviezen an wetgevende vergaderingen in het licht van de rechtspraak van het Arbitragehof* (Maklu 1999)

—— '"In foro interno et in foro externo": de internationale bevoegdheden van gemeenschappen en gewesten' in G Geudens and F Judo (eds), *Internationale betrekkingen en federalisme: Staatsrechtconferentie 2005—Vlaamse Juristenvereniging* (Uitgeverij Larcier 2006)

—— 'De Pariteit in de Ministerraad (Artikel 99, Tweede Lid van de Grondwet): Een Vereiste Met Een Louter Taalkundige, Een Communautaire of Ook Een 'Taalgroep-Parlementaire' Betekenis?' (2015) 1 Tijdschrift Voor Bestuurswetenschappen En Publiekrecht 4

Verellen T, 'The ERTA Doctrine in the Post-Lisbon Era: Note under Judgment in Commission v Council (C-114/12) and Opinion 1/13' (2015) 21 Columbia Journal of European Law 383

—— 'On Hybrid Decisions, Mixed Agreements and the Limits of the New Legal Order: Commission v Council ('US Air Transport Agreement')' (2016) 53 Common Market Law Review 741

—— 'Federalism and Treaty Enforcement in the European Union. Letters from America' (2017) Jean Monnet Working Papers (City University 2017)

—— 'Opinion 3/15 on the Marrakesh Treaty: The ECJ Reaffirms 'Minimum Harmonisation' Exception to ERTA Principle' (2017) 42 Revista General de Derecho Europeo 160

—— 'European Sovereignty Now? A Reflection on What It Means to Speak of "European Sovereignty"' (2020) 5 European Papers 307

—— 'Unilateral Trade Measures in Times of Geopolitical Rivalry' (*Verfassungsblog*, 25 May 2021) <https://verfassungsblog.de/unilateral-trade-measures-in-times-of-geopolitical-rivalry/> accessed 13 June 2021

—— 'When Integration by Stealth Meets Public Security: The EU Foreign Direct Investment Screening Regulation' (2021) 48 Legal Issues of Economic Integration 19

—— 'Common Commercial Policy and Customs Union' in M Scholten (ed), *Research Handbook on the Enforcement of European Union Law* (Routledge 2023)

—— 'Convergence and Divergence in EU External Action: The Very Slowly Emergent Doctrine of Shared Competence' in M Kos, J Kukavica, and M Sahadžić (eds), *The Dialectics in Multilevel Systems—Mechanisms of Divergence and Convergence* (Hart 2023)

Vermeule A, *Common Good Constitutionalism* (1st edn, Polity 2022)

Verrijdt W, 'EU Integration and the Belgian Constitution' in S Griller, M Claes, and L Papadopoulou (eds), *Member States' Constitutions and EU Integration* (Hart 2016)

Vladeck SI, 'The Exceptionalism of Foreign Relations Normalization' (2014) 128 Harvard Law Review Forum 322

vrtnws.be, 'Senaatsvoorzitter Stephanie D'Hose (Open VLD) wil Senaat afschaffen', 8 January 2022) <www.vrt.be/vrtnws/nl/2022/01/08/senaatsvoorzitter-wil-senaat-afschaffen/> accessed 1 February 2022

Wade HWR, 'The Basis of Legal Sovereignty' (1955) 13(2) The Cambridge Law Journal 172

Waelbroeck M, 'The Emergent Doctrine of Community Pre-Emption—Consent and Re-Delegation' in T Sandalow and E Stein (eds), *Courts and Free Markets*, vol II (Clarendon Press 1982)

Waldron J, 'Is the Rule of Law an Essentially Contested Concept (in Florida)?' (2002) 21 Law and Philosophy 137

Walker N (ed), *Sovereignty in Transition* (Hart 2006)

Walsh B, 'Why the Climate Bill Died' *Time* (26 July 2010) <http://science.time.com/2010/07/26/why-the-climate-bill-died/> accessed 6 November 2022

Walter BF, *How Civil Wars Start: And How to Stop Them* (Penguin 2022)

Walters MD, 'Written Constitutions and Unwritten Constitutionalism' in G Huscroft (eds), *Expounding the Constitution: Essays in Constitutional Theory* (Cambridge University Press 2008)

Wechsler H, 'The Political Safeguards of Federalism: The Role of the States in the Composition and Selection of the National Government' (1954) 54 Columbia Law Review 543

Weiler JHH, 'The Transformation of Europe' (1991) 100 Yale Law Journal 2403

—— 'The External Legal Relations of Non-Unitary Actors: Mixity and the Federal Principle' in JHH Weiler, *The Constitution of Europe: Essays on the Ends and Means of European Integration* (Cambridge University Press 1999)

Weiss W, 'The European Parliament's Role in the Operation of Trade Agreements: Parliamentary Control and Executive–Legislative Balance in External Action' in D Fromage and A Herranz-Surrallés (eds), *Executive–Legislative (Im)balance in the European Union* (Hart Publishing 2020)

Wessel RA, *The European Union's Foreign and Security Policy: A Legal Institutional Perspective* (Martinus Nijhoff Publishers 1999)

—— 'Legal Aspects of Parliamentary Oversight in EU Foreign and Security Policy' in J Santos Vara and S Rodríguez Sánchez-Tabernero (eds), *The Democratisation of EU International Relations Through EU Law* (Routledge 2018)

Wessels W, *The European Council* (1st edn, Palgrave 2015)

Wheare KC, *Federal Government* (Oxford University Press 1963)

White G, 'Traditional Aboriginal Values in a Westminster Parliament: The Legislative Assembly of Nunavut' (2006) 12 The Journal of Legislative Studies 8

Wilder M and Howlett M, 'Bringing the Provinces Back in: Re-Evaluating the Relevance of Province-Building to Theories of Canadian Federalism and Multi-Level Governance' (2015) 9 Canadian Political Science Review 1

Wilson LM, 'The Fate of the Dormant Foreign Commerce Clause after Garamendi and Crosby' (2007) 107(3) Columbia Law Review 746

Winckelmans W, 'Belgisch klimaatakkoord is voor een andere keer' *De Standaard* (10 November 2021) <www.standaard.be/cnt/dmf20211109_97712641> accessed 25 November 2021

Wouters J, *Internationaal Recht in Kort Bestek* (Intersentia 2017)

—— and De Smet L, 'The Legal Position of Federal States and Their Federated Entities in International Relations—The Case of Belgium' (2001) Working Paper. Leuven: Institute for International Law (KU Leuven)

—— Meester BD, and Ryngaert C, 'Democracy and International Law' (2003) 34 Netherlands Yearbook of International Law 139

Wright D, 'Rethinking the Doctrine of Legitimate Expectations in Canadian Administrative Law' (1997) 35 Osgoode Hall Law Journal 139

Wright WK, 'Facilitating Intergovernmental Dialogue: Judicial Review of the Division of Powers in the Supreme Court of Canada' (2010) 51 Supreme Court Law Review 625

—— 'The Political Safeguards of Canadian Federalism: The Intergovernmental Safeguards' (2016) 36 National Journal of Constitutional Law 1

Yoo JC, 'Laws as Treaties?: The Constitutionality of Congressional-Executive Agreements' (2001) 99(4) Michigan Law Review 757

Young EA, 'The Puzzling Persistence of Dual Federalism' [2012] Faculty Scholarship <http://scholarship.law.duke.edu/faculty_scholarship/2689> accessed 21 June 2017

—— '"The Ordinary Diet of the Law": The Presumption Against Preemption in the Roberts Court' (2012) 2011(1) The Supreme Court Review 253

Young OR, 'Political Leadership and Regime Formation: On the Development of Institutions in International Society' (1991) 45 International Organization 281

Zeigel J, 'Treaty-Making and Implementation Powers in Canada: The Continuing Dilemma' in G Schwarzenberger and B Cheng (eds), *Contemporary Problems of International Law: Essays in Honour of Georg Schwarzenberger on His Eightieth Birthday* (Taylor & Francis 1988)

Zubrzycki G, *Beheading the Saint: Nationalism, Religion, and Secularism in Quebec* (University of Chicago Press 2016)

Index

For the benefit of digital users, indexed terms that span two pages (e.g., 52–53) may, on occasion, appear on only one of those pages.

Tables are indicated by *t* following the page number